*Anonymous*

Anomalous

# Anonymous

## THE PERFORMANCE OF HIDDEN IDENTITIES

*Thomas DeGloma*

*The University of Chicago Press* CHICAGO AND LONDON

The University of Chicago Press, Chicago 60637
The University of Chicago Press, Ltd., London
© 2023 by The University of Chicago
Published 2023
Printed and bound by CPI Group (UK) Ltd, Croydon, CR0 4YY

32  31  30  29  28  27  26  25  24  23      1  2  3  4  5

ISBN-13: 978-0-226-82879-4 (cloth)
ISBN-13: 978-0-226-76513-6 (paper)
ISBN-13: 978-0-226-82880-0 (e-book)
DOI: https://doi.org/10.7208/chicago/9780226828800.001.0001

Library of Congress Cataloging-in-Publication Data

Names: DeGloma, Thomas, author.
Title: Anonymous : the performance of hidden identities / Thomas
    DeGloma.
Description: Chicago ; London : The University of Chicago Press, 2023. |
    Includes bibliographical references and index.
Identifiers: LCCN 2023001749 | ISBN 9780226828794 (cloth) |
    ISBN 9780226765136 (paperback) | ISBN 9780226828800 (ebook)
Subjects: LCSH: Social interaction. | Anonymous persons.
Classification: LCC HM1111 .D44 2023 | DDC 302—dc23/eng/20230207
LC record available at https://lccn.loc.gov/2023001749

♾ This paper meets the requirements of ANSI/NISO Z39.48-1992
(Permanence of Paper).

# Contents

1. ANONYMOUS ACTS                                                                                    1

    The Social Dynamics of Anonymous Acts                                         8

    Names, Namelessness, and Pseudo-Names                                         8

    Freedom and Constraint in the Breach of Personal Identity                    13

    The Exhibitionist and the Voyeur: Anonymity and
        Information Control                                       16

    Impersonal Agencies: Someone, Anyone, Everyone, and No One                   18

    Culture and Meaning in the Performance of Anonymity                          26

    Outline of the Book                                                          30

2. PROTECTIVE ANONYMITY                                                                             33

    Concealed Authorship and the Performance of Elena Ferrante                   39

    Social Ethics of Anonymity                                                   43

    Anonymous Altruism and Charity                                               44

    The Screened Confession and the Masquerade                                   46

    The Impartiality of Impersonality and the Performance
        of Academic Evaluation                                   50

    Anonymous Communities and Forums                                             55

    Anonymous Therapeutics and the Case of
        Alcoholics Anonymous                                     56

    Computer-Mediated Anonymous Forums                                           58

    Anonymous Consumption and Exchange                                           60

    Exploiting Protective Anonymity                                              63

3. SUBVERSIVE ANONYMITY                                                                             67

    Subversive Art and Literature                                                71

    Masked Social Movements and Anonymous Rebellion                              77

    The Religious, Theatrical, and Festive Roots of Masked
        Social Protest                                           78

Masked Movements and Their Subversive World Orders     81

The Anonymous Performances of Ku Klux Klan Terror     85

Performing the Digital Guerrilla Insurgency: The Hacker
    Networks of Anonymous     90

The Klan and Anonymous: Shared Characteristics of
    Subversive Anonymity     96

FBI Counterintelligence and the Anonymous Subversion
    of Subversive Activity     99

4.    THE ANONYMITY OF SOCIAL SYSTEMS     105

Institutions and Systems as Cover Representations     110

Wall Street and the Financial Crisis     110

Corporate Personhood and Electoral Politics     113

The NSA, Big Tech, and Electronic Surveillance     114

Distance Killing and the Nation at War     117

The Modern State as "Humane" Executioner     121

Anonymous Labor and Systems of Production     127

5.    THE ANONYMITY OF TYPES AND CATEGORIES     135

Typification and Social Performance     140

Anonymous Others in Situated Encounters     147

The Anonymity of Class and Occupation     147

Anonymous Sex     150

Racial Typification, Law Enforcement, and Police Violence     154

Cisgender Typification and the Segregation of Public Restrooms     160

Analytic Typifications     164

6.    THE SOCIAL CONTRADICTIONS OF OUR
HIDDEN IDENTITIES     169

Unmasking Acts     173

*Acknowledgments*     179

*Notes*     181

*References*     221

*Index*     257

# ✳ 1 ✳

# *Anonymous Acts*

I am in disguise tonight in order that I might speak freely, without conjuring up too much regard on your part about the particular who whom I happen to be. . . . As psychiatrists who are homosexual, we must know our place and what we must do to be successful. If our goal is high academic appointment, a level of earning capacity equal to our fellows, or admission to a psychoanalytic institute, we must make certain that no one in a position of power is aware of our sexual preference and/or gender identity. Much like the black man with light skin, who chooses to live as a white man, we cannot be seen with our real friends, our real homosexual family, lest our secret be known, and our dooms sealed.

"DR. H. ANONYMOUS" speaking at the 125th Annual Meeting
of the American Psychiatric Association, May 2, 1972[1]

At their annual meeting in May 1972, the American Psychiatric Association (APA) hosted a panel discussion titled "Psychiatry: Friend or Foe to the Homosexual? A Dialogue." The APA sponsored the panel in response to an ongoing campaign organized by gay rights activists to push the professional association to declassify homosexuality as a mental disorder. The APA is the professional organization in charge of the *Diagnostic and Statistical Manual of Mental Disorders* (*DSM*), the official diagnostic reference book of psychiatry and the professional psychotherapeutic disciplines. By listing homosexuality among the mental disorders of the DSM, activists charged, and perpetuating the harmful notion that homosexuality is a sickness that needs to be cured, the APA was responsible for facilitating discrimination against homosexuals in a variety of contexts. Psychiatrists, they claimed, were thereby complicit in the social persecution of homosexuals and, in their part, responsible for the personal suffering of many.[2]

The 1972 panel included gay rights activists Barbara Gittings, known

FIGURE 1. Dr. H. Anonymous (later revealed to be Dr. John Ercel Fryer) with Barbara Gittings and Franklin E. Kameny at the May 1972 meeting of the American Psychiatric Association. Photo by Kay Tobin. © Manuscripts and Archives Division, The New York Public Library.

for launching the New York chapter of the pioneer lesbian and gay rights group called the Daughters of Bilitis, and Franklin E. Kameny, another nationally prominent figure known for fighting discrimination after being fired from his US government post in 1957 because of his sexual orientation. The panel also included established psychiatrists Judd Marmor and Robert Seidenberg. However, a fifth panelist, quoted in the epigraph to this chapter and seated at the center of the table, was only identified as "Dr. H. Anonymous." He appeared masked, wigged, and costumed with his voice disguised (see fig. 1).

Unlike the rest of the panelists, Dr. H. Anonymous was the only speaker who was both homosexual and a psychiatrist. The combination of these identity attributes, rather than either one on its own, established a unique threat at that particular time and place. Not until 1994 did Dr. John Ercel Fryer publicly reveal that he was the person behind the mask. Fryer was a practicing psychiatrist and an untenured professor of psychiatry at Temple University at the time he spoke on the 1972 panel.[3] Not only was homosexuality grounds for termination of employment (or, in

Fryer's case, denial of tenure) and other forms of discrimination, but Fryer was a standing member of the very profession that deemed his sexual orientation to be pathological. Fryer's anonymity on this panel served the protective purpose of keeping his sexual identity disconnected from his professional identity so that, as his reference to race helps to make clear, he might safely and convincingly pass among most of his professional peers and colleagues as a straight man.[4] By obscuring his face and body with a mask and costume, disguising his voice with microphone distortion, and using a pseudonym, Fryer was able to speak publicly as a gay psychiatrist, on behalf of "psychiatrists who are homosexual," in an act that openly subverted the official position of the APA with the hope of affecting change.[5] In the process, he dramatically conveyed an important and meaningful message to a particular and situated audience that later broadened to include the public at large when news of the event, along with a photo of the masked speaker, spread. By appearing and speaking anonymously, Fryer framed the oppressive conditions experienced by gay psychiatrists and, by extension, gay men and women more generally.

While Fryer's presentation as Dr. H. Anonymous was an important step in the process that led the APA to declassify homosexuality as a mental disorder at the December 15, 1973, meeting of its board of trustees,[6] it also calls our attention to some of the more general and foundational characteristics of anonymity. As Fryer hid the "the particular who" that he "happen[ed] to be," he separated his masked actions from his personal identity, negating the relevance of personal identity to his critical testimony and social standpoint. *Personal identity* refers to that which we recognize as an individual's unique being in relation to others. It is "often . . . bound both to name and body" and manifests as our mental image of an individual and that person's unique position in a network of social relationships.[7] In most situations, we openly display or routinely reveal our personal identities. We offer a personal name, and we have no intention of hiding the connection between our personal identity and our various social roles and activities. On some occasions, we may wear a name tag, provide an identifying document (such as a work or student identification card or a state-issued driver's license), or use a personalized social media profile to communicate with others. Personal identification is a normal part of many routine interactions and relationships, and the basic details of our personal identities are quite commonly expected and often explicitly requested when we first meet and interact with others. In various circumstances, we may be required to state our name "for the record," supply a social security number, provide a signature in front of a witness, or show a passport. We also establish personal identity with other official documents (such as birth certificates), fingerprints, handwriting, voice recognition, facial recognition (either via visual comparison with a photo identification document or via the digital technologies that drive surveillance databases and social media image-tagging software), retina scans, radio-frequency identification (RFID) chips, DNA sequencing, credit cards, license plates, log-in credentials, and medical and dental records.[8] Much of the data underlying these personal identity markers are increasingly stored in digital form. We use such technologies to establish unique personal identities in relation one another—to mark, track, and verify distinct individual beings in the world.

Anonymous actors obscure their personal identities, which calls our attention to all the ways that people might avoid links to identifying information while acting in various situations. For example, some use cash rather than credit cards to make a purchase, "burner" phones rather than account-based phones when making a call or sending a text message, or anonymizing software and digital encryption systems when interacting with others online.[9] Others publish texts or produce art without using their personal names, wear masks and indistinct clothing at political protests to hide their physical features, or act behind the cover of a corporate entity or some third-party representative to engage in a financial transaction. In all of these cases and many others, actors dissociate and disconnect certain actions from the personal identities they carry in other aspects of their lives. As Kathleen A. Wallace argues, a key feature of anonymity involves a "noncoordinatability of traits," or "the lack of coordination between [an anonymous individual's] agency"—their activity *as anonymous*—and that individual's "other socially recognizable traits and locations in social networks of action."[10] Likewise, Julie Ponesse points out that the "nonidentifiability" at the core of anonymity "is accomplished by dissociability," which involves separating certain information from the "particular persons who occupy it."[11] Thus, anonymity is possible insofar as actors can successfully sever the link between certain actions and their personal identities.

In this book, I analyze a wide variety of historical and contemporary cases to develop a cultural and interactionist sociology of anonymity. In general, my arguments about anonymity (literally, "no name") also apply to pseudonymity (literally, "false name"). While I discuss important distinctions between them, and while I specifically address pseudonymity in reference to particular cases or to highlight its unique characteristics, my overarching objective is to present a general framework that allows us to better understand *how and why individuals act with obscured personal identities*. Broadly speaking, I am motivated by the following questions:

How should we understand anonymity and pseudonymity? Why, under various circumstances, do individuals act anonymously or pseudonymously? How do they accomplish these states? How do they use them and in what situations? When does it make sense to say an individual is anonymous rather than simply unknown in the way that so many strangers are unknown to us and irrelevant to our lives? What are the implications of anonymous activity for various relationships and for society in general, for better or for worse? To address these questions, I consider a broad array of different cases in every chapter. In the process, I hope to show just how prevalent and significant anonymity is in the world, and how a sociology of *anonymous acts* can provide critical insight with regard to a variety of important issues.[12]

My core argument is that anonymity and pseudonymity are best understood as *performances* in which actors obscure personal identities as they make meaning for various audiences.[13] When we think of anonymity, we often think of someone who is hiding and preventing us from knowing exactly who they are. Indeed, this is part of the picture, but anonymity is not simply hiding.[14] Nor does it involve invisibility, as some scholars suggest when they refer to Plato's parable of the Ring of Gyges (a hypothetical ring that allows its wearer to be invisible) to discuss the moral implications of anonymous behavior.[15] In fact, anonymity involves someone who is very obviously *acting* while intentionally blocking others from recognizing personal identity in outwardly meaningful ways. While John Ercel Fryer hid his personal identity, he also performed for an audience, presenting himself in a generic and mysterious fashion to convey a message. He was *actively* and strikingly anonymous rather than *passively* unknown, cloaked in his presentation of character and performance of purpose. In fact, in order to be relevant or meaningful at all, anonymity must be moved into action—brought to life in social situations or circumstances that involve dynamic relations or interactions with other people. As actors do the work of moving anonymity into action, they use their various physical or stylistic displays, pseudonyms or avatars, texts and vocalizations, and other modes of expression to shape the meanings of their situations and interactions for various purposes. Anonymity is a matter of performative accomplishment.

On the one hand, I am interested in how performances of anonymity influence the interactive construction of meaning as contingent and emergent in specific situations. These concerns are traditionally associated with philosophical pragmatism and the sociological perspective of symbolic interactionism. Anonymous activities are typically set in particular times and places, and, most significantly, they manifest in relation to particular audiences.[16] Thus, the meanings of anonymity emerge via the dynamic interplay between anonymous actors and those with whom they interact. Furthermore, while actors may be anonymous to the audiences for whom they perform, others may know exactly who they are (as some members of the "GayPA," an informal network of homosexual psychiatrists within the APA, knew all along who was behind the figure of Dr. H. Anonymous). In other words, anonymous actors exert different degrees of information control with regard to different audiences, and members of different audiences have different types of knowledge about the identities of those who perform anonymously.[17] Regardless of the material or technological measures one employs to act anonymously, and regardless of the social ethics or laws in place to protect people from being personally identified by others, anonymity breaks down when performances fail and performers can no longer control information in ways that shield personal identities.

From this perspective, anonymity is always contextually, situationally, relationally, and temporally bound, although these boundaries manifest differently on a case-by-case basis, depending on the circumstances at hand.[18] Those who act or write as if anonymity can be absolute or infallible, along with those who proclaim that anonymity is a "myth" and not (or no longer) truly achievable,[19] both misunderstand the fundamentally social and contingent character of anonymity. Rather, anonymity is simultaneously achievable and precarious. Thus, I am not particularly interested in taking a positivist or rationalist position on whether or not "true" anonymity exists, nor am I particularly interested in taking an evaluative stand on the moral character of anonymous acts (although both of these themes come up throughout this book as I analyze different cases). Instead, I am primarily focused on broad social and cultural questions with regard to how actors perform hidden identities in various contexts and relationships—how they bring anonymity to life and thereby make meaning in their times, places, and situations while obscuring personal identities.

On the other hand, I am equally interested in the ways actors draw on durable cultural codes and historically relevant symbolism, imagery, and scripted text—the rich elements of culture and deep-seated structures of symbolic communication—as they perform anonymity and pseudonymity in their various contexts and situations. When they block the signifiers of personal identity, such actors replace them with alternative signifiers that they use to express culturally relevant meanings. With this perspective, rooted in the strong program in cultural sociology,[20] I unpack the deeper layers of meaning that actors animate, often in creative and sometimes novel ways, when using anonymity to achieve their objectives.

In addition to considering the interactive dynamics and deep cultural logics of anonymity, I am interested in how anonymous acts share general properties across a range of otherwise different cases and situations. Adding a formal and comparative framework to this study, I approach anonymity from the perspective of social pattern analysis.[21] Social pattern analysts look for general similarities across otherwise different "cultural, situational, and historical contexts" in order to develop broadly relevant social theory.[22] Thus, I analyze and compare cases from various times and places and across levels of analysis—from small-scale interpersonal interactions to large-scale social systems—in order to reveal the patterned and most pervasive social characteristics of anonymity. I also explore anonymous acts in different spheres of social life, including the religious, political, economic, psychotherapeutic, theatrical, artistic, legal, erotic, academic, and celebratory.[23] I address cases that pertain to computer-mediated interactions and online behavior and many that do not.[24] In each chapter, I focus on one particular theme or dimension of anonymous activity and bring together different cases to highlight what all of them show—separately and together—about the dimension of anonymity at hand.[25] Consequently, I bracket out details that are not relevant to the current discussion but may be relevant in other chapters. Furthermore, I enhance my discussion in each chapter by developing deeper analyses of key cases. In order to strike a balance between the *depth* and *breadth* of my analysis, I attend to both the textures of meaning that emerge from the analysis of particular cases and the ingrained cultural patterns that are relevant across a variety of otherwise different cases.

Using this framework, I evaluate various types of data throughout this book. Engaging in a version of what Barney G. Glaser and Anselm L. Strauss referred to as "theoretical sampling," I have gathered and analyzed "different kinds of data" that allow for "different views or vantage points from which to understand" and develop a more comprehensive picture of anonymity in social life.[26] My data include textual documents of different types and sizes (such as journalistic accounts, historical and archival documents, works of literature, political treatises, official publications of organizations and institutions, web pages and online commentary, personal reflections and testimonies, and scholarly materials), images (including photographs, advertisements, and artistic works of various types), as well as film and video (produced by various agents for different purposes) and active performances (such as theatrical productions, performance art, social movement activities, and assorted types of rituals and interactions). My data also include various secondary-source materials originally introduced by sociologists, anthropologists, psychologists, folklorists, literary analysts, and scholars working in other areas who have studied some of the particular cases I address. I use their work, and sometimes analyze or reinterpret their cases, to further highlight the more generally relevant themes that transcend their particular concerns. I also draw on direct experiences and observations in every chapter.

With this multifaceted approach—stressing interactionist, cultural, and formal-comparative sociological visions while analyzing a diverse array of different cases and using a substantial and assorted collection of data—I illuminate the deep meanings and broad relevance of anonymity in social life.

## *The Social Dynamics of Anonymous Acts*

As they cloak their personally defining features, anonymous actors work to impact the world around them. To fully grasp the social significance of this phenomenon, we must carefully unpack the interactive and symbolic dynamics of anonymous acts. To this end, for the remainder of this chapter I will consider some general and foundational characteristics of anonymity and pseudonymity in social life. These characteristics will underlie and inform my discussion of the different social dimensions of anonymity in the chapters that follow.

### NAMES, NAMELESSNESS, AND PSEUDO-NAMES

The word "anonymous" is Greek in its etymological roots. To be anonymous literally means to be without a name. Therefore, a sociological inquiry into the character of anonymity can start by considering what it means to have a name. Why are names evoked and to what purpose in different contexts and situations?

Naming is about specifying individuals and objects and designating their proper place in relation to one another. Thus, naming requires establishing sociomental boundaries and is foundational to our acts of identification and personification.[27] It is about establishing the distinctiveness of individuals and objects, which is central to the process of bringing an amorphous and undefined world into focus. As Peter L. Berger and Thomas Luckmann argue:

> Every name implies a nomenclature, which implies a designated social location. To be given an identity involves being assigned to a specific place in the world. As this identity is subjectively appropriated by the child ("I am

John Smith"), so is the world to which this identity points. Subjective appropriation of identity and subjective appropriation of the social world are merely different aspects of the same process.[28]

In other words, naming is a primary mechanism by which we grasp the distinctions and relationships among objects and entities in the world. It is fundamental to both cognition and knowledge.[29] Consequently, the ability to name is crucial to our ability to attribute unique characteristics, actions, expressions, and ideas to particular persons. We can understand the act of naming as the antithesis of anonymity, but only when and insofar as naming allows us to establish, comprehend, and express the nature of an individual actor's unique personal identity in relation to the personal identities of other people.

In the early modern era, the word "anonymous" was first used to designate published works of literature that did not bear the name of an author.[30] Because literary texts were increasingly understood as works that needed to be attributed to identifiable persons, texts that were not linked to a named author were explicitly marked and labeled "anonymous." As with such cases, the lack of a name only becomes significant when, in a particular time and place, an audience expects "to identify a *specific* individual" responsible for a particular action or product.[31] However, because "[a] name could be ambiguous" and because there are many other ways of establishing unique identities, "anonymity should be understood to mean, more broadly, nonidentifiability rather than simply . . . 'namelessness.'"[32] If we read a poem attributed to "John Smith" posted to an internet forum, we have a name but we do not necessarily have knowledge of the author's personal identity. Moreover, in some cases, we may have access to an individual's name and yet remain blind to their personal identity because a social anonymity marks the dynamics of our interactions. Consider, for example, a police officer who writes a ticket. That individual might openly display a badge number and perhaps even a name tag, but to the individual who receives the ticket, he remains a "cop"; his personal identity does not matter to the interaction and, practically speaking, remains left out of the story and effectively unknown. Furthermore, all who are unknown to us are technically nameless to us as well, but like the countless people from other times and places who we will never encounter—neither in person nor by story, image, or reputation—they are not necessarily anonymous to us.[33] To be anonymous is to be without a name only because, and only when, names are meaningful as means of personally identifying social actors in particular situations. It is not namelessness in and of itself that equates to anonymity, but rather the act of obscuring one's name as a means to obscuring personal identity while acting for particular audiences.

Naming is also crucial to our ability to perceive an individual as the *same entity over time* and associate a sense of character or personality with that particular individual. Because "names are typically attached to selves and because most people go through life with the same name, a sense [of] continuity is, so to speak, built in."[34] Thus, naming allows us to string together otherwise discrete actions occurring at different times and places into the story that defines a particular and unique individual.[35] Carrying a name over time allows individuals to establish both "historicity and relationality"[36]—a "one-of-a-kind quality"[37] due to their unique biographical timeline and evolving standpoint in the space of social relations. Therefore, naming also allows us to attribute motive to a particular agent, hold a particular person accountable for his or her actions, assign blame or credit, and reasonably predict or anticipate the spirit of our future interactions with a particular person.[38] When we assign an individual's personal name to an action or product, we establish that individual's agency and link that action or product with the personal character of the individual who carries the name. We affect both the meaning of the person and the meaning of the action or product with that link. Insofar as these attributions of character, motive, responsibility, and agency have real and profound consequences, there is significant social power in the act of naming.

The significance of names to the continuity of personal identity calls our attention to an important temporal dimension of anonymity. To act anonymously is to temporarily split with one's personal and biographical past while also avoiding any future personal association with one's actions while anonymous.[39] It is to separate one's actions while anonymous from the continuity of being inherent in one's personal story and represented by the name that ties one's unique and personal identity together. Anonymous actors divorce their actions from the named person who is situated in time (with a past, present, and future) and in established relations to others (with enduring and evolving connections to particular individuals and communities). They effectively *suspend* their named personal identities while acting. Anonymous acts are thus divorced from an actor's *personal reputation*, as certain communities of others know that actor and their reputation by name, and they therefore exist outside of the "moral order and . . . economy of trust"[40] to which the actor is otherwise personally beholden.

Anonymous actors accomplish this suspension of personal identity by assuming a *cover representation*. Cover representations serve as *impersonal fronts* that stand in place of the signifiers we would otherwise use to establish personal identity.[41] The mask, in contrast to the face, is an archetypical cover representation; it is both a tool and a metaphor for acting anonymously.[42] By covering "the human face," masks obstruct "the primary means of our recognizing, and thus identifying, one another,"[43] as well as "the most important expressive tool human beings possess" in their relations with others.[44] Those who wear masks replace this important means of personal expression and recognition with the meaning conveyed by and with the mask itself. Masks, like cover representations in general, can be generically anonymous (as with a typical masquerade mask) or particular and pseudonymous (as with many contemporary Halloween costumes). They can also start out generic and take on the character of pseudonymity over time if an actor becomes known by the particular character of the mask they wield and is subsequently assigned a name. Actors use masks and other cover representations to facilitate the expression of different voices, feelings, personas, and characters and to make various meanings at different times and in different contexts.

Anonymous actors use many different types of cover representations. They can be material or digital, vocalized and/or visually displayed. They can also manifest as organizational fronts that actors use to obscure their personal identities, as third-party representatives that stand in for an unidentified actor,[45] or as generic social roles that actors use to define themselves and others in particular settings and interactions. In some cases, an actor's cover representation can be a particular product (e.g., like a work of art or political manifesto) that serves as the public front for an obscured personal identity. Moreover, actors can use multiple cover representations, sometimes simultaneously, to engage different audiences, such as when one individual acts anonymously or pseudonymously using different accounts in multiple forums online. In some cases, cover representations can be quite strong and durable, and it may be extremely difficult to discover an anonymous actor's personal identity. In others, they may be weaker and therefore more tenuous.[46] Moreover, cover representations can facilitate sincere expressions of underlying thoughts and sentiments or be fundamentally deceptive.[47] However, they all exist as *covers* insofar as they function as shields that prevent or undermine personal identifiability, and *representations* insofar as they have expressive and symbolic properties (which are often intertwined with their material, stylistic, technological, and functional qualities) that actors use to make and convey meaning. In fact, their function as *cover* influences their function as *representation*, and vice versa. Note that I am using the term "cover" actively, as a verb (as in "to cover one's tracks") but also as a noun (as in "to act under the cover of"). Despite their differences, actors use these various cover representations to bring anonymity and pseudonymity to life.[48]

Cover representations differ in degree along a spectrum that spans from the generic to the particular. While anonymity entails obscuring one's personal identity with a generic cover, pseudonymity entails obscuring one's personal identity with a specific name, face, or some other moniker (such as an online handle). Therefore, pseudonyms have many of the characteristics of names in general. Most significantly, pseudonyms allow us to link the actions of an obscured agent over time, providing for the establishment of a second narrative identity and biographical history rooted in an alternate name and split from one's personal narrative identity—a pseudonymous reputation that is disconnected from an actor's personal reputation.[49] Thus, naming does not need to establish personal identity for the attribution of *character* to be accomplished. Indeed, pseudonymous actors can build rich and elaborate *pseudonymous characters* that stand on their own, which allows some people (including social movement leaders, authors, artists, and serial killers) to be *both famous and unknown.*[50] Furthermore, "pseudonymous reputations" can certainly be "a source of esteem to the generator of the pseudonymous material," giving pseudonymous actors good reason to care about them.[51] For this reason, after she established her pseudonymous reputation, Mary Ann Evans maintained a strong commitment to using her nom de plume George Eliot, which became "a signifier for the authorial source of the text."[52] Finally, when people act anonymously, we always know they are obscuring their personal identities. However, when actors use pseudonyms, their cover representations can misleadingly appear to indicate valid or authentic personal identities in some cases, and they can be known as cover representations in others.[53]

Whether generically anonymous or particularly pseudonymous, actors make meaning while divorcing their covered performances from their personal identities. In this most fundamental sense, the differences between anonymity and pseudonymity are often blurred. For example, while the graffiti artist Banksy has risen to pseudonymous fame, his fans and critics alike often refer to his work as "anonymous." Consider also Rachel Cusk's review of Elena Ferrante's *The Story of the Lost Child*, where Cusk refers to the pseudonymous author as the "*famously anonymous* Italian novelist."[54] With regard to an audience's "speculation about authorship," John Mullan writes, "the distinction between anonymity and pseudonymity will often be indistinct or even immaterial."[55] When we commonly blur the distinction between anonymity and pseudonymity, we highlight the fact that both involve acting with a cover representation to engage an audience in the world.

Both anonymity and pseudonymity often allow individuals a greater degree of freedom to act and express themselves.[56] When one's actions are split from one's personal identity, one can be "freed from obligations, liabilities, and the restrictions imposed by guilt, shame, and fear."[57] One can also avoid personal consequences that would likely otherwise accompany their actions, including moral reproach, social alienation, or criminal prosecution, as well as unwanted praise and public appreciation. Indeed, "anonymity can certainly enable individuals to do what they could not do without it, and it may even encourage individuals to do what they *would* not do without it."[58] Such an enhanced freedom to act is depicted allegorically when Homer's Odysseus escapes the Cyclops, Polyphemus. After Polyphemus drinks enough wine to be impaired, Odysseus says, "Cyclops, you ask my name and I will tell it you; . . . my name is Noman; this is what my father and mother and my friends have always called me." When Odysseus blinds the Cyclops, Polyphemus shouts, "Noman is killing me by fraud! Noman is killing me by force!" Therefore, when the other Cyclopes hear Polyphemus's cries for help, they believe he is drunk and delusional. By answering Polyphemus with a pseudonym, which is both a clever cover name and so generic that it is no name at all, Odysseus avoids the fallout of his attack. He acquires an ability to act and escape that would have otherwise been impossible.[59] Affiliates of the hacker network Anonymous (which is also both a pseudo-name and a non-name) accomplish a similarly generic cover in their public actions and communications, which facilitates a freedom to attack powerful forces and violate the law. Likewise, when one sends an unsigned love letter or death threat, that individual is typically exercising a freedom of expression that they would not otherwise exercise.[60]

As Charles Horton Cooley, George Herbert Mead, and others have argued, a foundational part of our experience of self and personal identity involves our ability to take the perspective of others and thereby to see ourselves reflected in their points of view as we interact with them. Our vision of who we are and our understanding of how we should behave take form in the midst of social interaction, shaped by our relationships with others who enforce the expectations and values of the communities within which we are situated.[61] Acting anonymously or pseudonymously allows individuals to sidestep these social forces—to temporarily escape the interactive recognition and community norms that define and otherwise constrain their behavior. Anonymous actors often see the expressions, reactions, and evaluations of the others with whom they interact, but rather than seeing others oriented toward their personal selves, they see these others oriented only to their cover representations. Thus, by using a cover representation in place of personal identity, anonymous actors break out of the normative "interlocking of glances" that holds people *personally accountable* to a shared social and moral order.[62] They are freed from the weight of others' appraisals and judgments precisely because others are now only seeing and appraising their cover representations.

For example, with regard to social media forums in which participants remain anonymous, Abigail E. Curlew shows how individuals "perform renditions of their identity that they would not want associated with their overall reputation." Anonymity, Curlew argues, creates conditions for "undisciplined performativity" by undermining "the impact of socio-cultural norms in shaping user behavior."[63] The "dissociation between user-generated content and a social actor's overall sense of self" provides for "the freedom to post without user accountability."[64] Such a performative dissociation from personal identity can also be enhanced by geographic distance such as when people go *incognito* while on vacation, temporarily suspending and escaping the pressures and constraints of their everyday home identities. Such individuals "use long distances to consciously sort and separate identities" and "travel to a bounded space where they can indulge certain aspects of self and then return home, hoping for no overlap."[65] Thus, travel can allow "for relatively anonymous activity."[66] However, while escaping the interactive recognition that would otherwise hold them accountable to certain normative standards, anonymous actors are never truly "undisciplined" because they are never fully detached from social and cultural forces.[67] Rather, they often animate sentiments, ideologies, and perspectives that are suppressed in many contexts and communities while they are rooted, and even freely and openly expressed, in others. Both anonymity and pseudonymity can allow such suppressed sentiments and underground ideologies to emerge when and where social pressures would otherwise stifle them.

While anonymity typically allows actors a greater degree of performative freedom, such freedom can exist in tension with different forms of social constraint that are rooted in the ways others hold anonymous and pseudonymous actors accountable for their performances. On the one hand, anonymous actors may be accountable to others who are aware of their personal identities while they act anonymously. For example, corpo-

rate officers who act behind the cover of a corporate front may be anonymous to the general public, but held personally accountable by their board
of directors. In other situations, those who act anonymously together, as
an anonymous "performance team,"[68] often hold one another in check.
When members of the Ku Klux Klan don hoods and robes, they may be
anonymous to their victims and to the general public but remain aware of
one another's personal identities and hold each other accountable to the
normative expectations of the group.

On the other hand, a particular form of social constraint grows as
soon as actors take on a pseudonymous character profile and establish
a reputation.[69] When police detectives recognize a pattern in otherwise
anonymous criminal activity, they link multiple crimes to one criminal.
As with the cases of many serial killers, the criminal can then be assigned
a pseudonym (such as Jack the Ripper, Son of Sam, Zodiac Killer, or BTK
Strangler).[70] Police detectives can then induce a criminal's personal attributes and begin to predict his next move—a professional process known
as "profiling" that requires constructing a pseudonymous character to
which motive, style, tendency, and other particular qualities, even personal history, can be assigned. Profiling restricts the killer's freedom to
act and express himself as he becomes more recognizable and predict-
able by virtue of the pseudonymous character he has established in his
association with his victims and his public audience. The actor is even
more constrained if building a consistent pseudonymous reputation or
conveying a coherent message is part of his motivation (as in the case
of the anonymous actor dubbed the "Unabomber" and later exposed to
be Theodore "Ted" Kaczynski). Beyond the case of crime, many others,
including authors and artists, build pseudonymous characters that allow
for a freedom of expression but also become more confining the more
their audience develops performance expectations to which they hold the
pseudonymous actor accountable.

Finally, the members of anonymous or pseudonymous forums and
communities often police the behavior of one another. They require "communicative accountability" to their own system of norms and values,[71]
especially with regard to the prohibition against revealing personal identities. In pseudonymous settings, one's pseudonymous reputation provides
a particularly strong "esteem incentive to behave in accord with prevailing
values,"[72] a form of social control that is quite similar to the ways that
groups commonly hold personally identifiable individuals accountable
to group standards of behavior. In all such cases, the freedoms that stem
from acting in the breach of personal identity coexist with various forces
of social control and constraint.

## THE EXHIBITIONIST AND THE VOYEUR:
### ANONYMITY AND INFORMATION CONTROL

Considering the dynamics of information control,[73] anonymous actors adopt the formal characteristics of *controlled exhibitionism* and *concealed voyeurism*. With regard to controlled exhibitionism, anonymous actors reveal limited and focused aspects of their thoughts, actions, and sentiments in a controlled and often provocative fashion. While anonymity involves "a specific exercise of control, in which true pieces of information about a person are concealed from others,"[74] it simultaneously facilitates the social exposure of views, behaviors, and feelings that would likely otherwise remain hidden. While some may act like "mindless flashers" and others more like "practiced strippers,"[75] anonymous agents expose parts of themselves that they do not usually expose. This exhibitionistic character of anonymity is an important factor distinguishing it from privacy.[76] Both privacy and anonymity require sturdy boundaries around personal information. However, while privacy is about keeping something hidden, anonymity is about exposing something in a controlled and dramatic manner.

This characteristic of controlled exhibitionism comes with the risk of unwanted divulgence—of revealing too much in the process of acting the anonymous role.[77] For example, attempts to remain anonymous by hooded members of the Ku Klux Klan were sometimes foiled when their victims recognized them because they wore their wives' dresses as robes, rode distinctive horses, or failed to disguise their voices.[78] Likewise, during the Venetian carnival of the eighteenth century, "masks did not always disguise. . . . Neighbors . . . recognized the character of a walk, the height and build of a body, the sound of a voice."[79] People who act anonymously online can be betrayed by their IP addresses when authorities or hackers link such information to their personal identities.[80] Anonymous reviewers working for academic journals can accidentally reveal their identities by expressing strong opinions or directly referring to their own published work. Despite their careful attempts to hide identifying information, many anonymous actors "may leave clues about aspects of themselves" in the process.[81] Simultaneously, audience members are usually quite sensitive to clues about the personal identities of anonymous actors. Managing the tensions of controlled exhibitionism, which involves carefully maintaining an optimal balance between exposure and concealment, is crucial to a successful anonymous performance.

With regard to concealed voyeurism, anonymous actors can watch the consequences of their performances and revelations from a protected vantage point, often hidden in plain sight. They can see without *being seen* or *being known* as the particular person behind the anonymous act. For example, when FBI director James Comey acted with the Twitter handles @projectexile7 and, later, @FormerBu, both associated with the pseudonym "Reinhold Niebuhr," he was able to experience online interactions and exchanges without being seen and known as James Comey.[82] Likewise, when popular authors such as Stephen King and J. K. Rowling publish under pseudonyms (Richard Bachman and Robert Galbraith, respectively) to ensure the reception of their newer work is not influenced by their established personal reputations, they can observe audience reactions to their work in new ways. In a similar vein, parables of Elijah the Prophet visiting homes dressed as a beggar, or Jesus walking unrecognized among his disciples after his crucifixion and resurrection, both highlight how acting with a generic and anonymizing cover representation (beggar or stranger) can allow one to see without being personally identified as the seer—and to witness behaviors that one may not witness if one's personal identity was evident.[83] Claiming and expressing this voyeuristic dynamic in an eerie and frightening way, one individual harassed a family after they purchased a home in Westfield, New Jersey, by leaving ominous notes in their mailbox signed "The Watcher."[84] Whether occurring on the busy streets of large cities where one observes others while anonymously blending into the crowd,[85] in an interpersonal setting where someone wears a mask, via pseudonymous social media interactions and exchanges, or in some other case,[86] such a concealed voyeurism allows actors to observe others without being personally recognized.

Because it often facilitates such a voyeuristic perspective or vantage point, anonymity can afford actors the benefit of seeing what they would otherwise not see. Consequently, it creates a risk that one may acquire upsetting information—that one may see something that one does not particularly enjoy seeing. Returning to the case of the anonymous love letter, when the receiver is speculating with a close friend about who the letter writer might be, that friend might actually be the writer, secretly enjoying the ability to observe the reception of her letter. However, she also risks witnessing the receiver (who is unaware that the writer is actually present) freely mock, belittle, or reject her. In this regard, anonymous actors can experience the troubling voyeuristic insight afforded to individuals who pass as a member of another group, who render themselves "open to learning what others 'really' think of persons of his kind."[87] In a similar vein, when employers adopt pseudonyms and disguise themselves as employees of their own companies in the CBS television series *Undercover Boss*, they often gain information about the perspectives and practices of their employees that they find disturbing.

Given this characteristic of concealed voyeurism, we can consider anonymity not just as a mode of avoiding surveillance, but also as an important means of surveilling others. As Michel Foucault comments with
regard to Jeremy Bentham's panopticon prison, in which prisoners confined to cells in a ring are constantly observable by guards who are concealed in a central tower, it is a means of "dissociating the seen/being seen
dyad."[88] As with tinted windows on automobiles (police and civilian) or
tinted visors on motorcycle helmets, anonymity facilitates a voyeuristic
advantage and can establish a power imbalance centered on optical access,
information control, and knowledge.

Finally, these complementary characteristics of controlled exhibitionism and concealed voyeurism often take form in relation to "segmented
audiences" that have different degrees of knowledge with regard to the
personal identities of the actors in question.[89] Those who have insider
knowledge as to the personal identities of anonymous actors "form a
secret society of a kind."[90] Such *identity insiders* are positioned either to
enable the anonymous activity at hand (sometimes even being directly
complicit in the construction of the cover representation) or to expose
the personal identities of the anonymous actors. For example, the personal
identity of the artist Banksy is unknown to many but not to all, as the
artist has an inner circle of confidants and assistants who are well aware
of what others desire to know.[91] Likewise, while Jonathan Swift published
*Gulliver's Travels* anonymously, "Swift's friends had always been in on the
'secret' of its authorship."[92] Veiled Muslim women of Middle Eastern and
North African origin might be anonymous to the Western Judeo-Christian
gaze, but certainly not to their families, local communities, and personal
networks. The drone operator who bombs a target 7,000 miles away may
be anonymous to his victims and to the public at large, but not to his
coworkers and chain of command. In each case, one's audience standpoint shapes one's position in relation to the dynamics of knowledge and
information control, and thereby plays a vital role in the definition and
experience of anonymous acts.

## IMPERSONAL AGENCIES: SOMEONE,
## ANYONE, EVERYONE, AND NO ONE

While anonymous and pseudonymous actors block their audiences from
linking actions and expressions to personal identities, they prompt them
to comprehend and attribute agency in various impersonal ways. We can
explore these impersonal and somewhat amorphous agencies by considering the interrelated notions of *someone, anyone, everyone,* and *no one.*

Each of these notions represents a different way that audiences can conceptualize the forces behind anonymous action and expression.[93] They are variously relevant to the many different cases I discuss throughout this book, taking form to different degrees and in different combinations according to the particular case or situation at hand.

The notion of *someone*, as epitomized by the generic pseudonyms "John Doe" and "Jane Doe," calls our attention to the fact that a core feature of anonymity is *mystery*. Mystery breeds speculation. Indeed, anonymous and pseudonymous actors often prompt their audiences to wonder about the personal identities that are obscured.[94] Given the allure of mystery, audiences will often search for answers. For example, many have pondered the identity of the mysterious author known by the pseudonym B. Traven, who has been described as "the most shadowy figure in the history of literature."[95] Likewise, the Toynbee tiles, colorful tiles with similar cryptic messages embedded in the streets of cities across the United States and South America, have inspired serval speculations and investigations into the mysterious identity of the guerrilla artist who created and placed them.[96] Similarly, many have wondered about the creator(s) of the remarkable cryptocurrency Bitcoin, known only via the pseudonym Satoshi Nakamoto. As also evidenced by the vast amount of public speculation about the personal identity of the anonymous whistleblower who exposed the content of US president Donald Trump's July 25, 2019, phone call with Ukrainian president Volodymyr Zelenskyy, or the widespread guesswork about who authored the 2019 book *A Warning*, a purported exposé of the Trump White House by an unnamed "senior Trump administration official,"[97] anonymous actors cultivate curiosity. In each case, the anonymous or pseudonymous agents at work are perceived through their products or communicative activities, which serve as public representations of mysterious *someones*.

Such a mystery of personal identity calls our attention to important differences between secrecy and anonymity. While the act of keeping a secret involves "concealing information about us as already-known entities," acting anonymously involves keeping "bits of information [one has] revealed" from being linked to one's personal identity.[98] Furthermore, acting in secret involves concealing the act itself. When East German Stasi agents spied on citizens of the German Democratic Republic using hidden recording devices and informants, they used secrecy to their advantage in that they were present yet all evidence of their presence was typically obscured (despite a mounting general awareness of their activities). However, when US FBI counterintelligence operatives wrote unsigned letters to social movement leaders in the 1960s and 1970s, such as

KING,

In view of your low grade, abnormal personal behavoir I
will not dignify your name with either a Mr. or a Reverend or
a Dr. And, your last name calls to mind only the type of
King such as King Henry the VIII and his countless acts of
adultery and immoral conduct lower than that of a beast.

King, look into your heart. You know you are a complete
fraud and a great liability to all of us Negroes. White
people in this country have enough frauds of their own but I
am sure they don't have one at this time that is any where near
your equal. You are no clergyman and you know it. I repeat you
are a colossal fraud and an evil, vicious one at that. You
could not believe in God and act as you do. Clearly you don't
believe in any personal moral principles.

King, like all frauds your end is approaching. You could
have been our greatest leader. You, even at an early age have
turned out to be not a leader but a dissolute, abnormal moral
imbecile. We will now have to depend on our older leaders like
Wilkins a man of character and thank God we have others like
him. But you are done. Your "honorary" degrees, your Nobel
Prize (what a grim farce) and other awards will not save you.
King, I repeat you are done.

No person can overcome facts, not even a fraud like yourself.
Lend your sexually psychotic ear to the enclosure. You will find
yourself and in all your dirt, filth, evil and moronic
talk exposed on the record for all time. I repeat - no person
can argue successfully against facts. You are finished. You will
find on the record for all time your filthy, dirty, evil
companions, male and females giving expression with you to your
hidious abnormalities. And some of them to pretend to be ministers
of the Gospel. Satan could not do more. What incredible evilness.
It is all there on the record, your sexual orgies. Listen to
yourself you filthy, abnormal animal. You are on the record. You
have been on the record - all your adulterous acts, your sexual
orgies extending far into the past. This one is but a tiny sample.
You will understand this. Yes, from your farious evil playmates
on the east coast to          and others on the west coast
and outside the country you are on the record. King you are done.

The American public, the church organizations that have been
helping - Protestant, Catholic and Jews will know you for what
you are - an evil, abnormal beast. So will others who have backed
you. You are done.

King, there is only one thing left for you to do. You know
what it is. You have just 34 days in which to do (this exact
number has been selected for a specific reason, it has definite
practical signfficant. You are done. There is but one way out for
you. You better take it before your filthy, abnormal fraudulent self
is bared to the nation.

FIGURE 2. Anonymous letter sent to Dr. Martin Luther King Jr., drafted and covertly
delivered by agents of the FBI's Counterintelligence Program (public domain).

Dr. Martin Luther King Jr. (see fig. 2), they used anonymity to cultivate
political instability and achieve social disruption.[99] Like the writers of
anonymous threatening letters in eighteenth-century England,[100] or like
the Unabomber terrorist of the late twentieth-century United States,[101]
FBI agents cultivated a troubling mystery. While secrecy may be ideal for
spying, they used anonymity to create an atmosphere of suspicion and
speculation in order to foster paranoia and thereby to "modify the adver-
sary's conduct."[102] After all, an anonymous threatening letter must have
come from someone with malicious intent. But who?[103]

In general, "written communication" can be characterized by a "mixture of determinateness and ambiguity" and a "plurality of possible interpretations."[104] Even when authors are named, we "construct" that "entity" of the author by imaginatively imputing characteristics to their being according to certain social and cultural norms attached to their field.[105] However, the range of interpretations possible to the reader of any written communication immediately increases when the personal identity of the writer is concealed. The very form of any anonymous correspondence (whether a love letter, a death threat, or a passive-aggressive note left on one's car) requires the recipient to attribute authorship to a disembodied and impersonal *someone*. This mysterious *someoneness* of communication is characteristic of many online interactions and relationships where an actor's cover representation takes the form of a pseudonymous handle, an avatar, or simply anonymous text in an exchange.[106] Whatever the objectives of any actor may be, the disembodied character of digital media has made anonymous and pseudonymous communication more easily achievable and much more commonplace. However, all technologies that facilitate communication over a distance, beginning with the advent of written language (which might be left on a wall, recorded in a book and stored for a long time, or delivered by a third party—human or animal) and proceeding through the telegraph and telephone (long before the birth of internet technology), allowed for increased possibilities of anonymous (disembodied, nameless, faceless) and therefore mysterious communication.

While the notion of *someone* calls our attention to the mystery of anonymous agency, the notion of *anyone* evokes the impersonality and interchangeability at the core of various anonymous interactions and relations.[107] On a basic level, "anonymity is a function of there being a multiplicity of persons with whom the anonymous person may be confused," which "allows that they could be someone, or even anyone, else and hence interchangeable with any number of people about whom [certain] information might be true."[108] This notion is central to what the philosopher Maurice Natanson calls the "anonymous transcendental ego" in that our individual actions and objectives, while seemingly personal, are often not truly unique, but rather formulaic, socially structured, and therefore shared with many other similarly situated social actors.[109] Thus, the notion of *anyone* is expressed in the anonymity of generic social acts, social roles, and social types. It does not matter who produces the food I eat; it can be anyone. It does not matter which particular person processes my paycheck, as long as I get paid. Such an *anyoneness* of anonymity stands in contrast to the personal character of our more intimate social relationships that are based on the unique personal identities of those in our close social circles. In this regard, we can also consider anonymity as antithetical to conventional celebrity and personal fame, especially insofar as celebrity and fame foster public obsession with the unique and defining characteristics of the famous individual's personality.[110] When celebrities and high-ranking political officials walk among the common population incognito, they use disguise and concealment, or simply rely on a lack of recognition, to achieve a temporary anyoneness.[111] Such disguised interactions replace highly marked personal identities with unmarked generic modes of being, allowing famous individuals to experience and observe the world around them from a perspective that is often impossible due to the status they carry when their personal identities are exposed.

This characteristic of *anyone* is what allows for the anonymity imposed by (and experienced in) many jobs and occupations. For example, we might see someone we encounter as a postal carrier, a police officer, or a nurse. As long as such individuals don the attire and perform the duties associated with those roles, their personal identities remain secondary or even insignificant to their interactions in their respective professional capacities.[112] This notion of *anyone* is also a core part of the rationale behind random sampling and survey procedures in the social sciences, and why protecting the anonymity of the subjects of such research is thought to enhance rather than detract from the general quality and character of the findings, which are supposed to be generic and impersonal. The point is that anyone who fits the generic parameters of a population of interest can answer the questions and the results will demonstrate something about the population under study. Personal identity is not simply irrelevant, but explicitly excluded so that it does not interfere with these results. While the anyoneness of anonymity calls our attention to the impersonal structural positions people occupy in social systems, such a characteristic is also foundational to the stories we create and tell. While specifically named characters are often quite important to the content of a story, such particular characters are based on models and types that serve as building blocks of common plots and generic story formulas.[113] These scripted character-types can be filled by anyone who assumes the role, a phenomenon that is especially evident with regard to background characters and extras in film.

The anyoneness of anonymity provides for a *social leveling* because, as interchangeable beings, individuals are seen as basically equal. Some have deemed this leveling effect vital to public deliberations and civil interactions. Using the metaphor of the mask, and describing masked interactions as "the essence of civility," Richard Sennett argues that "masks permit pure sociability, detached from the circumstances of power, malaise, and private feeling of those who wear them." For Sennett, the characteristics of personal identity ("personality") ought to be left out of modern public life, and civic engagement should be fundamentally impersonal.[114] Therefore, anyone can take part, and it is the weight of their ideas and contributions that matter, not their personal attributes. Building on this basic idea, Alfred Moore argues that "pseudonymous communication can enable the meeting of strangers under terms of structured impersonality." While pseudonyms in online forums allow participants to be held accountable for their actions and communications over time, they also strip them of other markers of status and free them to speak without fear of repercussions reaching outside of that particular deliberative space.[115] Such a social leveling underlies the democratic principle of "one person, one vote" and the idea, however much it is actually impeded by the realities of social inequality, that anyone can run for political office in a democratic society.

Building on the characteristic features of *someone* and *anyone*, the notion of *everyone* evokes a collective mass and an anonymity that strives toward universality. With such a framework, ownership and credit for anonymous acts can be shared by all. In this regard, Virginia Woolf described premodern anonymous authorship as expressive of "the common voice singing out of doors."[116] Similarly, "the great majority" of anonymous threatening letters written by aggrieved actors and political dissidents in eighteenth-century England used "the collective pronoun 'we,'" allowing individual writers to frame their acts as expressing "the common sense of injustice of the poor as a whole . . . not the personal but the collective grievance."[117] Likewise, the anonymous passages of the Babylonian Talmud give this religious text a collective voice and sense of belonging to "everybody,"[118] as did the anonymous authorship of the 1914 Christian book *The Impersonal Life*.[119] Such an attribution framework can be used to create the appearance of widespread consensus (unanimity) or mass support without naming particular individuals, as when a politician constantly refers to the anonymous "a lot of people" to indicate popular approval for a policy, or when a speaker explicitly refers to the anonymous "everyone" in order to support an argument (as in "everyone is saying . . .").

Moreover, the *everyoneness* of anonymity accentuates homogeneity and obscures differences, as when the masked, hooded, and uniformed robbers of the Spanish television series *La Casa de Papel* (titled *Money Heist* for its English release on Netflix) force their hostages to wear the same red jumpsuits and Salvador Dalí masks that they are wearing to commit the crime, using one uniform cover representation to blend criminals and hostages into a homogeneous mass and thereby making it nearly impossible for authorities to know who is who. Furthermore, the notion of *everyone* illuminates a key aspect of anonymity as it is used by some masked activists to accentuate the mass character of their movement and mass support for their actions and objectives. The hacker network that goes by the name Anonymous articulates this characteristic of anonymity when they state, "We are everyone and we are no one."[120] Likewise, Rorschach, the masked villain of HBO's 2019 series *Watchmen*, which is based on Alan Moore and Dave Gibbons's graphic novel of the same title, states in reference to his masked movement, the 7th Cavalry, "We are no one. We are everyone. We are invisible."[121] Similarly, the masks worn by the Zapatista movement of southern Mexico allow for the sentiment that "'we are all Zapatistas.'"[122] Such an anonymous mass is also captured in communist theory and propaganda referring to the interests and will of the "masses" or the only slightly more specific "workers," and in the opening phrase of the preamble to the US Constitution, "We the people."

Additionally, individual names can indicate *everyone* when multiple others adopt them as mass pseudonymous covers, as in the famous scene from Stanley Kubrick's 1960 film *Spartacus*. As depicted in the film, after a slave uprising against the Roman state was suppressed, the rebellious slaves were promised their lives in exchange for identifying their leader, Spartacus. They then each stood and stated, "I'm Spartacus!," thereby transforming the individual name into a symbol of mass resistance. By jointly claiming to be Spartacus, each man rendered the claim meaningless as a personal identity and established it as a collective cover representation for their united will. A similar phenomenon occurs in the AMC Network's *The Walking Dead*, when the members of the tribe "The Saviors" refer to themselves as "Negan" and each claim "I am Negan" in reference to the name of their leader. Likewise, the final scene of the film *V for Vendetta* depicts the population of London collectively disguised as the masked character V, marching together to witness the bombing of the British Parliament building. This collective mass finally removes their masks in unison when their anonymity grew so universal that masks were no longer necessary. At some point, if everyone is indeed behind the mask, there is no longer any mystery about *who* is acting with the cover representation.

Finally, the attributional frame of *no one* calls our attention to the fact that generic and impersonal cover representations make it difficult to attribute actions and expressions to any particular person at all. In general, individuals experience the freedom provided by being no one whenever they act anonymously, as illustrated when Odysseus escapes the Cyclops under the cover of "Noman." A key aspect of this freedom is that it affords anonymous and pseudonymous actors (and everyone else for that matter) plausible deniability because their actions are not only detached from their personal identities, but from *all* personal identities. Such an experience of *no oneness* can also stem from the phenomenon of "deindividuation" described by Philip Zimbardo, which involves the diffusion of personal autonomy and responsibility when one becomes increasingly anonymous in the context of a group.[123] In such cases, anonymity "can strip persons of compassion and prevent them from seeing themselves as individuals with the full agential powers that can harm others."[124] It can also lead to a diffusion of credit, which is why many strong students are averse to group assignments.

The no oneness of anonymity is particularly evident when we attribute agency to a social system or collectivity itself, rather than the particular individuals with personal identities who inhabit them. In fact, this sort of collectivist or system thinking is foundational to the field of sociology, as articulated in the work of Émile Durkheim, who considered society to exist as an entity and agency in and of itself. Indeed, speakers often use the term "society," or "the system," colloquially to casually explain away the causes of certain human experiences. We create or express such a foundation for anonymity when we attribute responsibility to a bank, for example, or capitalism, or "human nature." Such general collective actors are only slightly more tangible than the amorphous "they" that individuals often use in both common expressions ("you know what they say") and conspiracy theories ("they are out to get us"). Indeed, Foucault clearly captures such a notion of the anonymous *no one* when he describes social systems of power: "The logic is perfectly clear, the aims decipherable, and yet it is often the case that no one is there to have invented them," which is "an implicit characteristic of the great anonymous, almost unspoken strategies which coordinate the loquacious tactics" that profoundly impact our lives.[125] For Foucault, while we commonly speak of sexuality with reference to scientific, psychological, or legal discourses and ideas we have constructed, and these discourses and ideas in turn define our experiences of sexuality in many ways, we attribute them to no one with the consequence of seeing them as fundamental truths. Finally, the notion of *no one* can also be used to degrade individuals and even strip them of their humanity, as when Africans were defined not as people but as chattel, and when Jews and other victims of the Holocaust were treated as "cargo" by political and bureaucratic actors, effectively rendering them not only anonymous but also inhuman.[126]

While anonymity and pseudonymity block our ability to attribute actions and expressions to particular actors with unique personal identities, they prompt us to comprehend and attribute agency in other impersonal ways. The notions of *someone, anyone, everyone,* and *no one* each capture important aspects of such attributions of impersonal and anonymous agency.

## CULTURE AND MEANING IN THE PERFORMANCE OF ANONYMITY

Anonymous and pseudonymous actors bring hidden identities to life in a wide variety of situations where they work to manage the impressions of others and define their particular circumstances and relationships.[127] In the process, they use anonymity and pseudonymity in creative ways that are particular to their situations. However, they also draw on broadly relevant cultural codes and symbols as they work to define their actions along with issues, events, and concerns that transcend their local settings and particular interactive dynamics.

Analyzing anonymity as performance, I build on the work of Erving Goffman and Jeffrey C. Alexander. While treating the self as a performative accomplishment, Goffman gives us a detailed account of the tools and techniques individuals and groups use to define their situations for their audiences. He explicates the nuances of the embodied work that actors do and the "expressive equipment"[128] they mobilize to assign meaning to certain scenarios and episodes of social activity. With regard to anonymity, we must attend to the ways that people mobilize their cover representations (whatever they may be) in particular situations to manage the impressions of those with whom they interact. For example, people who act anonymously or pseudonymously in different online environments often put considerable care and intention into designing their avatars, even purchasing symbolic decorative goods that allow them to perform the character persona they wish to bring to life.[129] Beyond simply being a technology that shields their personal identities, computer-generated avatars are a means to perform alternative identities. In such cases, like many others, hidden identities come to life in particular situations and exchanges and only in the flow of social interactions. The tools and techniques of such performances are important to the meanings such actors work to convey.

Moving beyond the local, interactive, and technical aspects of performance, Alexander builds on the historical anthropology of Victor Turner and the theatrically inspired performance theory of Richard Schechner to consider the rich cultural foundations that actors must creatively fuse with their performances in order to successfully reach their audiences on cognitive, emotional, and deep psychic levels.[130] Accordingly, actors work to emplot entrenched cultural codes and bring deeply rooted cultural symbolism to life in their situated performances, and they must do so convincingly if they want to win the hearts and minds of others. When viewing anonymous acts as performances, we must consider their particular, situational, and interpersonal dynamics, but we must also illuminate how anonymous actors mobilize deep cultural meanings in creative ways relative to their particular circumstances and concerns. Thus, it is not enough to simply address the tools and technologies that people use to obscure their personal identities. Instead, if we are to comprehend the social logic, significance, and impact of anonymous acts, if we are to understand the various ways that anonymous actors make meaning and thereby shape the world around them, we must analyze both the pragmatic use and cultural significance of their hidden identities in action.

For example, when multiple social movement participants wear masks of the same design at a protest event, they actively perform the repressive dynamics they are protesting by animating their collective need to hide from an enemy regime. Whatever the actuality of threat, they define and perform themselves as targets of repression as they create the political scene and define the issues at hand. As they use their masks to obscure their personal identities, they also use them to bring the contentious circumstances of the protest to life. Moreover, the symbolism associated with the specific style of mask that a social movement group collectively wields typically expresses some deeply rooted message about the conflict at hand and their position in it. In the case of the Ejército Zapatista de Liberación Nacional (EZLN), the southern Mexican revolutionary movement also known as the Zapatistas, the *paliacate* is often used to hide the faces of rank-and-file movement participants (see fig. 3). This distinctive Mexican scarf or bandanna is a traditional fabric worn by agrarian workers that has both stylistic and functional significance. Functionally, it can be used to gather produce, protect its wearer from direct sunlight, hold hair back or absorb sweat on a hot day, or provide a dirt and pesticide filter for the nose and mouth while working. During political confrontations, the materiality of this traditional scarf not only protects activists from being personally identified by surveilling authorities, but also symbolizes the working conditions of the folk population of southern Mexico. When activists use such symbolic garb to cover their faces at a public protest, they cast the movement as one of local and popular democratic resistance to the repressive conditions and authoritarian politics imposed by an outside force. By using the *paliacate* to guard against personal recognition, these activists advanced their collective social recognition.

In addition to the *paliacate*, Zapatista activists also don dark balaclavas

FIGURE 3. Women identified as Zapatistas cover their faces with *paliacates* (1996).
Photograph by Julian Stallabrass. From Wikimedia Commons (https://commons
.wikimedia.org/wiki/File:Ejército_Zapatista_de_Liberación_Nacional_IMG
006a-sm_(11450035824).jpg). Creative Commons Attribution 2.0 Generic license
(https://creativecommons.org/licenses/by/2.0/deed.en).

(sometimes referred to as "ski masks") that are typically used by tactical
police and military units but have been appropriated by poor guerrilla
movements. The balaclava came into fashion among the Zapatista ranks
and then achieved iconic status after it was worn by the Zapatista leader
and spokesperson known by the pseudonym Subcomandante Marcos (see
fig. 4).[131] Almost always pictured wearing a balaclava, Marcos came to
represent the cultural style of the masked Mexican freedom fighter, his
political allure and grandeur greatly enhanced by his hidden identity.[132]
By using the *paliacate* (a locally popular piece of functional dress) and
balaclava (a symbolically and functionally reappropriated piece of elite
military gear) as subversive masks, the Zapatistas made both into iconic
symbols of resistance[133] that carry folk tradition and reclaimed style
into social conflict and express something of the movement's popular
and democratizing character on a grander stage. As anonymous actors
don their cover representations, they not only hide their identities, but
also commonly animate deep-seated cultural codes and symbols as they
define their situations and their actions for audiences both local and
beyond.

Considering another example, when participants in anonymous sup-

FIGURE 4. Photo purportedly of the EZLN spokesperson known by the pseudonym Subcomandante Marcos (1996). Attributed to Jose Villa at Villa Photography. From Wikimedia Commons (https://commons.wikimedia.org/wiki/File:SubMarcos HorseFromAfar.jpg). Creative Commons Attribution-Share Alike 3.0 Unported license (https://creativecommons.org/licenses/by-sa/3.0/deed.en).

port groups refrain from asking one another particular questions because those questions would reveal identifying information, they implicitly communicate the social stigma associated with their common concerns, and their joint commitment to protecting one another from linking these concerns to their personal identities. Such a collective commitment to anonymity reinforces the boundaries around the group in space and time, clearly and strongly distinguishing it from the outer world.[134] This joint performance of anonymity also creates and reinforces the definition of the space as healing, safe, and transformative by providing for the expectation and imperative that participants will share their deepest truths with one another in their liminal and dialogically situated avoidance of personal identification. This performance of anonymity serves to define the relations and interactions among participants, the immediate context, and the situation of the individual interactants, but also relies on and reinforces deep-seated cultural meanings about specific illnesses, experiences, and behaviors and the stigmas and struggles they carry.

As with these and the many other cases I analyze in this book, actors perform anonymity and pseudonymity in culturally meaningful ways as they work to define their situations and relationships. Moreover, their performances of anonymity and pseudonymity often speak to more broadly relevant issues and concerns. By performing anonymity in their particular situations and circumstances, anonymous actors work to define their realities and influence the world around them.

## Outline of the Book

With all of these general characteristics in mind, I explore a different social dimension of anonymity in each chapter of this book. By focusing on a particular social dimension as the main theme of each chapter, I am able to address multiple otherwise different cases by showing how they each illustrate that broadly relevant theme. In the process, I show how the phenomenon of anonymity is of widespread social and historical significance, and more pervasive than we might assume.

In chapter 2, I consider the ways that individuals and communities make use of anonymity for *protective* reasons in various situations and contexts. First, I explore several cases to demonstrate how anonymity is used to protect individuals from various discreditable acts that might otherwise lead to embarrassment, shame, ostracism, or some other punitive consequence.[135] By using anonymity to escape these consequences, actors effectively sidestep the social power that operates to enforce compliance with normative rules and systems of meaning. However, they also reinforce these rules by performing the need to hide their personal identities while engaging in certain behaviors. Building on this discussion, I then show how various *social ethics of anonymity*, rooted in different circumstances and settings, provide protective covers that shield personal identities. I explore the cases of anonymous altruism and charity, Catholic confession, masquerade parties and festivals, and anonymity in academic research. I also explore various anonymous communities and forums including addiction and recovery organizations and various other mutual support communities, as well as more multifaceted anonymous forums and communities that exist solely online. Next, I address the protective dimensions of *anonymous consumption* and explore the ways some products are consumed by individuals who hide their identities. Finally, I conclude by discussing the ways that actors exploit modes of protective anonymity for deceitful or nefarious purposes.

In chapter 3, I take the protective character of anonymity as a given in order to explore the *subversive* dimensions of anonymity. I focus on the ways that actors subvert personal identity as a means to suspend, undermine, or otherwise subvert dominant interpersonal, cultural, political, and moral norms. After examining several preliminary cases, including the phenomenon of QAnon and the impact of anonymity on behavior in various online forums, I consider different examples of anonymous and pseudonymous art and literature, including graffiti art, political performance art, and both fictional and nonfictional texts. Building on these discussions, I then analyze the strategic performance of anonymity by two otherwise very different social movements: the Ku Klux Klan and the hacker network Anonymous. Despite their significant differences, these movements share some general characteristics that stem from their performances of subversive anonymity. I then address the ways that the US Federal Bureau of Investigation (FBI) used anonymity to disrupt social movements as a part of its counterintelligence program, or COINTELPRO, in the 1960s and '70s.

In chapter 4, I analyze the anonymity afforded to individuals who act behind the cover of social systems (including organizations, corporations, states, and nations). I focus on five cases—the early twenty-first-century housing crisis, corporate personhood in electoral politics, the electronic surveillance of US citizens by the US National Security Agency (NSA) and other powerful organizations, technologies of distant and mass killing that evolved to characterize war and terrorism over the last century, and state executions with a particular focus on the role of medical doctors and nurses in lethal injections. While addressing each of these cases, I focus on the ways that large systems and institutions of various types facilitate anonymous acts. Next, I discuss the social character and consequences of anonymous production and exchange, raising several examples to show how anonymity is a central feature of various economic activities and relationships in the world.

I then turn to discuss anonymity as a consequence of identity typification in chapter 5, which involves seeing and treating people as generic and impersonal types and categories rather than particular and unique individuals. First, I address the distinction between acts of self-typification and other-typification. The former involves the self-determined construction and use of categorical cover representations while the latter involves the imposition of categorical cover representations that obscure the personal identities and unique characteristics of others. Such anonymizing acts often involve imposing a social label that is meaningful within the context of power imbalances, rendering individuals anonymous in problematic ways. Following an introductory discussion, I explore several cases that each show, in different ways, how actors typify and anonymize others in situated encounters. First, I discuss the ways that actors anonymize others according to class and occupation. Next, I examine the social dynamics of anonymous sex. I then consider how racial typification anonymizes individuals in ways that facilitate racially marked or motivated police activity, including the perpetration of violence. Finally, I analyze contemporary controversies over the segregated use of public restrooms along conventional lines demarcating male and female bodies to explore how cisgender typification leads actors to disregard the personal identities of others in favor of generic categories and labels. I conclude this chapter with a discussion of analytic typification and anonymization in the social sciences.

This book concludes with a final chapter in which I summarize my discussion of the interpersonal and cultural consequences of anonymity. I address the remarkable social and moral contradictions that stem from being unable to attribute actions to actors with known and continuous personal identities. In the context of this concluding discussion, I briefly address the significance of *unmasking acts* that expose anonymous actors. Summing up this cultural and interactionist sociology of anonymity, I reflect on the prevalence and relevance of anonymity in the late-modern world.

# Protective Anonymity

I'm constantly repulsed by my own skin. I don't want to touch myself, can barely look at my own body. I can't help but think about the little child I was, once upon a time, the little pink-and-white baby who made her parents so proud, as my mother told me over and over. . . . So much love, so much bother with sunbonnets, bath thermometers, and evening prayers—and all for the filth I am now.

ANONYMOUS, *Eine Frau in Berlin (A Woman in Berlin)*[1]

The 1954 book *Eine Frau in Berlin (A Woman in Berlin)* is based on the diary that Marta Hillers kept over an eight-week period from April to June 1945, when she lived in Berlin during the Soviet occupation following the defeat of the Nazi army. Hillers published the book anonymously and was only identified as its author in 2003, two years after her death. As part of her account, she describes her personal experience as a victim of multiple rapes, along with the pervasive sexual assault of German women by Soviet soldiers. When Hillers published the book in 1954 in English (which was only later published in German in 1959), it was controversial on both sides of the Cold War divide. For some, her words stood "as a shattering indictment"[2] of the episode and an attack on the character of the Soviet liberators. For others, Hillers's anonymous revelations about sexual victimization stoked German shame associated with the era, and she was "accused . . . of 'besmirching the honor of German women.'"[3] Moreover, as a German national who lived and worked in Berlin during the Third Reich, Hillers had at least a general affiliation with, and some professional ties to, the Nazi regime.[4] Her association with notorious perpetrators complicates and intersects with her personal victimhood. Thus, in Germany, "the book was met with either hostility or silence" in a climate of widespread collective denial about the war era.[5]

Hillers's anonymity served a complex protective function. Broadly speaking, it shielded her from the multifaceted backlash she would have faced for telling her story if her personal identity was attached to it. Furthermore, as the brief excerpt reproduced in the epigraph above indicates, her anonymous authorship allowed her to share her deeply troubling experiences and complex feelings, including a strong sense of personal mortification, without carrying a public association with sexual assault and traumatic victimization throughout her life. Additionally, her anonymity shielded her from potential accusations of complicity with the Nazis. As both rape victim (one who sought out a sexual relationship with a Soviet officer in order to protect herself from assaults by multiple soldiers) and German national under the Nazi regime during World War II, Hillers embodied multiple dimensions of trauma and shame. Her positionality tied her to interpersonal, local, and international dynamics of power in complex and contradictory ways. Her anonymity as author depersonalizes all of these difficult circumstances and experiences and detaches them from her postwar personal reputation and identity, allowing her to quietly break from this past episode while also telling her story, thus keeping the past alive publicly yet impersonally. Moreover, Hillers's anonymity allowed the story of her personal experiences to be more generalizable. As "Anonyma," Max Färberböck's way of referring to Hillers in his 2008 film portraying the account, she takes on the characteristic of anyoneness with regard to women who face and navigate sexual victimization, especially those who experience it as part of the horrors of war and military occupation.

In this chapter, I consider various circumstances in which individuals and communities perform anonymity and pseudonymity for protective reasons.[6] To some extent, all anonymous acts are protective in that they shield actors from social stigma and other potentially detrimental or simply unwanted consequences.[7] Such a protective shielding of personal identity is evident in many cases of anonymous testimony, confession, and authorship. It is also exemplified by the pseudonymous actions of "Jane Roe," the plaintiff in the controversial 1973 US Supreme Court case *Roe v. Wade*, or "Deep Throat," the whistleblower and press informant who exposed the Nixon Watergate scandal, as well as Bill W. and Dr. Bob, the pseudonymous cofounders of Alcoholics Anonymous.[8] In these and many other cases, the protective character of anonymity and pseudonymity facilitates the controlled exhibition of behavior or information that would otherwise remain hidden, and establishes a concealed standpoint from which anonymous and pseudonymous actors can witness the impact of their actions and revelations while avoiding personal fallout. Protective anonymity also allows for various forms of experimentation with identity, for better or for worse, which might not otherwise occur.

On the one hand, such actors *perform while protected*. They use the protective covers of anonymity and pseudonymity to act in risky, controversial, or provocative ways that might otherwise lead to undesirable outcomes including embarrassment, shame, ostracism, retaliation, and persecution, or simply to shield themselves from unwanted attention (such as that which might come after making a charitable contribution or after winning a large sum of money).[9] Thus, the protective character of anonymity can provide a temporary liberation or escape from stifling social forces and corresponding social anxieties, freeing individuals to act. In this vein, anonymity and pseudonymity facilitate the function of suicide prevention and other support lines, "safe haven" boxes that allow people to abandon unwanted babies,[10] two-way mirrors during police lineups, and tip lines for solving crimes or conveying information to authorities (see fig. 5).[11]

For these same reasons, governmental offices along with mainstream news organizations (such as the *Guardian* and the *New York Times*) and alternative news outlets (such as the website WikiLeaks) promise to shield the personal identities of whistleblowers who take great risks to reveal information about powerful actors.[12] Likewise, anonymity and pseudonymity are used to protect individuals in different legal contexts, as when law enforcement agents promise future pseudonymity via witness protection programs in exchange for testimony against a powerful defendant, or when courts protect the personal identities of witnesses, victims, and perpetrators alike due to their age. In general, when institutions (such as courts or news media outlets) shield the personal identities of some actors due to their age, they express the cultural notion that one can be too young to be publicly identified with controversial experiences or held personally accountable for their actions. In other cases, courts in various nations shield the personal identities of judges and jury members "to protect them from inappropriate influence (whether persuasion, coercion or bribes) and retribution."[13]

Actors also use anonymity to act and express themselves in ways that are deemed morally improper, offensive, seditious, or criminal. For example, some use anonymity to express vulgar, racist, sexist, or otherwise aggressive sentiments that they would likely keep quiet or disavow if their personal identities were exposed. Likewise, both thieves and activists use costumes and masks to protect themselves from retaliation by powerful forces. Moreover, from the Scarlet Pimpernel to Batman, fictional super-

FIGURE 5. Poster on a bus stop soliciting anonymous tips about crime. Seventh Avenue and Union Street, Park Slope, Brooklyn. Photo taken by author.

heroes (who typically start out anonymous and later become pseudonymous) wear masks or otherwise shield their personal identities to protect themselves from the social ramifications of vigilantism (Zorro, the Lone Ranger, Kick-Ass), the threat of retaliation to friends and family (Spider-Man, Daredevil), and the obligations and constraints that personal relationships would otherwise impose. Illustrating a characteristic shared by all anonymous and pseudonymous actors, their cover representations allow them to lead dual lives.

On the other hand, actors *perform their need for protection*. As they obscure their personal identities to act and express themselves, they also communicate something about the ways that power regulates behavior and voice in their particular situations and circumstances. When nurses who worked during the coronavirus pandemic shared their stories anonymously via an online document, they not only revealed important information about hospital conditions at the height of the pandemic, but also demonstrated their fear of retaliation from hospital administrators.[14] Likewise, in 2017, when women working in the media industry anonymously shared experiences and levied accusations of sexual harassment and sexual assault using an online document titled "Shitty Media Men,"[15] they not only called attention to the pervasive character of such behaviors throughout the industry, but also to the fact that they faced retaliation from powerful forces for telling their stories. Similarly, women in Saudi Arabia used the anonymity afforded by computer-mediated communication, along with pseudonymous representations via news media, to campaign against the legal and cultural system of Saudi male guardianship. Engaging in communication that risked harsh punishment, some of these women posted anonymous photographs of themselves on Twitter, donning an abaya with a niqab that covers both body and face, while standing in a nondescript setting and holding placards (sometimes over their faces) displaying various messages in protest of the system in which men are granted extensive control not only over their lives and bodies, but also their voices.[16]

By acting with anonymous and pseudonymous cover representations in various situations, actors frame their actions and expressions as socially stifled, personally repressed, stigmatized, incendiary, or otherwise in need of protective cover, and thus more authentic and revealing of some deeper and suppressed "truth." In this regard, the hidden identity of an actor can make the information they reveal seem especially illuminating and therefore more valuable.[17] Thus, in a story published by *Elle* magazine, anonymity offers us "an all-access pass to four men's inner thoughts" and sexual fantasies, as if anonymity makes the story more psychologically revealing and honest.[18] In another case, a pseudonymous author explained to academics who read the *Chronicle of Higher Education* that he was commonly paid to write a variety of master's theses and PhD dissertations for their students.[19] Without a pseudonymous cover, it is implied, the story would have remained secret. With it, we have an honest confession. Consider also the air of authenticity artists create when they shirk fame and embrace anonymity, thereby making their work seem more honest and prompting us to "see them as more real."[20] In all of these cases and many others, the hidden identity of the source shapes the extraordinary value of the content, which would not be exposed, it is implied, without the protection of an identity cover.

Given their controversial character, the performances of protective anonymity are often multivocal; they convey different meanings to different audiences. For example, one actor's use of anonymity to attack another might be seen as a courageous expression of truth that breaks through repressive social constraints, or a cowardly assault that unjustly violates cherished moral principles. An anonymous financial contribution might be perceived as a noble and selfless act or a cunning attempt to manipulate a situation. The pseudonymous blogger who wrote and interacted online as Shpitzle Shtrimpkind while questioning and eventually leaving her Hasidic Jewish community might be seen as a role model by those critical of ultra-Orthodox life, while simultaneously being viewed as a dangerous heretic by those who remain committed to her former worldview.[21] Likewise, while it was "for fear of retaliation" that former employees of a powerful media corporation spoke to the press anonymously to reveal details about the political affairs of their former employer,[22] the employer likely viewed their anonymous actions as a treacherous betrayal. Indeed, the very character of the protection afforded to the performer(s) depends on one's standpoint in relation to the anonymous act.

Conflicting perspectives on the protective character of such anonymous acts often sync with legal and scholarly debates about the merits and pitfalls of anonymous speech.[23] Proponents of anonymous speech, spoken or written, point out that anonymity allows ideas that would otherwise be suppressed to flourish, facilitating the expression and discovery of truth. In two landmark US Supreme Court cases, *Talley v. California* (1960) and *McIntyre v. Ohio Elections Commission* (1995), the court ruled that anonymous political speech is protected under the Constitution's First Amendment for this very reason.[24] As Supreme Court Justice John Paul Stevens stated in his majority opinion for *McIntyre v. Ohio Elections Commission*, "anonymity" can serve as "a shield from the tyranny of the majority."[25] Thus, "anonymous speech has, in general, enabled individuals to avoid persecution in climates of oppression."[26] Furthermore, proponents of anonymous speech point out that when we detach ideas and actions from personal identities, we also obscure the various statuses individuals carry, allowing us to judge ideas and arguments on their own merit, untainted by the biases of various social inequalities. In this vein, positing an "equalization phenomenon" or "equalization hypothesis," some have argued that the disembodiment made possible by computer-mediated communication has a leveling effect among users, which allows for greater freedom and equality of expression.[27]

However, as those who are leery of anonymous speech point out, anonymity can also facilitate harmful communication and behavior, including hate speech, libel, public shaming, bullying, doxing (publishing another individual's personal or private information online as a form of harassment or intimidation), flaming (making aggressive, insulting, or incendiary comments online), and trolling (the practice of intentionally inciting discord online by antagonizing and provoking others), as well as various other types of deceptive or criminal communication, such as blackmail or terroristic threats.[28] In his dissenting opinion to the *McIntyre* ruling, Justice Antonin Scalia argued that anonymity effectively protects individuals who engage in deceptive "uncharitable and uncivil expression" by "eliminating accountability, which is ordinarily the very purpose of anonymity."[29] Proponents of such a position often argue that this lack of personal accountability effectively undermines the core virtues of deliberative speech in a democratic society.[30] Moreover, the protections afforded by anonymity and pseudonymity also facilitate the exploitation of vulnerable others. Alfred Moore offers a cogent summary of the debate about anonymous speech, writing, "The discussion of anonymity and deliberation has repeatedly circled around two contradictory normative positions. One is that anonymity is valuable because it enables expression free from fear of repercussions. The other is that anonymity is destructive because it enables expression free from fear of repercussions."[31]

From a sociological perspective, which transcends the frame of this normative debate, acting and speaking with a hidden identity is not inherently positive or negative. Rather, one's assessment of any anonymous act depends on one's standpoint in relation to the performance at hand, and to the particular situation that the anonymous actors are working to define with their actions and expressions. As we will see with the various cases discussed below, when actors use protective cover representations to shield their personal identities, they animate the very dynamics of social control that they evade. In the process, they use anonymity and pseudonymity to create characters, make meaning, and define various situations and circumstances by virtue of their covered and protected state.

## Concealed Authorship and the Performance of Elena Ferrante

In the world of literature, many writers have published anonymously or pseudonymously to protect themselves (and occasionally others) from the consequences of their work, or inversely to shield their work from judgments that might result from their open authorship. "The motivations for publishing anonymously," Robert J. Griffin argues, "have included an aristocratic or a gendered reticence, religious self-effacement, anxiety over public exposure, fear of prosecution, hope of an unprejudiced reception, and the desire to deceive,"[32] all of which involve some intention to guard against the consequences of unwanted social attention. For example, one reason Charlotte Brontë published as Currer Bell was to curb the unsettling pressures of public recognition.[33] Likewise, Mary Ann Evans published as George Eliot in part to deflect attention from "her scandalous social situation," which involved living with a married man.[34] Lord Byron reportedly published his satirical poem *Don Juan*, which some deemed morally scandalous, anonymously so that it would not be used against him in divorce court.[35] A similar desire to avoid moral and political reprisal likely motivated the author of the 1554 Spanish novella *The Life of Lazarillo de Tormes and of His Fortunes and Adversities*, which was critical of the Catholic Church and ruling aristocracy in Spain, to remain anonymous.[36] Eric Arthur Blair is said to have adopted the pseudonym George Orwell "to spare potential embarrassment to his parents" who "could have been distressed" by the contents of his early autobiographical account in which he describes his experiences as "an out-of-work drifter and penniless tramp."[37]

Others published anonymously simply to hedge their bets with a first book or poem, protecting themselves from potential public humiliation in case the work flopped, or when using a literary form from which they wished to distance themselves in order to protect their social status.[38] As some cases of anonymous authorship imply, protective anonymity can serve "as an insurance strategy" or "a mechanism for managing . . . risk" when the consequences of publication are simply unknown.[39] Thus, those authors and other artists who appear to have used pseudonymity as a strategic way to establish their fame[40] can only appear to have done so in retrospect. Prospectively speaking, when such actors set out on their course, they have no idea how their work will be received. If they are ultimately celebrated, artists can then reveal their personal identities and frame their prior pseudonymity as a matter of ego modesty. However, if the work flops, which is more likely, they can keep their personal connection to the work hidden "with no effect on . . . reputation one way or the other."[41]

Discussing the question of authorship, Michel Foucault argues that anonymity only became a marked and conspicuous phenomenon in the early modern era.[42] Prior to this period, stories circulated anonymously without much concern for naming an individual author. However, with new understandings of storytelling as intellectual property, new legal practices of copyright, and the growing commercialization of text, the idea of authorship became significant in new ways. The practice of designating and defining authorship became a way for audiences to "characterize the existence, circulation, and operation of certain discourses within a society." In this moment, "literary anonymity" became "a puzzle to be solved."[43]

For Foucault, we construct authors via our engagement with texts and "the subject," or author, is ultimately "a complex and variable function of discourse."[44] Thus, on the one hand, Foucault helps us to see that audiences imagine and define authors according to socially and historically rooted processes of comprehending words and stories. However, on the other hand, Foucault fails to adequately acknowledge the performative capacity of authors. Whether they choose to expose or obscure their personal identities, authors are performers who actively work to create meanings with their texts and their authorship. Those who publish anonymously or pseudonymously for protective reasons use their chosen cover representations to frame their work as something that merits the personal obscurity of its author, who is deemed significant at least in part because of this personal obscurity. They actively cultivate a public mystery around their true personal identities, one that often defines and enhances their literary reputations.

The renowned contemporary Italian novelist Elena Ferrante is well-known for her pseudonymity as well as her passionate defense of her personal obscurity. The literary critic James Wood described her choice to hide her personal identity as "wisely self-protective" given the "intensely, violently personal" nature of her work.[45] While Ferrante initially decided to hide her personal identity because, in her own words, she "was frightened at the thought of having to come out of [her] shell,"[46] she soon developed a number of other reasons that reinforced her commitment to a protective pseudonymous posture. Echoing Mary Ann Evans/George Eliot, who "feared being constructed by the popular media" and sought to prevent her "personal life" from serving as a lens for "public interpretations of her novels,"[47] Ferrante's reasons evolved to include "hostility toward the media" which "*invents* the author," shifting attention away from the written work itself and focusing instead on "the author's reputation" and "'external' credentials" while imposing a "demand for self-promotion" that "diminishes the actual work of art."[48] Thus, Ferrante argues that her hidden identity is essential to the purity and integrity of her craft. Like Charlotte Brontë, whose pseudonymous cover as Currer Bell served as "a kind of creative principle—what allowed her to make life into fiction" and became "a sign of creative defiance,"[49] Ferrante states that both the process and product of her writing are shaped by, and would not be the same without, her protective pseudonymity.

Indeed, according Ferrante, her cover representation frees her to write by detaching her words from her self.[50] Regarding the "absence" of her personal identity over the course of her pseudonymous career, Ferrante comments, "What has never lost importance for me, over these two and a half decades, is the creative space that absence opened up for me. Once I knew that the completed book would make its way in the world without me . . . it made me see something new about writing. I felt as though I had released the words from myself."[51] Thus, without the constraints imposed by personal identity, Ferrante argues, the author can live through the text alone and nothing of her personal self can muddle the reader's relationship with that text, nor should it. Many of her fans agree. "The fact that Ferrante has chosen to be anonymous," writes Alexandra Schwartz of the *New Yorker*, "has become part of [the] contract" between author and readers, "and has put readers and writer on a rare, equal plane" where they can "meet on an imaginative neutral ground, open to all."[52] This imagined equality and connection stems from the fact that the author's hidden personal identity allows her to make her otherwise personal and exceptional voice more generic, creating an everyoneness that allows readers to more easily share in, and identify with, her storytelling. In this way, Ferrante is seen to be like Sir Walter Scott, who also made "the places he knew seem known to his readers," and whose "anonymity was a way of turning . . . personal experience into impersonal fiction."[53] In Ferrante's case, her work contains strong themes of "disappearance" and the "erasure" of self, whether through violence or other difficult life circumstances, along with the "manipulation" or "cancelation" of identity, and she enhances these themes with her passionate pseudonymity in ways that invite her readers to relate.[54]

However, many of the characteristics of personally identified authorship that Ferrante repudiates are actually vital to her performance of pseudonymous authorship as well. "True miracles," Ferrante wrote to her publishers before the release of her first novel in 1991, "are the ones whose makers will never be known."[55] Yet Elena Ferrante is quite well-known. Only the personal identity of the individual behind the pseudonymous cover is obscured, and it is obscured with effect. Ferrante, as a complex author-character with a history, has a reputation via the string of novels and other writings, including interviews and personal letters, that she has produced and published over the course of three decades. Despite her critical position on the media, she has a media-generated image, which is progressively enhanced, perhaps *mostly*, by the mystique of her personal identity and the controversies that have ensued when some try to unmask her.[56] Regardless of the author's intent, there is great value in the mystery and meaning she creates with her pseudonymity. Furthermore, a quick glance at Ferrante's website will reveal that the author, in league with her publishers, is certainly engaged in the work of authorial promotion, despite the fact that the identity being promoted is split from her personal identity.

The author known as Ferrante wields her cover representation and the very fact of her hidden personal identity, along with her expressed reasons for hiding it, as a *character frame* that imparts meaning to her work. In other words, she creates, uses, justifies, and defends Elena Ferrante to code her writing as authentic and pure, free from the corruption and pollution of market and media-driven authorial fame and publicity. She also uses her pseudonymity to call attention to her text—to foreground and elevate it as she creates her authorial persona via its public circulation. As she performs her pseudonymity, she uses it to perform the meaning of her text and its/her relationship to audiences of readers. Upon reading the opening note of an interview with Ferrante, conducted by her publishers Sandro and Sandra Ferri in 2015, I was struck by how the entire affair was directed by Ferrante, who determined the setting of the interview and supervised the final organization of the text.[57] Her publishers worked with the author as a performance team to produce and release the interview, which conveyed many of Ferrante's views on the importance of her pseudonymous authorship, just before the English-language release of *The Story of the Lost Child*, the fourth and final novel of her Neapolitan series. Thus, Ferrante presented her views on her concealed personal identity, and several other matters related to her writing, just in time to frame the meaning of the words in the book for her audience of readers. While serving as a protective pseudonym, Elena Ferrante is every bit as much a performative literary act.

## Social Ethics of Anonymity

In many cases, individuals shield their personal identities, or obscure the identities of others, to conform to ethical standards and moral norms. These standards and norms are rooted in different communities and institutions that determine how, why, and when the masking of personal identities serves a valued social purpose. In some of these cases, even when the personal identities of actors are privately known or knowable, participants in the scene cooperate to ignore them and protect them from public revelation. Understanding how such social ethics of anonymity operate is vital to grasping the performance and impact of hidden identities in various domains of social life.

## ANONYMOUS ALTRUISM AND CHARITY

Not all acts of protective anonymity shield actors from negative attention. By separating their personal identities from their charitable or kind behaviors, some use anonymity to "escape adulatory attention"[58] and thereby enact the selflessness at the core of an ethic of altruism. Of course, such protection is of a different character than the protection one seeks from threatening circumstances, but it is protection nonetheless, in this case from a type of personal credit that threatens to undermine or destroy the purity of one's good deed. This link between anonymity and the goodness of charitable acts is a common ethical principle, one established in Jewish, Christian, and Islamic doctrine. The Jewish tradition of *tzedakah*, a righteousness that takes form as charitable giving, was regarded by the rabbi philosopher Maimonides to be of a higher ethical level when done anonymously as opposed to publicly.[59] Likewise, the New Testament book of Matthew states, "Be careful not to do your 'acts of righteousness' before men, to be seen by them. . . . So when you give to the needy, do not announce it with trumpets . . . do not let your left hand know what your right hand is doing, so that your giving may be in secret."[60] In this scripture, the segregation and secrecy of the act (metaphorically represented by the division between the actions of the right hand and the knowledge of the left hand) creates the information control necessary to render the deed anonymous and therefore truly righteous. A similar principle is expressed by a verse in the Quran, which states that giving "to the poor privately is better for you, and will absolve you of your sins."[61] Capturing a similar point, Georg Simmel discussed "the case of the noble individual whose subtle shame makes him conceal his best in order to not to have it remunerated by eulogy and other rewards; for, otherwise, he would possess the remuneration, as it were, but no longer the value itself."[62] By compartmentalizing his virtuous deeds, and thereby separating them from his personal reputation (his "eulogy"), Simmel's "noble individual" keeps his deeds truly good and possesses them on some ethically pure level. Likewise, describing this concealment as necessary to the purity of righteousness in the Christian tradition, Hannah Arendt argued that "the moment a good work becomes known and public, it loses its specific character of goodness, of being done for nothing but goodness' sake," and "goodness must go into absolute hiding and flee all appearance if it is not to be destroyed."[63]

Beyond purifying the altruistic act, anonymity can also protect donors "from additional demands" and from "advertising their wealth."[64] Whatever the motivation might be, anonymous charity is typically marked in contrast to gifts that result in one's name being printed in a bulletin or inscribed on the face of a building.[65] However, while individuals who give anonymously shirk a public recognition attached to personal identity, anonymous giving itself is often announced, praised, and publicly celebrated for its particular quality of goodness. In this regard, recipients and others can advertise anonymous donations to establish the quality of a particular charity to future donors,[66] or simply to elevate the principle that anonymous giving is truly noble. Thus, for example, representatives from Toronto's Centre for Addiction and Mental Health publicly praised an anonymous donor for giving one hundred million dollars in 2018, calling the gift a "phenomenal act of generosity, courage, trust, foresight and leadership."[67] While reporting on an anonymous donation to an animal shelter, one journalist subtitled her post, "There are good people in this world!"[68] The renowned musician Prince was publicly praised after his death for his long-standing habit of anonymous giving.[69] Recognition after death voids the anonymity of the giver but protects the ethical character of anonymous giving as the altruistic donor can no longer personally benefit from public recognition.

The ethics of anonymous altruism establish a meaningful framework for its character as a performative act. While charitable actors can use their named donations as a "signal" to others that they personally carry a certain social status or class standing,[70] anonymous donors signal valued humility with their contributions. As they shield their personal identities, they enact and convey cultural and moral meaning with their anonymous charity. Consider the case of one anonymous benefactor who deems himself "Secret Santa." In December 2018, this individual, who has been defined as a "wealthy businessman," recruited a homeless man as a third-party proxy to pass out hundred-dollar bills to anyone who stopped to "pay him some attention" while he was panhandling.[71] Such an act, which inverts the charitable dynamic between giver and receiver while rewarding the behavior of those who initially showed generosity or care to a needy individual, was also carefully staged and coordinated for television news cameras and then edited and packaged for a public audience. The homeless agent and surprised recipients are all drawn in to serve as characters in a carefully scripted narrative with both plot and moral, a modern enactment of a Christian ethic of charity during the Christmas season. Furthermore, like anonymous authors, artists, and whistleblowers, many anonymous philanthropists are known to be the person behind the act by friends, family, associates, or others in their closest networks, which likely boosts their reputations among those in their close social circles, not only because of their generosity, but also specifically because they shirked public recognition.[72] While this particular "Secret Santa" remains anonymous behind his panhandling proxy, his face cast in shadows or turned away during his televised appearance that is publicly available online, he is likely known to his entire performance team, which appears to include many local officials and other accomplices. Even if and when an anonymous donor manages to make a gift without any other person linking the gift to their personal identity, such an act can still be performed for one's self or one's God. In such cases, one's self-as-audience can serve as the evaluator of one's self-as-righteous-actor. Furthermore, from the perspective of the believer, God is also watching and judging. After Jesus's instruction, as conveyed in the book of Matthew, "not to do your 'acts of righteousness' before men, to be seen by them," he states, "Then your Father, who sees what is done in secret, will reward you."[73] Likewise, the Quran instructs anonymous givers that "Allah is All-Aware of what you do."[74]

## THE SCREENED CONFESSION AND THE MASQUERADE

As with many of the cases I have already discussed, protective anonymity allows actors to reveal potentially compromising information while detaching it from their personal identities and reputations. For this reason, *both* confidentiality and anonymity are core principles of the traditional Catholic ethic and practice of confession, which is facilitated by the private, partitioned, and screened confessional booth. Before the early thirteenth century, confession "was not individual but collective."[75] The practice of confession was used to openly address problematic social actions that deviated from standards of acceptable behavior and were thus seen as causing a rift between the sinner and the Church as community. When Catholic authorities privatized the sacrament, they shifted focus "from the social to the personal" and "interiorized the notions of sin and repentance."[76] With his design and formal introduction of the confessional box in the sixteenth century, Archbishop Charles Borromeo gave material and practical form to the Church's increasing focus on deeply personal revelation.[77] Writing for the Institute for Sacred Architecture, John J. Coughlin notes, "The traditional confessional . . . serves to safeguard the inviolability of the seal of the Sacrament of Penance," which "functions to ensure the faithful that they may freely confess their sins and receive God's forgiveness without the danger of public revelation by the confessor."[78] In this sense, the confessional booth, with its closed doors or curtains, is a structural expression of an ecclesiastical emphasis on privacy and confidentially. By concealing one's expressed sins from a public audience, it encourages confessants to speak otherwise unspoken personal truths. Indeed, the words "confess" and "confidential" share the Latin root prefix *con* (derived from *com*), which means "together, with," conveying the shared and yet exclusionary nature of what is said in the *con*fines of the booth.[79]

However, in another sense, the visually obstructive screen or grate that separates authoritative clergy (as confessor) from the confessant, when used, allows for an additional layer of protection that manifests as an interactive anonymity during the ritual process.[80] Simultaneously shielding the face of both confessor and confessant, the screen renders individual confessants as *anyones*, obscuring and leveling their otherwise meaningful personal identities and accentuating their general status as sinner under the jurisdiction of the religious community. In addition, the screen likely functioned at times to make the confession box similar to a contemporary anonymous crime tip line, making it easier for confessants to expose neighbors and family members as they probed the depths of their own infractions. In our contemporary era, it also protects the priest from knowing the personal identity of anyone who confesses a serious crime, and therefore from any legal obligation to report such a confessant to state authorities.[81] Moreover, Catholic authorities also use the anonymity of the screen to depersonalize the priest's power and authority so that any individual priest can stand *in persona Christi*—as general proxy for God and light.[82] The barrier gives the priest the freedom and power to transcend his personal identity and assume an impersonal and omniscient status as a voice of God. With regard to his mortal personal identity, he, also, could be anyone. Thus, while the anonymity of confessants frees them to reveal sin, the anonymity of the priest-as-confessor enhances his confessional authority along with his interpretive, proscriptive, and remedial power, allowing him to steer the confession ritual more freely and forcefully.[83]

The anonymity of the confessional screen is replicated and enhanced today by the computer screen when religious authorities hear confession online.[84] Such online confessionals can even be automated, allowing one to confess one's sins to a generic authority that offers ready-made penance and absolution according to the type and degree of sin one confesses.[85] A protective anonymity of confession is also enabled by an array of physical and online platforms where individuals confess intimate and secret details of their lives to a public audience, such as the website and various affiliated exhibition spaces of the PostSecret project.[86] In such "intimate economies,"[87] individuals anonymously share all kinds of otherwise private and deeply personal information, revealing "I smoked crack," "I faked a miscarriage," "I made my dog go down on me," or "I am addicted to Internet Porn," to list just a few examples.[88] Such confessants are anonymous to their audience, and their audience (an amorphous public at large) is mostly anonymous to them. The anonymous format of such projects shapes, and perhaps enhances, the performative character of the confessional utterance, which is typically shocking in its directness and, in the case of PostSecret, often presented on an artistic background designed by the confessant for the purpose of framing the emotionality of the revelation. In the words of one commenter, many online confessions manifest "as a live performance of sin," which is a big part of what makes "this confessional worth peeking at."[89]

In a similar sense, the traditional Catholic confessional box not only enables the articulation of sin, but actually frames (structurally and performatively) and defines what sin is to practitioners. The act of performing confession in such a private and screened manner actively codes sin in its antithesis to those thoughts and activities that we openly declare and willingly link to our personal identities. Sin is a hidden inner truth that must be revealed despite our resistance to its revelation,[90] a resistance that can be overcome with the protective negation of personal identity. However, even when a screen is used, the personal identity of the confessant might be known to the confessor (and vice versa). In a more general sense, the screen provides an important structural expression of a cooperative ethic of anonymity that is infused into the social performance and interactive practice of the confession by the players themselves, who tactfully avoid or ignore personal identity as a matter of normative value. In such cases, the personal identity of the confessant is *socially ignored* even if *privately known* so that the ritual becomes depersonalized, which allows the sin to be the matter of concern rather than the personal identity of the sinner, and the generic ritual interaction with God and general reconciliation with the Christian community to be stressed rather than one's personal relationship with the individual priest behind the screen. The individual confessant is not besmirched by the otherwise damaging revelation, but purified. Personal identity and reputation remain unscathed.

In a similar vein, the masquerade mask protects one from the stigma associated with taboo actions and expressions, but in this case frames such actions and expressions as frivolous play or contextually confined and acceptable deviance, enabling activity that would otherwise not occur for the embarrassment, shame, or other degradation it would impart to the actors involved. Masquerade masks, with their roots in carnivals that created a temporary breach of the normative social order,[91] carry a culturally rich meaning that actors creatively mobilize when they use them to shield their personal identities at a party or festival. By using these rich symbolic covers, in all their ornate variations, actors create a particular type of interactive dynamic, one rooted in a shared spirit of ambiguity and a jovial "challenge to categories of identity."[92] In this case, performances of anonymity are typically reciprocal as multiple people wear similar masks, which allows for a leveling of social status that would otherwise shape interactions.

Taking a famous and telling theatrical example, a masquerade ball provides the protective time and space that allows Romeo and Benvolio to attend a Capulet party under cover of their masks, and such masks facilitate Romeo and Juliet's first meeting and strong attraction, which famously defies the boundaries of their families' rivalries. After their encounter, Romeo is shocked to learn of Juliet's identity as a Capulet. Likewise, after learning of Romeo's personal identity and family affiliation, Juliet cries, "My only love sprung from my only hate! Too early seen unknown, and known too late!"[93] Her exclamation carries the contradiction of the scene; her love for Romeo was sparked when she saw him cloaked in an anonymity that split his personal identity from their encounter. The context of the ball protected him from the impression she would have otherwise formed if his personal identity and family affiliation were exposed.[94] As with Shakespeare's setting, masquerade parties give participants permission to ignore personal identities and thus the social categories and statuses they signify, allowing for a freedom of interaction that would otherwise be restricted if personal identities were publicly exposed and openly acknowledged.[95]

Yet this freedom of interaction stems from the social and cooperative ethic of anonymity and norms of identity play that individuals create with their masks in these particular settings. The ethic of the masquerade party, like that of the confessional, is utterly social and performative. Even when the identities of actors who don masks at a party are known to one another, which is common, their mutual and simultaneous wearing of masks carries the meaningful impact of this device as a tool that both shields personal identities and enables otherwise risky, or risqué, expressive activities. Thus, in eighteenth-century Venice, where masks were a common fashion accessory even outside of carnival, "the identities of maskers were often known."[96] However, "in general, maskers did not address one another by name," and, furthermore, "to strip someone of his mask was a supreme insult," even when one recognized another mask wearer.[97] Using such masks in a festive context, actors practice a shared ethic of anonymity that allows them to behave and interact in the breach of personal identity, and to thereby maintain an alternative social order—one that is separate from the reality of their everyday lives.[98]

## THE IMPARTIALITY OF IMPERSONALITY AND THE
## PERFORMANCE OF ACADEMIC EVALUATION

We can take a similar approach to better understand official rules of assessment and procedures of evaluation that require the anonymity or pseudonymity of actors to protect against biases that stem from prejudice, favoritism, or fear of retaliation.[99] In such cases, actors are not simply unknown, but rather actively and purposefully depersonalized to perform social ethics of impartiality, fairness, and/or privacy.

For example, by anonymizing applicants, contestants, or examinees who compete for some valued reward, we express the principle that the evaluation of individuals' performances and achievements should not be influenced by their personal characteristics or any prior personal relationship with the evaluator. Nor should our evaluations be affected by ascribed statuses such as race, ethnicity, gender, class, age, physical disability, or perceived attractiveness.[100] We create and use such depersonalizing procedures to level the playing field, treating others (who are often made to be generic "subjects" or "candidates") as impersonal anyones in order to focus our perceptions and judgments on the performances and products we evaluate. The FOX network's television show *The Masked Singer*, an elaborate version of the more conventional screened audition,[101] reveals how anonymity can focus attention and hone judgment on one variable (vocal performance, in this case) while generating mystery and speculation about the person behind the mask. Likewise, judges in NBC's program *The Voice* turn their backs to the contestants (via rotating chairs) during the initial round of evaluation. In the same vein, contributors to the contest to design the Vietnam Veterans Memorial in Washington, DC, were anonymous, focusing the panel of eight judges on the quality of the design proposals alone. After a decision was rendered, the contributor of the winning design was revealed to be twenty-one-year-old Maya Lin, an undergraduate student at Yale University at the time. Given the controversy that ensued when Lin's personal identity was revealed—which brought her Asian ethnicity, her age, and her undergraduate status to the fore of public attention—it indeed seems that the initial anonymity of the process was important to shield against biased assessments. Lin's design may not have been chosen, it is implied, if Lin herself was attached to her submission. Such institutionally mandated shielding procedures also apply to anonymous admissions protocols, anonymous grading systems, and anonymous tryouts of various types.

Alternatively, when we obscure the personal identities of those who conduct the evaluations, we express the notion that they should not face retaliation or reward for voicing their opinions, and that depersonalization thereby purifies their assessments, rendering them more honest. Such a principle shapes our reception of the evaluations conducted by anonymous literary, art, and food critics.[102] It also provides the rationale for gathering anonymous feedback from a discrete and particular constituency (as with anonymous course evaluations at colleges and universities) and from broader communities and publics at large (as with opinion polls and large-scale surveys). Furthermore, the notion that obscuring personal identity renders evaluations more honest explains why anonymous and pseudonymous online review platforms (such as Rate My Professor) are widely used by consumers looking for information about a particular product, service, or institution.[103] In such cases, anonymity allows for critique without fear of retaliation, but perhaps more significantly, without the social embarrassment or shame that might otherwise come with criticizing someone more directly and openly, an act that often blemishes the social face of both the criticized and the criticizer (as would also occur in cases that involve excessive or inappropriate praise).[104] By shielding the evaluator from such an interpersonal and emotional force, anonymous reviews allow individuals to speak freely. However, anonymity might also facilitate both critical and supportive communication that is unwarranted, and which would otherwise not occur if evaluators were held personally accountable for their comments.

We create and use systems of anonymous assessment to shape the meanings of our evaluative acts. By removing personal identities from the evaluative process, anonymizing agents establish the sense that they are accessing pure information that might otherwise be unavailable or tainted. They thereby perform the legitimacy of their evaluations and judgments. For example, the "double-blind" peer-review system used by many academic journals (one in which authors are anonymous to those who assess their papers, and the reviewers are also anonymous to the authors) is widely regarded as a method of ensuring fair and impartial assessment of academic scholarship according to the standards of a scholarly community.[105] However, this system of anonymous review is also, and more generally, "a legitimating resource" that "functions as a 'strategic ritual' which lays a general foundation for journals to claim credibility and legitimacy."[106] Journal editors use this system of protective anonymity to perform the scientific integrity of their platform while justifying their own authoritative decisions as gatekeepers in the process.[107] Likewise, student evaluations of college and university faculty are often deemed "a more accurate representation of teaching performance" when student evaluators remain anonymous.[108] However, researchers have shown that this system of anonymous evaluation can produce racist and sexist assessments, ratings that vary by the age and perceived personal attractiveness of the faculty member under review, and critical evaluations based on receiving fairly assigned but poor grades.[109] Despite the fact that anonymous student evaluations of faculty do not really measure the quality or effectiveness of teaching, and despite other increasingly obvious problems with the procedure, college and university administrators continue to use them to legitimate their judgments and decisions regarding faculty performance.

The protective character of anonymity is also one of the primary reasons for rules requiring the anonymization of human subjects in scholarly or scientific research. Academic Institutional Review Boards (IRBs) and other agencies establish procedures mandating the anonymity of human subjects in order to shield research participants from potential harms and biases that might stem from linking the characteristics exposed by research to their personal identities. However, these rules and procedures often create a "false promise of anonymity" and therefore lead well-meaning researchers to vastly overstate the protections they offer.[110] In many cases, supposedly anonymized data are quite linkable to personal identities.[111] With regard to ethnographic research in the social sciences, despite the default practice of using pseudonyms to disguise the identities of human subjects and communities, researchers often expose information that can be used to identify people and places simply by publishing deeply insightful, nuanced, and revelatory ethnographic accounts.[112] Identifying subjects can be especially easy for "knowledgeable community insiders,"[113] suggesting "that anonymization is likely to be most problematic precisely where it would be most useful—at the local level—and that it can do little to protect the identities of participants from intimates and associates or from . . . the very people likely to be in positions to react or retaliate against them."[114] The rise of modern internet connectivity and the ease with which we can search for information compounds this issue, especially insofar as it allows curious readers to link "private information (conveyed in an interview under guarantees that research participants' real names will not be used)" with "public information out there for anyone to see."[115] Thus, although they often craft detailed protocols to anonymize or pseudonymize the people they study, scholars and their IRBs are primarily performing an ethic of protective anonymity without any guarantee that the personal identities of research participants will not be connected to the stories that scholars tell about their lives and activities.

One way to strengthen the anonymity afforded to ethnographic research subjects might be to "dissemble our descriptions of individuals" by altering "gender, class and ethnicity" or other variables key to a subject's identity.[116] Cases in which a researcher is studying an especially vulnerable population might merit such "extensive masking."[117] Catarina Frois resorted to such measures when studying twelve-step recovery groups.[118] Alice Goffman also employed such extensive measures in her now quite famous study of individuals living a "fugitive life" in an inner-city neighborhood. To protect her subjects from retaliation, not only did Goffman change the names of individuals and places, but she also altered other aspects of people's identities, the details of certain situations, and the temporal sequencing of events. Her deep commitment to protective anonymity led many critics, some of them anonymous themselves, to question the veracity and legitimacy of her analysis.[119] Furthermore, the anonymization of research subjects might also protect researchers who study violent or dangerous populations from being targeted by those subjects who feel threatened by exposure.[120] However, despite careful and extensive measures, reporting anything distinctive about a subject's comments and/or actions still risks exposing their personal identities to peers, authorities, or even strangers.[121] When readers are made aware that such details have been changed, they might try to decode the covers the ethnographer has constructed. Ultimately, the anonymizing mandates and protocols of our academic Institutional Review Boards seem best suited to protect colleges and universities from liability, rather than protecting research participants from harm or supporting researchers who face possible retaliation or legal intervention.[122]

Furthermore, as "a representational strategy with interesting ontological and political implications,"[123] the scholarly practice of anonymizing or pseudonymizing human research subjects can have serious consequences for the integrity of an analysis.[124] Abiding by "the canons . . . of ethnographic ethics," which "seemed reasonable and necessary" when conducting and publishing his research, Charles L. Bosk altered a crucial characteristic of identity for one of his subjects in a way that ultimately narrowed the range of interpretations that readers might develop with regard to an important situation.[125] While studying the surgical department and training program of a major university-affiliated hospital (pseudonymously deemed "Pacific Hospital"), Bosk detailed the deliberations of "the promotion meeting at which surgical faculty [met] to decide the fate of second-year surgical residents."[126] In his initial account, Bosk described how members of the surgical faculty argued that one particular second-year resident, who Bosk referred to with the pseudonym "Dr. Jones," was not only ill-suited to be a surgeon, but also unfit to practice medicine at all.

They cast doubts on Jones's mental health, questioned whether or not the resident was "on drugs," and argued that Jones was unable to take criticism or even hold a constructive conversation. All the while, Bosk referred to Jones (like all of the other surgical residents and all of the faculty) as a man. In fact, as Bosk admits many years later, in an "Amended Appendix" to the 2003 edition of the 1979 book, "Jones was the sole female in the cohort of surgical residents [he] observed."[127] Initially, Bosk changed Jones's gender to ensure a protective anonymity. As the only women in the program, accurately ascribing gender would have revealed her personal identity.[128] Thus, standards of anonymization, as Bosk retrospectively points out, not only blocked any potential interpretation of the situation with reference to Jones's gender, they also "offered more protection to the surgeons of Pacific Hospital than [they] did to Jones," left the analysis "theoretically impoverished," obscured the culture of sexual harassment at the hospital, and otherwise rendered a serious problem invisible and an important critique impossible.[129]

When qualitative researchers pseudonymize their participants, they perform their own ethical standing as researchers and define their reports as legitimate works of social science rather than journalism or some other form of storytelling. Furthermore, pseudonymization allows researchers to breathe more freely with regard to their own interpretations and representations of the people and communities they study—a measure of self-protection against pressures and anxieties related to the accuracy of their interpretive work.[130] After all, by using cover identities to obscure their subjects' personal identities, the researcher could be writing about anyone. While the relationship between the scholar and informant, or the scholar and community, will often be quite personal, the relationship between author and pseudonymous character can become impersonal and generic, perhaps, as Nancy Scheper-Hughes argues, leaving ethnographers "too free with [their] pens, with the government of [their] tongues, and with [their] loose translations and interpretations of…life."[131] Moreover, "giving people or places pseudonyms and strategically deleting identifying information turns them into usable examples or illustrations of generalizing theoretical categories," which allows the researcher to use the subject as a "stand in for social classes, ethnic groups, genders, institutions, or other theoretical constructs."[132] Thus, by masking the individuals and places they study, ethnographers effectively make them generic and therefore representative of other cases.[133] In sum, while their promises to shield personal identities can never be guaranteed, ethnographers use procedures of pseudonymization to perform a variety of ethical and representational meanings that are central to their scholarship. Most fundamentally, anonymity and pseudonymity are tools that many scholars use to define their scholarly standpoints and craft their theatrical assessments.

## Anonymous Communities and Forums

Anonymous communities and forums involve multiple people who co-operate to obscure their personal identities as they gather with common purpose. Such groups come together for different reasons, but all of them maintain a *culture of reciprocal anonymity or pseudonymity* that shapes patterns of interaction, norms of attention, and practices of information control in group settings.[134] Whether cohering in physical or virtual space, participants create a protective refuge to share their experiences, tell stories, discuss issues, express feelings, or otherwise communicate with one another while avoiding stigma and other consequences that would likely result from their comments and revelations.[135] Even though, in some cases, participants might be able to personally identify others, and in certain situations some may reveal identifying information, most shield their own personal identities while actively ignoring or showing indifference to the personally defining characteristics of others. They also monitor one another's compliance with these group values and contextual norms (which can be, but are not necessarily, explicitly defined).[136]

Such communities and forums often take form as alternative lifeworlds, or "liminoid" zones.[137] For Victor Turner, the liminoid refers to times and places set apart from the mainstream social order, "along the margins, in the interfaces and interstices of central and servicing institutions," where participants escape many of the constraints they face in their day-to-day lives. They are "independent domain[s] of creative activity" and "settings for all kinds of freewheeling, experimental cognitive behavior as well as forms of symbolic action" that often have a "subjunctive" character.[138] Because those who participate in anonymous communities and forums temporarily act in the breach of their personal identities, where they can escape many of the pressures that personal identification places on their performances in other venues, they are able to bring new identities and patterns of behavior to life, along with new narratives, memories, and definitions of social events and experiences.[139] Thus, such communities and forums can be "empowering, liberating, and transformative."[140] However, by shielding their personal identities, the participants of such communities and forums also reinforce the notion that the content of their communicative activity is risky or problematic. They often enact and re-create the very stigma and marginality that led them to obscure their personal identities in the first place.

## ANONYMOUS THERAPEUTICS AND
## THE CASE OF ALCOHOLICS ANONYMOUS

Some anonymous communities and forums are primarily therapeutic. Such groups provide participants with a social space to express their vulnerability (along with suffering, fear, loneliness, and other related emotional states), seek support for a problem they would otherwise deny or keep secret, and perform support for others by relaying their own experiences.[141] These include and array of addiction and recovery organizations (also known as twelve-step groups) such as Alcoholics Anonymous, Narcotics Anonymous, and Al-Anon (for family members and loved ones of people suffering from addiction and substance abuse). They also include various groups that address other issues based on the twelve-step/recovery model, such as Co-Dependents Anonymous,[142] Sex Workers Anonymous, Debtors Anonymous, Racists Anonymous, and many more.[143] Today, the anonymity and pseudonymity afforded by computer-mediated communication allows for a wide variety of therapeutic communities and forums with either explicit or implicit cultures of anonymity or pseudonymity to cohere online. These include groups of self-identified survivors of childhood sexual abuse and other traumatic experiences, individuals who have abandoned a major religious affiliation, those who are embracing a new sexual orientation or gender identity, and many others that facilitate the sharing of deeply sensitive, painful, or traumatic issues.[144] On a fundamental level, "the strategic use of anonymity on the Internet" offers "a vital form of self-protection from potential perpetrators"[145] and other agents of social control, which is crucial given that those who share personal stories online may not be safe, or be able to freely discuss their concerns, in their physical environments and communities. The publicly accessible character of such online spaces also allows for an enhanced degree of "anonymous spectatorship"[146] and therefore a broader social reach. It allows anyone to anonymously discover the space and its participants' stories, which may enhance their impact but also puts participants at greater risk of being personally identified by outsiders who recognize the details of their accounts. In all of these cases, the anonymity or pseudonymity practiced by the group allows participants to create a transcendental or transformative space where they can freely experiment with new identities while redefining their situations and experiences.

The prototypical anonymous therapeutic and recovery community is Alcoholics Anonymous (A.A.). The anonymity referred to in the program's name stems from the normative routines and interactive practices that define its meetings and events—what Norman K. Denzin calls "the social worlds of recovery."[147] As with other anonymous communities and forums, A.A. uses anonymity and pseudonymity to form a protective space that frees participants to express themselves in ways that they wish to separate from their personal identities.[148] In addition to the stigma carried by addiction itself, meeting participants commonly engage in "talk that in ordinary conversation would be defined as displaying a 'loss of face.'" This includes "crying, the revelation of deviance while under the influence of alcohol, discussions of bouts of insanity, mentions of crippling fears or depressions, and talk of failures in marriages and social relationships."[149] New participants quickly learn they are expected to shield their own personal identities and avoid the personal identities of others in various ways—most basically by refraining from using or asking about last names or other identifying information.[150] The use of a first name on its own has a generalizing, pseudonymous quality.[151] Moreover, first-name-only policies do not require that the first name used be the first name legally and otherwise associated with one's personal identity. More generally, participants enact a "double wall" of avoidance[152]—a "don't ask, don't tell" practice with regard to personal identity—along with a moral imperative to never expose someone as a meeting attendee outside of the context of the meeting (which would break the segregation of identities at the heart of the anonymous culture).[153] Furthermore, the social architecture of the meeting spaces, often tucked away in church basements or otherwise secluded from the public, helps to bring the anonymity of the group to life.

During A.A. meetings, which are usually held in person but increasingly offered online (a practice enhanced by the COVID-19 pandemic for many recovery groups), attendees are encouraged and ultimately expected to share their life experiences while shielding their personal identities, which generalizes their accounts and allows participants to focus on what they hold in common. In the process, participants assume the general identity of "alcoholic." Often referring to one another as "A.A.'s,"[154] the alcoholic thus becomes a depersonalized anyone rather than a unique individual.[155] In the widely known (and sometimes parodied) conventional A.A. introductory line, "My name is _____, and I'm an alcoholic," the stigmatizing yet generic identifier (alcoholic) is uttered and embraced while the personalizing feature of a last name is avoided. In practice and performance, the term "alcoholic" stands in for a last name. By ritually deleting and replacing the surname with a shared signifier, participants experience the recovery community as a type of family.[156] Furthermore, the formulaic character of the impersonal introduction (as indicated by the blank space in my illustration above, which can be filled with *any* first name) provides a common framework that facilitates and defines the shared character of the confessional revelation, a revelation that "sets the stage for subsequent constructions of the self" to fall in step with a shared interpretive framework and recovery narrative.[157]

Like other anonymous communities, A.A. is a particular example of the "reinventive institutions" discussed by Susie Scott.[158] Participants use anonymity and pseudonymity to engage in ritualized performances of self-reflexive transformation during meetings where the shared identity of "alcoholic" is embraced and applauded despite being stigmatized in other settings. However, while telling their stories under the protective covers of anonymity and pseudonymity, A.A. members simultaneously convey their need for protection, defining their shared condition as a matter of shame or embarrassment on some basic level. Thus, as "members . . . renegotiate their identities" in line with collective norms, they simultaneously reproduce and institutionalize the group itself.[159] They both comply with and ritually reaffirm the need for A.A.'s foundational *Twelve Steps and Twelve Traditions*, which establishes anonymity as "the spiritual foundation"[160] of the community and all of its practices. Indeed, the group holds that each participant "takes part in the weaving of a protective mantle which covers our whole Society and under which we may grow and work in unity."[161] Such a culture of anonymity not only protects individual members, but also protects the group itself as an alternative world of meaning and a sanctuary of sobriety and recovery.

## COMPUTER-MEDIATED ANONYMOUS FORUMS

The evolving capacities of computer-mediated communication have led to a radical proliferation of anonymous forums of various types.[162] Online forums can allow for either synchronous or asynchronous interaction among disembodied participants who may be anonymous or pseudonymous, and who may be acting with one or multiple cover representations. Many also provide a platform for individuals to communicate in view of public or semi-public audiences that are made up of equally anonymous others (including co-participants and spectators). Thus, such forums often function as "alternative publics"[163]—parallel spaces of dialogue and debate that have "a distinctive discursive character" due to the ways participants collectively shield and avoid personal identities.[164] While "true technical anonymity" may not exist in many online forums (because website operators typically log the IP addresses of their users), the interactive "culture of [such sites] revolves around the *idea* of anonymity," which functions as a strong social imperative.[165]

Online anonymous forums include various crowdsourcing or information-sharing sites that cater to particular populations, such as those where medical doctors share cases that confound them and ask for input from one another,[166] or sites where individuals on the academic job market share information about job searches while expressing frustrations, anxieties, and opinions about various matters in their field.[167] Yik Yak, an anonymous social media application, allows anonymous forums to temporarily form according to users' geographic proximity. Anonymous forums also include much larger multifocal online venues such as 4chan (the now quite famous anonymous internet imageboard that as of this writing claims over twenty million unique monthly users and around one million posts per day),[168] and Reddit (a well-trafficked pseudonymous online discussion site that claims over 430 million "average monthly active users" and over 130,000 "communities").[169] Both 4chan and Reddit are structured around different topical subforums or thematic discussion threads where participants focus on particular issues or themes such as current events, video games, food, sports, sex, pornography, and much more.[170] Certain anonymous networking spaces are also rooted in the more amorphous "dark web" (where individuals can anonymously interact for various purposes, especially to engage in illicit activities).[171] These include sites that function as "cryptomarkets" where anonymous individuals (who often use digitally encrypted code names, or cryptonyms, and cryptocurrencies) buy and sell illegal drugs or other contraband.[172]

In the tradition of carnival and masquerade, some online anonymous forums allow participants to performatively engage in play and fantasy, or act outlandishly and even aggressively in ways they wish to keep divorced from their personal identities. In his cogent and illuminating discussion of 4chan and similar forums as "Internet masquerade," David Auerbach describes the unique patterns of interaction and style of communicative behavior within such anonymous forums as "A-culture."[173] In line with other anonymous communities and forums, Auerbach notes that A-culture can simultaneously involve both shame and pride. Creating what amounts to a counterpublic or parallel world, participants perform the *shame* in their acts by virtue of the fact that they hide their personal identities, and their *pride* by virtue of their reclaiming and glorifying behaviors that would otherwise be shameful. This peculiar combination of shame and pride can provide for a sense of exceptionalism (which Auerbach recognizes as "elitism") among participants, as "the individual stigma that someone might feel is replaced by a *collective* stigma belonging to the entirety of A-culture, as sites like 4chan are branded cesspools of hate and obscenity—to the delight of many of their participants."[174]

While much communicative interaction in these anonymous forums is focused on particular topics or themes, the underlying culture allows for and even encourages obscenity, trickery, trolling, various forms of crude humor and fictitiousness, maliciousness, and other deviant acts that can be captivating, engaging, and ultimately cohesive in effect. As Abigail E. Curlew argues with regard to the anonymous forums facilitated by the social media app Yik Yak, a "dampening of disciplinary power" experienced by participants in such forums "is often associated with a proliferation of vitriolic behavior," including comments that are racist and sexist in nature.[175] However, above all, Auerbach argues, "A-culture is a space for playing with unrestricted notions of identity and affiliation and for the establishment of a private set of in-jokes and references" that bind participants together as equal members of an alternative community.[176] While trolling, obscenity, hate speech, and other aggressive acts are common, along with rampant "suspicion" and "a general sense of unreality," these dimensions of A-culture are all brought to life by the identity play enabled by anonymity. "The world" of the anonymous forum becomes "an immensely large playground" that is "carefully regimented and circumscribed," a world that "is distinct and detached from the real one."[177] The protective covers of anonymity and pseudonymity spur the creation of such parallel social worlds, where people who would not otherwise come together gather to say and do things they would not otherwise say and do, performing new versions of self and enacting new realities that are split from the mainstream social order.

## Anonymous Consumption and Exchange

Some products and services are purchased and consumed by individuals who obscure their personal identities to protect themselves from shame and embarrassment, evade punishment, or simply avoid unwanted social attention. Whereas Thorstein Veblen defined "conspicuous consumption" as a "means of reputability" for the wealthy leisure class, a way of openly demonstrating one's social status or membership in an elite group,[178] we can think of *anonymous consumption* as a way of splitting one's use of certain products or services from one's personal reputation and social standing. People often purchase or consume commodities and services like pornography, prostitution, certain health and sanitary goods, medications, certain books, illicit drugs, and various other products, both legal and illegal, in an anonymous fashion. The less exposed and susceptible to personal identification, either via social recognition or record keeping, the more likely consumers may be to purchase certain products such as condoms[179] or books,[180] for example.

For these reasons, some industries establish normative protections that shield their patrons' personal identities.[181] Therefore, while medicines for depression and erectile dysfunction must be prescribed by name to particular individuals who consume them (leaving a relatively permanent record that renders their personal identities traceable), official HIPAA (Health Insurance Portability and Accountability Act of 1996) rules of confidentially and privacy, combined with normative patterns of avoidance and discretion, allow the consumption of such medications to be relatively anonymous in most cases. When delivered via physical mail, taboo merchandise like pornography or incontinence products are often contained in discreet envelopes. Likewise, retail stores that deal in sexual or pornographic material often lack windows (or cover them).[182] Such covered windows create a dual effect; they protect passersby from accidentally seeing what they might not want to see, but also allow consumers to shop while shielded from a more public gaze—a measure of privacy that facilitates a protective anonymity while shopping. Furthermore, as the display in the Babeland window pictured in figure 6 suggests, such protective covers can send a contradictory message that promotes pride in its overt communication while simultaneously conveying shame in its obstructive design. In a similar vein, various online markets facilitate anonymous consumption while also providing forums for consumers to unabashedly yet anonymously discuss their tastes and preferences.[183]

The distinction between anonymity and personal identifiability in commerce calls our attention to the different social characteristics of transactions that involve cash and those that involve credit or bank debit,[184] as well as the differences between transactions conducted while physically co-present with others and those that take place online or are otherwise mediated by a third party. While cash is generic and universal and therefore can be used without leaving a traceable record,[185] it is most often used when the parties engaged in the transaction are present in the same physical space. Consumers and sellers (who see and are perhaps known to one another) are likely to be more personally exposed at this level of physical interpersonal exchange. Alternatively, credit cards are unique and particular, leaving a relatively permanent record that can typically be linked to the personal identity of the consumer. However, credit cards and other account-based means of purchasing goods facilitate more distanced transactions that can occur by physical mail, over the phone, online, or via some other form of mediated communication, thus depersonalizing those

FIGURE 6. Despite its unambiguously sex-positive and proud message, the store Babeland, which specializes in sex toys, obscures its windows. Bergen Street, Park Slope, Brooklyn. Photo taken by author.

transactions at the level of interaction. In other words, different payment systems allow actors to anonymize themselves in different ways, in relation to particular audiences in different situations. Today, online commerce facilitates a practical anonymity by providing a technologically mediated cover for buyers *and* for the producers and distributors of the goods and services they consume, rendering transactions more automated and impersonal.[186] However, computer mediation also makes surveillance more routine and facilitates personal profiling through detailed activity tracking and record keeping. To block such personal exposure, cryptocurrencies such as Bitcoin blend the anonymizing characteristics of cash and digital commerce by allowing consumers to make electronic payments that are not linked to personal accounts. Rather, Bitcoin transactions and stored Bitcoin currency are linked to pseudonymous alpha-numeric keys called "Bitcoin addresses," which can be unique for each transaction. While the record of all transactions is public and transparent, the IP addresses and personal identities of spenders and receivers are not part of this record, allowing users to obscure their personal identities and evade the forces and technologies of electronic surveillance.[187]

In many cases of anonymous consumption and exchange, third parties, such as business owners and website operators, serve as intermediaries who protect personally identifying records and other information. In such cases, either buyer or seller or both may remain anonymous to the other and to the outside world. When purchases are made online using a pseud-onymous cover, the web platform or email server technically serves as a third-party actor that shields the link between a buyer's and/or seller's cover representation and their personally identifying account information or IP address.[188] Such is also the case when individuals make purchases via a corporate account, or by other types of legally established proxies such as trusts and "private associations" that shield their personal iden-tities.[189] The anonymous purchasing of real estate can be accomplished through a limited liability company (LLC), for example. Likewise, some auction houses preserve the anonymity of buyers and sellers. In the case of *Tattered Cover, Inc. v. City of Thornton* (2002), the Colorado Supreme Court ruled in favor of a bookstore owner demanding to protect the per-sonal identities of her customers. Siding with the plaintiff, who argued that disclosing the personal identities of book buyers to state authorities "would have a substantial chilling effect" on the purchasing and reading of books, the court recognized anonymity as vital to the free consumption of information.[190] However, while many third parties promise to guard their clients' personal information, such promises are often not totally fail-safe. As we witnessed with the 2015 Ashley Madison data breach, in which information personally identifying the users of a website facilitating extramarital affairs was stolen by hackers and published online, measures of protective anonymity are always somewhat violable and precarious.

Actors adopt a range of practices and use various structures, relation-ships, and technologies as they work to achieve anonymous consumption and exchange in different situations. In the process, they protect them-selves for different reasons but also reinforce the social imperative to ob-scure personal identity. The message is that one needs to hide to consume certain products and services and while engaging in various relationships of exchange.

## Exploiting Protective Anonymity

Deceitful actors can exploit the architectures, technologies, rituals, and policies that afford protective anonymity by using them to commit fraudu-lent acts. Acting behind protective covers, they can spread misinformation for various opportunistic purposes. For example, any individual might exploit the protections of anonymous crime tip lines to falsely accuse a personal enemy and/or shift the attention of authorities away from the actual perpetrator of a crime—just as those who made anonymous denunciations during the Spanish Inquisition, or those who post accusations in anonymous online forums today, might very well be taking advantage of the protective cover afforded by the situation to make bogus claims while dodging personal accountability. In fact, the ease with which a deceitful or malevolent actor can assume an anonymous or pseudonymous cover online, along with "the speed with which reputations can be made and altered" over the internet, creates fertile ground for the exploitation of protective anonymity for various harmful purposes.[191] In a similar fashion, an individual researcher or reporter, or alternatively one of their informants, might exploit academic or journalistic policies that shield the personal identities of sources in order to circulate false or misleading information, whatever their reason may be. Because this potential for manipulation or deceit is a feature of anonymity in general, a particular type of *trust* is required of the audience to an anonymous performance. Thus, the value and effectiveness of anonymous sources in the news media depends on the extent to which readers trust the media outlet, the reporter, and, via their professional vetting, the anonymous source as well. In any case, audience members will trust in the validity of an anonymous act or expression only when they imagine that the actor behind the cover representation is genuine and sincerely represented.

Likewise, one might exploit the anonymity or pseudonymity of online review platforms to damage the credibility of a business competitor (which is a particularly deceptive type of libel) or to falsely inflate the positive reputation of one's own business (an illegal practice known as "astroturfing" because of the false positive impression it creates).[192] Similarly, students may use their anonymous course evaluations or online review platforms for various reasons that stray from an honest assessment of the course and its instructor.[193] The protective covers of anonymous evaluation allow for false claims that are particularly insidious because they capitalize on our normative assumptions that anonymity allows for a more truthful account of a reviewer's actual experiences. In a similar vein, political candidates have sent anonymous mass mailings that besmirch and undermine their opponents while bolstering their own campaigns, creating the false impression that the communication comes from some unaffiliated member of the public or some "grassroots" association.[194] In all such cases, deceitful actors exploit the widespread perception that protective anonymity facilitates the articulation of suppressed truths in order to promote a lie or mischaracterization that can positively or negatively misrepresent the target of the action.

In other cases, snooping actors can opportunistically exploit cultural assumptions about, or promises of, protective anonymity to gather otherwise inaccessible personal information for their own gain, or in order to publicly expose others who believed they were acting in a protected space or forum. Consider the ways that anonymous and pseudonymous architectures allow snoops, voyeurs, and spies to slip in undetected. For example, anyone might step behind the screen in the confessional to assume the role of confessor,[195] or use a pseudonym to join a support group and assume the role of participant, thus acquiring access to the privileged information revealed by others in these seemingly protected confines. The protective characteristics of anonymity are not just available to individuals seeking refuge from various social threats, but also to individuals seeking to perpetrate harm—to those who want to engage in deceitful activities or otherwise attack or malign others while avoiding personal accountability for their actions. In this vein, the protective cover representations afforded by computer-mediated communication can allow criminals to extract personal information from their marks in order to manipulate or exploit them in various ways. Even before the internet, some exploited the protective anonymity of telephone hotlines for their own nonconsensual sexual gratification.[196] In all such cases, actors perform anonymity or pseudonymity in ways that are misleading, often at the expense of others and for their own benefit.

## Conclusion

In all of the various cases I have explored throughout this chapter, which cover a wide variety of circumstances and situations occurring at different times and in different places, actors use anonymity or pseudonymity for protective purposes. Whether obscuring their own personal identities, the personal identities of other people, or both, they work to bring otherwise suppressed behaviors, sentiments, and perspectives to life. In the process, such actors also perform the social and cultural dynamics of protection, animating and dramatically defining normative forces of power and social control as they work to evade these forces. In many cases, as actors bring protective anonymity to life, they express deeply rooted social ethics or principles associated with personal privacy, equality, and fairness, or the need to shield vulnerable people from retaliation by more powerful forces. However, while achieving voice that would otherwise remain muted, actors who perform protective anonymity often reinforce the stigmatized or marginal character of the actions and sentiments that they dissociate from personal identity, bolstering the notion that people must hide to be heard, be obscured to be seen, and generally protect themselves from personal association with certain issues, conditions, and behaviors.

Whether involving individual or cooperative efforts, performances of protective anonymity illustrate the thoroughly social, relational, and situationally contingent character of our hidden identities. Anonymity and pseudonymity are always brought to life by actors working in particular times and places to define situations for their audiences. As they use their various cover representations to obscure their personal identities, they free themselves to animate ideas and sentiments that they would otherwise refrain from expressing—to define various situations and circumstances by virtue of their covered and protected state. Given the freedom associated with this protected form of expression, the meanings of anonymous acts are often subversive in that they challenge or undermine dominant norms and perspectives in various ways. I explore this subversive character of anonymity, and further discuss how performances of hidden identities can be rooted in social dynamics of contention and power, in the next chapter.

# * 3 *

# *Subversive Anonymity*

Q is everybody. We don't know who particularly Q is; Q is a movement.
QANON SUPPORTER at a "Blue Lives Matter" rally in Brooklyn, New York[1]

We are everywhere.
Q[2]

In late October 2017, someone identified as "Q Clearance Patriot" (now simply known as "Q") began posting conspiratorial and often cryptic political messages in the anonymous internet forum 4chan. This actor claimed to be a high-level Washington insider holding a level Q security clearance.[3] Q further claimed to be strategically leaking sensitive information about Donald Trump's ongoing efforts to expose and arrest an "evil corrupt network of players" (often referred to as the "Deep State") who routinely subvert American democracy.[4] Q was purportedly using 4chan "to drop crumbs" of information while adding that, in its entirety, "the truth is mind blowing and cannot fully be exposed."[5]

Over the next three years, the actor (or multiple actors, as some claim) known as Q used three online forums to post thousands of messages.[6] During this period, and especially during the first year of the COVID-19 pandemic and the political drama surrounding the 2020 US presidential election, the movement of believers known as QAnon grew from a small network to a relatively significant popular crusade.[7] This growing community of followers viewed messages posted in the name of Q, or "Q drops," as coded revelations, and they used various social media sites to share their interpretations.[8] Many of these followers claimed that Q's posts were a calling to true "fellow patriots" to support the political leadership of Donald Trump as he worked to liberate the United States from a morally corrupt cabal that includes highly ranked Democrats, well-known Hollywood personalities, and other powerful figures. Some of these nefarious elites, some QAnon followers believe, engage in Satan worship, child sex trafficking and pedophilia, and the murder of children to extract and consume a rejuvenating chemical derived from the adrenaline in their blood.[9] The overall QAnon narrative uses a Christian apocalyptic theme to spur political revolt, prophesizing the victory of righteous forces fighting against the forces of evil,[10] culminating in "the storm" (the mass arrest and imprisonment of Deep State agents) and "the great awakening," where evil will be defeated and faithful followers will be rewarded with a free and glorious new world order.[11]

The case of QAnon shows how actors can perform anonymity and pseudonymity in *subversive* ways. On one level, any actor masquerading as Q subverts identity itself. The pseudonymous cover "Q" allows an actor to escape the constraints and transcend the limitations that personal identity would otherwise impose (whomever that person may be). However, on another level, pseudonymity allows that actor to bring a *subversive character* to life. Pseudonymity facilitates the performance of a noble insider with special knowledge, a concerned rebel who is taking great risk to reveal deeply important "truths" for the purpose of undermining a powerful and corrupt machine and awakening a righteous mass army. As Adrienne LaFrance has argued, "The story of Q is premised on the need for Q to remain anonymous," and "QAnon adherents see Q's anonymity as proof of Q's credibility."[12] In other words, Q's subversion of personal identity enables this mysterious actor's politically, morally, and culturally subversive acts. Furthermore, Q's pseudonymity also allows followers to imaginatively project themselves into the Q moniker, to collectively claim the character identity of Q, as when supporters echoed the famous scene from Stanley Kubrick's 1960 film *Spartacus* by holding signs that read "We are Q" at Donald Trump rallies.[13] It allows them to universalize their shared moral and political standpoint, as when supporters describe Q as "everybody," or when Q claims to be "we" and "everywhere," as in the epigraphs to this chapter. Such a sense of collective identity is further evident in the QAnon slogan "Where we go one, we go all." Using the Q cover representation as a claim to collective authority, movement adherents have worked to subvert long-accepted and mainstream ways of thinking about politics. In the name of Q, they have striven to undermine the legitimacy of the US political system and mainstream social institutions and to encourage subversive actions that have sometimes been violent and illegal.[14]

In this chapter, I explore the ways that individuals and communities perform anonymity and pseudonymity to engage in subversive acts.

Taking the protective dimensions of anonymity discussed in chapter 2 as a given, I focus on how actors obscure their personal identities to suspend, undermine, and otherwise subvert established interpersonal, cultural, political, and moral norms. In the process, such actors typically bring alternative meanings and counternorms to life. The protective and subversive dimensions of anonymity are inseparably intertwined. Recall three cases addressed in chapter 2 with regard to the protective character of anonymity: the nurses who risked administrative backlash in order to share frontline stories of the COVID-19 pandemic anonymously online, the women working in the media industry who anonymously exposed rampant sexual harassment by powerful male colleagues and employers, and the Saudi women who campaigned anonymously against the system of male guardianship in their country. All of these actors also perform anonymity subversively, using it as a means to critique and undermine status quo inequalities and systems of power while expressing alternative values in the process. This subversive dimension of anonymity requires our distinct attention if we wish to more fully understand the performance and impact of hidden identities in these and many other situations.[15]

Philip Zimbardo was among the first to systematically explore the link between anonymity and the subversion of social norms. For Zimbardo, who was concerned with destructive and violent actions that occur during protests and riots, anonymity promotes "deindividuation," which he described as a psychological state in which individuals lose their sense of personal identity and become detached from the social forces that hold them in check.[16] Deindividuation often precipitates "antisocial behavior," or "behavior in violation of established norms of appropriateness," Zimbardo argues, because it occurs during "conditions [that] minimize self-observation and evaluation as well as concern over evaluation by others."[17] In an important experiment, he found that people who were anonymized (those who were required to wear hoods and oversize lab coats while the experimenters refrained from using their names) acted to deliver longer painful electric shocks to others (accomplices to the experiment who were pretending to be shocked) compared to those whose faces were exposed and personal names were used. In other words, anonymity led to increased aggression and willingness to harm others, as primarily measured by the duration of the shocks experimental subjects believed they were delivering to other human beings.[18] Claiming that his experiments shed light on social unrest and upheaval, Zimbardo argues that "where social conditions of life destroy individual identity by making people feel anonymous," one will see a "great expenditure of energy and effort directed toward shattering traditional forms and institutionalized structures."[19] For Zimbardo, anonymity is linked to "chaos" and the "darker side" of human action and expression,[20] to a "loss of control over one's own behaviour," a "loss of rationality," and a general disruption of social norms.[21]

Over the past few decades, some social psychologists have rightly criticized Zimbardo and other classical deindividuation theorists for relying on "a desocialized model of the self."[22] These researchers have developed and advanced a Social Identity model of Deindividuation Effects, or SIDE model,[23] arguing that "anonymity does not produce a loss of identity so much as a switch to or an increase in the salience of social identity in group contexts."[24] In other words, those who experience obscured personal identities in group contexts often conform to and express norms rooted in those groups, rather than acting without reason or against social norms altogether.[25] Thus, anonymity is not *anti*social. Rather, anonymity and pseudonymity can free individuals and groups to break norms and resist powerful social forces by spurring them to assert alternative social norms and values that would otherwise remain muted.[26]

While helping us to understand how anonymity detaches individuals from various forms of social control, both classical deindividuation theorists and SIDE researchers typically treat anonymity as an imposed "input variable"[27]—as a social condition that produces psychological and behavioral changes, one that they attempt to create in laboratory settings. Moving beyond the limits of both frameworks, I stress the ways that anonymous actors creatively perform subversive anonymity and pseudonymity as they actively work to make meaning in the world. Such actors design and wield their anonymity and pseudonymity to subvert identity itself in creative ways that allow them to confront, alter, or transcend some normative part of the social order, including normative relations of power. In the process of subverting social norms, they actively make alternative meanings with their anonymous acts. Even when actors use anonymity and pseudonymity to perpetrate harm, to voice hateful or discriminatory attitudes and viewpoints, or to engage in aggressive or destructive behavior (the types of behavior that concerned Zimbardo), they are subverting some order of social norms and values while bringing counternorms and alternative values to life. In this vein, for example, those who objectify women in anonymous online forums, "treating them as mere sets of body parts, mere appearances," use their anonymous covers to animate deeply rooted ideologies of misogyny.[28] Such anonymity is subversive not simply because actors use it to escape social control, but rather because actors use it to violate mainstream civil norms by performing alternative behaviors and values, thereby creating an alternative openly aggressive and misogynistic social order in their online forum, one that has "real-world consequences for . . . women."[29] Even anonymous acts that promote discord and destruction also typically facilitate some form of cohesion and construction insofar as subversive actors give life to alternative ways of understanding and being in the world.

In order to more fully understand the social dynamics of subversive anonymity, we must explore how individuals and communities use their cover representations to performatively express certain beliefs, ideologies, values, moral sentiments, and feelings while undermining others. In this regard, authors and visual artists of different genres and time periods have obscured their personal identities for various subversive purposes. Subversive anonymity is also evident in the masked performances of masquerade and carnival when participants embrace that which is conventionally regarded as deviant or taboo.[30] Likewise, political dissidents throughout history have acted behind various cover representations to accomplish their subversive aims. The subversive quality of obscured personal identity is evident in the French term for pseudonym, *nom de guerre*, the literal translation of which is "name of war," which establishes an etymological connection between pseudonymity and "guerrilla" activity, a theme I will discuss with regard to both art and political protest. Only by analyzing subversive anonymity as performance in all such cases can we grasp how actors use cover representations to animate alternative and rebellious meanings in their contexts and situations.

## Subversive Art and Literature

For the producer of any text or work of art, the act of obscuring one's personal identity involves a fundamental subversion of contemporary norms that govern the ways we attribute authorship and define the connection between a creation and its creator. In our reading of visual art, fictional literature, music, poetry, autobiography, philosophy, or political propaganda, we often see the meaning of the work, and the social performance more generally, as directly related to the identity of its author. We wish to know the author in order to fully comprehend the work, which we attach to the social standpoint, moral orientation, motive, and other characteristics of those who create.[31] By obscuring their personal identities and often establishing an air of mystery in the process, anonymous and pseudonymous artists and authors sabotage this process in different ways. Furthermore, they use their cover representations to buck rules, express alternative meanings, or promote subversive values with their work.

For example, by adopting the common pseudonymous signature "By a Lady," early eighteenth-century female authors were able to speak more freely and subversively to an audience of women, "to and for a group of sympathetic readers, but speaking against the appropriate norms." In other words, they adopted the gendered yet generic title "Lady" in order to subtly undermine norms of gender expression and communication, thus achieving "subversion through the mimicry or ironic performance of the cultural expectations of the dominant group in power."[32] In the nineteenth century, Charlotte, Emily, and Anne Brontë published under the names Currer, Ellis, and Acton Bell, choosing these first names because of their gender ambiguity (rather than their gender specificity). Beyond simply subverting their own gender, they consciously subverted gender itself as a part of the mystery they sought to cultivate with their work.[33] When Charlotte published *Jane Eyre* as Currer, such a consciously ambiguous cover representation provided "an invitation to speculate about the sex of the author," and many marveled at, or simply rejected, the possibility that the author was a woman.[34] Likewise, when Mary Ann Evans published anonymously early in her career, she created an "ambiguously gendered narrative voice" that led readers to "develop a sympathy that crosses gender lines."[35] Later adopting the pseudonym George Eliot, she continued to subvert gender norms of the literary world that shaped expectations and interpretations of the contributions of women.[36] As her "masculine pseudonym was a claim to authority,"[37] Evans led readers to appreciate her work when a conventionally female name may have been an obstacle to their appreciation. In a similar fashion, the author born Amantine Lucile Aurore Dupin, who sometimes dressed and lived as a man and at other times as a woman, wrote as George Sand while publishing novels that addressed politically charged themes related to gender and class inequality in nineteenth-century France, often centered around the constraints of marriage. Dupin's pseudonymous authorship expressed something of the author's "transgressive style of dress and behavior," and further subverted entrenched norms of gender identity as a literary accomplishment.[38]

Different types of cases abound. Ralph Waldo Emerson's 1836 book *Nature*, which established the moral and practical foundations of transcendentalism, was first published anonymously because it challenged mainstream religious ideologies of nineteenth-century America. While Emerson espoused the belief that God pervaded the natural world, he simultaneously outlined the core tenets of a spiritual movement that undermined the authority of (and ultimately spurred nonconformity with) the dominant religious and governmental institutions of his day. Romain Gary, the celebrated French novelist and winner of the 1956 Prix Goncourt (the highest literary award in France) played with and subverted the impact that his fame would have on the reception of his subsequent work by publishing under several pseudonyms. Gary won the Prix Goncourt a second time in 1975, despite the fact that the rules prohibited the award being given to any individual more than once, because he published his 1975 Goncourt-winning novel, *La vie devant soi*, under the name Émile Ajar, a bogus identity he sustained until after his death. Gary's ability to play with multiple literary identities prompted an air of mystery around his persona and character, and led some to define him as "the greatest literary impostor of all time" or to raise questions like "Is Emile Ajar the greatest writer who never lived?"[39] In these and many other cases, authors used anonymity and pseudonymity to perform subversive challenges to dominant norms, values, practices, and/or rules.

Such a subversive anonymity is further evident in the case of graffiti and related forms of street art, much of which is produced anonymously or pseudonymously.[40] Pseudonymity is typically established when the art is made with or in the form of a tag (an ornate moniker), or with an established and recognized style. Graffiti is often politically subversive in its social contexts in that artists use it to call attention to issues and causes that might otherwise remain "plagued with silence."[41] However, it is also *artistically subversive* (insofar as graffiti challenges the definition of art along with the structure of artistic authority and legitimacy in the field), *aesthetically subversive* (in that it challenges the definition of what makes for a visually appropriate and beautiful urban landscape), and *legally subversive* (insofar as graffiti artists violate rules governing the right to alter both public and private property, including bathroom stalls,[42] external walls, streets, neighborhoods, semi-secluded and controlled spaces,[43] or the natural landscape[44]). Thus, Jean Baudrillard described graffiti as an "insurrection of signs"—a revolt against "the dominant culture" that governs space and structures social relationships.[45]

While graffiti is inherently communicative and performative, its underground and transformative character also makes it an ideal medium for delivering subversive social critique and promoting social change.[46] For example, activist-artists blended rich local themes with globalizing forms when using graffiti to undermine the legitimacy of Hosni Mubarak's presidency during the 2011 Egyptian uprising.[47] Others spread various subversive messages by "chalking on the walls and pavements" in eighteenth-century England,[48] and some create graffiti today "to resist the capitalist colonization of space in . . . Berlin"[49] or to advance the cause of Puerto Rican independence.[50] Likewise, the artist known as Black Hand uses a pseudonymous cover to play a subversive role in Iran, producing public art critical of the state while bucking state censorship and legal definitions of acceptable art in the process. In subversive acts that prefigured the

Me Too movement, women at Brown and Columbia Universities graffitied bathroom walls with the names of men they accused of sexual assault and harassment, spurring public dialogues and changes to campus policies.[51] In the Brown and Columbia cases, "graffiti are an alternative means of expression for women."[52] In general, "graffiti can be seen as a parallel text within a culture"[53] but also as a way of creating "alternative spaces."[54] To this end, in an unusual case, a group known as the "guerrilla grafters" covertly graft fruit-bearing limbs onto public trees, effectively subverting and transforming the normative distinctions between city and country, the tamed and the wild, an urbanized environment and the natural world.[55] The Israeli artist known as Dede Bandaid transforms urban structures that would otherwise fade into the background, shifting our attention by giving them new, visually marked meanings that are often absurd or out of place.[56] By "redirecting attention" and turning "*non-places into places,*" graffiti "can also change our movement through a space . . . effectively changing its experienced form and temporality,"[57] transforming the world not only via its message, but also its form. In all of these cases, artists obscure their personal identities in acts that reclaim and transform social spaces. In the process, they subvert mainstream or dominant meanings and promote alternative visions of the world in which they work.

Perhaps the most famous pseudonymous street artist in the world today is Banksy, who uses his work not only to criticize war, police violence, and policies that lead to climate change, for example, but also to subvert the mainstream values of the traditional world of high art. In one 2005 performance designed to undermine the exclusivity of museum culture, Banksy covertly hung various unattributed politically and culturally subversive images in four mainstream New York museums—the Museum of Modern Art, the Metropolitan Museum of Art, the Brooklyn Museum, and the Museum of Natural History. He had previously pulled similar stunts in London and Paris.[58] Furthermore, by titling his 2010 film *Exit Through the Gift Shop*, Banksy took a critical stand against the commercial character of museum culture. In August 2015, Banksy opened his critical exhibit *Dismaland*, a mock theme park that made use of a variety of artistic techniques to lambaste the corporate character of the Disney brand. In each case, Banksy pits his obscured identity and underground style against the exclusivity and profit orientation that defines the dominant institutions of art and culture. In the process, he promotes a subversive artistic ethic as an alternative to the mainstream world of art—"a new art world for a new audience, running alongside the existing world and now, slowly but surely, within it."[59]

Furthermore, Banksy often plays with the contradictions of being fa-

FIGURE 7. Banksy image of a portrait artist sketching a masked person. Courtesy of Pest Control Office, Banksy, Image from Banksy.co.uk, 2022.

mous in his pseudonymity (of being widely appreciated yet personally unknown), a contradiction he expresses in his depiction of a portrait artist sketching a masked subject (fig. 7). Portrait artists are known for capturing the particular and distinctive aspects of a person's face and/or body, as illustrated by the portraits of various famous people in the background of the scene. However, ski masks and balaclavas are used to obscure all distinctiveness in order to project a generic front. With the image in figure 7, Banksy creatively illustrates the contradictory phenomenon of being *distinctively unknown* in the world.

In this sense, while the person behind the pseudonym (or "mask") forgoes personal fame, Banksy is world-famous for forgoing personal fame.[60] His cover of pseudonymity (and the mysterious allure of someoneness it fosters) has become an inseparable part of the artist's rebellious character, which is intertwined with the meaning, significance, and value of his art. Thus, "anonymity, once a necessity, has become something of a marketing tool" and has "created its own interest."[61] By performing a well-known character who is personally unknown, the mysterious vandal became an international sensation.

Well before the rise of Banksy, the Guerrilla Girls collectively brandished gorilla masks to criticize sexism inherent in the mainstream institutions of the art world.[62] This anonymous collective of female artists originally formed in 1985 to protest an exhibit at the New York Museum of Modern Art for its male-dominated program,[63] thereby criticizing the gendered characterization of high art while simultaneously establishing an alternative feminist voice in the field. The group also sought to subvert the "class-bound" character of mainstream museums and galleries.[64] In 1990 they published *Guerrilla Girls' Code of Ethics for Art Museums*, which is an attack on the corporate and male-dominated nature of museum culture. Thus, the collective worked to "undermine the idea of a mainstream narrative by revealing the understory, the subtext, the overlooked, and the downright unfair."[65] In the process of calling attention to the absence of certain voices in the dominant institutions of the field, the group also brought their own critical feminist art to life while individual members reclaimed the names of dead female artists as pseudonyms. By breaking mainstream norms and pushing an alternative artistic order, the Guerrilla Girls subverted the gatekeeping "role of the curator and collector."[66]

While Banksy produces his subversive art with a unique individual pseudonym, the Guerrilla Girls have primarily performed as an anonymous group; the tributary pseudonyms used by members blend into their anonymous collective front. Anonymity is not only the foundation of the Guerrilla Girls' uniquely subversive and underground style, but it also allows these activists to take a stand *as* and *for* women in general, demanding more attention and recognition for women in their field while simultaneously shirking individual recognition in their activist performances. As one member who uses the pseudonym Alma Thomas notes, the anonymity of members primarily served "to maintain the symbolism of the Girls intact"[67] as a collective movement. Thus, while Banksy primarily cultivates a mysterious someoneness with his individual pseudonym, the Guerrilla Girls primarily cultivate a feminist form of everyoneness with their shared anonymity. The former allows for *vicarious ego aggrandizement*—the performative promotion and celebration of an alternate individual identity. The latter involves *ego deprecation*—a minimization of individualism via the accentuation of a mass and amorphous community. Such ego deprecation, as I discuss in the following sections of this chapter, is a key characteristic of all anonymous social movements.

The Guerrilla Girls used anonymity to democratize artistic identity and authority, directly claiming, "We could be anyone. We are everywhere."[68] Indeed, from the perspective of their fans and general audience, anyone could be behind the gorilla mask. However, by using anonymity to eschew personal fame and individual recognition in favor of a collective identity and amorphous artistic movement, some members have suggested that they may have ultimately undermined a vital objective. In a reflective and critical note, the Guerrilla Girl who uses the pseudonym Alice Neel argued, "In a way, being anonymous goes against what we are fighting for. We are actually keeping ourselves from being fully acknowledged and recognized and part of history."[69] Another member who uses the pseudonym Kathe Kollwitz has argued that one consequence of anonymity was that "it kept anyone from getting credit. . . . We don't get personal credit for it, although the work is so fantastic and interesting to do."[70] While the subversive art of this anonymous movement boosted recognition of an underrepresented group, the collective character of their anonymous work simultaneously hindered the recognition of individual artists by blending their performative contributions into a shared cover representation.

## Masked Social Movements and Anonymous Rebellion

Activists representing social movements that span the spectrum of political ideology have used masks and other various cover representations to express their rebellious positions and engage in insurgent activities. Such movements include the American Ku Klux Klan and the hacker network that bears the very name Anonymous, as well as the contemporary anarcho-activist network Antifa (short for "anti-fascist") along with various underground or guerrilla movements from different periods and contexts, including the Ejército Zapatista de Liberación Nacional, or EZLN. As the actors behind these otherwise very different movements engage in masked anonymous performances, they confront and undermine established meaning systems in order to subvert different forms of power. In the process, they actively advance alternative values and systems of meaning.

My analysis here builds on the work of E. P. Thompson and James C. Scott. Thompson discussed "the anonymous tradition" and "counter-theater" as two of the three most important "characteristics of popular action" in eighteenth-century England.[71] Scott developed this perspective to systematically discuss anonymity as one of "the manifold strategies by which subordinate groups manage to insinuate their resistance, in disguised forms, into the public transcript."[72] Subversive acts of anonymity, as Scott realized in his own way,[73] often involve the movement of meanings developed in alternative lifeworlds and underground spaces into the contentious public realm. However, both Thompson and Scott viewed anonymous protest within the Marxian framework of class power dynamics. Both described anonymity as a tool that the masses of the subordinate class(es) use to counter the will and policies of the dominant class. Here, I build on their work to illuminate the ways that different types of movements use anonymity to cast and perform themselves as the *everyone and anyone populous* rising against an oppressive power when such an interpretation is not structurally evident or universally accepted. While "the masked face" may have "the potential to make the previously unseen majority visible,"[74] it also, and more commonly, generalizes the stance of a vocal minority. In other words, anonymity is not simply an expressive tool to give voice to objective mass interests. Rather, the movements I analyze in this chapter use anonymity as they work to assert the popular character and establish the meaning of their claims. In my view, while their actions often express underlying social tensions, these actors use the tools and cultural symbolism of anonymous subversive action to engage adversaries and define particular antagonisms. They use their masked performances to define issues, events, and experiences, and to advance alternative meanings of oppression, injustice, and emancipation.

THE RELIGIOUS, THEATRICAL, AND FESTIVE

ROOTS OF MASKED SOCIAL PROTEST

In order to fully grasp the subversive anonymity practiced by different modern and late-modern social movements, we must first delve into the historic use of masks in religious rituals, theatrical performances, and carnival. Modern masked social protests evolved from these historical and cultural antecedents and retain some of their central characteristics. These accumulated characteristics include the use of masking to facilitate (a) the symbolic expression of social solidarity and collective identity, (b) the transformation of individuals into culturally coded characters, (c) the production of a critical and socially reflexive theatrics, and (d) the cultivation of alternative and seditious meaning systems. In this sense, contemporary masked social protest is a cultural phenomenon that emerged over time while retaining the legacies of past eras.

Masking has historically been used to suspend or subvert quotidian norms and to achieve ritualistic transformations during religious ceremonies in societies with collective polytheistic or animistic worldviews. Taking a range of different examples, we might consider the social use and cultural significance of masks during the rites of the early Greek cult of Dionysus, indigenous Shintō rituals in Japan, and some Native American ceremonies (from different Mesoamerican societies to the various communities of the Pacific Northwest). In each case, despite their otherwise significant differences, masks were used to create sacred ritual space and time in which known members of the community were transformed into deities, spirits, demons, or other totemic characters in order to enact shared beliefs about the nature of the world and the order of the cosmos. With regard to some indigenous Mesoamerican cultures, "when donned in ritual, the mask allowed men to become gods," and "the world of the spirit and the world of daily existence met."[75] Likewise, in some *Kagura* (Shintō dance rituals) that took place at night, participants wore masks to animate demons that would "return to *their world* at daybreak."[76] In such ceremonial contexts, it does *not* make sense to speak of the anonymity of the actors behind the masks. They were not hiding their personal identities. Nor were they seen as agents who manipulated or acted "behind" the beings they became in sacred settings. Rather, their personal identities temporarily disappeared to be replaced during the sacred episode. These transformations—of living persons into sacred characters—were possible and powerful because they expressed the metaphysical worldview and shared sentiments of the community behind them.[77]

In classical Greece, the rise of professional drama, which evolved from Dionysian religious ritual, marked the establishment of an artistic sphere of performance that was separate and distinct from the religious sphere, one that facilitated a new intellectual and critical reflection on society.[78] Greek actors continued to use masks, but they used them as tools to create culturally and politically coded characters—dramatis personae—that they animated in order to construct alternative worlds of meaning into which they hoped audiences would be cognitively and emotionally absorbed.[79] In other words, theater masks facilitated transformation, but of a different quality—defined by an artistic rather than a religious frame and "a conscious and pragmatic effort to create dramatic effect" in an era of increasing "social and culture complexity" when such an accomplishment of dramatic realization could not be taken for granted.[80] In this sense, masks allowed actors to express and embody a very flexible notion of identity and "the idea of letting go one's individual self in order to become . . . a character . . . was therefore neither threatening nor problematic."[81] They also allowed "a single actor to play multiple roles (including different ages and genders) in the same play."[82] Moreover, masks allowed actors to "say and do things that could not be said and done in everyday life, and . . . present to the audience events, actions and ideas that were horrifying or ridiculous, inspiring or fantastic."[83] However, as with masking in religious rites, it still does *not* make sense to speak of the anonymity of the actors behind theater masks. Instead, theater became an art defined by the skillful and creative manipulation of persona.[84] Professional actors were known (and sometimes celebrated) creative agents who used masks to consciously subvert personal identity in order to convey meaningful (and often politically subversive) messages about the world.[85]

With the growth of Christian cultural and political power in the West, ecclesiastical authorities sought to replace the pluralism and polytheism inherited from the classical and Hellenistic world with a society unified by a singular moral code. At its core, Christian authority was fundamentally hermeneutic, or interpretive, as the Church fought to establish a monopoly on the meaning of selves, texts, ritual activities, performances, and behaviors of all types. As Christian authorities attacked the polytheistic world order, they redefined Greek theater (as expressed in the Roman off-shoot that included elaborate festivals in the name of Bacchus, the Roman version of Dionysus) as deceptive and evil. Tertullian (c. 155–c. 220 CE) compared theater to a sewer and specifically attacked its character as a space in which quotidian norms were breached, arguing that "never and nowhere is it right to do what you may not do at all times and in all places."[86] Furthermore, Tertullian was "particularly reproachful of actors regarding the mimesis that is central to their craft" and argued that "God specifically hates hypocrisy and false things, including masks, dressing as another gender, or trying to sound or look like anyone besides yourself."[87] Two centuries after Tertullian, Augustine was also highly critical of the false and corrupting character of Roman theater and saw it as a sinful distraction from a proper and true Christian orientation.[88] "In short," as A. David Napier states, "the stage was seen by Christians as not only immoral but as completely antithetical to the Christian world view."[89]

As they rallied against the theatrical arts, Christian authorities redefined the mask as a means to hide one's true identity and motives. They associated masking with evil and sin (on a moral level) and rebellion (at the level of social and political structure).[90] Thus, "in the Christian and post-Christian world," the flexibility of identity at the heart of masking practices was viewed as "abandoning responsibility for one's own individual soul or self," which "became intolerable."[91] In fact, the very essence of masking contradicted the Christian idea of the "'moral person'" as a "metaphysical entity," as a singular and essential "being possessing metaphysical and moral value,"[92] and thereby undermined efforts to hold individual persons accountable to the Church and its vision of God. In this moment, masking comes to be coded with deceit, falsehood, illusion, and sin, cast as the antithesis of honesty, truth, authenticity, and goodness. Masked activities, and indeed the very notion of fluid or flexible identity, came to be seen as mendacious, strategic, and even sinister in character.[93] It is here that we see the emergence of a subversive anonymity that would become a key feature of carnival and, later, masked social protest. As Christians sought to unify the social and moral order, and as masks were now seen as hiding actors with subversive intent—as separating their true and only identities from their masked actions—actors increasingly used masks to obscure their personal identities as they worked to challenge dominant definitions of the situation and subvert power.

Over time, as Efrat Tseëlon explains, "the mask moved from the ritual to the theatre and ultimately to the streets."[94] As masking became a central feature of carnival in the feudal era, carnivalgoers "built a second world and a second life outside officialdom," creating what Mikhail Bakhtin called a "two-world condition," or a "double aspect of the world and of human life."[95] Revelers accomplished this second world order by using masks and costumes to obscure their personal identities while violating normative constraints on behavior, often thwarting Christian rules and restrictions in the process (e.g., those associated with the asceticism of Lent).[96] This was the world "of folk consciousness, of folk culture" that stood against the "monolithically serious" official world and subverted its "prevailing truth and . . . the established order,"[97] expressing a "very real power struggle."[98] As a mass popular theatrical activity, carnival "does not acknowledge any distinction between actors and spectators."[99] The people and the play become bound into one alternative and subversive lifeworld. On such occasions, as with the case of rural Austrian Krampus actors in the latter half of the twentieth century, "masks . . . facilitate . . . behavior in which people are led to transform their normal selves, to transcend everyday roles, or to soar beyond the level of commonplace reality."[100]

I have sketched this brief cultural history to show that key features of modern masked and anonymous social protest were inherited from the historical and cultural antecedents outlined above. These include masking as a means of embodying sacred and iconic characters in ways that express the shared values and collective identity of a movement community, engaging in critically reflexive performances to shape political culture and impact broad audiences, and creating parallel alternative worlds of meaning in the midst of the dominant social order, all while subverting personal identity and thereby escaping personal association with seditious motives and actions. These characteristics have accumulated to define a modern mode of masked social protest in which actors suspend and transcend their personal identities for various moral and political purposes. Modern masked social movement actors bring iconic rebellious characters and alternative political meanings to life in pluralistic and contentious public arenas, drawing rich symbolism from their cultural milieus to suit their political situations and objectives.

## MASKED MOVEMENTS AND THEIR SUBVERSIVE WORLD ORDERS

At the inception of the modern era, revolutionaries often used anonymity and pseudonymity to articulate their political positions and perform insurgency. François-Marie Arouet, French Enlightenment thinker and critic of the Catholic Church, wrote under the pseudonym Voltaire. The famous American Revolutionary pamphlet *Common Sense*, now widely known to have been written by Thomas Paine, was first published and circulated anonymously. The American *Federalist Papers*—written by

Alexander Hamilton, James Madison, and John Jay—were published under the pseudonym "Publius," the first name of one of the founders of
the Roman Republic, Publius Valerius Publicola, and a name that is very
similar to the Latin word *publicus*, which means "public" or "of the people."
Like the British Liberals John Trenchard and Thomas Gordon, who published their widely influential essays under the name "Cato" decades before Hamilton, Madison, and Jay used "Publius," many Enlightenment-era
revolutionaries used the names of classical Greek or Roman partisans as
pseudonyms to performatively link their modern revolutionary ideals to
the birthplaces of democracy and republicanism. These pseudonyms came
to life as "ancient roles . . . acted out" in a modern context where they
signified cultural values such as "public virtue and patriotism," along with
honor, sacrifice, and experience, as well as "tradition and authenticity."[101]
Moreover, the Boston Tea Party was a costumed and largely anonymous
act that dramatically realized a mass popular hostility to British taxation
of the American colonies, a "collective performance" that "successfully
dramatized colonial opposition to the British crown, clarified a key issue in
the antagonism, and mobilized fervent public support."[102] The costumed
character of this protest likely broadened its appeal, allowing people of
all backgrounds to identify or experience affinity with the anonymous
heroes of the defiant and subversive act. In such cases, anonymity and
pseudonymity focus attention on the revolutionary performance and
content of the message while downplaying the personalities of the individuals responsible. This also allowed actors to obscure or misrepresent
their class status, as when John Adams wrote newspaper editorials under
the name "Humphrey Ploughjogger," assuming the cover representation
of a common farmer.

    After the political forces behind the revolutions of modernity achieved
power, the act of hiding one's identity was more commonly associated
with undermining modern values of public accountability, truth, and
transparency.[103] In 1790, just months after Revolutionary forces took
power in France, masks were officially banned as they were seen to violate the dignity of the new social order and to symbolize "the servitude . . .
of life under a tyranny."[104] Likewise, in the mid-nineteenth century, John
Stuart Mill argued: "Disguise in all its forms is a badge of slavery," and "it
is high time now that people should be taught the duty of asserting and
acting openly on their opinions."[105] The image of hiding one's identity, especially while occupying a public role, was deemed uncivil and a threat to
reason, truth, and justice. Such a view remains a bedrock principle of most
deliberative bodies (congresses, senates, community associations, etc.) in

democratic societies.[106] This historical contradiction in the liberal position on obscuring personal identity—embraced in revolutionary practice but rejected as principle of governance, "praised for freeing citizens" in some cases and "condemned for providing convenient cover to harmful or democratically undesirable behavior" in others[107]—shows just how the moral evaluation of anonymity and pseudonymity is socially structured around dynamics of power.

In our post-revolutionary era, social movements with very different objectives and ideologies have used anonymity to escape the constraints of the dominant social order and bring subversive (and sometimes illegal) activity to life. Using standardized masks, costumes, and other cover representations, movement actors transform themselves into rebellious characters to cooperatively advance critical alternatives to status quo social conditions and relations. On a general level, such subversive performances convey a *deprecation of the ego* and an *accentuation of the mass*. Despite significant differences across a variety of cases, the deprecation of egoism, facilitated by "stylized garb in which . . . personal outlines disappear,"[108] serves to focus audiences (both public and internal to the movement community) on the impersonal political meanings, motivations, and objectives behind social movement acts, rather than on the personal identities of the actors.[109] Such a deprecation of ego also blurs and levels in-group distinctions, providing group members with a certain interchangeability and anyoneness.[110]

While the deprecation of egoism emphasizes a certain anyoneness of movement participation, the accentuation of the mass gives the group itself the character of everyoneness.[111] Social movement actors use their masks to convey the notion that a great many people privately believe in the movement but fear retaliation from powerful and repressive authorities, and that their masked actions express suppressed beliefs and values held by a mass community. Because anyone can don the mask, which serves as the shared face of subversive performance, movement participants often claim it represents all the members of a particular population, a collective "we" that may strive toward mass inclusion while simultaneously excluding outsiders based on ideology or some other variable (such as class or race). Moreover, from the perspective of the masked individual, acting behind the shared cover representation blends one's personal identity (including one's motives, agency, and responsibility) into the collective identity of the movement community and a shared common purpose pitted against an oppressive force.[112] Thus, the cover representations used by anonymous subversives can establish a *symbolic uniformity* and "a striking vision of solidarity"[113] in contraposition to the uniformed front typically displayed by official representatives of the dominant social order (often police and/or military forces).[114]

Social movement anonymity can also change the dynamics of state repression. On the one hand, by obscuring personal identities, masked movements make it harder for authorities to surveil their activities, identify leaders, and discipline actors. On the other hand, the anonymity of subversive agents allows authorities to justify casting a wide net when identifying activists and punishing lawbreakers. Such a political dynamic allowed John Cookenboo and Vincent Yochelson to be arrested in Berkeley, California, on April 15, 2017, the day after masked activists physically confronted right-wing protesters, "on *suspicion* of wearing masks while committing a criminal offense."[115] Furthermore, to counter the impact of social movement anonymity, anti-mask legislation has been adopted at different times and places around the world. In many cases, these laws do not just criminalize "the obscuring of identity while committing a crime but simply the obscuring of personal identity in itself."[116] By targeting and seeking to expose individuals who wear masks, such law enforcement practices serve to chip away at the ability of a movement to perform itself as a mass collective force.[117]

Beyond these general characteristics, subversive activists wield anonymity in other culturally meaningful ways. Their masks, cloaks, and other cover representations often carry deep, historically entrenched symbolic meanings.[118] Moreover, masked social movement activists animate and mobilize this entrenched cultural symbolism using popular scripts, vocabularies, and theatrical formats.[119] They bring deep symbolic references and cultural codes to life as social dramas with familiar plots, character-types, and morals that audiences can understand (whether or not these audiences agree with movement claims). They then use their anonymous acts to advance parallel social orders as a threat or challenge to dominant systems of meaning. Thus, the symbolism of the masks, cloaks, and other cover representations used by anonymous movement actors, and the ways these symbols are moved into action, need to be interpreted and understood with regard to the cultural, historical, and political milieu in which the subversive activity unfolds. When social movement actors engage in anonymous performances, they pit their masked characters *with* some people and *against* others in order to define situations, problems, and personas in the world, as well as to define various events, experiences, issues, places, and actions as they challenge dominant social orders and power structures.[120] Over time, their masks and other cover representations come to carry a broad cultural and iconographic force.

## THE ANONYMOUS PERFORMANCES OF KU KLUX KLAN TERROR

The iconic cover representations and other symbols used by the Ku Klux Klan since its second iteration in the early twentieth century carry deeply rooted meanings about race, religion, and nation in the United States. The whiteness of the hood and robes along with the Christian legacy of its symbols serve to frame Klan actions, including lynchings and other forms of violence and terrorism, as the fulfillment of a racist religious destiny that stands above and beyond any individual's personal identity or any specific interpersonal encounter.[121] The "fiery cross," or *crann tara*, previously used to gather Scottish clans and villages together to face a foreign enemy, constructs a symbolic ancestral link to medieval Europe and historical continuity with an imagined ethnic-religious community.[122] With these uniform symbols, Klan members not only obscured their personal identities but also, and simultaneously, mobilized durable cultural codes to define boundaries between the *pure* and the *polluted*, the *holy* and the *depraved*, the *authentic* and the *foreign*, and the *civilized* and the *barbarous* in order to performatively claim the goodness and rightness of white Protestant-Christian nationhood in the United States.[123] Thus, Klan members used their anonymity as a means to performatively subvert progress toward racial equality, and to assert what adherents claimed to be a right and natural classificatory order in the world.

All of this symbolism was inspired by D. W. Griffith's 1915 film, *The Birth of a Nation*, which was based on the 1905 novel by Thomas Dixon Jr. titled *The Clansman: A Historical Romance of the Ku Klux Klan*.[124] The film provided a model for Klan anonymity as we know it today. It also provided a narrative script that set the masked Klansman as a new American hero acting on a masculine protective code of honor and duty to defend family, nation, and civil society from a barbarism imposed by Black men with political power. A burning cross is depicted in one of several illustrations in Dixon's novel with the caption "The Fiery Cross of old Scotland's hills!"[125] It was also wielded by a hooded and robed Klansman mounted on a rearing hooded and robed horse in the image widely used to promote Griffith's film, an image that reflected a key scene of Klan action toward the end of the film (see fig. 8).[126] As Klan rebels moved the white hoods, robes, and burning crosses from the film screen to the streets, they established these symbols as an iconic force of white supremacy and racist terrorism in American life.

The Klan of the 1920s operated with split performative fronts—one open and uncovered, the other secretive and masked. Both, however, were fronts performed for audiences in the public sphere.[127] On the one hand,

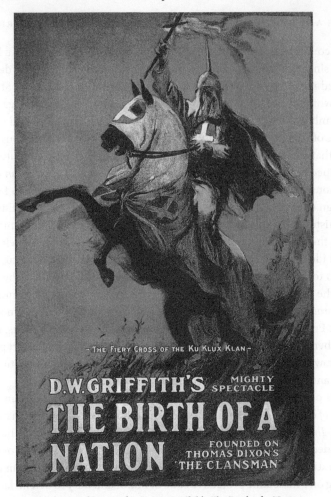

FIGURE 8. Promotional poster for D. W. Griffith's *The Birth of a Nation*.

the open and uncovered front consisted of "organized mass public events" in the form of festivals, parades, and religious ceremonies held all over the country, "mass performances, staged for audiences," and "extravagant productions that offered entertainment for all" who attended.[128] The personal identities of many Klan leaders were well-known and rank-and-file members often did not wear masks at these Klan-sponsored events. On the other hand, the secretive and masked front consisted of hooded and robed rituals that conveyed a sense of mystery and exclusivity, providing a magnetic draw to potential recruits while striking a clear boundary between insider and outsider communities.[129] These masked rituals often overlapped with public festivals and celebrations, where they served to showcase Klan power and organization and convey public threats to those the Klan defined as its enemies. This front also included a great deal of masked vigilante violence and terrorism that typically occurred under the cover of darkness, only to be publicized after the fact.[130] Thus, the Klan was at once *both* public and secret, open and exclusive, familiar and anonymous. These two performative fronts complemented one another as the movement worked to advance its vision of "Americanism,"[131] a vision defined by a white supremacist social and political order that countered liberal visions that linked growing diversity, inclusivity, and globalism with American progress.

However, the original iteration of the Ku Klux Klan arose approximately five decades earlier in the Reconstruction era. During this first wave, early Klan members adopted a performance style from popular southern theatrical, musical, and festival practices, which included costumed parades and nighttime performances.[132] Using a carnival format blended with the theatrics of minstrelsy, Klan rebels of the Reconstruction era adapted and animated these "popular cultural forms" as they worked to extend the racial and political power relations of the antebellum order into the postwar world.[133] As they engaged in anonymous acts of racist terror and "nocturnal violence" against recently freed Black southerners, Klan members used an array of readily available materials to disguise themselves, including cloth or burlap (e.g., "painted meal sacks"), paper, animal skins, carnival and masquerade costumes, military uniforms, and women's clothing (fig. 9).[134]

These early Klan activists often used their masks to perform as Confederate soldiers returning from the grave, sometimes donning Confederate military regalia as they acted out their subversive scenes.[135] Just as the masks worn in mummers' plays facilitated the rites of "revivification" that are central to those plays,[136] Reconstruction-era Klan radicals used masks and costumes to revive dead Confederate soldiers and the social order for which they fought. In this sense, the early performances of Klan terror accomplished what Claude Calame regards as an essential innovation of Greek drama. Whereas the "spatiotemporal frame" of storytelling (narrative alone) was past oriented, dramatic performance allows the audience to meet anachronistic characters in "the here and now" and "face to face." From the perspective of the audience, "the mask in part reestablishes by visual means . . . the mythical narrative's actorial and spatiotemporal framework and the world of possible others that it constructs."[137] However, whereas the formal theatrical stage creates a "distance" between character and audience,[138] the masked terror acts of the Klan eliminated this bound-

FIGURE 9. Illustration drawn from a photograph depicting captured Ku Klux Klan members in 1871. This image was originally published in *Harper's Weekly*, January 27, 1872, with the caption "Mississippi Ku-Klux members in the disguises in which they were captured." From Wikimedia Commons (https://commons.wikimedia.org/wiki/File:Mississippi_ku_klux.jpg). Image in the public domain.

ary and brought racist "ghosts of the Confederate dead"[139] directly into the local communities and neighborhoods of the postwar era. In the process, the Klan forced their targets/victims to become part of their violent subversive scenes, which they played out for local and national audiences.

Thus, Klan activists used their nighttime theatrics to frame their terroristic acts, and also to continue the methods of social-psychological control commonly used in the antebellum South to discipline slaves, which included "the promotion of suspicion" and the perpetuation of "a continuing state of anxiety and fear."[140] These tactics were designed to restrict movement, curtail social and political organization, and limit economic engagement.[141] The anonymous character of Klan activity, enhanced by the night as a performative mise-en-scène, facilitated these objectives as "no one knew who his enemy was."[142] In other words, the Klan made it so that any white person might be one who dons a hood and plays the ghost. Freed Black southerners therefore had to worry about the Klan day and night, and whenever they interacted with a white person, that person might as well be Ku Klux. Such a mechanism of general surveillance, along with a mysterious and persistent threat of violence conveyed in the form of a haunting, is also evident in the case of a letter written in 1868 to Davie Jeems, a Black man elected to serve as sheriff in Georgia, by an anonymous actor claiming the moniker of the Ku Klux Klan. This letter writer claims to have died "at Manassus [sic] in 1861" and now exists "as a Locust in the day Time" while stating "at night I am a Ku Klux sent here to look after you and all the rest of the radicals and make you know your place."[143]

Both present and obscured, simultaneously forcible and mysterious, Klan activists used anonymity to accentuate the mass character of resistance to federal control as they worked to undo the moral, cultural, political, and, most directly, racial social reconstruction imposed by the North in the aftermath of the Civil War, a social order deemed "oppressive" and "radical" by the earliest Klan leaders.[144] This accentuation of the mass character of the Klan movement is evident in the 1868 claim of Nathan Bedford Forrest (former Confederate general and early leader of the Ku Klux Klan) that the Klan commanded "about 550,000 men" in the South.[145] Though many doubted this claim, the anonymity of the Klan made it impossible to prove or disprove. The accentuation of the mass is further evident in William Joseph Simmons's proclamation to revive the Klan in 1917, which begins with the preamble: "I, and the citizens of the Invisible Empire through me, proclaim to you as follows."[146] The term "invisible empire," first used in the title of the third book of the Dixon trilogy, *The Traitor: A Story of the Fall of the Invisible Empire* (1907), also expresses the Klan's performance *as* an alternate political order—an oppressed mass political entity poised to assert control over society.

In both its first and second waves, the power of Klan terror relied on the way that Klan cover representations stood above individualism and personal identity to signify a collective meaning system and social order—a parallel world that was defeated but not dead, in abeyance, of the night, and behind the hood. In this sense, the subversive anonymity of Klan terror has always stood (and continues to stand) in semiotic contrast to the Reconstruction vision of a racially inclusive democratic society. Anonymous Klan actions, in addition to terrorizing freed slaves and their descendants, sought to define Black Americans as incompatible with civil society—a performative attempt also directed at audiences of northern whites who were advancing the causes of Reconstruction and civil rights.[147] In this way, anonymity became a central tool of the subversive force directed against the legitimacy of a reconstructed society and democratic racial equality, a force that sought to maintain a system of white supremacy and racial oppression throughout the postwar era.

PERFORMING THE DIGITAL GUERRILLA INSURGENCY:
THE HACKER NETWORKS OF ANONYMOUS

Taking a thoroughly different and more contemporary example of social movement anonymity, we can consider the masked hacker networks
known by the name Anonymous. "Beyond a foundational commitment
to the maintenance of anonymity and a broad dedication to the free flow
of information, Anonymous has no consistent philosophy or political program."[148] Furthermore, Anonymous is not a formal organization with a
defined structure and leadership. Gabriella Coleman aptly describes this
mysterious movement as "a hydra—comprising numerous different networks" and discusses the "internal feuds and sectarian impulses" that are
quite common among participants.[149] In fact, soon after this movement
formed and began to engage in direct activism, the entity fractionalized
into "several sects and splinter groups, each with unique enterprises and
campaigns."[150] Yet Anonymous is widely perceived as an organized social
movement with a rebellious hacktivist agenda.[151] Over time, different activists have brought this sense of organized coherence to life by using a
shared cover representation to perform their subversive anonymity.

    After first emerging in the internet forum 4chan, where participants up-
hold a strong ethic of anonymity, those acting under the moniker of Anonymous transcended this setting in 2008 and began to coordinate various
public campaigns and confrontations. Their targets have included organizations like the Church of Scientology, the Ku Klux Klan, the Westboro
Baptist Church, and ISIS, as well as multiple corporate and governmental
agencies in the United States and around the world. Using various hacking
tactics and propaganda work (which has often involved the production
and circulation of videos and posters online), Anonymous has worked to
reveal information or otherwise intervene to support various high-profile
causes in the name of social justice and public accountability. These activities have included, for example, exposing information pertaining to
the 2012 Steubenville (Ohio) High School rape case and the 2014 police
shooting of Michael Brown in Ferguson, Missouri, as well as supporting the Arab Spring uprising and Occupy Wall Street. Anonymous actors
pride themselves on maintaining a decentralized and leaderless structure,
and most individuals who act as Anonymous (while typically referring to
themselves as "Anons") choose to keep their personal identities hidden.
As a rule, "personal identity and the individual remain subordinate" to the
collective identity and public posture of the broad community.[152]

    The most recognizable and iconic cover representation associated with
Anonymous is the mask worn by the fierce, savvy, and poetic rebel-hero of

Alan Moore and David Lloyd's 1982 graphic novel, *V for Vendetta*, which was adapted and made into a popular film directed by James McTeigue in 2006 (fig. 10). As a masked and pseudonymous vigilante character with a revolutionary agenda, V is similar to both the protagonists and villains of the superhero genre.[153] He wears a mask depicting the face of Guy Fawkes, who was a member of a radical Catholic group that planned to set off an explosion in the British House of Lords in 1605 in an attempt to assassinate King James I. The failure of this attempt, which came to be known as "the Gunpowder Plot," has been celebrated in Britain over the course of centuries on November 5 with festival-style gatherings where revelers, who often wear costumes and masks, have at times been anti-authoritarian and even riotous.[154] By reclaiming the image of Fawkes in their graphic novel, Moore and Lloyd symbolically revived his ghost and recast his failed (and unfinished) mission to now involve an attempt to overthrow a fascist regime set in a fictional dystopian England. Fawkes, a villain in the popular story of the 1605 Gunpowder Plot, became a symbol of political alienation — a symbol that was inverted and transformed into the face of a popular yet mysterious hero by the novel and then the film that followed over two decades later. Like Thomas Dixon's *The Clansman* and D. W. Griffith's *The Birth of a Nation* but with very different politics, *V for Vendetta* is the story of a once-failed rebellion rising again.

In the name of Anonymous, many activists have donned the Guy Fawkes mask while issuing warnings or threats in online video messages or appearing in person at public protests. Subsequently, the mask and its image, which has also been used in a wide array of political art and propaganda, was embraced by many other left-leaning activists engaged in popular protests around the world, including by participants of the Occupy movement (figs. 11 and 12).[155] Thus, while becoming a significant political force in and of itself, Anonymous also became the archetypical expression of an iconographic style that grew well beyond any single group, organization, or political event.[156]

However, as recent and visually distinctive as this political iconography might be, the masked subversive activity of Anonymous represents a new version of older practices. In order to fully grasp the rich cultural and political significance of the Guy Fawkes mask today, and to more thoroughly understand the subversive anonymity of those who wear it, we must see this cover representation as a performative tool used to facilitate *a contemporary manifestation of a historically precedented mode of anonymous political performance.*

In the mid-1990s, well before the rise of Anonymous, the Ejército Zapatista de Liberación Nacional (EZLN), or Zapatistas of Chiapas, Mexico,

FIGURE 10. The protagonist V dons a Guy Fawkes mask in James McTeigue's film
*V for Vendetta.*

established a model for masked political activism in the post–Cold War
era. On the one hand, the Zapatistas were working in the tradition of
the many guerrilla insurgencies of the Global South that preceded them,
movements that also influenced activists across the Global North. On the
other hand, the Zapatistas expressed a new late-modern style of political
resistance and insurgency. In the wake of their uprising on January 1, 1994,
which was an act in opposition to the North American Free Trade Agreement (NAFTA), the Zapatistas became one of the most widely influential
movements of their era. Expressing a local folk culture of resistance to
counter the global forces of neoliberalism and state militarism, Zapatistas typically masked their faces with *paliacates* (Mexican bandannas) or
black balaclavas. Via their masked and pseudonymous representative, Subcomandante Marcos, the Zapatistas promoted a vision that stressed the
integrity of local movements while simultaneously accentuating a universalism of subversive struggle. They advanced what Thomas Olesen refers
to as a "global consciousness" and a spirit of "mutual solidarity . . . that
blurs the distinction" between activists from richer and poorer nations and
"emphasizes similarities between physically, socially and culturally distant
actors, while at the same time respecting and acknowledging local and
national differences."[157] Activists around the world and across the Global
North celebrated the Zapatistas as an inspirational revolutionary force
against the oppressive fallout of globalized capitalism, embracing their
emphasis on local democratic egalitarianism, their tactical opposition to

FIGURE 11. Protesters camped during Occupy Wall Street, October 31, 2011. Photo by Lee Hassl (Leepower). From Wikimedia Commons (https://commons.wikimedia .org/wiki/File:Occupy-Wall-Street.jpg). Creative Commons Attribution-Share Alike 3.0 Unported license (https://creativecommons.org/licenses/by-sa/3.0/deed.en).

FIGURE 12. Protesters at a demonstration in Madrid, June 17, 2016. Photo by Daniel López García. From Wikimedia Commons (https://commons.wikimedia.org/wiki /File:Manifestación_Puente_de_Vallecas._24_(27645807402).jpg). Creative Commons Attribution 2.0 Generic license (https://creativecommons.org/licenses /by/2.0/deed.en).

the swelling technologies of state surveillance, and their symbolic appeal to a global and inclusive movement for social justice.[158] As the influence of the Zapatistas grew, late-modern generations of northern activists not only adopted political principles from this popular movement of the Global South but also dramatic aesthetics and practices as they crafted and performed political opposition.[159] As neoliberal political power and culture were globalizing on an increasing scale, so was a new political culture of resistance, one that encouraged meaningful performances of subversive anonymity.[160]

When masking themselves in political action, the Zapatistas linked symbols of southern Mexican and indigenous culture to an anyoneness and everyoneness that they expressed via the generalizing force of their anonymity. While embracing this mode of subversive performance in principle and form, northern dissidents around the world initially lacked a defined cultural iconography that they could call their own. With the March 2006 mass release of the Warner Brothers film *V for Vendetta,* James McTeigue (who notably claims *The Battle of Algiers* as inspiration) and the Wachowskis (as screenwriters) provided that icon when they transposed Moore and Lloyd's earlier (1982) graphic narrative to the big screen. Only after the release of the film was the Fawkes mask reappropriated for memes in 4chan and various other internet forums.[161] And then later, beginning in 2008, the image of V/Fawkes was used by activists in public campaigns.[162]

By adopting the Guy Fawkes mask today, activists around the world,[163] including those who act under the banner of Anonymous, animate the iconic character V, who embodies revolutionary ambitions, anti-authoritarianism, and an underground posture, along with a witty, playful, and transgressive carnivalesque style. In print and on screen, V is a marginalized, passionate, and rebellious figure who is always and only known via his cover representation. Donning the V/Fawkes mask, subversive actors express their willingness to take extreme action and their aversion to taking personal credit, establishing personal leadership, or achieving personal fame for such actions. However, they also express a formal and ideological affinity with the model of indigenous guerrilla insurgency advanced by the Zapatistas. From this perspective, just as the scarved subaltern rebel is to the local conflicts that stem from the globalizing world order, the masked hacker is to the multifaceted global network of the World Wide Web. The latter is a late-modern, relatively privileged, and technologically enhanced version of a guerrilla freedom fighter.

On multiple occasions, individuals acting under the banner of Anonymous have posted ominous videos online to address a situation of con-

FIGURE 13. A version of the emblem associated with the group Anonymous at the center of a flag. Author: Anonymous. From Wikimedia Commons (https://commons .wikimedia.org/wiki/File:Anonymous_Flag.svg). Image is in the public domain with the following description: "This flag is fictitious or proposed but not adopted. It may be named as it would be as an official flag of a geographical or other entity and have some visual elements that are similar to official logos or flags of that entity, but it is not official and doesn't have any official recognition."

cern.[164] As a form of communication, these videos often emulate a scene from the film *V for Vendetta* in which V hijacks a television studio and delivers a televised address to the people of England (as shown in fig. 10). Sometimes donning a Guy Fawkes mask, at other times simply displaying the group's emblem of a person in a dark suit with a question mark in place of a head (fig. 13), and typically using computerized vocal distortion, an anonymous spokesperson usually articulates a grievance that serves to justify threats of direct retaliation or a more general promise of popular revolt.

Whether confronting Scientology, attacking the Federal Reserve, challenging the Los Angeles Police Department, or issuing a public warning to some other target, such performative video decrees combine more traditional masking practices with the tools of electronic social media to render a double cover of anonymity and mystery. They provide a clear example of how "virtual space" can serve "as a performance region" that allows actors to "control information" and shield identity in new ways.[165] At the same time, those acting in the name of Anonymous use this dual cover representation to claim that they represent the popular will, or even to *be* "the people."[166] The nature of the electronic medium, which allows messages to be hosted on multiple sites and links to be widely shared, serves to reinforce the everyoneness conveyed by the masked and anonymous act.

Sincere in tone though often outlandish in content (and commonly framed with overtly dramatic music), videos posted under the banner of Anonymous give the illusion of being an official statement representing the position of an organized underground movement. In fact, however, these video performances could have been produced and posted by anyone who adopts the network's iconic style and symbolism. On the one hand, this uncertainty of authorship stems from the deprecation of ego that is embraced as principle by those who act as Anonymous.[167] As one mysterious actor states in a video posted to relaunch "Project Chanology" (Anonymous's coordinated and public attack on the Church of Scientology), "we are faceless, leaderless, and decentralized to a degree that it will be impossible to stop us."[168] On the other hand, the fact that anyone can claim to speak as, or on behalf of, Anonymous also fuels conflict between factions and leads to speculation about the authenticity of some public messages. For example, several commenters openly questioned the legitimacy of an Anonymous video titled "Message to the President of the United States (Donald Trump)," which is quite supportive of Trump's 2016 political victory, critical of Islam, and opposed to the US policy of accepting migrant refugees.[169] Such commenters questioned the authenticity of this video performance simply because the content did not fit with their ideas of Anonymous, despite the fact that the form of the message was identical to most precedents and *as if* other videos released in the name of Anonymous are somehow more official or sanctioned by an authority.[170] Such disputes highlight the fact that a diversity of actors might work behind the iconic Guy Fawkes mask and other collective symbolism, and that this shared and homogenizing cover representation is the only way that the phenomenon of Anonymous appears as a discernible and distinctive social movement.

THE KLAN AND ANONYMOUS: SHARED
CHARACTERISTICS OF SUBVERSIVE ANONYMITY

Despite their many significant differences, the Ku Klux Klan and Anonymous share some general characteristics that stem from the masked and anonymous form of their subversive activity. These general characteristics show that, regardless of their particular politics and concerns, their performance styles are shaped in many ways by their use of anonymity for subversive purposes. For example, in both cases the use of uniform masks allows participants and supporters to comprehend the movement as a general *idea* that manifests via particular anonymous performances. When white Americans wore Klan hoods and robes, they embodied the "immutable principles" of the "Invisible Empire"[171] and translated them into particular acts of violence and terror. Thus, the anonymous character of Klan terrorism allowed for what Elaine Frantz Parsons calls "the *idea* of the Ku-Klux" to flourish—a "disembodied" and "composite notion of the Klan" that took form prominently in the accounts of national media.[172] Consequently, "the Klan attack was always the imposition of a translocal idea not only onto the bodies of real victims but also onto concrete communities."[173] With regard to a very different political standpoint, this general phenomenon is also expressed by Anonymous with their variations of the phrase "you can't kill an idea."[174] Those acting under the banner of Anonymous commonly express variations of this sentiment, such as "We will never be destroyed. . . . We, as an idea. Ideas cannot be arrested, killed, or broken."[175] In both of these cases and in others, when donning masks, individuals suppress their personal identities and egos in order to animate such impersonal ideas and collective principles. By stressing the vitality of the impersonal and imperishable idea, such groups accentuate both their mass character and their fate. While individuals will come and go, they claim, the idea, which serves as the immortal soul of the movement, will prevail.

Both the Klan and Anonymous have origins in trickery and dark comedy, central characteristics of carnival. Both have used humor, play, and a Dionysian style as frames with which to shame, humiliate, and attack their targets. While we tend to think of the Ku Klux Klan by envisioning those scenes of direct racist terror that came to define the group's most salient acts, the earliest manifestations of this activity were often "conceived and popularly received as comic" by white southerners who served as an audience to Klan drama, and such acts were indeed initially performed as dramatic "practical jokes" that facilitated "the terrorization of African Americans and intractable Republicans."[176] In other words, Klan members framed racist terror "as a proper extension of their original comic play, the carnival space of enacted fantasy quickly metamorphosing into an actual site of torture."[177] These violent acts were also presented to the broader public as "a comic commodity" by the southern Democratic press.[178] Likewise, a foundational motivation for Anonymous, as well as modern hackers and internet trolls in general, is to sow disruption and publicly shame their targets for the "LULZ," a term derived from "LOL," the abbreviation for "laughing out loud." The LULZ is a particular type of humor and laughter that stems from the humiliation or victimization of others, "unmistakably imbued with danger and mystery" stemming from "the pleasures of transgression."[179] The emotional core of the LULZ involves the externalization of shame onto a victim, which becomes a powerful way of cultivating solidarity among the shamers themselves. As Mikhail Bakhtin argued with regard to medieval carnival, such "dark" humor is subversive because the laughter it provokes "builds its own world versus the official world, its own church versus the official church, its own state versus the official state."[180] It creates a boundary between insiders and "those not in on the joke."[181] In both cases, serious movements with serious consequences were born out of actions framed as humor, and the link between dark humor and aggression was blurred.

Both the Ku Klux Klan and Anonymous have used the privileges afforded by their masks to escape the surveillance of official forces while simultaneously surveilling others. In both cases, anonymity facilitates a protected voyeurism, or watching from behind the mask. Consequently, such movements create atmospheres of fear and paranoia for their targets and those outside their inner circles. From this position, both movements practice a threatening form of vigilantism. The vigilantism of the Klan extended the legalized antebellum violence of slave discipline into the post-emancipation era. However, the vigilantism of Anonymous "includes reprobative punishment rather than violence" and often involves attempts to mar the public image or undermine the interests and objectives of their targets.[182]

Over time, the masks and other symbols used as cover representations by the Ku Klux Klan and Anonymous evolved to achieve iconic status. Setting significant differences aside, in both cases subversive symbolism was popularized as iterations of a masked character model appeared in print (in Dixon's trilogy and Moore and Lloyd's graphic novel) and later in film (Griffith's *The Birth of a Nation* and McTeigue's *V for Vendetta*). In both cases, popular media (aided by print propaganda and press in the Klan's time, and digital propaganda and internet technology for Anonymous) was key to the cultural diffusion of the narrative and imagery that was later mobilized by anonymous subversives. As the masks in both cases attained "iconic status . . . after transcending page and screen,"[183] they were eventually mass produced and sold commercially to meet popular subversive demand. However, while in both cases print and film media provided a cultural and technological mode and means of diffusion, rank-and-file activists did the work of giving these masked characters new life via their performances of subversive anonymity.

All of the masked social movements I have discussed evoke figures and events of the past, drawing historical analogies and bridging the past and present in various ways.[184] Whereas the Guerrilla Girls animated the personas of dead female artists, and the EZLN used their masks to channel the spirit of Emiliano Zapata (the early twentieth-century southern Mexican revolutionary),[185] Klan radicals used them to revive dead soldiers of the Confederacy. Continuing this tradition, the Klan of the twentieth century professed itself to be the "revived, reconstructed, remodeled, refined and expanded" version of its Reconstruction-era predecessor.[186] Likewise, Anonymous uses the evolving historical image of Guy Fawkes. In all cases, masked actors revive past characters who have unfinished business and performatively reinvent these figures in an attempt to make future-oriented change. As described by Karl Marx while reflecting on modern French Revolutionary history, such social movement actors "anxiously conjure up the spirits of the past to their service and borrow from them names, battle cries, and costumes in order to present the new scene of world history in this time-honoured disguise and this borrowed language."[187] Such a temporal bridging strategy is also evident in the motto printed with W. J. Simmons's 1917 Klan treatise, "ABC of the Invisible Empire," which states, "We were here yesterday. We are here today. We will be here forever."[188]

As the participants of each group split their personal identities from the subversive characters they perform, they express deeper cultural tensions (with both moral and political implications) underlying the social situation at hand. Using this division between person and character, masked subversives create and advance alternative social orders as a threat or challenge to dominant political frameworks, cultural codes, and systems of meaning. Thus, the Klan created a drama of resistance to the federally imposed Reconstruction vision of society and defined Black enfranchisement as a menacing evil. In the process, they sought to revive the antebellum social order. The hacker networks of Anonymous also created a drama of resistance, but to an increasing and unchecked centralization of state and corporate power and to corresponding and pervasive forms of surveillance in the late-modern era. In the process, participants advanced new ideas about freedom and accountability rooted in open public access to information and a mass egalitarian will. Despite their significant differences, both groups used their masks to play their heroes and define their villains as they worked to dramatize conflict and shift relations of power.

## FBI Counterintelligence and the Anonymous
### Subversion of Subversive Activity

In 1956, under the direction of J. Edgar Hoover, the American Federal Bureau of Investigation (FBI) established a counterintelligence program

(COINTELPRO) in order to "expose, disrupt, misdirect, discredit, and otherwise neutralize the activities" of a number of prominent social movements rooted in the United States.[189] COINTELPRO was kept secret until 1971, when activists broke into a Pennsylvania FBI office and stole documents that they anonymously mailed to multiple press outlets in order to expose the covert operation. Over the course of this program, the FBI strategically used a subversive anonymity, along with a number of other tactics, to accomplish their objectives. Recall their anonymous letter to Martin Luther King Jr. displayed in fig. 2, for example. While acting anonymously, FBI agents frequently engineered clues in order to manage the impressions of their targets and lead them to particular though erroneous conclusions, often prompting their marks to suspect that the actor behind the anonymous cover was a member of a dissenting faction or another organization. In fact, a core intent of COINTELPRO was to manipulate the imaginations (and stoke the paranoias) of social movement activists while discrediting and undermining movement leaders in the process.

Consider the following case. In December 1969, the FBI anonymously released a cartoon in order to drive a wedge between members of the Socialist Workers Party (SWP) and other groups participating in the coalition known as the National Mobilization Committee to End the War in Vietnam ("Mobe"). The anonymous flier depicted a goose marked "SWP" raping another marked "New MOBE" in midflight with the caption "Fly United? Balls!" followed by text highly critical of the impact of SWP leadership on the activities and overall integrity of the Mobe coalition.[190] The intent of this anonymous act (which was preceded by several anonymous letters crafted to achieve the same objective) was not simply to besmirch the SWP, but also to provoke suspicion among the members of all constituent groups as to who authored the flyer. The overarching objective was to factionalize the coalition opposing the war in Vietnam. In such cases, as imaginations wander, fingers are pointed. Mistrust and paranoia grow. The social foundations of organization, coordination, and unity are subverted and destabilized. The FBI used similar tactics with similar objectives to disrupt the Puerto Rican Independence movement, organizations affiliated with the civil rights movement (such as the Student Nonviolent Coordinating Committee, or SNCC), various groups associated with the New Left, the American Indian Movement (AIM), and more.[191] In such cases, FBI agents used anonymity to create rifts between individuals and groups, discredit leaders, dissuade rank-and-file participants, and generally thwart organized subversive political activity in the process.

The subversive anonymity of FBI COINTELPRO agents differs from that of social movements like the Ku Klux Klan and Anonymous. In most cases, when social movement participants don masks and obscure their personal identities, they typically use a *sincere representational* form of anonymity to symbolize a particular subversive community and its cause. However, when COINTELPRO agents hid their identities, they typically crafted a *deceptive misdirectional* form of subversive anonymity to engineer the impression that they were someone or something other than FBI agents (e.g., often pretending to be other activists). They crafted ambiguous, deceptive, and intentionally misdirectional cover representations to achieve their goals. The distinction between these two subtypes of anonymity—sincere representational and deceptive misdirectional—is often not directly evident during the interaction at hand, which shows how anonymity is ripe for "false flag" operations in which actors intentionally misrepresent both the source and motive of their actions. While actors in both cases use subversive anonymity to create an air of mystery around their activities, agents who use the deceptive misdirectional type strategically combine elements of the *mask* and the *disguise*. "Masks hide a true identity in a visible way. Disguise asserts an identity, a *false* identity, but the concealment is concealed."[192] Layering these elements so that the anonymous cover is also simultaneously a disguise, FBI agents created false anonymous fronts in that there was a greater "discrepancy between fostered appearances and reality" as crafted by "an imposter" who worked to "dissemble, deceive, and defraud."[193] In the case of COINTELPRO, agents worked to direct assumptions about source, motive, and responsibility with regard to the anonymous act away from the FBI and toward other sources. Thus, anonymous COINTELPRO agents achieved an additional layer of obscurity and held even less accountability than more sincerely masked activists. In general, those who perform a deceptive misdirectional anonymity enjoy a greater freedom to manipulate the definitions of their situations and are typically well poised to frame others.

Moreover, as can be determined from the case of the SWP/Mobe cartoon, the deceptive misdirectional type of anonymity employed by the FBI is ideal for carrying out the strategy of *divide et impera* (divide and rule) discussed by Georg Simmel, in which a third party opportunistically provokes and benefits from conflict between the other two (or more) "in order to gain a dominating position."[194] For example, as part of their coordinated attempts to disrupt the Puerto Rican Independence movement, COINTELPRO agents conspired to craft and distribute hundreds of anonymous letters, leaflets, and cartoons designed to provoke suspicion, conflict, and overall discord in organizations like the Movimiento Pro-Independencia de Puerto Rico (MPIPR) and the Federación Universitaria Pro Independencia (FUPI).[195] One such letter, "purportedly by an anonymous veteran MPIPR member," would allege a "Communist takeover of the organization" in order to provoke factionalism around members' views of communism and Cuba.[196] Others publicly targeted established MPIPR leader Juan Mari Bras with various accusations, condemnations, and warnings in order to prevent unity between the MPIPR and other local groups.[197] In such cases, COINTELPRO agents strategized about how to manipulate assumptions about the sources of these documents and went to great lengths to create "secure conditions to protect the Bureau as the source."[198] While casting doubts about movement leadership, the FBI was strategically working to incite conflict between different pro-independence organizations that might otherwise forge bonds of political solidarity. As Ward Churchill and Jim Vander Wall argue, "These methods were used not only to divide *Puertorriqueños* among themselves, but to forestall alliances between any of the various elements of the *independentista* movement and progressive groups on the U.S. mainland."[199] While clearly deceptive and misdirectional, such a strategic and subversive use of anonymity is designed to direct the suspicions, accusations, and hostilities of two or more parties against one another, thereby backgrounding their similarities and weakening their common cause.

In all of these cases, the exposure of previously classified FBI memoranda and official directives (once protected internal communications) revealed the segregated "back region" where such anonymous performances were planned. In such back regions, members of the "performance team" (those who operate behind the covers of anonymity) strategize and coordinate their efforts to manage the impressions of their targets.[200] According to the plan, the very existence of the FBI in the dynamic should have remained unknown, obscured behind the constructed cover. Such operatives used their anonymity to subvert the subversive activities of others while remaining invisible as a party to the situation.

## Conclusion

In this chapter, I analyzed a wide variety of cases from different times and places to illuminate the ways that actors use anonymity and pseudonymity for subversive purposes. In each case, actors bring subversive characters to life and perform their hidden identities in ways that undermine some interpersonal, cultural, political, or moral norms while advancing alternative ideas, values, and ways of seeing and being in the world. As they subvert personal identity itself, they work to make meaning—to define situations, events, issues, and relationships while challenging or undermining some form of social power.

Whether acting as individuals (as with many of the authors and artists I discussed) or collectives (as with masked social movements), anonymous subversives bring anonymity to life in their particular contexts to perform for their particular audiences. Taken together, these performances of subversive anonymity demonstrate the utterly social and situational character of our hidden identities. Actors craft and animate their cover representations to advance certain causes—for better or for worse—that are rooted in their social and historical circumstances. We need to interpret the rich semiotic significance of their cover representations, along with the formal, dynamic, and interrelational dimensions of their anonymous performances, to fully understand the subversive character of their anonymous acts. As I will discuss in the next chapter, actors can also use various impersonal institutions and social systems to shield their personal identities as they act and make meaning in the world around them.

# *The Anonymity of Social Systems*

Consider the following exchange involving a sharecropper defending his home from a tractor driver employed to raze several farms, as portrayed by John Steinbeck in *The Grapes of Wrath*.

> "I built it with my hands. Straightened old nails to put the sheathing on. Rafters are wired to the stringers with baling wire. It's mine. I built it. You bump it down—I'll be in the window with a rifle. You even come too close and I'll pot you like a rabbit."
>
> "It's not me. There's nothing I can do. I'll lose my job if I don't do it. And look—suppose you kill me? They'll just hang you, but long before you're hung there'll be another guy on the tractor, and he'll bump the house down. You're not killing the right guy."
>
> "That's so," the tenant said. "Who gave you orders? I'll go after him. He's the one to kill."
>
> "You're wrong. He got his orders from the bank. The bank told him, 'Clear those people out or it's your job.'"
>
> "Well, there's a president of the bank. There's a board of directors. I'll fill up the magazine of the rifle and go into the bank."
>
> The driver said, "Fellow was telling me the bank gets orders from the East. The orders were, 'Make the land show profit or we'll close you up.'"
>
> "But where does it stop? Who can we shoot? I don't aim to starve to death before I kill the man that's starving me."
>
> "I don't know. Maybe there's nobody to shoot. Maybe the thing isn't men at all."[1]

With this passage, Steinbeck creates a scene and dialogue that captures the desperation of farmers displaced in the midst of the 1930s dust bowl, but one that could easily be transposed to the twenty-first-century housing market crisis. In fact, writing about the frustrations of struggling homeowners who applied to the Obama administration's Home Affordable Modification Program to stave off foreclosure, David Peterson and Daina Cheyenne Harvey comment, "Respondents voiced their irritation over the failures of the program . . . yet their responses lacked the unity that would be expected if there were a clearly responsible agent. Like the man from the country waiting to see the Law [a reference to Franz Kafka's *The Trial*], it was unclear who or what was responsible."[2] Central to both situations is the anonymity of the actors who, shielded by financial or governmental institutions, took measures that impacted countless lives. Steinbeck's sharecropper is left perplexed about the personal identities of those who would destroy his farm and starve him. Those who are foreclosing on the farm are provided a significant degree anonymity due to their ability to act behind the cover of a bank, or the even more bewildering "East," both of which represent a large and impersonal system that stands in contrast to the personal character of the sharecropper's house. Their anonymity comes to life in the act of repossession and demolition that prompts the tenant's question, "Who can we shoot?" Notably, this anonymity does not fully extend to their conspicuous pawn-like surrogate driving the tractor who is the local face of the operation. While Steinbeck refers to him as "the driver," he is also recognized as "Joe Davis's boy" by the tenant.[3] However, as the driver insists, if he did not do the job, someone else would. Despite the fact that he is seen and known, it could be anyone acting on behalf of the powerful and impersonal system.

As Steinbeck illustrates with this scene, actors can use impersonal institutions, including committees, organizations, corporations, states, and nations, along with the general social systems in which they are rooted, as cover representations for their actions. Such institutions take on a life of their own, allowing individuals operating within them, and especially those with the power to steer them, a certain freedom to act while avoiding personal recognition, accountability, and liability for their actions.[4] However, such institutions also shape and constrain the actions of their functionaries at various levels who often act according to broad system logics, "led by an invisible hand to promote an end which" is not their own by design.[5] Even personal interests and rational thought can be assimilated and scripted by institutions and social systems that actors, working in complex arrangements according to system logics, collectively deploy to accomplish daunting and sometimes horrifying objectives without the weight of personal responsibility.[6] By acting behind the covers of impersonal institutions, actors bring these powerful social forces to life in ways that shape the meanings of various experiences, situations, and events in the world.

Formal organizations and bureaucratic institutions obscure personal identities by casting particular individuals as generic anyones. As Max Weber recognized, and Talcott Parsons later elaborated, bureaucratic environments are characterized by instrumental-rational logics expressed in the form of official rules and procedures that render the particular and personal identities of individuals irrelevant.[7] Such impersonal systems, often defined by strategic objectives and calculated tactics—what Weber called "the specifically modern calculating attitude,"[8] can be contrasted with the more personal and intimate character of what Jürgen Habermas referred to as "lifeworld" settings.[9] We tend to see actors as generic in the former and uniquely distinguishable in the latter, which shapes the ways we relate to others in each type of situation. Thus, we tend to see the functionaries of bureaucratic institutions or complex systems as completely replaceable by anyone else who could do the same job.[10] While I may exchange pleasantries with the person behind the counter at a bank, an officer of my state division of motor vehicles, or a technician working for a computer support service, I really do not care *who* they are, nor do I care if someone else steps in and replaces them, as long as the individual is competent with regard to the requirements of the functional role.

Our experience of institutional actors as anonymous anyones can be enhanced by the sheer scale of the systems in which they work. As Georg Simmel famously argued, large and complex cities provide for an experience of anonymity that contrasts with life in small towns, villages, and local communities.[11] In the former, people blend into the crowd; in the latter, they carry their personal identities with them (and those who are not personally known are often marked and conspicuous). For Simmel, the larger the group, the less personalized and more anonymous are its members, which allows for heightened degrees of both obscurity and freedom.[12] Such an anonymity, provided by the cover of mass groups and populated environments, accounts for the relative ease with which one can observe strangers in populated public places,[13] or while at crowded nude beaches,[14] where the act of seeing is depersonalized. The anonymity provided by large groups also accounts for the fact that students enjoy a greater ability to hide in jumbo lectures compared to small seminars, the different regard with which we hold mass emails versus direct personal messages, and the ways that personal distinctions are blurred into an undifferentiated mass during some large religious pilgrimages,[15] for example. In each case, the crowd provides an impersonal cover for individuals who can blend into the collective.[16] Even when some insiders are personally known to other insiders, as is commonly the case in large crowds,[17] such environments depersonalize interactions with others who are not known.

They render actors anonymous to spectators both inside and outside the group.

In addition to these dimensions of impersonality, we tend to see groups, institutions, and systems as sui generis actors, as agents that exist and persist "over and above [their] individual elements," assuming an independent character of their own.[18] Especially as institutions and social systems become more organizationally or technologically complex—requiring significant degrees of internal differentiation and highly specialized forms of knowledge—their complexity greatly enhances their *social opacity*.[19] It becomes harder for outsiders to understand how such institutions and systems actually work and to know who is responsible for their operations. In fact, "individual contributions may not be identifiable at all" and often "cannot be distinguished significantly from other people's contributions."[20] Thus, we tend to attribute such actions and operations to the institution or system itself. Even when the personal identities of those who act on their behalf are known or easily traceable, when functionaries are personally exposed and high-profile officers are widely recognized, and even given that insiders to such systems are often personally known to one another, actions are often impersonal, and responsibility is often diffuse and unclear. We experience the system itself as the primary actor and locus of agency while its representatives lack the power to do much beside follow its rules and facilitate its larger objectives. Therefore, any meaningful "decision appears to be made by some super-individual authority,"[21] an anonymous no one that holds great power without being a definite and accountable *who*.

These dual characteristics of anyoneness and no oneness complement and reinforce one another to establish the anonymity of social systems. Thus, we commonly attribute the actions of real people who bring these systems to life to the "ideal type of the social collective."[22] Such a logic pervades common language as "we frequently use sentences in which ideal types like 'the state,' 'the press,' 'the economy,' 'the nation,' 'the people,' or perhaps 'the working class' appear as grammatical subjects. In doing this, we naturally tend to personify these abstractions."[23] In other words, we treat and experience the system and its institutions as responsible for the actions of its anonymous functionaries.[24] Consider the ways we attribute different decisions (as well as legal powers and responsibilities) to organized collectives such as parole boards, organ transplant committees, and grand juries; or the ways we attribute agency to social movement groups, corporations, society, or even "civilization";[25] or simply explain various phenomena with vague reference to "the system." Such ways of thinking and speaking, which involve attributions of motive and agency to impersonal social forces, shape the meaning of various actions and events for different audiences.

When we ascribe agency to an impersonal entity or system, we often focus our attention on its major operations and ignore a variety of particular activities, decisions, and interactions that occur behind the scenes.[26] We void personal agencies in light of impersonal system proceedings. In the process, we also let real people off the hook, including those who steer these institutions and use them for personal gain. Such a way of comprehending agency also prompts people acting within (or on behalf of) the system to detach their individual actions from their consequences, to experience their contributions as relatively insignificant and impersonal, and even to perceive those whose lives might be impacted by the broader institution or by systemic forces as *anonymous units* rather than particular people.[27] Such system functionaries can "view the world through a set of particularistic codes" linked to system objectives "that involve a certain blindness to the wider social effects of their operations."[28] Thus, the anonymity afforded by social systems can detach persons from their actions in ways that define social interactions and relationships for all parties involved.

In this chapter, I explore the ways that anonymous actors use institutions and social systems as cover representations to shape certain relationships, accomplish particular tasks, and define situations for various audiences. While acting with such system fronts, actors make meaning in the world. They also marshal the power of particular institutions to accomplish both personal and system objectives. To this end, I present focused analyses of five cases: the early twenty-first-century financial crisis, the concept of corporate personhood and the 2010 US Supreme Court ruling in *Citizens United v. Federal Election Commission*, the electronic surveillance of US citizens by the National Security Agency (NSA) and "big tech" companies, the phenomenon of distance killing that evolved to characterize war over the last century, and modern state executions in the United States with particular attention to the method of execution most commonly used today—lethal injection. While addressing each of these cases, I focus on the ways that institutions and social systems of various types facilitate anonymous acts. In each case, those who act within and through social system fronts create and define events and situations that are deeply consequential for others. They bring social systems to life and endow them with agency, responsibility, and power. Others then experience the system as the actor, which renders the personal identities of the operators obscured or negligible in the relationship—anonymized in various ways by structures, technologies, procedures, and rules. Next, complementing my discussion of anonymous consumption in chapter 2, I briefly discuss the social character and consequences of anonymous labor and production. While developing all of these discussions, I consider how the anonymizing force of social systems can promote social alienation, apathy, and a diffusion of responsibility that can run counter to our ideals of community, democratic participation, and public accountability.

## Institutions and Systems as Cover Representations
### WALL STREET AND THE FINANCIAL CRISIS

The massive financial crisis that unfolded from late 2006 through 2010 took off with an unprecedented wave of foreclosures on homes, which then had "a catastrophic domino effect"[29] that hobbled the US economy and rippled throughout the world. In the years building up to this economic meltdown, lending agents issued millions of unsustainable subprime and adjustable rate mortgages to borrowers who were eventually overcome by their mounting debt and unable to make payments. As debts surged and housing values plummeted, many homeowners ended up owing more than their homes were worth. The resulting flood of defaults and foreclosures devastated the housing market, which ultimately tanked the stock market and crippled several massive investment banks that used bundles of these mortgages to back the investments of various clients. In September 2008, Lehman Brothers, one of the oldest and largest investment banks in the United States, filed for bankruptcy. Several others, many on the brink of collapse, would soon take billions of taxpayer dollars as bailout funding. The overwhelming strain on public coffers led to years of debilitating social austerity measures.

The financial crisis was marked by an asymmetrical structure of accountability that illustrates the anonymity of institutions and social systems. On the one hand, the millions of people who defaulted on their mortgages made financial decisions that turned out to be detrimental, personally and cumulatively. These individuals, many of whom ultimately lost their homes, were personally targeted when banks initiated foreclosure actions. They were held accountable according to an *ethic of personal responsibility* and suffered consequences in line with an *ethic of personal liability*. On the other hand, mortgage brokers and investment bankers worked to maximize profit despite obvious risks, and regardless of the impact of their actions on millions of lives. For years building up to and during the crisis, in a cultural milieu marked by weak regulation and fraudulent conduct,[30] these agents acted in ways that brought the crisis to fruition. However, while defaulting homeowners suffered personal consequences, most actors within the financial industry avoided personal scrutiny and responsibility for their actions. Most remained anonymous as banks and the broader financial system bore the brunt of the blame in line with an *ethic of institutional responsibility*. Moreover, the public carried a significant financial burden for corporate losses in line with an *ethic of socialized liability*. Despite the fact that real people in the financial arena made strategic decisions and benefited in various ways from the situation, corporate institutions and systems served as covers that effectively anonymized most of the actors behind the operation.

In general, people form and use corporations to achieve goals they would not otherwise be able to achieve as individuals. In the process, individual actors split themselves from the actions of the corporate entity, which stands independently and operates according to its own rules and procedures. By structuring their actions according to the official bureaucratic rules and calculated procedures of their corporate institutions, actors in the finance industry depersonalized their work and distanced themselves from the consequences of their pursuits. With regard to the financial industry in general, "people working in this domain often make decisions that do not seem to have implications for specific salient individuals." Furthermore, they "make their decisions in a relatively anonymous manner which does not create a sense of the ownership of the act." Consequently, their actions "can feel victimless" as they "work within larger organizations and institutional systems" that create the sense "that many are actually not directly responsible for their own decisions."[31] While "the break between a person's identity and their deed is not total or altogether untraceable, . . . the connection is blurred" enough to diffuse personal responsibility and give everyone involved, including corporate actors themselves, the sense that the system is ultimately at fault.[32] Such a mode of operation establishes the corporate institution as the locus of agency and responsibility. From this perspective, foreclosure is a performative accomplishment enacted by individuals and teams carrying out economic acts on behalf of a constructed corporate financial entity. In the process of confiscating or repossessing property, actors mobilize the legal discourse and deep cultural codes of capitalism (which foreground the individual responsibilities and liabilities of the homeowners and the economic fairness of instrumental bank actions) in an attempt to legitimate such acts and define them as legally and morally reasonable. Operating according to official procedures designed to benefit those institutions, powerful corporate actors depersonalized and legitimated the actions that led to the crisis itself, pursuing private gain at a social cost and skirting personal responsibility in the process.[33]

When we recognize a corporation as an actor, we give it motive, interests, agency, and even personality. We also blame it for problems. Given this attribution of agency and structure of accountability, dispossessed and struggling homeowners were typically unable to identify particular individuals who could help them with their personal predicaments. They struggled to find answers and to locate responsible agents as the banks they dealt with "remained nearly totally opaque."[34] While desperately searching for effective assistance, the large majority of homeowners felt that "the real locus of agency" was "their bank" itself, while the people they interacted with were "mere functionaries" with "little power." Some felt the real problem was the entire financial system itself.[35] At every stage of the crisis, homeowners had similar experiences.[36] Even when the personal identities of corporate actors are publicly exposed or traceable, they stand either as inaccessible symbols of the greater corporate agency (as is the case with board chairs and CEOs) or as insignificant pawns (as with service representatives). In the social interactions that defined their experiences, homeowners ultimately faced anonymous corporate systems.[37]

In line with homeowner perceptions, many pundits raised some version of the argument that "Wall Street," the "big banks," the "mortgage industry," the "government," or the unbridled system of capitalism was at fault. In the broadest sense, some even blamed everyone participating in the economic system and argued that "the American public, by default, was complicit."[38] Blaming everyone, or even a broad and diverse range of players, in effect holds no one accountable and reinforces our sense that the crisis was caused by a complex and nebulous system. Indeed, for many the crisis itself became an agentic force, a juggernaut that instilled fear, ushered in "a new wave of pessimism," and undermined trust in the economy, a force that "could drive the country into a full-blown recession."[39] Thus, the public discourse addressing the situation was marked by both an "extraordinary breadth for assigning blame for the financial crisis" and a sense that "the structure of the present financial system, its culture, and its collective practices and policies" were ultimately at fault.[40]

While those who lost their homes were frequently named and personally profiled in various news media accounts detailing their hardships, most financial actors remained anonymous behind institutional and system covers.[41] In one typical account, the struggles of Dirma Rodriquez and her disabled daughter, Ingrid Ortiz, are pitted against the behemoth Bank of America. In this and many similar public narratives, the bank is represented by a named spokesperson who, like Steinbeck's tractor driver featured in the quote at the beginning of this chapter, merely represents an otherwise impersonal institution that operates outside of anyone's personal control.[42] Likewise, Jennifer Ryan Voltaire is pitted against Wells Fargo.[43] Similarly, while meticulously detailing the complicated and difficult ordeal of Sheila Ramos, who lost her Florida home to foreclosure, one journalist points to "the Wall Street mortgage machine" (with its various institutional parties) as the power behind the crisis.[44] A great number of stories fit this model in which named people suffer due to the actions of institutions that create harm through the fault of no one in particular. Even activists, such as those affiliated with the Occupy movement, commonly identified systems and institutions, such as "Wall Street and the Banks,"[45] as responsible agents. The very fact that commenters can publicly assign and debate responsibility in such vague terms with regard to such a serious global situation, and typically while blaming impersonal institutions, creates an atmosphere of plausible deniability for everyone involved. Thus, the "big banks" (as institutions) and "Wall Street" (as metonymic code for the financial system) function both as the actors that are central to the financial crisis *and* covers for "the position and concentration of power in the hands of certain privileged agents."[46]

## CORPORATE PERSONHOOD AND ELECTORAL POLITICS

Corporate organizations function as cover representations for individuals in a wide variety of economic, political, and legal activities. This phenomenon has been reinforced by court decisions upholding the principle that corporations have rights of personhood under the law, thereby enhancing the anonymity of the individuals *acting as* such entities in certain situations. The concept of corporate personhood originated in the late nineteenth century with the notion that the Fourteenth Amendment clause guaranteeing every "person" equal protection under the law applied equally to corporations. However, more recent Supreme Court decisions, especially those rendered in *First National Bank of Boston v. Bellotti* (1978) and *Citizens United v. Federal Election Commission* (2010) (along with several related cases) extended this logic by recognizing First Amendment constitutional protections of free speech for corporations, freeing individuals to use them to finance political initiatives and electoral campaigns.

While the courts have generally upheld the basic requirement that political campaigns name their donors in line with democratic principles of transparency and public accountability, the *Citizens United* case opened new avenues for wealthy financiers to exert disproportionate influence on electoral outcomes while masking their identities behind layers of corporate cover. The decision specifically overruled previously established restrictions on corporate funding in politics, freeing corporations to spend massive amounts of money to influence elections as long as they do not officially coordinate with the campaign they act to support. Practically speaking, the ruling created a framework that allows agents to form "super PACs" (political action committees), which, in addition to raising unlimited amounts of corporate money, are often funded by "shadowy nonprofits" that themselves raise corporate funds but "don't disclose their donors."[47] This allows powerful actors to act behind various organized groups, often with "innocuous names,"[48] to steer democratic politics anonymously.[49]

Using an organized political action group as a front separates political speech acts (such as print, television, or web-based advertisements) from the personal identities and interests of their financial sponsors. It also obscures motives for political endorsements and attacks and distances them from the benefiting candidate, generalizing and popularizing the opinion while enhancing perceived credibility and objectivity.[50] Despite contradicting the general democratic tenet of personal accountability to the public, and the mandate to disclose political funding sources established by the Federal Election Campaign Act of 1971, such "dark money" has become a powerful force in the contemporary political arena. In such cases, wealthy actors and even foreign agents can obscure their identities behind multiple layers of corporate cover while shaping US democratic processes and outcomes. They can "mask their values and policies behind a deceptive veil of anonymity"[51] while using the super PAC as a front with which to manage the impressions of the public.

## THE NSA, BIG TECH, AND ELECTRONIC SURVEILLANCE

In early 2013, Edward Snowden, a computer consultant who worked for the National Security Agency (NSA) contractor Booz Allen Hamilton, began leaking classified information to the press. In June 2013, several major media outlets including the *Guardian* and the *Washington Post* started publishing stories based on this leaked information, detailing previously undisclosed NSA surveillance operations, most notably the highly controversial PRISM program. Under the rationale of state security, the NSA—in coordination with several major private technology and communications companies (including Google, Facebook, Verizon, Yahoo, Skype, and others)—was secretly tracking, logging, and analyzing the personal internet and mobile phone activity of millions of American citizens and people around the world, including many high-ranking leaders from different nations, friend and foe. The extent of governmental and corporate surveillance, Snowden showed, was both deep (monitoring the most intimate aspects of people's lives) and global.

The Snowden revelations serve to make us aware of the fact that we are being surveilled. Even if, pre-Snowden, we suspected, we now know that our lives are continually monitored and recorded while we are personally profiled for various governmental and commercial purposes. In the wake of these revelations, large media and technology corporations like Facebook, Google, and Apple have repeatedly come under fire for their routine approaches to the privacy rights of individuals, both users and those indirectly connected to their platforms.[52] Snowden showed us that state institutions depend on these corporations for access to the "big data" (the aggregated and searchable content of the online activity of millions of users) and metadata (which includes IP addresses linked to specific devices, location information about mobile activity, details about relationships and contacts, and other information that can, often quite easily, be directly linked to personal identities) upon which their massive surveillance practices are based.[53] These private technology companies follow a business model that involves the regular collection and storage of data that users generate with their activities, data that is routinely shared with third parties. The NSA and other state agencies then use this big data for profiling, predictive, and preventive purposes in the governmental and political sphere.[54] Many users now have a basic awareness of this fact and have even become accustomed to these normal terms of our late-modern lives. Indeed, such surveillance by large and powerful agencies is complemented and facilitated by new norms of self-exposure as individuals regularly, both knowingly and unwittingly, expose their personal information online in various public or semi-public forums, or simply by carrying and using the devices that connect them with others.[55]

Whistleblowers like Edward Snowden expose the secrets of powerful institutions, giving a public audience the message that the once-hidden, now-exposed operations of these agencies pose some threat or cause some harm that should be addressed and remedied.[56] While "challenging and interrupting dominant system codes" and "abandoning instrumental reasoning" central to the institutions they betray, they perform "a democratic persona" in service to the civil sphere.[57] They then take a personal stand against the impersonal system they once inhabited, often achieving personal fame (either being celebrated or vilified) in the process. However, the Snowden leaks also leave the identities of our unnamed voyeurs hidden behind massive state agencies and private corporations. In other words, "the surveillers" continue to "remain anonymous to the surveilled."[58] This social dynamic, in which our personal exposure is contrasted with the anonymity of institutions and systems, shapes the character and impact of mass surveillance in our lives.

From one perspective, we might expect a growing awareness of surveillance to have a controlling effect, rendering the surveilled intimidated and disempowered.[59] Such an awareness can "induce . . . a state of conscious and permanent visibility that assures the automatic functioning of power." It can create an "anxious awareness of being observed" that pushes those "subjected to a field of visibility" to regulate their behaviors and discipline themselves.[60] Thus, the agents of surveillance often want us to know (or think) they are always watching us and monitoring our behavior. Frederick Douglass realized this when he observed the tactics of the brutal overseer Mr. Covey. Because Covey would often sneak up and surprise working slaves, or let himself be seen watching them from behind a fence or tree, the slaves assumed he was always watching even when he was not visible, and "work went on in his absence almost as well as in his presence; and he had the faculty of making [slaves] feel that he was ever present with [them]."[61] However, Covey was not an anonymous force. He was a conniving, violent, and potentially deadly force who maintained a direct personal relationship with the people he watched.

Alternatively, when watchers operate behind the cover of massive institutions and are integrated into complex social systems of technology and communication, their anonymous and ubiquitous character may dampen the direct impact they have on individual actions. A "peeping Tom" at one's window or even an anonymous hacker who steels password-protected information will likely inspire righteous indignation, but the diffuse effects of nameless and faceless operators who use massive institutions to steer an omnipresent system of watching feel more distant and thus more easily evade the sustained concern of those whose privacies are violated. Their operations, and the technologies of big data surveillance, are also bewildering and "opaque for outsiders, including lawmakers and citizens."[62] Moreover, the rationale for such ubiquitous surveillance is meshed with the broader functions of these institutions in our lives. While opponents of surveillance culture see it as an oppressive practice, others may accept it as a necessary condition and measure of personal freedom and security.[63] Likewise, anonymous surveillance is now deeply associated with tailored and personalized experiences and inseparably linked to our ability to maintain interpersonal relationships (professional, casual, and intimate) facilitated by our chosen social media and communications platforms.[64] To do without depersonalizes our experiences and disconnects our lives.

Post-Snowden, little has actually changed. With the flood of media coverage detailing NSA and corporate surveillance practices, there was a corresponding spike in internet searches for the anonymizing web browser Tor, suggesting that more people sought to establish a protective anonymity online.[65] However, despite this limited growth of interest in anonymous web browsing, Snowden's revelations were met with an astonishing degree of nonchalance among the majority of the general population and "brought few new users to privacy-enhancing technologies."[66] Furthermore, both state and private institutions continue to engage in substantial surveillance activities as a part of their normal modes of operation. Private companies that engage in routine internet-based surveillance often promise to protect user privacy by anonymizing the information they collect and share, which is generally aggregated ("big") and thus "often [goes] beyond direct representation to simulation, and from narrative to numerical form,"[67] turning particular people into obscure no ones. Yet corporate promises of anonymity (which are often stated in ethical terms) can be contrasted with the increasingly personalized character of the online services and advertisements individuals receive via their web browsers, email, and social media platforms, clear evidence that "the subject of surveillance is hence not simply population, . . . but above all the individual subject of communication."[68] The assurances we receive about anonymous data-collection procedures can also be contrasted with the increasingly common phenomenon of data breaches that expose our personal information to public scrutiny. Currently, our personal information can be retrieved by anyone with technological know-how, and such skills are more commonly "reappropriated by lay persons"[69] as computer technologies saturate our lives. In short, the practitioners of mass surveillance are obscured by opaque institutions and complex technological systems while our personal identities are actively profiled, digitized, stored, and distributed. The anonymity of institutions and social systems is a key factor shaping the dynamics of surveillance and information control in our rapidly changing world.

### DISTANCE KILLING AND THE NATION AT WAR

Acts of war, always carried out by real people who bring violence to life, have historically been performed by organized armed forces. Armies typically blend the personal identities of individuals into a formal system to express violence on behalf of a kingdom, state, or nation. Uniform regalia and collective symbols (often national or religious) serve as fronts that organize, motivate, and justify the coordinated actions of individual soldiers.

For centuries, the typical mode of combat was face-to-face, "within arm's reach," and soldiers saw one another on the battlefield.[70] Even though the personal identities of combatants were obscured by a collective identity and the military front, killing was an intimate act. However, as the technologies of war developed with the Industrial Revolution, and especially throughout the twentieth and into the twenty-first century, "killing from a distance" became "the normal form of combat."[71] This ability to kill from a distance expanded with the development of weapons technologies that allow for mass killing (e.g., the dropping or launching of explosives, including atomic and nuclear bombs, from afar) and targeted long-range killing (as facilitated by increasingly precise and powerful guns and, more recently, drones). Despite the fact that one mode of killing is indiscriminate (mass) and other discriminate (targeted), these technologies of war deepen the cover for the individual agents carrying out acts of violence, further depersonalizing the act of killing in the name of the nation, rendering the agents of death even more anonymous to their victims.

With mass killings, including many acts of terrorism, victims are also typically anonymous to their killers. In such cases, the perpetrators of mass violence usually target nations, governments, or financial systems, and sometimes entire religious or ethnic groups, rather than particular individuals whose deaths are deemed part of the broader objective.[72] However, acts of targeted or "precision" killing, such as those carried out with unmanned aerial vehicles, or drones, are intended to be more personal in their objective. While often criticized as a form of summary execution, targeted drone strikes are typically justified as a means of avoiding mass casualties that would result from other forms of assault. They have become more common in modern conflicts that are deemed "asymmetrical" because state militaries are engaging nonstate agents and paramilitary organizations.[73] Moreover, these acts of war rely on "virtual technologies that mediate both combat and decision making."[74] Such technologies facilitate "respatialization dynamics" that make conflict even more asymmetrical, separating "weapon and weaponeer" by great distances.[75] Thus, a core dimension of this form of warfare involves the fact that the targets of violence are surveilled and personally exposed (some are named and hunted) while the perpetrators are sheltered and anonymized, not just behind the cover of a military institution, but via the distance between them and the weapon itself. Given this distance, the weapon (via its violent effect) serves as the cover representation for its anonymous operator, which is evident in the language we use to describe drones and their operations. When the military refers to drones as "*unmanned* aerial vehicles," or when we refer to them as "machine assassins,"[76] name them "predators," or run headlines like "Obama Apologizes after *Drone Kills* American and Italian

Held by Al Qaeda,"[77] we depict the technology as an independent actor rather than a tool of agent-operators who, however far away, *do* the acting *with* a drone. From this perspective, the operators could be anyone; their status as generic functionaries liquidates their personal relevance to the operation, a phenomenon that whistleblowers attempt to undo by publicly outing themselves as operators and taking personal responsibility for acts of killing.[78]

In contrast to the fact that the personal identities of drone operators are typically obscured, the US Central Intelligence Agency refers to its drone attacks as "*personality* strikes" when a known individual is targeted for assassination, and "*signature* strikes" when particular individuals, whose personal identities are often unknown, are targeted after surveillance reveals "patterns of life associated with terrorism."[79] Both terms convey the notion that the violent act is justified by the personal guilt of those who are targeted and killed. From the perspective of the attackers, these specific individuals are targeted because they have orchestrated violence (usually indiscriminate terrorist violence) in the past and/or, it is claimed, will likely do so in the future. Thus, using their technologies and systems of "precision" killing, violent actors anonymously perform acts of war as smart, surgical, civilized, and humane endeavors that remove and prevent evil and harm in the name of the good and peace-loving civil society.

Yet the extent to which such violence is "precise" is disputed. While "evidence suggests that drones are technically capable of satisfying the condition of discrimination," the practice of intelligence gathering and data interpretation is imperfect and "often suffers from insufficient and potentially unreliable ground information to contextualize the tactical situation."[80] With regard to the targeting process, "it has become clear" that drone operators "often do not know who they are killing, but are making an imperfect best guess."[81] Because "signature strikes" are often based on surveillance profiles that rely on metadata gathered from mobile phones, any innocent person might be mistakenly deemed a terrorist or enemy combatant and executed via Hellfire Missile, along with anyone in the vicinity, without any sort of legal process and without warning to the local community.[82] Thus, critics claim that drones regularly cause large numbers of civilian deaths and foment outrage among the general populations of the nations in which they are deployed, where "they are viewed as fearsome indiscriminate killers of civilians."[83] Estimates regarding the number of civilian casualties vary. Some claim that up to fifty civilians are killed per every targeted militant.[84] While US government representatives have typically denied or downplayed civilian casualties resulting from US drones strikes, in effect rendering these victims either invisible or anonymous to the world outside their local communities,[85] mounting evidence and a growing number of cases, including the August 2021 strike that killed an Afghan aid worker and multiple children, serve to undermine those denials.[86]

From the perspective of those who are attacked, such acts of violence represent an oppressive foreign system. The weapon—an impersonal force of death—becomes the face of the national entity that wields it. For example, as Farea Al-Muslimi stated in his testimony to the US Senate Subcommittee on the Constitution, Civil Rights and Human Rights, "drone strikes are the face of America to many Yemenis."[87] Furthermore, even before they strike, drones can indeed be noticed by those living below, as in one case of a Pakistani village where it was reported that "the buzz of the hovering drone terrifies the villagers, who live in constant fear of an explosion from the sky."[88] Given all of these factors, drones are experienced as faceless agents that perpetrate terror and ongoing trauma on behalf of the nation they represent.[89]

Considering the asymmetries of identification and meaning that characterize targeted drones strikes allows us to better understand how other long-range precision weapons anonymize the perpetrators of violence. Sniper rifles allow operators to remain unseen while zooming in to target a specific person. Likewise, consider the M230 Chain Gun mounted on US Apache helicopters, which has an attack range of up to 4,000 meters (2.49 miles). This weapon is featured in a video that was leaked by whistleblower Chelsea Manning via the WikiLeaks website, where it was dubbed "collateral murder."[90] The video shows an attack that took place in Baghdad on July 12, 2007, from such a great distance that the targets appear completely unaware that a helicopter was surveilling them. The perpetrators are totally shielded by the distance afforded by their weapons technology. Those operating the helicopter and its weapon, and we who view the video online, see the men on the ground only as technologically mediated images, their beings transformed into avatars not unlike those encountered in war-themed video games, thereby making it very difficult "to distinguish between combatants and non-combatants" during the operation of war.[91] In this case, the distance also allowed particular individuals on the ground to be erroneously defined as combatants and therefore as legitimate targets (at least two were professional journalists, carrying cameras that were defined as weapons). From the perspective of people on the ground, the US soldiers in the helicopter are represented only by the act of violence itself, which becomes the manifestation of the United States as nation in that moment. We can contrast such depersonalized violence with the more personal character of violence in past eras, as captured by the American Revolutionary War command "Don't fire until to you see the whites of their eyes."

With "the increasing use of impersonal forms of warfare," especially "among affluent states," and especially with the rise of war "by remote control,"[92] violence commonly manifests as an anonymous act. Very soon, we will likely see the deployment of automated or robotic weapons that further anonymize violence and death.[93] From this perspective, war is a performative accomplishment enacted by individuals and teams perpetrating violent acts while shielded by organized military fronts and their technological systems. Such individuals act behind, and with, the fronts of nations or paramilitary organizations for particularly violent purposes while divorcing their own personal identities from their actions.

## THE MODERN STATE AS "HUMANE" EXECUTIONER

When medical doctors and other healthcare professionals perform state-mandated executions by lethal injection in the United States, they typically do so while anonymous to the condemned prisoner, attending witnesses, and the public at large. Their names are usually withheld from official records, "and they are often paid in cash."[94] Several states have established laws reinforcing the anonymity of those who facilitate executions, arguing that such measures are necessary for their safety and security, as well as to protect the integrity of the system itself.[95] Beyond simply keeping the personal identities of individual participants hidden, some—like the state of Missouri, for example—deem anyone who knowingly identifies participants in the execution process legally liable for damages.[96] Indeed, modern executions in the United States are characterized by anonymity, along with a more general strategy of concealment and obscurity—what John Lofland calls "a concealed dramaturgics."[97] Keeping the personal identities of executioners concealed allows us to define the modern state, with its impersonal legal-rationale authority, as the punitive agent of the execution process. Such an attribution of agency to the state system is evident in the way we communicate, allowing us to assert and understand that "Texas has executed 33 people since 2017" or, pitting the impersonal system against the personal prisoner, "Alabama has executed Nathaniel Woods despite looming doubts."[98]

In contrast, during premodern and early modern eras in Europe, executions were typically open acts of public spectacle that often involved large crowds and conspicuous theatrics.[99] During these eras, a sovereign or some state authority employed a professional executioner to organize and carry out the act. The professionalization of execution served to displace mob killings, centralize the authority behind corporal punishment, and "symbolize the power and wrath of the state."[100] Executioners did not hide their personal identities. Rather, they actually "comported themselves in ways that endowed them with distinctive public and personal identities," and each was publicly known for their "personal style."[101] In fact, the image of the hooded and anonymous medieval executioner appears to be a myth of modern design, one that serves to make modern state killings appear civil and just in contrast.[102] As the modern era advanced, state-mandated killing became increasingly controversial (both morally and politically), its legitimacy and fit with modern liberal ideals of civil society repeatedly questioned. Thus, in the United States, political authorities became more and more concerned with establishing refined and enlightened methods of execution. Growing concerns and mounting controversies spurred changes in method and stimulated the impetus to anonymize the executioners behind state systems and institutions.

Over the past four decades, lethal injection has, by far, been the most common method of penal execution in the United States. In the wake of several legal challenges to the constitutionality of the death penalty,[103] states began to adopt lethal injection protocols, claiming the method to be humane, backed by medical science, and, therefore, legally sound and in line with Eighth Amendment protections against cruel and unusual punishment. The new procedure emerged as an alternative to death by electrocution (which was increasingly seen as grotesque and painful despite previously being adopted as the humane method of choice), hanging (which was deeply associated with "the conduct of southern lynch mobs whose savage violence had recently given new and unwelcome meaning to the age-old symbol of the noose"),[104] and firing squad (which was, at its roots, a military method that likely seemed at odds with the civil autonomy of the penal system in modern society). These previously established methods often made the pain, bodily harm or disfigurement, and even suffering of the condemned individual plainly visible for those witnessing the act. As an alternative, the basic protocol used in executions by lethal injection was designed in 1977 by Dr. Jay Chapman, medical examiner for the state of Oklahoma, and reviewed by Dr. Stanley Deutsch, an anesthesiologist at the University of Oklahoma.[105] These doctors marshaled the insights of modern medicine to control the pain and suffering of the condemned.

This is not the first time a new form of capital punishment was justified as more humane because it was designed and sanctioned by doctors. The famous French doctor Joseph-Ignace Guillotin used the same rationale to push a method that became quite famous in the wake of the French

Revolution.[106] However, lethal injection was not simply designed by medical authorities; it actually medicalizes the entire killing act. Thus, as Atul Gawande explains,

> officials liked this method. Because it borrowed from established anesthesia techniques, it made execution like familiar medical procedures rather than the grisly, backlash-inducing spectacle it had become. . . . It was less disturbing to witness. . . . And officials could turn to doctors and nurses to help with technical difficulties, attest to the painlessness and trustworthiness of the technique, and lend a more professional air to the proceedings.[107]

Despite its medical design, however, legal challenges persisted and plaintiffs continued to allege the unconstitutional cruelty of the process. Today, the method of lethal injection (along with the death penalty in general) remains utterly controversial, both morally and politically.[108]

Given that this new process relied on medical expertise, state authorities were now faced with the practical and legal necessity of soliciting the participation of doctors and nurses. In order to secure their cooperation, prison wardens and state officials promised healthcare professionals that their work would remain anonymous. Anonymity protects participating doctors and nurses from the possibility of rebuke by their peers and from potential damage to their reputations in the eyes of the public at large, both of which may have consequences for their careers and professional standings. However, given the quite serious implications of execution, this promise of anonymity has itself become a matter of legal and political controversy. Many have argued that the condemned prisoner, the press, and the public at large have a right to know the personal identities of execution team members in order to ensure that they are qualified to provide legally appropriate and constitutionally sound executions.[109] If named healthcare practitioners oversee lethal injections, we can evaluate them based on their personal reputations. However, when an anonymous medical doctor conducts or oversees the killing, the depersonalized medical degree and license to practice medicine—that symbolic capital shared by all practicing doctors—is foregrounded over the personal identity and history of the individual actor, allowing a general medical authority to grant legitimacy to the act while the specific individual ducks personal accountability. Moreover, such an arrangement also allows for *one* doctor to participate in multiple executions over the course of his career while his anonymity leaves open the possibility, and can even generate the perception, that *many* doctors have been involved.[110] The anonymous doctor could be *any* doctor, reinforcing the impression that the penal act is sanctioned by the *institution* of modern medicine.[111]

By assimilating an anonymous and impersonal medical authority, state officials have blended the otherwise contradictory social logics of medical and penal institutions into a complex system front that shapes the meaning of state-sanctioned acts of killing.[112] They merge the medical professional role with the penal role, an act of care with an act of killing, dissolving otherwise significant moral boundaries that separate our institutions of healing and punishment. Human life is coded differently according to the values of each social sphere—sacrosanct in one and forfeitable in the other. Bodies are the target of nurturing repair and healing in one, and disciplinary force and harm in the other. Moral questions of guilt and innocence are irrelevant to one and central to the other. The aim of healthcare is liberation from disease and escape from death; the aim of the penal system is bodily confinement, mortification, and social or, sometimes, physical death.

The contradictions of this blended system front allow actors rooted in one sphere to justify their actions by referring to the other. Thus, medical professionals often justify their killing actions by pointing to the fact that they are compliant with state law and democratic mandate.[113] At the same time, state authorities justify their killing actions as humane and even caring according to the logic of modern medicine. The very presence of healthcare professionals, hospital equipment, a medicalized room, pharmaceuticals, and the use of medical language serves to make the activity appear less brutal, even painless and peaceful, and therefore more agreeable to a public audience, generating what David Garland calls "a civilized aesthetic."[114] By assimilating the general characters and props of the medical system to set the mise-en-scène of the killing ritual, state actors are able to code the execution as modern (vs. primitive and antiquated), clean and sterile (vs. dirty/bloody/odorous/defiled), and civilized (vs. barbarous). As some witnesses and critics have observed, the setting of an execution by lethal injection resembles a hospital room, and the act "mimics a procedure performed thousands of times a day in hospitals across the United States."[115] Some doctors and nurses even dress for medical procedures and use sterilization techniques when participating in the process, as if the prevention of post-operative infection was a concern.[116] Furthermore, the mandated use of a pharmaceutical paralyzing agent intended to prevent the body of the condemned from signifying struggle for life furthers the presentation of the scene as peaceful and surgical. From this perspective, execution is a performative accomplishment steered by anonymous medical professionals who sanitize the ritual act of state killing and package it for the conscience of the public.

As some have argued, the "image of a white-coated symbol of care working with or as the black-hooded executioner is in striking contrast to established physician ethics."[117] Indeed, the American Medical Association takes the position that "as a member of a profession dedicated to preserving life when there is hope of doing so, a physician must not participate in a legally authorized execution."[118] Other professional medical associations take similar positions.[119] Nevertheless, by blending medical and penal logics, state actors use the anonymous medical credentials of their execution team members to legitimate their otherwise controversial actions, framing the modern state as humane executioner.

✳

The anonymity of social systems is a performative accomplishment. On the one hand, actors use social systems and institutions, like corporate banks, intelligence agencies, national militaries, or state departments of corrections—with their rules, procedures, and technologies of operation—as impersonal fronts with which to act and define various situations. On the other hand, when we attribute an economic crisis to Wall Street, when we speak of surveillance by "big tech," when we say a nation is at war, or a state executes a prisoner, we actively anonymize the agents involved in these activities. We attribute motive and agency to institutions and systems, which are often opaque and quite impervious to outsiders, rather than the particular people who bring them to life. By facilitating anonymity, these organized social systems license individuals to act in ways that they would not likely otherwise act if they were held directly and personally accountable. While this anonymity thus provides a degree of freedom, it also imposes its own form of social constraint. When individuals act within these system structures, they render themselves subservient to the purpose and power of those collective agencies. As a result, their actions and relationships can become molded by institutional objectives and strategic practices; they are assimilated into the impersonal system that they perform.

When Stanley Milgram conducted his famous electric shock experiments, he was primarily concerned with understanding how and why individuals would obey the commands of an authority figure who required them to act in ways that they might otherwise find morally objectionable. Deeply concerned with understanding the circumstances that prompted millions to follow the genocidal Nazi regime in Europe, Milgram explored the conditions under which authority figures could successfully command ordinary people to harm others. The more removed or distant his research subjects were from another human being, Milgram found, the more likely the subjects were to obey the commands of the experimenter to shock that person (a confederate to the experiment) at increasingly painful and dangerous levels. The greater the divide, the less they saw "the act of depressing a lever"—the lever they were told would deliver the shock—to be "relevant to moral judgment, for it [was] no longer associated with the victim's suffering."[120] As he explored the implications of his research for understanding the dynamics of interpersonal and mass violence, Milgram made a more general point that pertains to the ways that certain social contexts cultivate impersonality via their social logics and normative definitions of action. He speculated that the greater the boundary between the research subject and the confederate who supposedly received the shock, the more the subject could be wholly or primarily concerned with his performance as a good assistant to the experimenter, "so concerned about the show he is putting on for the experimenter that influences from other parts of the social field do not receive as much weight as they ordinarily would" in other situations.[121] In other words, being *good* meant performing according to the codes of the experimental frame, which required actions (in this case, electric shocks) that made sense according to the instrumental-rational logic of the scientific process. The more anonymity was a factor, the more easily and thoroughly these actions were made meaningful and legitimate according to the logic of the research and its setting—what Milgram refers to as the "background authority" of institutions.[122]

When individuals act as anonymous functionaries of institutions and social systems, they become "enmeshed in a social structure" with its own logic, objectives, relationships, and strategic rules of operation.[123] Their personal motives are subsumed and reshaped by institutional forces that functionally depersonalize and anonymize them in particular situations, and in situated relations to others, while defining those situations (and the nature of their actions) according to impersonal institutional objectives. To be good means to act in compliance with these impersonal objectives—to animate the will of the system one inhabits. From such a standpoint, we hone our moral focus on "the job to be done and the excellence with which it is performed."[124] Moreover, we shift our assessment of responsibility away from the personal and to the system.[125] Even though the personal identities of many who act with system covers are publicly knowable or traceable, the social system itself allows for their anonymity to emerge as a fundamental part of the performance of system objectives. This can lead to what Zygmunt Bauman has called "a free-floating responsibility" in which "the organization as a whole is an instrument to obliterate responsibility."[126] By anonymizing its functionaries and thereby depersonalizing their actions and relationships, not only do institutions and social systems make it difficult to assign personal responsibility, but sometimes to ascertain responsibility in general—to hold anyone or anything accountable in any meaningful way. A similar liquidation of personal identity and a general anonymization of labor characterizes many social systems of production in the world today.

## Anonymous Labor and Systems of Production

Modern economies have rendered many types of labor invisible. In such cases, we fail to acknowledge that work exists. We may see the laborer (as in the case of those who routinely work in the home while their work is ignored, conditions traditionally experienced by women[127]) or not (as in the case of those who clean offices at night while others are not present), but in both cases we are blind to the work itself. It "remains hidden from view," and people often act as if it doesn't exist.[128] However, in many situations the activity of work and/or its product are quite visible while the laborer remains anonymous. In such cases, we are aware of the fact that someone is working to produce the commodities and services we consume, but we divorce those products and services from the personal identities of those who do the actual work. Instead, we experience some corporation, industry, or brand, or in some cases a famous individual, as the agency behind the act. Such an anonymity of labor has become an increasingly prevalent part of our late-modern economies as a growing number of people perform their work as generic and interchangeable functionaries of broader corporate systems of production or institutionalized service relationships.

As he developed his critical analysis of the capitalist system of production, Karl Marx illuminated the roots of both invisible and anonymous labor. For Marx, workers who engage in the industrial activities of capitalism are detached in various ways from their work (which is depersonalized) and their product (which is abstracted from its human character) as a routine matter of course.[129] To the capitalist (or, we might add, more generally from the vantage point of many corporate systems), the worker is like any other tool, and their labor is like any other raw material in that it is indispensable yet generic and replaceable. Following this logic, as the processes of production (and today we can include service provision) become more systematized, they also become more impersonal and anonymized. The producers of goods and the consumers of their products often experience one another as distant, "abstract," and "absolutely anon-ymous."[130]

Developing a related set of ideas in his discussions of commodity fe-tishism, Marx explored how the relationships among people take "the fantastic form of a relation between things," and therefore "the products of labour" appear to us as if they are independent of their producers, di-vorced from the real human and social conditions that would otherwise give them meaning.[131] Thus, as consumers in the world, we see the com-modity (labor's product) as an abstraction, as something separate from work, and "the social character of labour appears to us to be an objective character of the products themselves."[132] Such a separation of the prod-uct from the circumstances and history of those who work can render the work itself invisible in some cases (it disappears into the product, the existence of which we take for granted) and the workers anonymous in others (the product appears to exist independently of anyone's per-sonal contribution).[133] With regard to the latter situation, even in cases where workers can be seen, heard, or named, they often work as part of a system front that renders their personal identities irrelevant to the entire process, to the product, and to the economic exchanges of their field. Such workers are typically *not* anonymous to their local employ-ers, colleagues, and communities, but with regard to the broader public and to consumers at large, their personal identities are obscured by a corporate front or by some named producer who gets all of the personal credit.

Consider food production in the industrial world as one of many pos-sible cases. Consumers in industrial and post-industrial economies are typically unaware of who produces their food. Rather, food products are more commonly represented by corporate brand names, to which con-sumers attribute credit and responsibility for the act of production. If one purchases Tyson chicken or craves Campbell's Soup, Tyson and Campbell (both the last names of company founders that are no longer associated with particular people) are named as the agencies behind the product. Such impersonal brands are foundational to commercial culture but also render the people who work and bring them to life generic and replaceable *anyones*—anonymous functionaries who are personally irrelevant to their product. One indication of our attribution of productive agency to the corporate brand is that we expect the product to be consistent and predict-able across time and space, despite the fact that different people actually do the work of producing it. When we order a McDonald's cheeseburger, for example, we expect it to taste the same whether produced in a Cali-fornia plant and cooked in Seattle or produced in Germany and cooked in France. In any of its roughly 39,000 locations (as of 2020), McDonald's makes the food while the workers are anonymous.

In some cases, entrepreneurs seek to personalize food products and undo the anonymity that characterizes most contemporary food production. To this end, local food movements, farmers' markets, food cooperatives, and community-supported agriculture (CSA) initiatives often facilitate a direct connection between consumers and farmers and other food producers (such as bakers and fishing crews). These and other agents promote such connections as an ethical practice, thereby working to dissolve the anonymity of labor and the invisibility of the productive process. Moreover, as a result of such movements, the personalization of food has become a way of signifying superior quality. Within this cultural milieu, some local and personal operations have grown into large-scale corporate enterprises, while other more traditional corporate firms have worked to connect their products to particular people. The eggs I sometimes purchase feature photographs of the family that owns the farm along with information about their chicken-raising and egg-farming practices. The chicken I recently purchased advertises "meet your farmer" with a web address. Such entrepreneurs work to counter consumer alienation from food by stressing the consumer's relationship to the named food producer (providing personal information about the farmers) and often by locating production practices (providing information about the farm). By foregrounding such information, which is typically hidden by more traditional corporate production systems, they work to transform our relationship to the product itself.

Consider also the practice of branding a commercial food product with a named family member (Tia Lupita hot sauce) or simply the first names of the company founders (Ben and Jerry's ice cream) or the founders' daughter (Amy's soups). Likewise, consider the contemporary practice of distinguishing food products by associating them with a named celebrity chef who claims personal credit for the recipe and responsibility for the culinary quality of the product, or cases in which a notable personality takes responsibility for the ethical standards of production and thereby safeguards the moral quality of consumption (as with Paul Newman's charitable Newman's Own food company). Such cases of *personality branding* call our attention to the fact that most food products are indeed *not* marked in this way; most are not directly associated with any personal identity.[134] By adding a personal name to a product, or developing a brand around a personal identity, companies attempt to create trust around the portrayal of personal accountability and perhaps even an illusion of personal connection. The person behind the brand in effect becomes the "author" of (the one who *authorizes*) the product. Their personal character is written into the meaning of the food and the experience of consumption. However, despite such efforts to personalize food, the vast majority of those who produce it remain obscured behind the personality brand.

Likewise, while some anonymous authors and artists produce an unsigned piece of work, ghostwriters and art restorers obscure their personal identities behind the name of another more celebrated person who typically gets credit.[135] These systems are engineered and contracted by publishing corporations and museums, which are also credited with producing or curating the product. When the contributions of ghostwriters and art restorers are unacknowledged, the labor can remain invisible. However, when the fact of assistance or restoration is known but the craftspeople employed are unnamed, the labor is anonymous despite the fact that it creates or fundamentally alters the product. Indeed, ghostwriters are most commonly employed to help celebrities write autobiographies.[136] Thus, "ghostwriting can also be seen . . . as the apotheosis of the star [i.e., celebrity] system," one that "precludes anonymous publication as absolutely as it requires anonymous composition."[137] In other words, ghostwriters are anonymous specifically in their contrast to the identified people to which the texts they compose are attributed. In a similar vein, "designers Frederick Law Olmsted and Calvert Vaux scored much of the credit for" the construction of New York's Central Park, but those who did the physical work of building the park remained relatively anonymous.[138] Likewise, journal reviewers in academia engage in an officially anonymized form of labor that generates credit for named authors and profit for corporate publishers.[139]

In this regard, consider the case of the *Stammaim*, the anonymous editors ("redactors") of the Babylonian Talmud. Critical Talmud scholars distinguish "between two primary literary strata: *meimrot*, traditions attributed to named sages (the Amoraim, c. 200–450 CE), . . . and *setam hatalmud*, the unattributed or anonymous material," which were added by Stammaim over the course of several later generations (~450–650 CE).[140] These anonymous scholars "did not act as passive conduits" but rather were creative anonymous agents who "added extensive discussions and commentary" while organizing, contextualizing, and ultimately changing the meaning of the sacred text.[141] Like contemporary ghostwriters, their contributions are distinctly anonymous in contrast to the named rabbinical authorities credited within the text. Moreover, the anonymity of the Stammaim allowed them to perform a generalized, authoritative, and even ancient and divine voice that framed their interventions into the text and their contributions to its meaning.[142] However, their interventions were always based on their evolving perspectives and social concerns.[143] Thus, the Talmud was produced over time as anonymous actors continued to inject their contemporary understandings and practices of Judaism into the text, revising past understandings in the process.[144]

Moreover, as Jeffrey L. Rubenstein convincingly suggests, the Stammaim actors were in fact anonymized in the context of an emergent institution of their era—the formal rabbinical academies that were "permanent organizations with corporate identities that transcend the individuals present at any given time."[145] The academies were bustling and competitive arenas of discussion and interpretive debate—what Rubenstein calls "dialectical argumentation"—that likely replaced earlier more intimate and personalized practices of the Amoraim.[146] Thus, the Stammaim "were speaking on behalf of the institution that" itself served as "the sage whose tradition they were conveying."[147] Their redaction of the Babylonian Talmud led to a multivocal, complex, and even argumentative text that reflected generations of dialogue and debate among large groups of scholars in the academy. The text ultimately came to express a social system of retroactive interpretive authorship that anonymized many producers of "a document that became the basis of the rabbinic curriculum, the foundation of Jewish law, and a source of biblical interpretation, customs, theology, and ethics."[148] In short, this system of anonymous production defined a core aspect of the religion of Judaism itself, both in its product and in the process reflected in those sacred writings.

Anonymity is also a core feature of various service relationships and modes of economic exchange. Consider the common practice of outsourcing customer service (as when call centers are organized and based in different parts of the world). Globalized communications technologies shrink geographic distance and integrate otherwise disparate time zones,[149] yet they simultaneously enhance the anonymity of the workers who are masked by technologies and corporate scripts that facilitate their generic roles. In such cases, even when voices are heard over telephones or faces are seen by clients on computer screens, and even when names are used (or are easily traceable via an employee identification number, an email address, or an internet chat log), these markers of personal identity often do not matter to the relationship because workers are, in effect, mediated impersonal functionaries. Furthermore, the computer-mediated character of other forms of support labor (such as website design or database management) converts the work itself into "a disembodied flow of signs and symbols" transmitted electronically,[150] which can render the personal identities of the laborers obscured by the system and its technologies. Likewise, retail companies can also serve as mediating agents while their brands serve as cover representations that mask the identities of those who produce the commodities on the shelves. When consumers buy clothing from a Gap store, for example, they often think of "Gap" as the agent behind the product, despite the fact that clothing sold by Gap, Inc., is produced by workers in factories in various locations around the world.[151]

The now common practice of ordering an increasing variety of products online allows for an enhanced social distance and a deeper anonymization of labor and production. When we order our food, clothing, or books, or even purchase a car or a home from a website or phone app, we do not even see or directly interact with another individual. While buyers are often identifiable via their credit card information or delivery address, the producers of goods and others involved in production, distribution, and exchange processes are more deeply anonymized. In this regard, the impersonal and anonymous character of labor is enhanced by the medium of the computer code and hardware.[152] As the product shows up at our door, the system is convenient but entirely opaque. In many cases, online commerce may create the illusory feeling that items produced in other parts of the world are "local" in character. We order clothing from our personal computer and it shows up at our personal residence, despite the fact that it was produced by anonymous others working in foreign conditions unseen. As Ethel C. Brooks shows with regard to the globalized conditions and gendered character of work in the garment industry, the lives of those who produce our clothing often remain obscure. We experience the product as real but the labor as abstract. As Brooks argues, "The provision of living proof—in the forms of testimony and the bodily presence of Third World women as witnesses—lays bare the impossibilities of abstract labor."[153] In other words (addressing her point within the frame of my current discussion), what Brooks calls "living proof" personalizes the conditions and experiences of workers who are otherwise masked and anonymized by global systems of production and exchange.

## Conclusion

Throughout this chapter, I have shown how actors use and experience organized social systems—including corporations, states, nations, and other institutions—as cover representations as they work to accomplish various tasks and achieve their goals. In the process, they obscure personal identities while bringing these system entities to life, defining various situations for their audiences, which include the people who are directly impacted by their actions. While actors use social systems and institutions in ways that obscure their personal identities, audiences play a part in the meanings such actors create when they accept that, and speak as if, the system itself acted. In other words, the anonymity of social systems is an utterly social and performative accomplishment that manifests when and only because people use system covers to define actions, situations, events, products, and issues in the world.

Social systems and institutions can free individuals and teams to act, but can also constrain them by molding their actions and experiences (along with their motives and rationales) to system logics, creating various tensions between the ethics and values to which we typically hold individuals accountable and those we apply to impersonal agencies like corporations and states. In the words of Louis Wirth, these powerful entities have "no soul,"[154] meaning that when such entities act, or more precisely when people act through such entities, their depersonalized actions become bound to no one in particular. Thus, when individuals use systems and institutions as cover representations, they can accomplish goals that would otherwise be out of reach, but they can also act in ways that transcend or violate moral standards associated with personal behavior. Furthermore, in many of the cases I discuss throughout this chapter, individuals can experience greater degrees of alienation, replaceability, and even dehumanization, both when working as generic functionaries of the systems that anonymize them *and* when acted upon by those who are anonymized by a system front.[155] In general, the anonymity of social systems might feed a more pervasive manifestation of the psychological malaise and political frustrations that C. Wright Mills associated with a distinctly bureaucratic form of modern life.[156] In some cases, such feelings lead to social apathy. In others, they spur rebellion. However, in all of the cases I have discussed in this chapter, the anonymity of social systems raises profound issues of moral and political concern, prompting us to consider ways of enhancing personal accountability and personal recognition in the world. In the next chapter, I build on this discussion to consider the tensions between personal recognition and the anonymity we create when we see people as types and categories.

# The Anonymity of
# Types and Categories

Within the first few pages of *The Souls of Black Folk*, W. E. B. Du Bois described a childhood experience in which his visiting card was rejected by a white classmate. The girl, a "newcomer" to his integrated school in Massachusetts in the era following the Civil War, "refused it, peremptorily, with a glance." Reflecting on the impact of this encounter, he wrote, "Then it dawned upon me with a certain suddenness that I was different from the others; or like, mayhap, in heart and life and longing, but shut out from their world by a vast veil." With these words, Du Bois captured an important dimension of the lived experience of racism. He evoked the metaphor of the veil to describe being seen *as* his darker skin and "shut out" from the world of his white peers. Furthermore, Du Bois tells us, the divisive force of the veil creates a duality of self-consciousness. He saw "himself through the revelation of the other world . . . that looks on in amused contempt and pity" but could also see out from behind the veil, "gifted with second-sight," a vision that allowed him to know the world from a perspective that his classmates lacked.[1] In just a few words, Du Bois portrayed a key social-psychological dimension of oppression. A core aspect of his experience involved being rendered anonymous, judged and dismissed as a generic member of a detested group, stripped of personal identity within a structured relationship defined by a social imbalance of power.

While Du Bois used the metaphor of the veil to describe the inter-personal and social-psychological experience of racism, his famous introductory remarks to *The Souls of Black Folk* also provide a particular example of the more general phenomenon of *typification*. Typification involves seeing and treating people as generic types or categories rather than particular and unique individuals with distinct personal identities. Alfred Schutz developed the general theory of typification as a central component of his sociological view of knowledge. He also connected this way of seeing and experiencing people to anonymity.[2] For Schutz, social life involves "a system of relevances and typifications," a social structure of perceptions, classifications, and expectations that "transforms unique individual actions of unique human beings into typical functions of typical social roles, originating in typical motives aimed at bringing about typical ends." Furthermore, "the incumbent of such a social role is expected by" others "to act in the typical way defined by this role."[3] According to Schutz, we see many of the actors we encounter *as types* rooted in the structure of social relations, often obscuring their individual personhood while imposing generic labels and routine modes of behavior. Thus, over the course of our interactions and encounters, we impute social identities that eclipse the personal identities of others.[4] When we act toward others based on the way we perceive their type or categorical standing, and anticipate their motives and behaviors based on such "acts of typification,"[5] we essentially anonymize them. In such cases, the other is "anonymous in the sense that [their] existence is only the individuation of a type."[6] This idea was later expanded by Peter Berger and Thomas Luckmann, who briefly discussed "the anonymity of the type" and argued that "every typification, of course, entails incipient anonymity."[7] According to these scholars, we organize many elements of the world (including other people) into general types and categories as we interpret them and grasp their significance, and such interpretive work is always shaped by social norms that structure the meanings that those types and categories have for us.

Georg Simmel also addressed the general phenomenon of typification to describe the perilous existence of certain people who "are not really conceived as individuals, but as *strangers of a particular type,*" a social situation that "contains many dangerous possibilities."[8] From Simmel's perspective, we objectify and type people who embody a "unity of nearness and remoteness,"[9] meaning those who are both present in our lives and simultaneously outside of our more familiar and intimate circles. When we encounter such strangers, we may interact with them, even frequently, but they remain distant in a *sociomental* sense. From this perspective, we can typify someone as we meet them for the first time or someone we have encountered for years (such as a janitor or store clerk in either scenario) just as we can typify someone in our physical environment, someone we read about or see in a photograph, or someone we interact with online. In any case, when we see an individual *as* a type and therefore anonymize them, we often express and reinforce this *sociomental distance* when we relate to them. We construct a meaningful boundary that excludes intimacy or personal knowledge of the other.

In this chapter, I build on this foundational work. I explore how the anonymity that stems from typification manifests within and gives meaning to various encounters, situated interactions, and socially structured relationships. Putting people into types and categories does not necessarily make them anonymous. However, socially established typification schemes provide ontological frameworks that we often use to *eclipse personal identities in meaningful ways* that make actors anonymous units rather than particular people in certain situations. As opposed to recognizing a group membership or categorical designation as an important part of an individual's personal identity—which preserves the individual's autonomy and also allows for multiple groups, classes, and identifying traits to converge in the unique person who carries them[10]—such acts of typification obscure the personal identities of particular individuals behind an ascribed *categorical cover representation* and an associated set of assumed qualities based on generalized characteristics and expectations. For example, when during the course of an encounter or a social interaction, an actor sees and refers to another individual as "the nurse," a "homeless person," or "the waiter," or when she describes someone as "the old woman," a "terrorist," or "the Jew," that actor renders the personal identities of those individuals irrelevant to the portrayal. This process of typing people requires the sociomental accentuation of one or a small number of generalized characteristics (which are sometimes imagined or invented) that are used to label and define all members of a category while a much greater number of potentially meaningful and more personal attributes are ignored.[11] Furthermore, the labels actors use to type others are themselves inherently impersonal. Thus, "no matter how many people are subsumed under the ideal type, it corresponds to no one in particular."[12] Such labels include a vast and diverse array of widely used categorical designations and official titles, as well as common slang terms that can consist of historical references, euphemisms, dysphemisms, metonyms, synecdoches, or other linguistic devices, and that can be derogatory, deferential, or relatively neutral.[13]

While this anonymity of types and categories involves obscuring another's particular and unique characteristics on an individual level, it simultaneously involves accentuating homogeneity and ignoring heterogeneity on a group level. Individuals who are typified as "members of culturally marked social categories are thus often seen as 'representing' other members of those categories,"[14] further reinforcing the sociomental homogenization of the group and leading "outsiders [to] make general inferences" about the characteristics of all individuals who are lumped together.[15] Furthermore, such *homogenizing portrayals* often involve *essentialist logics*, as typifying others can entail associating members of the type with intrinsic and immutable characteristics, manifesting in the expectation that *all* members of the category are *always* the same.[16] The anonymity at the core of this process is expressed by the fact that actors often see those they typify as interchangeable with other individuals *of the same type*.[17] Such a perception of interchangeability allows for the rather awkward experience of mistaking one member of a typified group for another, a phenomenon that reveals the classificatory and discriminatory assumptions that underlie our perceptions of others.[18] Such logics of typification also guide profiling practices in multiple spheres of social life, which involve creating descriptive and predictive categorical generalizations with which to sort individuals. As a sorting practice, acts of typification primarily seek to answer the question of *what kind of person is this*, rather than the question of *who is this*. As we lump individuals into a type or category, we also split them off from others, essentializing or naturalizing the distinctions between groups.[19] In the process, actors express and reinforce *typification norms* rooted in cultural and interactional settings.

On a basic level, typification is fundamental to human thought and knowledge. Without this ability, we would not be able to organize and know the world in any meaningful way. However, typification always occurs within a social system of types and categories—in a socially structured "matrix of abstractions."[20] Furthermore, such a matrix of abstractions is often organized and expressed as what Patricia Hill Collins calls a "matrix of domination."[21] Thus, typification norms are often organized around entrenched power dynamics that characterize the structured relations of race, class, occupation, sex, gender, disability, citizenship, and more. As we typify others, we often define them, along with ourselves, according to culturally coded inequalities, bringing those inequalities— along with conflict and contention—to life in our interactions and relationships. In this way, anonymity by typification stands in contrast to the leveling effect that can occur when anonymous actors escape social cues that signify status, rank, class, or category and thereby establish a more equal position vis-à-vis one another.[22] Instead, certain characteristics of otherwise different persons serve as culturally meaningful markers with which we (often somewhat automatically) position them as anonymous representations of certain standpoints within complex power structures, leading to both a perception and an experience of anonymity that is rooted in dynamic relations of privilege and oppression, as well as normality and stigma. In such a social environment, uniforms (with regard to occupation and class), clothing styles (with regard to class, gender, ethnicity, or religion), skin color (with regard to race), body parts (with regard to sex or ability status),[23] voice (with regard to age, race, and/or sex),[24] and hair color (with regard to age) all do signifying work. They function as "signs in a system of sign relations"[25] that are structured according to various dynamic axes of power. My focus on the anonymity of types in social interaction is therefore also a query into a *social semiotics of power*—an exploration of how actors use various social signs and imputed characteristics to organize people (others and themselves) into impersonal and categorical relations of inequality.

Considering this anonymity of types and categories calls our attention to the fact that categorical cover representations can be voluntarily donned or imposed. Thus, we need to distinguish between *acts of self-typification* (the self-driven performance of a type to obscure one's personal identity) and *acts of other-typification* (which involve the performative ascription of categorical covers to others in our social interactions and relations).[26] With regard to the former, individuals actively type and anonymize themselves. With regard to the latter, individuals type and anonymize others, so we must distinguish between *typifier* and *typified* in the social dynamic. However, we also need to keep in mind that our social interactions can be structured by a "reciprocity of anonymity: I am anonymous to most Others just as most Others are anonymous to me."[27] In other words, in "my social relationships with my contemporaries," typification is often "mutual." For example, "corresponding to my ideal type 'engineer' there is the engineer's ideal type 'passenger,'" and "we think of each other as 'one of them.'"[28] I am the customer to the store clerk, and she is the clerk to me. I am the white man to the pedestrian I pass on the street, and she is the Asian woman to me. Those who we type and anonymize often type and anonymize us in return.

Furthermore, actors who are typified and anonymized in one context, interaction, or relationship are often simultaneously known personally and uniquely in another context, with regard to another community or set of relationships. In general, while "most of the time, most of us are anonymous in public," where one is often "seen as a member of a category, not as an individual, by the signs he produces—inevitably or by choice, accident, or compulsion,"[29] we are simultaneously seen as unique persons by our close friends and family members. Thus, over the course of our lives and each particular day, our different relationships are defined by "varying degrees of intimacy and anonymity."[30] Consequently, whether one recognizes and experiences another as personally distinguishable or generically anonymous depends on one's particular standpoint in the world—within the fold of some communities and outside the boundaries of others.[31] Finally, we may be aware of, or have access to, the personal identities of individuals and still typify them. Du Bois's classmate may have known his name (or at least she was able to easily learn it), yet she still saw him as a racial type in the context of a racist society. A waiter serving a customer might be wearing a name tag yet still be seen as "the waiter," just as the customer may use a credit card to pay but still be seen as "the customer." Police officers usually display badge numbers and license plates yet are often experienced as "cops." In these examples, the impersonal type defines the individual in particular interactions and situated relationships with others while the individual's personal identity is ignored and rendered irrelevant. Despite the presence of unique identifiers, a social anonymity marks the dynamics of such interactions and situations.

## Typification and Social Performance

As they work to define their situations for various audiences, actors often use categorical covers to cast others and themselves as culturally coded *character-types*. In the process, they anonymize the parties involved in particular circumstances, encounters, and exchanges.

On the one hand, actors perform self-typifications using a categorical front. In this regard, when anonymous authors of the early eighteenth century signed their work "By a Lady," they performed "a particular type voice," that of "a wise, educated, older woman with a moral mission, a type of 'universal' wise woman," regardless of who was behind the categorical cover. This had the "effect of appealing to a female community as having shared interests—an authoritative woman speaking to women." Furthermore, it gave rise to "a shared community of writers and readers, not distinguished by individual features, but a shared femininity and shared concerns."[32] Such cases, in which one's pseudonymous cover is also a categorical designation, show how types and categories can more generally serve as fronts for various activities, even when the actors do not explicitly hide their personal identities. For example, when members of an antiwar social movement speak as war veterans, when individuals criticize a political policy as Christians, or when advocates demand political reform as members of the LGBTQ community, they de-emphasize their personal identities and emphasize their categorical standing to establish political authority. Such acts of self-typification often serve to establish one's right to speak on behalf of, or to otherwise represent, a group or community. Thus, actors accentuate the general characteristics they share with the group over their personal identities. They act as a type or category of person to make their voice and actions meaningful and generalizable in that regard.

Actors can also typify themselves in ways that deceive others by falsely claiming a type or category, a phenomenon that is more easily achieved and therefore more common in the age of computer-mediated communication. For example, when in two cases men used pseudonyms to pose as lesbian bloggers, they adopted a categorical cover to establish an authoritative voice on behalf of the lesbian community. When the personal identities of these bloggers were exposed, critics and readers expressed feelings of anger and betrayal for their transgressive performances.[33] Such a betrayal is less about the general fact that these writers adopted pseudonyms to disguise their personal identities, and more specifically about the fact that in doing so they deceitfully used a categorical cover that conflicts with the social standpoint they routinely and genuinely occupy. Some expressed a similar sense of anger and betrayal after three men (Jorge Díaz, Augustín Martínez, and Antonio Mercero) revealed themselves to be the award-winning female author Carmen Mola,[34] or when a white woman used "a distinctly South Asian name" to publish a children's book "featuring a brown-skinned main character."[35] In general, when authors obscure their personal identities using a misleading categorical cover, they acquire an authoritative voice that allows them to market stories centered on the perspectives and experiences of others for their own gain.[36] Furthermore, "the ability to masquerade as others" whether online or via some other medium, can "perpetuate stereotypes" when actors pseudonymously perform in line with harmful portrayals while legitimating such portrayals by presenting themselves as members of the category portrayed.[37]

On the other hand, actors cast *others* as character-types, actively anonymizing them while establishing meaningful boundaries between groups of people as they define their situations. For example, Iddo Tavory shows how non-Jews typify religious Jews during everyday interactions, and occasionally while making anti-Semitic remarks, due to the yarmulkes and other signs that religious Jews wear on the body. Such items, which are routinely taken for granted and disattended by the individuals who wear them, become highly marked indicators of "ethno-religious belonging" and create meaningful boundaries in socially situated interactions. As people perceive the yarmulke, "the wearer is re-constituted as a 'Jew,'" even when the wearer is not consciously focused on his or her Jewishness.[38] Outside typifiers act toward the typified Jew in various ways (benignly and hostilely) that make the Jewish type meaningful and relevant in the encounter. As Tavory wore a yarmulke during the course of his ethnographic research in a Hassidic community, he "became both visible and invisible," marked as a religious Jew yet typed as one too.[39] Such a process illustrates how, from an outside perspective, others see religious signs (yarmulkes) and not personal identities, actively typifying the observant

Jews they come across. Echoing Du Bois's theory of double consciousness and the veil, Tavory argues that these typifying acts impacted the identity and self-consciousness of those who were typified, in this case bringing "the marginal consciousness of Jewishness" to life in the midst of social interaction.[40]

Typifying others simultaneously involves self-typification.[41] As one lumps others into a group or category, one also situates oneself as member of an alternative group or category, separating *other* from *self* and *them* from *us*, establishing the social anonymity of both camps in relation to one another.[42] Thus, antithetical and interdependent character-types come to life in our performances and interactions, and in the stories we tell, forming "relationship schemas" that we "use . . . to enact the obligations of solidarity"[43] while simultaneously expressing divisions and contentions between typified groups in the world. Such interrelational typifications can involve a basic designation of complementary duties (as in Schutz's example of the passenger and the engineer). However, other-/self-typifications are also commonly structured according to morally and politically charged binary codes, such as the antitheses of weak and powerful, subservient and dominant, barbarous and civilized, polluted and pure, dangerous and safe, or sick and healthy, as well as corresponding emotion codes that usually revolve around feelings of fear and trust, contempt and pride, or hatred and love. In such cases, acts of other-/self-typification structure and express social relations of power, inequality, conflict, and contention. In many cases, actors degrade or dehumanize others as they typify and anonymize them,[44] justifying certain feelings and actions toward those others that they would deem morally reprehensible if perpetrated by others against members of their own group. As they vilify others with their acts of typification, they sanctify themselves (or, in some cases, they may sanctify others as they vilify themselves) while defining and justifying their motives and actions.

The famous Stanford Prison experiment, conducted by Philip Zimbardo and his team, demonstrates how such other-/self-typifications can come to life in situated social interactions.[45] In this experiment, researchers divided the subjects (male college students) into two groups—guards and prisoners—and constructed a mock prison in the basement of the Stanford University Psychology Department in which these participants were placed to play their assigned roles. Guard-participants were given power and authority. They were "dressed in identical uniforms" and "all wore . . . silver-reflecting sun-glasses [that] prevented anyone from seeing their eyes or reading their emotions," which "helped to further promote their anonymity."[46] Meanwhile, prisoner-participants were removed

from their homes by police, stripped of their personal belongings, and assigned a generic uniform and an impersonal prison number that replaced
their personal names. Each was also made to wear a "stocking cap on the
head [as] a substitute for having the prisoner's hair shaved off," which
was "designed in part to minimize each human being's individuality."[47]
The prisoners were also frequently blindfolded. As the regular blocking
of eye contact (via sunglasses and blindfolds) between guards and prisoners signified, "strict impersonality was the rule" in this experimental
drama.[48] The guards quickly committed themselves to controlling the
prisoners. They justified their oppressive actions under the experimental
frame of law and order, and the most dominant among them even became
rather sadistic—"extremely hostile, arbitrary, inventive in their forms of
degradation and humiliation, and appeared to thoroughly enjoy the power
they wielded when they put on the guard uniform and stepped out into
the yard, big stick in hand."[49] In contradistinction, and in direct response
to the depersonalization and degradation imposed by the experimenters
and their guards, the prisoners were forced to act *as prisoners*, whether
through deference or resistance to authority, and ultimately to fear and
obey the guards. In this case, the participants were made to be anonymous
character-types in a social drama, one that brought culturally coded distinctions and power dynamics to life.

Historically, powerful actors have created and imposed other-/self-
typification schemes to justify violent and oppressive actions while
anonymizing the parties involved. For example, as Europeans typified
non-European others throughout history, Edward W. Said shows, they
simultaneously typified themselves, establishing a rationale for exclusion
and colonial exploitation.[50] Thus, "the Orient is an idea" that Europeans
produced to construct "the idea of Europe" in contrast, anonymizing millions with broad categorical covers and "reiterating European superiority over Oriental backwardness" in the process.[51] Powerful agents have
used more particular variations of this broad and evolving typification
scheme to anonymize enemies in warfare, cast them as evil or inhuman,
and to thereby justify violence against them. Consider the blanket use of
the acronym "VC," or the related slang term "Charlie," to designate Vietnamese people as anonymous enemy-communists during the American
war in Vietnam,[52] along with the racist term "gook"[53] used in reference to
anyone of Asian appearance. As Vietnam War veteran and conscientious
objector Edward R. Sowders testified to a congressional panel on May 24,
1973, "the Vietnamese were . . . all considered less-than-humans, inferiors.
We called them 'gooks,' 'slopes.' Their lives weren't worth anything to us
because we'd been taught to believe that they were all fanatical and that

they were all VC or VC sympathizers, even the children."[54] By typifying any and all Vietnamese people as "VC" and "gooks," American military personnel coded millions of individuals as anonymous manifestations of a homogeneous, uncivilized, and evil enemy force. They simultaneously established themselves as the antithetical heroic and good counterforce. By virtue of the racialization of the contrast, such a typification scheme also excluded Vietnamese Americans, and Asian Americans more generally, from the category of "American" underlying the moral of the war. In comments that illustrate how such a typification of the enemy-other rendered all who were lumped into that category morally legitimate targets of violence, General William Westmoreland, commander of the US armed forces in Vietnam from 1964 to 1968, stated, "The Oriental doesn't put the same high price on life as does the Westerner. . . . Life is cheap in the Orient. . . . Life is not important."[55] Such acts of typification, of other and of self, thereby framed the drama of war and justified acts of violence against anonymized people in the name of righteousness, freedom, and "life" itself.

More recently, US and other "Western" forces have typified and anonymized Arabs and Muslims as evil menacing terrorists, thus coding themselves enlightened, civil, and free in contrast.[56] Such cultural codes are directly evident in the titles given to international campaigns of violence such as the "War on Terror" and "Operation Enduring Freedom" (names given to the US-led military assaults in the Middle East in response to the attacks of September 11, 2001), both of which provide interpretative frameworks that prompt participants and observers to define the anonymous character-types engaged in conflict and to understand their actions. Those who bring military violence are civilized and valiant freedom fighters called to duty against savage terrorists.[57] The "fundamental brutality" ascribed to "the opponent" complements and reinforces "a heroic or patriotic mythology" that frames the image and actions of one's own team.[58] Such a typification and anonymization of the enemy as terrorist is made visible in widely circulated photos of men deemed terrorists who have been imprisoned at Guantanamo Bay, Cuba, and made to wear bright orange uniforms and caps, signifying both extreme danger (in color) and criminality. However, the typification and anonymization of this enemy-other is perhaps most visibly blatant in the widely circulated images of hooded detainees being tortured by US military personnel at the Abu Ghraib prison in Iraq (fig. 14). Faces covered, stripped of clothing, and totally depersonalized, they are rendered generic and anonymous in acts of brutal humiliation.[59] Notably, such codes and categories are often contested by the parties to conflict who compete "over the

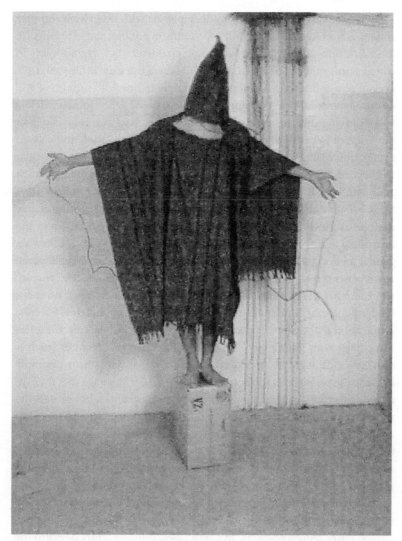

FIGURE 14. Hooded and tortured prisoner at the Abu Ghraib prison in Iraq. Photo taken November 4, 2003. From Wikimedia Commons (https://commons.wikimedia .org/wiki/File:AbuGhraibAbuse-standing-on-box.jpg). Image in the public domain.

legitimacy of violent acts."[60] From the perspective of many who live in Middle Eastern or Southeast Asian countries, anonymous Westerners are deemed the "terrorists." As with the dynamics of conflict in general, the moral quality of the character-types corresponds to the standpoint of those performing the typifications. Consequently, typification schemes often express various positions within relations of power.

While all acts of typification reduce people with otherwise complex and multifaceted personal identities to uniform profiles, and many involve the ascription of invented or fabricated characteristics, certain cases in which actors misrecognize and *mistypify* others can expose how multiple axes of power intersect to anonymize people in line with dominant and discriminatory cultural assumptions.[61] For example, when someone refers to a child's mother as her "nanny" because her raced skin tone is darker than that of her child's, the ascription of a gendered, raced, and classed occupational label obscures both her personal identity and her particular connection to that child. Deeply entrenched cultural judgments associated with race and gender, along with normative beliefs about the ways these identity attributes intersect with the work of child rearing, guide the mis-ascription of the "nanny" label and the anonymization of the individual in this hypothetical (though not uncommon) case. Likewise, gender and occupational status are intertwined in acts of mistypification when patients refer to female doctors as "nurse" or male nurses as "doctor," an experience that various healthcare workers commonly share on social media platforms. Illustrating another form of anonymization via mistypification that operates by an intersectional logic, when an actor refers to a citizen as an "immigrant" based on perceived ethnic features (such as skin tone, clothing style, or accent), visible religious symbolism, or simply because the typified person is speaking a particular language that the typifier deems foreign, the ascription of the "immigrant" label reveals the ways that ethnicity, religion, and linguistic proficiency can intersect with normative modes of distinguishing between citizen-types and foreigner-types to establish social frameworks of inclusion and exclusion. When actors typify others in such ways, they anonymize them while reinforcing powerful cultural visions of national purity and fears of foreign pollution.

Actors who are typed and anonymized by others might performatively embrace and conform, refuse and resist, or otherwise adapt to their categorical cover representations. In some cases, typified actors perform the character-type, fulfilling the expectations of their designated role and maintaining a functional (and sometimes protective) degree of personal obscurity.[62] In other cases, they challenge the social position assigned to their ascribed character-type, but in the process they reclaim and perform the very types and categories that render them anonymous. When an actor works to publicly protest the unjust treatment of a particular class or categorized group of people, for example, "one is acting more as a member of a category than as an individual."[63] Measures designed to address historical wrongs by mandating the inclusion of previously excluded groups, such as policies widely known as affirmative action, indeed require typification to boost categorical representation. In these cases, the typifications imposed by others are claimed and often redefined by the typified actors for various reasons. Yet, in other cases, actors may actively defy the classificatory logics of types and categories.[64] In such cases, noncompliance with a normative typification scheme can be deeply rebellious, but it is also often marked as dangerous and pathological by those adhering to the dominant social norms of types and categories.

## Anonymous Others in Situated Encounters

I will now address several cases to illuminate the ways that actors use categorical covers to typify and anonymize people in the midst of different situated encounters, experiences, and interactive scenarios. In the process, I explore what the anonymity of types and categories tells us about common dynamics of power and the connection between interpersonal relations and broadly relevant cultural structures of classification.

### THE ANONYMITY OF CLASS AND OCCUPATION

In 1946 the photographer Walker Evans published a series of photographs in *Fortune* magazine. The subjects were all unidentified people passing by the same intersection on a Saturday afternoon in downtown Detroit, Michigan. These people were all typed and framed under the title of the spread, *Labor Anonymous*, to be experienced by reader-viewers as individuations of a national and economic class—"the American worker."[65] With the exception of one woman who is accompanying a man, all of the subjects in the eleven published photos are men, and only one of those men appears to be Black, signifying the gendered and raced character of the American working class as imagined by those who produced this piece.[66] The people featured in this series of photos were certainly not anonymous to their families, friends, colleagues, and local communities. However, each is anonymous to the general viewer, who is prompted to ponder them as manifestations of a class type. From this outside perspective, while we might find their particular features interesting, each is only generically present in the display and might as well be any other person of the same demographic. Each individual becomes an expression of "labor anonymous" because of the way Evans and *Fortune* present them to a community of viewers. They are not engaged in anonymous acts. Rather, they are typified and defined by the photographer, publisher, and viewers, who anonymize them in the process of *doing* art and media.

As Evans worked to present images of unsuspecting strangers as individuations of American labor, his status as foreigner to both class and local community certainly shaped his perspective. Evans came from an upper-middle-class Protestant and "white-collar" background,[67] a class outsider looking at his subjects as anonymous manifestations of a group that was strange to him, and *Fortune* indeed catered to a similar professional class of readers. This social distance, manifest in the act of standing on an unfamiliar street corner covertly snapping images of strangers as they went about their local business, is key to the reader's frame of reference and their ability to experience the individuals displayed as a class type. In this sense, Evans's photo spread calls our attention to the more general and common experience of encountering and engaging strangers, whether via print or digital photographs, in film or video, or in person. In such cases, deep cultural norms and situational frames commonly call our attention to signifiers of class, occupation, race, gender, and other categorical standpoints, prompting us to see people as anonymous manifestations of social types. While such categorical anonymity emerges in various situated and mediated social encounters, it also takes form according to deeply rooted cultural norms of classification that structure the distinctions we make and the meanings they carry.

In addition to the more general category of class, we can also consider how typification according to profession or occupation obscures the personal identities of individuals working various jobs, leading others to see them as janitors, nannies, retail clerks, doctors, or police officers, for example, rather than particular people. We commonly make assumptions about individuals based on their presentation of occupational role or professional standing, whatever their particular abilities may be and regardless of their personal identities (which allows occupations and professions to make great covers for spies, thieves, and con artists). When actors typify individuals with an occupational category, they hold them accountable to both the functional responsibilities and social status associated with that position.[68] In this sense, Schutz reflected, "I am always expecting others to behave in a definite way, whether it be postal employees, someone I am paying, or the police . . . , merely as anonymous entities defined exhaustively by their functions."[69] Thus, "the particular individuals who are involved with the mail are and remain almost entirely anonymous. Their identities are irrelevant to the act of mailing a letter."[70] In a similar vein, some otherwise famous and personally celebrated musicians can go incognito and remain unrecognized when they perform in quotidian spaces like urban metro stations precisely because they are seen by most via the label and status of street buskers.[71] Likewise, when we refer to someone as "the maid" or "housekeeper," we obscure personal identity with a classed and gendered label and act toward that person according to the power relations such a categorization entails. Alternatively, when we refer to someone as "the manager," the categorical cover grants them status and authority in the situation, regardless of one's personal identity or particular abilities. Such a cover granted by a position of high status is depicted in the Old Testament book of Genesis, when Joseph's ten brothers traveled to Egypt to buy grain. Upon their arrival, they failed to recognize their brother, who "was the governor of the land." They saw him not as Joseph, but as "the man who is lord over the land."[72]

Consider also the synecdochic character of labels such as "blue collar" (referring to manual laborers) and "white collar" (referring to professional or managerial staff), or the derivative label "pink collar" (which borrows the established synecdochic framework to reference those who work jobs traditionally filled by women). The material symbolism of these labels, which refer to conventional characteristics of dress or normative class and occupational "uniforms" (or in the case of the "pink collar" label, a sex/gender color code) serves as a mechanism of typification that allows various otherwise different persons to be reduced to generic types.[73] The same process of symbolic typification and anonymization occurs when we refer to corporate executives as "suits," farmworkers or rural laborers as "rednecks," or bureaucrats as "paper pushers." With regard to "cops," a term that evolved from the verb "to cop," which in the eighteenth century commonly meant "to seize, to catch, capture or arrest as a prisoner,"[74] various individuals are often anonymized behind their general status and authority in relation to "civilians." Their occupational typification is also facilitated by the symbolism of their uniforms. As public servants, police officers are generally supposed to be personally identifiable, yet others frequently typify them during the course of their interactions. However, when cops in uniform evade personal identification, as was the case when some officers covered their badge numbers with black bands while working to police protests against the 2020 murder of George Floyd by police officer Derek Chauvin,[75] or when activists use the acronym "ACAB" (which stands for "all cops are bastards") on their protest signs, they reinforce the occupational cover and anonymity that shields individual police officers, freeing each individual cop to act, and to be seen, as any or all cops. Laws requiring police officers to personally identify themselves to civilians, such as New York City's 2018 Right to Know Act, are intended to undo this anonymity of the type.[76]

In addition to the typification and anonymization of people based on categories of work and occupation, the status of homelessness, especially with regard to those who reside or dwell in public places, serves as a categorical cover with which various individuals are typified and anonymized as members of a social underclass. Actors commonly use a normative set of signifiers to define people as "the homeless," including unclean and un-groomed bodies, the wearing of unseasonably warm clothing or excessive layers, the carrying of a large quantity of personal belongings, sitting or sleeping on a public walkway, or carrying a sign and asking for money.[77] Often lumped together, marked and visible yet undifferentiated and de-personalized in public spaces, those typed as the homeless are simulta-neously rendered outside the boundaries of civil society, both present and coded as sick (physically or mentally), dangerous, and unlawful.[78] In this regard, the discourse of the "homeless problem," while often used by well-intentioned social actors, reinforces the typification and anonymization of an otherwise diverse lot of people who lack an officially recognized place of residence.[79] Somewhat ironically, while commenters frequently ex-plain homelessness as a problem that stems from personal faults, personal identities are simultaneously obscured by the social type.[80] Furthermore, homeless people also typify the homeless, either to distance themselves from the stigmatized group or to embrace their membership in the home-less category and distance themselves from the normalized population of domiciled people.[81] In all of these cases such acts of typification obscure personal identities with categorical covers.

## ANONYMOUS SEX

Sexual encounters can be impersonal and anonymous, involving the typi-fication of the interactants. In such cases, the performance and experience of a sexual type or generic role obscures the personal identities of the participants and renders them irrelevant to the interaction (in contrast to cases in which the personal identities of the partners are fundamental to their sexual exchange). In fact, anonymity and typification can even contribute to the sexual intensity of the experience, enhancing the allure of the other and of the situation itself.[82]

Anonymous sexual interactions occur between relative strangers in public parks, public restrooms,[83] pornographic movie theaters, bath-houses, and clubs, as well as at group sex parties, where the number of participants establishes their relative anonymity during sexual activity. In each case, participants engage with one another because of their generic types. Bodies and actions are foregrounded while the personal aspects of identity are irrelevant.[84] Today, such impersonal sexual encounters are facilitated by websites and smartphone apps that allow participants to communicate and locate one another. However, an archetypical structural expression of the anonymous sexual encounter that predates the internet is the "glory hole"—a hole cut through the wall that partitions stalls in a public restroom.[85] The glory hole allows participants to engage in anonymous sexual contact (with the penis of one participant inserted through the hole) or to anonymously observe one another. In its basic structure, the glory hole expresses an anonymity of typification. It is not the person in which the fellator is interested, but the penis, and participants are reduced to fellator and fellatee. Likewise, it is not the personal identity of the masturbator that attracts the voyeur, but the act of masturbation, and participants are reduced to voyeur and exhibitionist. In effect, the hole reduces the encounter to its basic impersonal elements (penis and mouth, or eye and act of masturbation) while the surrounding wall blocks out everything else. It is an archetypical structural expression of the information control at the heart of sexual typification and anonymity.

We can also consider various types of sex work.[86] While some sex workers—including pornography actors, erotic dancers, peep show performers, phone sex operators of the late twentieth century, web cam workers of the twenty-first century, and prostitutes and escorts of various stripes—work without concealing their personal identities, many work anonymously and many others use professional pseudonyms. The act of concealing personal identity expresses something of the deep normative stigma that characterizes the sex industry, and those who participate in it, whether the sex work involved is legal or not. When participants obscure their personal identities, they separate their sexual actions from their personal relationships and histories, which serves a protective function in many cases but can also facilitate exploitation and victimization in others. However, participants in many commercialized sexual encounters are often further anonymized via their typification in the situation. In general, the commodification of bodies and sexual activities, which are performed and consumed, sold and bought, depersonalizes the product and the consumption, reinforcing the fact that personal identities are insignificant. Thus, pornography is most commonly a mutually anonymous, or an anonymous-to-pseudonymous, encounter. Consumers usually remain anonymous, confined to private spaces while consuming the bodies and actions of characters who either use stage names or who are simply unnamed, viewed solely for their performed character-type.

Likewise, in its most basic form, prostitution is an exchange relationship first and a sexual relationship second. Whereas many sexual relationships are characterized by a high degree of personal intimacy and are generally limited to the exclusive involvement of two particular people, exchange in many cases of sex work occurs between professionals (who often use occupational pseudonyms and are most generally referred to as "prostitutes," or with some synonymous slang term or euphemism) and clients (who often obscure their personal identities and are most generically referred to as "johns"). In the most formal sense, it is typically not the person that the client buys, but the sex act itself (or temporary access to another's body). Conversely, it is not the person that the sex worker pursues, but the client (or possession of the impersonal money). Consequently, each typifies and anonymizes the other to the degree that it is primarily the objectified representation of the other that comes into play during the association, making it a "striking instance of mutual degradation to a mere means." In this sense, the typification and anonymization of the interactants facilitates the temporally bounded and focally bracketed character of the situation, which is "fleetingly intensified and just as fleetingly extinguished,"[87] allowing both parties to focus on their primary objective while bracketing out the many aspects of their lives linked to their personal identities. Expressing the significance of the boundary that separates commodified sexual encounters from personal lives, one anonymous sex worker reported that she never works close to where she lives, never too close to personal acquaintances and family, "because," in her words, "I never want *anyone* to find out what I do."[88] Likewise, a client reports, "*Nobody* knows I do this. *Nobody* knows."[89] In these statements, the words "anyone" and "nobody," seemingly all-encompassing terms, actually exclude those with whom these individuals engage in commercial sexual relationships (those who very clearly know what they do) and thus their comments express the segmentation of identity at the heart of anonymous activity.

However, within the general framework of these formal characteristics, particular interactions between sex workers and their clients are more complex and situationally variable. They involve different concerns and objectives and, consequently, different performances of anonymity and pseudonymity that shape the character and mark the boundaries of the commodified sex act. In many cases, these bounded encounters and relationships involve a situated intimacy, performed by the sex worker and experienced by the client.[90] Furthermore, when prostitutes and clients have "regular" interactions, otherwise bounded encounters become bounded relationships with their own histories and particular interactive routines.[91] While situated intimacy and repeated meetings might undermine the strong sense of anonymity experienced in more fleeting encounters, such commodified sexual relationships often take on more of a pseudonymous character. Despite the fact that feelings of intimacy may grow for clients in such situations[92] and that "commercial sexual relationships can mirror . . .

'ordinary' relationships" in many ways,[93] they are often still bounded and separated from the personal lives of both participants. Even when personal names are known or personal homes are used as meeting places, an interactive typification continues to define the roles of both parties (in terms of who they are to one another *and* what they can and cannot do in one another's lives), which segments the commercial relationship from their respective personal relationships (such as with spouses or long-term partners). In other words, this element of intimacy does not necessarily negate typification—it simply changes the character of the performance.

The connection between typification and intimacy is illustrated by the phenomenon of the "girlfriend experience," a particular form of commercialized sexual encounter analyzed by Elizabeth Bernstein, which is marketed and performed by sex workers and preferred by many clients.[94] The girlfriend experience promises physical and emotional intimacy "in denaturalized and explicitly commodified form."[95] Such an encounter is performed so that it seemingly transcends the impersonal character of more traditional forms of commercialized sex, but it nevertheless remains strongly typified *as* the "girlfriend experience" (an interaction in which the sex worker is clearly and necessarily distinguished from an actual girlfriend in the view of both parties). In other words, the "girlfriend experience" is a categorical cover that frames the interaction as personal/intimate/ authentic yet can also obscure and bracket out the personal identities and personal relationships of the interactants in the scene. The pseudonymous character-types—"girlfriend" and "boyfriend"—are vital to the meaning of the distinctive experience *and* to maintaining strong "barriers between 'real life' and the commodified encounter."[96] In a similar sense, sexualized food servers in "breastaurants," usually "attractive young women who are dressed in revealing, sexually provocative costumes," perform their food service duties while "offering customers vicarious sexual entertainment and *simulated intimacy*."[97] Such "simulated intimacy" is performance work that involves "aesthetic labor and erotic capital" as the worker is reduced to a typified being—"the embodied brand of the breastaurant"[98]—in her commercial interactions and is only hired and tipped to be that type.

In addition to the ways that interactive typification anonymizes or pseudonymizes the participants in commercial sexual encounters, various moral crusaders—including religious authorities, politicians, state agents, and others—have historically typified sex workers and their clients in different ways. Many have defined the anonymous prostitute, for example, as dirty, diseased, immoral, and threatening to family and civil society.[99] In the late twentieth century, a sex workers' rights movement began to challenge this moralizing typification scheme, advancing a labor-oriented framework to advocate for the rights of sex workers to consensual, safe, and legally protected sex commerce.[100] Around the same time, some began to see sex workers as victims while defining clients as lewd, immoral, and threatening actors, as well as, in some cases, perpetrators of sexual violence.[101] Shifting over time, such broad discursive frameworks serve to typify and anonymize the participants to the sexual exchange, defining them as morally coded character-types regardless of their personal identities while often reinforcing the shame associated with sexual commerce.[102] Authorities seek to personalize such shame when they threaten to publicize the names of men who have been caught with a sex worker, thereby threatening the anonymity of the client in order to deter the act of prostitution.[103]

### RACIAL TYPIFICATION, LAW ENFORCEMENT, AND POLICE VIOLENCE

In a racialized society like the United States, actors typify and anonymize others by obscuring their personal identities behind racial categories. Such acts of typification rely on norms of "racial signification" by which actors classify people according to the ways they perceive and demarcate "different types of human bodies," using historically rooted processes of racialization to make assumptions about individuals and define distinctions between those who they assign to different racial groups.[104] However, beyond a mere classificatory measure, this process of racial typification often involves the attribution of deep-seated racial character codes that bring structured inequalities to life in situated interactions and events.[105] While the ascription of a typified racial character is indeed a social accomplishment, this process creates and perpetuates "the notion that members of different 'races' *have* essentially different natures, which explain their very unequal positions in our society."[106] Moreover, because race is such a pervasive mode of classifying and defining people, "persons involved in virtually any action may be held accountable for their performance of that action as members of their race category," and "engaging in action" means doing so "at the risk of race assessment."[107] As "race becomes . . . a way of comprehending, explaining, and acting in the world,"[108] the nuances and particularities of personal character and personal identity are obscured behind racial types and categories in the process.

People are variously subjected to coded racial typifications, and thus anonymized and defined as different racial character-types, depending on the category to which they are assigned in time and place. Bringing the ideas of Alfred Schutz and Maurice Natanson to bear on the critical work of Frantz Fanon, the philosopher Lewis R. Gordon has argued that racism imposes "peculiar forms of anonymity" on "black bodies," a phenomenon that takes form "in an antiblack world." This is, according to Gordon, a "perverted" and "racially relative form of anonymity" in which "the black's individual life ceases to function as an object of epistemological, aesthetic, or moral concern."[109] Notice Gordon's use of the phrase "the black," which stresses objectification, genericity, and typification.[110] In addition to being stripped of individuality, "the black" in the racist world, Gordon argues, "*is* crime and licentious sexuality" along with other manifestations of threat, pollution, and evil, as well as "inadequacy, failure, perversion, pathology, weakness, irrationality, and a host of deficiencies."[111] Thus, for Gordon, the moral coding at the core of racism defines the Black experience of anonymity. Like the unnamed narrator and protagonist of Ralph Ellison's *Invisible Man*,[112] "to be seen in a racist way is an ironic way of *not being seen* though *being seen*."[113] In other words, Black personhood and even individual Black consciousness is rendered invisible and only the racist characterization of *blackness as a type* remains, which is, in the words of Fanon, "*fixed*" by the "white gaze" that sees only a "type" and "species" rather than a person.[114]

Given the normative character of race and racism in the United States and other societies, a darker skin color, as W. E. B. Du Bois recognized, is symbolically linked to these moral and political qualities regardless of the personal identities of those deemed "black." Lighter or "white" skin is typified in contrast, establishing goodness and superiority through a cultural and political antithesis, regardless of the personal identities of those deemed "white." Whatever the racial category used to classify any individual, none are anonymous to their families, friends, or any other intimate acquaintance. However, given the durable and pervasive character of racial typification, the anonymization of people in many public encounters and other situated interactions is often "color-coded" according to this dominant scheme, as Elijah Anderson has observed. As people perceive strangers, "white skin denotes civility, law-abidingness, and trustworthiness, while black skin is strongly associated with poverty, crime, incivility, and distrust."[115] Thus, racial typification, with its concomitant ascription of racial character-types, usually anonymizes individuals in ways that express the entrenched power dynamics of racism. Actors bring these racial character-types to life through acts of other- and self-typification in particular situations, which are often rooted in, and structured by, durable institutions.

With regard to law enforcement, racial typification often shapes the practices of police agencies in the field—from common surveillance to the use of lethal force. In 1999 the American Civil Liberties Union released a groundbreaking report titled "Driving While Black," which detailed several cases and presented newly compiled data on race and policing that was gathered over the course of three lawsuits.[116] These testimonial and statistical data revealed clear patterns of racial profiling in which Black and Latinx drivers were targeted for stop, search, and arrest in numbers that were quite disproportionate to general population and road-use demographics, and also radically disproportionate to frequencies of criminal activity, all of which showed these police practices to be "based on race, not results."[117] Moreover, the evidence for racial profiling also reveals that white drivers are disproportionately seen as law-abiders, and, furthermore, police agents often perform racist acts of typification to patrol and guard the geographic boundaries of racial segregation. For example, when a Black state politician was pulled over while driving through a majority-white area, police agents asked him if he knew where he was. When one Black pastor was approached by police, they asked her if she knew anyone in the area, and when a Black reporter was pulled over in a predominantly white neighborhood, police agents asked him: "Are you lost?"[118] In such cases, personal identities and other defining characteristics are obscured behind the categorical cover of blackness, which is marked and typed as threatening and out of place in contrast to whiteness.

Consider also New York City's controversial "stop-and-frisk" policy, which refers to the police practice of stopping, searching, and sometimes using force against civilians. This practice is disproportionately used to police people of color and, despite recent decreases in overall frequency, "black and Latino people have continued to be overwhelmingly the targets of stop-and-frisk activity."[119] Notably, the most commonly reported justifications for stops in recent years have been that the targeted civilian "fits a relevant description" or "matches a specific suspect description," and most other reported justifications are also based on police agents' perceptions of suspicious activity on the part of the targeted civilian.[120] Thus, most of the time, such police interventions occur regardless of whether or not the targeted person actually committed a crime. Whether on a highway or a neighborhood sidewalk, officers commonly use "pretext stops" (stops under the pretext that the officer has observed or reasonably suspects some criminal activity) to justify further intervention (search and/or the use of force) with the hope of actually revealing evidence of a crime.[121] However, as the data show, race becomes a significant prompt to suspicion—a signifier of potential criminality and thus the de facto pretext in the situation. Such practices of racial typification, despite being done under the guise of legitimate law enforcement concerns, reveal that darker skin color serves as "a proxy of criminality"[122] in particular situations and on a collective scale.

As these cases show, the mental conflation of people of color with the category of *criminal* and the cultural code of *guilt*, along with the tacit conflation of white people with the category of *lawful* and the cultural code of *innocence*, is evident in the ways that police agents surveil citizens, perform their interventions, exercise state authority over bodies and movements, and sometimes apply force and perpetrate violence.[123] During the dramatic realization of these judgments and actions, such acts of typification render many targets of police intervention anonymous behind a systematized dynamic that downplays their personal characteristics and particular circumstances while accentuating a generic racialized justification scheme. In other words, those who become the objects of police intervention and violence are often typed and anonymized as the act unfolds, even though their personal identities will be known, and sometimes they become quite well-known, as a consequence of that intervention and violence.

Consider the case of Amadou Diallo, the Black immigrant from Guinea who was killed by police officers in the Bronx in 1999 after, they claimed, they mistook his wallet for a gun. Before the officers shot and killed Diallo, they profiled him, consistent with New York Police Department stop-and-frisk practices of the time, as a suspicious character for standing outside late at night, in front of his apartment in a poor Black neighborhood. Their assessment expresses an entrenched racial typification scheme with which particular signifiers attached to bodies and spaces communicate meaning according to underlying racist codes. This typification scheme, which existed before those four police officers approached Diallo that night, likely shaped their preliminary interpretation of his character, actions, and motives. It is very difficult to imagine a similar situation occurring with a white man standing in front of his expensive residence in an affluent neighborhood on New York's Upper West Side. Incidents that follow this pattern cannot simply be explained as information-processing errors stemming from the stress of the situation, as Malcolm Gladwell suggests. They are not simply "mind-reading failures" or cases of "temporary autism."[124] Rather, police agents are typifying and anonymizing the subjects they approach in line with a culturally coded racial system (one that intersects with class distinctions as well). They bring racial character-types into being as they exercise state authority. In other words, high-stress confrontational circumstances do not make "wallets invariably look like guns."[125] Rather, police agents type poor Black people as suspicious criminals with guns regardless of their personal identities or characteristics and animate this definition in their encounters. As is evident in the high-profile killings of Trayvon Martin and Ahmaud Arbery, who were both typed as criminal while simply moving about in public, vigilantes use the same ascription of racial character-types to justify their interventions and, ultimately in many cases, their violent actions.

While there are many other cases that we might consider to illustrate the operation of racial typification in police work, I discuss the following case because of the way it shows the complementary character of the racial typification structure as it unfolded in a dynamic social situation. On June 5, 2015, police officers in McKinney, Texas, responded to a call about a high school pool party that had grown large and boisterous. The following day, video of the incident appeared online and quickly went viral.[126] The video showed multiple officers on the scene while an irate police corporal Eric Casebolt (who is white) aggressively chased Black teenagers in bathing suits and ordered them to sit on the ground, handcuffing some before wrestling a fifteen-year-old girl, Dajerria Becton, to the ground, pinning her down with both of his knees, and eventually handcuffing her as she screamed for her mother and cried.[127] During the incident, Casebolt pulled his gun to threaten two Black male teenagers who were attempting to help Becton. About two and a half minutes later, two other officers (both white) return to the frame of the video escorting a handcuffed Black teen, one of the two Casebolt threatened, who now appears to be bleeding from the mouth, and sit him on the ground.

The racial dynamic in this video is evident as white police officers target and apprehend children of color. However, an additional key to understanding this event as an instance of racial typification lies beyond the frame and behind the production of the video itself. Brandon Brooks, the fifteen-year-old partygoer who was able to stand unscathed amid the chaos of the scene and shoot the seven-minute video, is white. He would later explain to a reporter, "Everyone who was getting put on the ground was black, Mexican, Arabic. . . . [The cop] didn't even look at me. It was kind of like I was invisible."[128] Apparently, he was never ordered to the ground, never questioned, and never even acknowledged by the police officers all around him. In other words, the typification of this white teenager, from the perspective of police agents, rendered him an anonymous, innocent, lawful, and harmless bystander, and therefore unmarked to the discriminating eye of law enforcement.[129] The signification power of his white skin typed him as a sociomental antithesis to the darker-skinned children who, in the same space, were defined and targeted as threatening and criminal. In other words, the racial typification scheme at work during this incident anonymized all of the children in the situation, but in different ways according to different character-types. In all cases, their

particular identities, personal characteristics, and degree of personal cul-
pability were irrelevant to police actions. While this anonymizing force
classified darker-skinned children as criminal problems, it simultaneously
rendered the lighter-skinned amateur videographer outside of the problem, even outside of the scene, and left him free to look back in.[130] Acting
in their official capacity on behalf of the state, police agents performed the
typification of blackness and whiteness via their engagement with young
civilians on the scene.

Racial typification also shapes the meanings that members of the public
at large attribute to visible cases of police violence, and thus the debate
over the moral and political character of these violent acts. More generally,
such acts of racial typification guide the ways that actors define individual
subjects in relation to the power and authority of the state. With regard
to public interpretation of such situations, the racist perspective is often
that Black subjects, despite their innocence, perform criminality (e.g., they
"looked suspicious," appeared to be a "thug," wore a "menacing" hoodie,
or resisted police authority when they should have complied). Such vocabularies of racial typification blame Black individuals for police or vigilante actions. Instead, however, police and vigilante actors often perform
the criminality of Black people when they typify and anonymize them
according to the racial codes of the dominant order. They then use their
acts of typification to justify aggression and violence. Such a performance
of racial typification is also evident in the actions of many individuals who
threaten to call the police and report Black individuals who have broken
no laws. In such cases, along with those discussed above, criminality is
ascribed as a property of the racial type. In many cases, those who define
the Black person as a criminal character-type are also performing their
own whiteness in contrast—as pure and innocent protectors or enforcers
of the law and moral order. From this perspective, *blackness* and *whiteness*
take on meaning in performative acts of typification and anonymization in
the context of a racial hierarchy. Until we grasp how such culturally coded
racial typification schemes shape perceptions, structure accounts, and
provide for vocabularies of motive with regard to acts of police violence,
we will not fully understand the cultural and interactionist foundations
of this social problem.

There are a great many cases in which Black people have been typed as
dangerous and criminal by agents who ultimately killed them. To counter
this anonymizing racial characterization, activists have worked to call
public attention to the names and personal characteristics of those who
have been killed by police officers. For example, the campaign to publicize and oppose police violence against Black women is called "Say Her

Name" (#sayhername),[131] which is also the title of Kate Davis and David Heilbroner's 2018 HBO documentary focused on the case of Sandra Bland, an African American woman who suspiciously died in police custody in Waller County, Texas, after being pulled over for a traffic violation and detained.[132] Likewise, the chant "Say their names!" is a common refrain at protests against police brutality. Similarly, when activists produce posters and placards featuring the names and faces (either as photographs or artistic renditions) along with other personal details of individuals who have been killed by police officers, they counter the anonymizing force of racist typification that shapes the phenomenon of police violence[133] (see fig. 15). The artist Kadir Nelson used the same tactic in his cover illustration for the June 22, 2020, issue of the *New Yorker*, titled "Say Their Names," which features the faces of several contemporary victims of police violence along with renditions of several anonymous enslaved people of the past.[134] Consider also the choice of activists to lead a 2014 march protesting the police killing of Eric Garner in New York with enlarged panel photos of Garner's eyes produced by the artist JR. The eyes are the feature of the face that is most personal. As A. David Napier notes, "*Prosōpon* [the Greek word meaning both face and person] derives from the Greek *pros*, meaning 'to,' 'toward,' or 'at,' and *ōpa*, 'the face,' 'the eye.'"[135] Furthermore, eyes typically peer out from behind most veils, which is evocative of the notion of "second-sight" that Du Bois associated with the self-affirming perspective of those who are oppressed in a racial hierarchy. By calling attention to names, faces, and eyes, activists highlight the personal identities of victims who are otherwise anonymized behind a racist typification scheme.

## CISGENDER TYPIFICATION AND
### THE SEGREGATION OF PUBLIC RESTROOMS

Social theorists have long established that the characteristics of sex and gender reinforce one another to function as a system for classifying otherwise diverse individuals into polarized male and female types.[136] In the dominant cisgender frame of interpretation, female birth sex (usually defined and assigned according to genitalia) coincides with female gender attributes and feminine appearance. In contradistinction, male birth sex coincides with male gender attributes and masculine appearance.[137] Moreover, these polarized male and female categories are culturally coded and associated with distinct personality traits, tastes, preferences, emotions, and behaviors that are commonly treated as *natural* characteristics of people based on their impersonal cisgender designations.[138]

While such cisgender designations do not obscure personal identities

FIGURE 15. Activists at "a vigil in remembrance of Black women and girls killed by the police." Photo by The All-Nite Images. From Wikimedia Commons (https://commons.wikimedia.org/wiki/File:-SayHerName_(17729657368).jpg). Creative Commons Attribution 2.0 Generic license (https://creativecommons.org/licenses/by/2.0/deed.en).

in many intimate relationships, where they may be seen as partial aspects of more complex and unique persons or simply inappropriate or inapplicable to some lives, cisgender notions of "male" and "female" often serve as categorical covers that obscure personal identities in various social encounters, situated interactions, and institutional relationships.[139] In such cases, actors use culturally coded *cisgender character-types* to make assumptions about others in ways that typify and anonymize them. Thus, "regardless of how an individual personally identifies . . . , others will still interact with them based on cisnormative gender expectations."[140] At the core of this process of attributing a cisgender character-type to others (or to one's self) are deep-seated social norms that govern "what it means to *be* a male or a female,"[141] and actors often hold people accountable for performing in line with these coded prescriptions.[142] In sum, these cisgender characterizations are deeply engrained in culture, actors use them to typify and anonymize others in particular situations and interactions, and such cisgender typifications are often structured and reinforced according to institutional conventions.

On the one hand, cisgender typification involves using dominant social logics and definitions of sex to lump various individuals into the same gender.[143] In such cases, gender is assigned and assessed "in relation to normative conceptions of appropriate attitudes and activities for particular sex categories."[144] This mode of cisgender typification is quite evident in the contemporary phenomenon of "gender reveal parties," in which expectant parents, after learning the medically assigned in utero sex of a fetus, publicly announce its gender as if information about gender was available to them. At such events, parents effectively cisgender-type fetuses, associating male sex with the color blue, mustaches, bow ties, and footballs, while associating female sex with the color pink, eyelashes, hair bows, and pom-poms.[145] Such cases not only show how cisgender characteristics are generalized and impersonal, but also that they can even be *prepersonal*, imposed before birth, prior to the assignment of a name, and indeed before the acquisition of most other aspects of personal identity.

On the other hand, cisgender typification involves using gender expression to determine an individual's "correct" or "proper" biological or anatomical sex, which is often defined as an essential element of one's being. Such acts of typification involve "treating appearances (e.g., deportment, dress, and bearing) as if they were indicative of underlying states of affairs (e.g., anatomical, hormonal, and chromosomal arrangements)."[146] They involve assigning what Suzanne J. Kessler and Wendy McKenna call "cultural genitals," which are commonly "assumed to exist" by others who believe and act as if specific genitalia "should be there."[147] This mode of cisgender typification is evident in the common assumptions adults make when they perceive children with long hair to fit the sex category "girl" and children with short hair to be rightfully classified as "boys," or when people rather automatically perceive a stranger with facial hair to be male.[148]

These dual modes of cisgender typification underlie normative assumptions behind the common practice of segregating public restrooms and other spaces, such as locker rooms and saunas, along conventional lines demarcating the categories of male and female. The conventional signs on restroom doors—a human figure either in pants or a skirt, or perhaps the common male symbol ($\male$), which was originally associated with Mars, the Roman god of war, or female symbol ($\female$), which was originally associated with Venus, the goddess of beauty—are abstract signifiers of general and impersonal categories. As such, they convey information about who can rightfully walk through the door of a public restroom, sorting people into anonymous types. When actors encounter strangers in such segregated spaces, they ordinarily perceive them as anonymous men or anonymous women, depending on the room they use. For many, the room itself regularly serves as a normative frame signifying the cisgender type of its occupants regardless of their particular and personal identities.

In recent years, several US states have introduced legislation, commonly referred to as "bathroom bills," designed to legally restrict access to public restrooms and related spaces according to some notion of biological sex.[149] Perhaps the most famous of these efforts is the North Carolina Public Facilities Privacy and Securities Act (also known as House Bill 2, or HB2), which was passed by the state legislature in March 2016 and then partially repealed in 2017 after a year of national controversy with the remaining components expiring in 2020.[150] This legislation required individuals to use public restroom facilities based on the sex assignment that appears on their birth certificates, thereby prohibiting many transgender individuals from using restrooms in accordance with their gender identities.[151] Under such a framework, when individuals who were born with male genitalia and live as women (presenting with a female gender identity) enter restrooms designated for women, they risk reproach, assault, and arrest because they are legally sex-typed as men. However, when individuals who were born with female genitalia and live as men (presenting with a male gender identity) enter that same room, the same risks exist when they are gender-typed as men.[152] In all cases, people are at risk when their gender expression is determined by others to be incongruent with their sex designation, which is consistent with the reports of many trans individuals.[153] When actors (whether state agents, private security guards, or vigilantes) police bathrooms based on such determinations, they are policing normative cisgender types and categories—the expected norma-tive alignment of birth sex, physical body, gender, and sexuality.[154]

Social anxieties about restroom segregation, and the interpersonal in-terventions that result (from stares and direct questions about an occu-pant's legitimacy in a segregated space, to verbal harassment and physical assault), reveal exactly how normative acts of cisgender typification render trans people out of place in the public world. Using cisgender typification norms, some actors commonly mark transgender individuals as dishonest deviants who violate the "true" and "natural" order of types and catego-ries.[155] Such actors also define trans people as problems or contradictions that can and should be resolved by placing them into the "proper" category, thereby denying and negating their personal identities while affirming a cis-gender reality and solidifying the boundaries between mutually exclusive cisgender types.[156] The same actors also tacitly use a cisgender typifica-tion scheme to anonymize most of the other individuals they encounter in public and semi-public contexts (including trans individuals who incon-spicuously pass in accordance with their gender identities) by automati-cally designating them as unproblematic and unmarked versions of *either* maleness *or* femaleness, imposing cisgender character-types that obscure individual nuances, personal identities, and lived experiences. These un-marked others are the hardly noticed co-occupants of public restrooms and other spaces, both segregated and integrated. In other words, such a deeply rooted cisgender typification scheme, which obscures personal identities and nuances among individuals who are put into normative cis-male and cis-female categories, provides the social framework within which the per-secution of trans individuals can occur. Only by imagining that all or most people we see are anonymous cisgender types—and only by obscuring the fact of considerable variation in the composition of sex, gender, and sexual-ity in the human population—can we mark and target some as threatening anomalies in relation to the rigid boundaries of the dominant social order.

## Analytic Typifications

As social scientists and other scholars seek to explain various aspects of the world, they commonly typify and anonymize the people they study. From the organization and aggregation of large-scale survey and census data to the formulation and presentation of anonymous or pseudonymous ethnographic and psychoanalytic case studies, researchers commonly ac-centuate various impersonal variables (including class, income bracket, occupation, race, sexuality, gender, age, location, or political orientation) over personal identities. In the process, they are not simply using those variables in a descriptive sense, but constructing them—establishing or refining their meaning and significance. To this end, scholars create "models of actors [that] are not human beings living within their biographical situation" but are instead "defined by ... the social scientist,"[157] and essentially used as abstract and generalizable character sketches to explain the experiences and behaviors of certain categories of people in the world. In other words, the models that scholars use are "not peopled with human beings ... but ... with *types*."[158] In constructing these analytic types, social scientists outline a typical set of characteristics, including motives and "typical course-of-action patterns," which, they imagine, apply to all the individuals who fall into the category they have created for their purpose of study and explanation.[159] Thus, scholars treat their research subjects as typified and anonymous illustrations of more broadly relevant social phenomena in order to develop generalizable social insights and theories.

Both Max Weber and Georg Simmel, each in their own way, established typification as an analytic strategy for sociology, and more specifically for comparative social analysis. Weber argued that social scientists ought to create abstract models, or ideal types, via "the synthesis of a great many" characteristics "into a unified *analytical* construct."[160] Such ideal types then serve as analytic tools with which researchers can study, compare, and know observable cases in the world.[161] However, it was Simmel who explicitly developed the method of constructing anonymous character models, or abstract theoretical portraits of actors defined by their positions vis-à-vis others in generalized "forms of sociation." Simmel stressed that otherwise different people can be regarded as being *of the same social type* based on their commonly held position within a social "pattern of coordination and consistent interaction," regardless of any individual's idiosyncratic characteristics or personal identity.[162] Thus, "the type becomes what he is through his relations with others who assign him a particular position," and "his characteristics are seen as attributes of the social structure," not personal characteristics.[163] Both Simmel and Weber explicitly developed theories of analytic typification as methods of comparative sociology (with Weber highlighting differences as deviations from a type and Simmel highlighting typical similarities as shared formal properties across otherwise different cases).[164] However, both theorists were also articulating a more general process of abstraction, typification, and, when it comes to human subjects, anonymization that has come to underlie research practices and theory construction in the social sciences.

As Alfred Schutz argued, scholars base their analytic typifications on the more common and fundamental typifications that people tacitly use and rely on in their routine interactions and encounters. In other words, "the thought objects constructed by the social scientist . . . have to be founded upon the thought objects constructed by the common-sense thinking of [people], living their daily life within their social world." Therefore, analytic typifications are "constructs of the second degree, namely constructs of the constructs made by the actors on the social scene."[165] These "second-degree" or "second-order" analytic typifications often bring into view the more tacit and routine typifications employed by everyday actors. When they are theoretically sound, they give us insight into the ways that actors commonly typify others and themselves in their routine circumstances and situated interactions. In other words, analytic typifications "give us a purely anonymous reality through which we are able to comprehend the correspondingly anonymous 'first-order' constructs of human beings in daily life."[166] Thus, Simmel's notion of "the stranger" highlights the ways that people commonly typify others who occupy such a position of strangeness—who are "near and far *at the same time*"—in their particular contexts and situations.[167] Likewise, scholarly typifications of the working class, sex workers, blackness and whiteness, and cisgenderism and transgenderism (typifications discussed in this chapter) are analytic constructs that help us to grasp the ways that people type and anonymize others based on these categories. However, when analytic types and categories are well established, they also, in turn, become common referents and categorical designations that influence how people typify others and themselves in everyday situations and encounters.

Consider the analytic typification and anonymization of people via the categorical cover of class, for example. Theories of class illuminate the ways that actors typify others and themselves during situated encounters and interactions in various contexts, actively classifying people according to style of dress, mannerisms, tastes, speech, and more. The work of Pierre Bourdieu can in part be read as a theoretical elaboration of such class typifications.[168] However, social theorists also typify and anonymize people while defining the abstract category of class, which shapes the ways that everyday actors use class as a categorical cover that obscures personal identities. Karl Marx, the iconic father of modern class theory, thoroughly typified and anonymized people while developing his historical analysis of class conflict and critique of capitalism. While observing the rise of the modern factory system across Europe, Marx conceived of the growing and increasingly centralized and homogenized proletariat as a social force of production. Thus, Marx could conceive of the proletariat's ability to act as a class "for itself," and therefore as a collective revolutionary force, rendering particular people irrelevant to the class, the economic system, and to history.[169] Typed as representatives of an economic category and its historically situated interests, individual members were mere embodiments of an exploited and alienated social location with a shared condition and a collective revolutionary destiny. The same holds for individual members of the bourgeoisie, who were equally anonymized as an analytic type. This analytic typification scheme has continued to shape common notions of class affiliation, solidarity, and conflict into the present era, which has also structured the ways that actors typify and anonymize people in everyday life settings and encounters, as with the Walker Evans photographs previously discussed. In fact, the analytic notion of class has become so deeply engrained that actors experience class types as a fundamental part of their commonsense realities. Such analytic typifications can, and often do, affect the ways actors perceive and classify others and themselves. In sum, scholars use such analytic types to illuminate broadly relevant social patterns and characteristics that transcend the idiosyncrasies of particular individuals and cases. However, these analytic tools depersonalize and anonymize research subjects in the process, creating new frameworks that shape acts of typification in everyday life.

## Conclusion

Typification is a basic function of perception and knowledge that takes form according to deeply rooted social norms. To comprehend the world in a meaningful way, we need to organize its component parts into types and categories, employing normative structures of typification with which we recognize similarities and distinctions among things and people, along with events and experiences, as we go about our lives. In various situations, encounters, and interactions, when actors typify others and themselves, they use socially established and culturally coded character-types to obscure personal identities, biographical situations, and the nuances of people's lives. They use categorical masks to anonymize people. In such cases, even when one might be able to know or trace another individual's personal identity, the encounter or interaction is defined by a social anonymity of types and categories. We produce this dimension of anonymity in particular times and places, and experience it as characteristic of certain socially patterned relationships.

As many of the cases I discuss in this chapter show, actors often typify and anonymize others in ways that reflect and reproduce structured relations of power and inequality. There is clarity to be gained, and possibly some potential for liberation, in understanding how the anonymity of types and categories shapes our experiences and expectations of others in line with these established power dynamics. If we can comprehend how typification norms and patterns facilitate the anonymization and objectification of people in ways that perpetuate harmful or oppressive social relations, we might also develop new insights about overcoming the most detrimental dimensions of these anonymizing acts in various social contexts and situations. In other words, by unpacking how the anonymity of types and categories blinds us to otherwise important information about personal identities and lived experiences, we can potentially alter the ways that such acts of typification facilitate problematic and harmful social relationships by rendering people to be formulaic characters in the social dynamics of power, conflict, and contention.

# * 6 *

# The Social Contradictions
# of Our Hidden Identities

In the future everyone will be anonymous for fifteen minutes.

BANKSY, words printed on a television screen atop a pedestal,
*Barely Legal* exhibit, Los Angeles, 2006

When the renowned pseudonymous street artist Banksy made the comment reproduced in the epigraph above (which is an inversion of the well-known predictive quip attributed to Andy Warhol decades earlier, "In the future, everyone will be world-famous for 15 minutes"), he was calling attention to the increasingly precious yet fleeting character of anonymity as an alternative to ever more prevalent forces of surveillance and social control. In a world marked by the intrusive monitoring of personal behavior, routine self-exposure via social media, obsession with fame and celebrity, public acts of narcissism, public shaming, and conspicuous consumption, anonymity provides a powerful yet temporary and elusive counterbalance to these social forces. However, from another perspective, the rebel artist may have been cleverly referring to the fact that a well-performed hidden identity can lead to a new and valuable type of fame—that it is becoming more common for anonymous and pseudonymous actors to capture the spotlight. Banksy, like so many others, has indeed profited from his obscured personal identity—from being famously unknown. In both readings, his aphorism captures something of the contradictory character of hidden identities in the world today. Anonymity and pseudonymity are increasingly precarious and even impossible to guarantee, yet simultaneously more common. Anonymous actors are obscured and unknown, yet they can simultaneously be prominent and well-known. They hide themselves as they actively perform and engage the world around them.

Throughout this book, I have explored several ways that anonymity and pseudonymity manifest in the world, along with a great variety of cases. Despite the many significant differences among them, all of these cases show how anonymity and pseudonymity come to life as social performances that involve the use of impersonal cover representations to obscure personal identities in particular situations and relationships. When actors perform anonymity or pseudonymity, they work to define their situations and impact the world around them. As such, anonymity and pseudonymity always take form as *meaningful* acts in relation to particular audiences. These states of being are never pure or permanent; they are social accomplishments that always and only exist insofar as an audience lacks awareness of an actor's personal identity. In this final chapter, I reflect on the social significance of those situations in which actors avoid personal recognition for their actions. To this end, I briefly summarize some key contradictions inherent in anonymous and pseudonymous acts. I then ask how the *unmasking* of anonymous actors can deepen our understanding of the social character of hidden identities.

As we saw in chapter 2, the protective character of anonymity shields individuals from punitive consequences, frees people to act in ways that might otherwise be suppressed, provides for fair and nonbiased assessments, and allows for the creation of transcendent "safe" spaces where individuals can jointly explore difficult conditions and situations in their lives. As they obscure personal identities in various ways, actors bring protective circumstances and spaces to life. They use various cover representations and practice various ethics of anonymity to make the meanings of protection and to establish certain freedoms. Therefore, in its protective character, anonymity facilitates a refuge from otherwise stifling or repressive social forces. It allows people to raise issues that they would not otherwise raise. However, the protection afforded by anonymity also frees individuals to engage in morally problematic behaviors while avoiding social accountability for their actions. In some cases, this means that actors who are protected by anonymity or pseudonymity can continue to harm or victimize others while enjoying (and even exploiting) the benefits of an untarnished (or perhaps even favorable) personal reputation, one that is divorced from their anonymous acts. Furthermore, in shielding small groups of individuals from the weighty social stigmas associated with various conditions and experiences, protective anonymity can liberate people from harmful social constraints and moral judgments. However, such a protective concealment might also reinforce the marginalization, isolation, and stigma accompanying those issues and situations. As decades of various pride-oriented movements show, positive social change often requires public recognition. Thus, the protective covers of anonymity may have a latent consequence of enhancing social foundations and personal feelings of shame.

As we saw in chapter 3, the subversive character of anonymity allows actors to challenge dominant cultural, political, and moral norms in order to affect change in the world. Anonymous and pseudonymous art and literature have been, and continue to be, important means of critiquing power and expressing alternative ideas and values. The contemporary trend of wearing masks at political protests, or obscuring one's personal identity while otherwise engaged in political activity (whether acting online or in physical space), allows activists to convey rich and deeply critical meanings and sentiments, express solidarity with their fellow partisans, and perform on behalf of a cause or movement while avoiding persecution for their politics. As they obscure personal identities, subversive actors bring alternative social meanings to life. However, such masking practices can also be used to propagate morally troublesome or heinous ideologies that would otherwise wither, and to facilitate deeply controversial and problematic political actions. They can also be used to deceive or misdirect audiences. Moreover, such subversive anonymity often frames the basic democratic rights of free speech and assembly (which are foundational to our modern ideals of the public sphere) *as if* they are illegal. In some cases, activists who obscure their personal identities act as if they are personally disenfranchised and split from the public forum when they might instead act as if they are part of it and accountable to it. While an open and transparent politics defined by personal voice and accountability raises the possibility of public dialogue with fellow citizens, even around difficult and contentious issues, a masked and anonymous politics inhibits open public dialogue in various ways. Somewhat ironically, in performing a dynamic in which we need to hide our faces in order to express our political views, activists might contribute to normalizing such a repressive environment.

The anonymity afforded by social systems, as I explored in chapter 4, is a consequence of the sui generis activity of powerful collective forces. While organized social systems often allow us to transcend our previous limitations, to engage in otherwise unfeasible operations and accomplish otherwise impossible tasks, they also often obscure the personal contributions of those who bring them to life and inhibit the personal accountability of those who steer them or profit from their activities. As such actors obscure their personal identities behind the covers of impersonal institutions and social systems, they act in ways that give these institutions and systems meaning in the world. They use the covers of states, nations, and various corporations in ways that impact the lives of countless people in different ways, both positive and negative. All too often, those whose lives are impacted by powerful social systems have no recourse when they are harmed. They face an opaque and impersonal system that appears to act on its own. While they may be vital to our lives, the anonymity created by such social systems can facilitate personal opportunism and corruption at the expense of social well-being, which can foster powerful forms of alienation and apathy in the world.

The anonymity that stems from typification, the subject matter of chapter 5, is a consequence of our ability to group people into types and categories, which allows us to organize our experiences and coordinate our expectations of the people we encounter in various situations and circumstances. Typification is a basic property of human thought that allows us to comprehend the complex world in an ordered and predictable way. When we typify and anonymize others and ourselves, we do so in ways that make the meanings of relationships and justify actions. We bring patterns of discrimination to life, whether that discrimination involves relatively neutral acts of drawing boundaries that demarcate social roles and responsibilities, or morally and politically charged ways of fostering social solidarity and division. Thus, as an anonymizing force—as a social blindness to the personal identities and characteristics of those we lump together and reduce to categorical labels—typification allows us to acknowledge groups and their unique collective identities and experiences. However, it is also at the root of our most problematic forms of hate and oppression, along with routine expressions of favoritism and unequal distributions of privilege.

As we can see from each of these discussions, the general consequences of hidden identities are not so clear-cut or straightforward. They can be inherently contradictory and often vary according to one's situated assessment of the particular anonymous or pseudonymous performance at hand. By approaching anonymity and pseudonymity as social performance, we can make better sense of these contradictions and develop a more thorough understanding of any particular case we analyze. Such an approach requires us to consider anonymous acts in their social and historical contexts, and to unpack the deep cultural meanings that anonymous and pseudonymous actors create for particular audiences. Thus, this approach requires us to interpret the cover representations actors use to obscure their personal identities, along with the characters they create in their interactions with others. Only by analyzing these fundamentally social dimensions of anonymity and pseudonymity can we grasp the significance of hidden identities in the world.

## Unmasking Acts

To complement our understanding of the meanings of anonymity and pseudonymity, we can consider the performance and impact of *unmasking acts*—efforts that expose or attempt to uncover the identities of anonymous or pseudonymous actors. If anonymity involves obscuring the particular characteristics of identity and accentuating a generic cover representation, unmasking acts involve removing the generic to get to the particular and specific. They involve linking detached actions and expressions to personal identities. Such unmasking acts often reveal even more about the motives, meanings, and consequences of anonymous activity via its breach. Some unmasking acts are slow and processual, such as when police detectives work to reveal the identity of a serial killer by piecing together clues. The logic of such a processual unmasking is evident in the mid-twentieth-century game show *What's My Line?* (CBS, 1950–67), in which blindfolded panelists sought to reveal the identities of celebrity guests by asking yes-or-no questions. Others involve a more rapid, shocking, and momentous revelation, such as when a social movement or whistleblower exposes a profiteer who was hiding behind the cover of a corporation, or when those who presumed they were acting anonymously online are suddenly exposed due to a hack or via subpoena by authorities. In either case, the revelation provides us with new information and often prompts a reevaluation of the situation at hand.

Audiences are often quite eager to discover the personal identities of anonymous and pseudonymous actors, and many even enjoy the challenge of unmasking an obscured author, artist, criminal, activist, internet troll, institutional power broker, or mysterious stranger. For example, as James H. Johnson writes, "Part of the fun of carnival was therefore in guessing the identities of other maskers. If you couldn't place them or didn't known them, you could examine the small telltale signs that might reveal their status—things like the cut of the costume they wore or the quality of its cloth."[1] John Mullan notes a similar excitement on the part of those who sought to discover the personal identities of pseudonymous nineteenth-century authors.[2] In fact, the mystery of authorship often became a "topic of conversation" that could add a whole additional layer of public attention to the book.[3] Because anonymous and pseudonymous actors establish a mystery of personal identity as they perform for their audiences, they stimulate curiosity and invite speculation. Such a social tension can make revelations of personal identity particularly dramatic. In many ways, the character of anonymous performance incites its undoing.

In some cases, the unmasking of anonymous actors might expose them to potential harm, retaliation, or punishment. For example, a vengeful motive appears to underlie attempts by US president Donald Trump and his allies to unmask the anonymous whistleblower who filed a complaint about Trump's July 25, 2019, phone call with Ukrainian president Volodymyr Zelenskyy.[4] Furthermore, a punitive motive underlies many unmasking laws targeting social activists, including pro-democracy activists in Hong Kong and Antifa (anti-fascist) activists in the United States.[5] As of this writing, the Unmasking Antifa Act of 2018 has been introduced to the US Congress and is currently under review by the House Subcommittee on Crime, Terrorism, Homeland Security, and Investigations.[6] Moreover, many criminal investigations are in fact unmasking efforts, but some, like the international effort targeting illegal activity on the dark web, suitably called "Operation Onymous," are explicitly designed to personally identify actors who use anonymizing technologies to commit crimes.[7] In a similar vein, many vigilante acts of hacking and doxing (publishing the personal information of others online) are indeed malicious acts of unmasking. While working to expose personal identities, unmaskers can also attempt to undermine the legitimacy of anonymous or pseudonymous agents by showing that their personal characteristics conflict with the character they have performed, as when Mexican government officials revealed that the Zapatista leader Subcomandante Marcos was of a different social class background than the movement for which he spoke.[8] Likewise, computer scientists have recently attempted to show that the famous Q of the QAnon movement is not, in fact, a high-ranking Washington insider, but rather a fictive character performed by two rather ordinary men.[9] Such retaliatory, punitive, or discrediting motives for unmasking underscore the protective character of anonymity by openly displaying the risks associated with personal identification. Thus, unmasking agents also bring certain power dynamics to life when they work to expose actors who shield their personal identities.

In other cases, actors who previously obscured their personal identities unmask themselves to take a social stand and pave the way for others in similar situations to more openly connect their circumstances to their lives. Consider, for example, Greg D. Williams's 2013 documentary, *The Anonymous People*, in which notable individuals openly discuss their struggles with addiction and recovery, thereby shattering the protective anonymity that traditionally accompanies this social standing in an attempt to challenge the associated stigma.[10] In this vein, some argue that anonymity can interfere with recovery by steeping the process in shame when, they claim, sobriety should be a matter of personal pride. Thus, one advocate argues that unmasking herself kept her "sober and accountable" while allowing her to be "proud" of herself and "comfortable" with her recovery.[11] Such a self-driven defiance of anonymity is also evident in the case of Chanel Miller, whose book, aptly titled *Know My Name*, exposes her as the victim of a highly publicized 2015 sexual assault by Stanford University student Brock Turner. In telling her story, Miller, who was publicly known as "Emily Doe" throughout the criminal proceedings, also details her struggles with her prior anonymity, linking it to a sense of isolation, shame, and typification stemming from the assault itself. Miller opens her story by stating, "I introduce myself here, because in the story I'm about to tell, I begin with no name or identity. No character traits or behaviors assigned to me."[12] Miller contrasts her anonymity and isolation with the support she received upon publicly releasing her victim statement in her own name.[13] Such cases of self-unmasking show how anonymity might serve to obstruct valued social progress and enhance a sense of isolation or shame by separating a crucial part of one's personal experiences from the personal identity one presents to others and to the world at large.

In many ways, Miller's choice to foreground her personal identity and claim authorship with regard to her personal story, along with the title of her book, is quite similar to the "say her name" campaign discussed in chapter 5, which was organized by those calling attention "to the often invisible names and stories of Black women and girls who have been victimized by racist police violence."[14] With a similar motivation to personalize the victims of racist violence, those who designed the National Memorial for Peace and Justice in Montgomery, Alabama, combat historical anonymity by openly naming victims of lynching.[15] While some unmaskers work to name and acknowledge victims, others, including whistleblowers and documentary filmmakers, attempt to unmask actors wielding the power of (and often profiting from) large institutions, thereby working to break through the anonymity of social systems as described in chapter 4. In this vein, Michael Moore's groundbreaking 1989 film, *Roger & Me*, popularized the process of calling public attention to the personal identities of powerful corporate agents who were previously shielded by their corporate organizations. Such unmasking acts ascribe motive and responsibility to real power brokers by pulling back the figurative curtain that obscured them.

Consider also how medical workers, who were essentially anonymized by generic and impersonal protective gear (gowns, masks, face shields, and gloves) during the COVID-19 pandemic, symbolically unmasked themselves by wearing name tags and large photographs of their exposed smiling faces on their torsos. Such an unmasking act, which transforms generic representatives of a medical institution into particular people, was first conceived by artist Mary Beth Heffernan to address the same issue with regard to Ebola in West Africa.[16] These unmaskers work to personalize their interactions with their patients as they deliver care.[17] Likewise, when people from different backgrounds and traditionally divided communities come together and cooperate to achieve a common goal, the anonymity that stems from typification can dissolve as personal friendships are formed and camaraderie grows.[18]

Unmasking can also confer an additional degree of honor and prestige when the source of an anonymous good deed is exposed against their will. Hannah Arendt's reflection on the Christian ethic previously discussed in chapter 2, that "the moment a good work becomes known and public, it loses its specific character of goodness,"[19] does not apply to many cases in which the personal identity of a benefactor is publicized by someone else. In such cases, the goodness of the deed is protected and the perceived good standing of the actor is enhanced by their now-known aversion to personal credit. For example, when the source of an anonymous charitable contribution is exposed by the receiver, the previously anonymous contributor reaps a double benefit—they are honored by the charitable act *and* by their seemingly genuine attempt to keep it anonymous. If such a charitable actor organizes their own unmasking by subtly and inconspicuously guiding observers to discover their personal identity, we have a self-aggrandizing variety of the same enhanced honor. The character of this ethical enhancement is hilariously portrayed and deconstructed in a season 6 episode of Larry David's *Curb Your Enthusiasm*, titled "The Anonymous Donor." In this episode, David attempts to orchestrate the seemingly accidental exposure of his identity as an anonymous charitable donor in order to reap this dual social reward. When his motives are exposed, however, he loses all positive recognition and the goodness of the deed dissolves, just as Arendt described. The precarity of such ethical enhancements, and the need to carefully perform unmaskings with this in mind, is also evident in the case of anonymous authors and artists who develop strong positive reputations when those who praise their work are additionally impressed by their personal modesty. While the revelation of such an artist's personal identity "would add to . . . reputation and esteem overall if it were to occur by accident, deliberate action on [the artist's] part to bring that integration about . . . runs the risk of seeming immodest."[20]

Finally, unmasking is also always a performative process that exists in social tension with performances of anonymity and pseudonymity. In March 2016, Marco Santagata, a professor of Italian literature at the University of Pisa, suggested that the pseudonymous author Elena Ferrante was University of Naples historian Marcella Marmo.[21] In October of the same year, the journalist Claudio Gatti claimed it was Anita Raja, an Italian literary translator and editor.[22] These suggestions sparked a considerable controversy in the months surrounding the English-language publication of Ferrante's *Frantumaglia: A Writer's Journey*, a book of personal essays, letters, and interviews centered on the author's life and writing process, including her poetic musings about her reasons for obscuring her personal identity.[23] Many have criticized these unmasking efforts, arguing in various ways that they reek of sexism in their unjustified attempt to undermine the artistic self-determination of a female writer who wishes to protect her personal identity as a way of crafting her work.[24] Some accused Gatti of acting like "a mafia magnate" and unleashing the "polluting power of journalistic innuendo" that "shadows one's reading of" the personal revelations and accounts offered in *Frantumaglia*.[25] Without insinuating any strategy or intent, all of these voices of 2016 (Santagata's and Gatti's, those of their many critics, and Ferrante's in *Frantumaglia*) came together in performative and dynamic relation to one another, making for a social drama of identity obscuration and speculation that was set out for a public audience. Thus, the unmasking acts became inseparably entangled in the performance that is Elena Ferrante.

A contemporary battle between the hacker network Anonymous and the Ku Klux Klan also shows just how complicated the politics of unmasking can get. In the fall of 2014, during the large-scale internationally televised protests against the police shooting of eighteen-year-old Michael Brown in Ferguson, Missouri, and before the name of Darren Wilson, the police officer who shot Brown, was publicly released, Anonymous pressured Ferguson authorities to identify the shooter. Those acting under the moniker of the hacker network later threatened to dox (to publicly release the personal information of) Ferguson police officers if they harmed those who were protesting the killing of Brown.[26] During this same period of protest, a local group called the Traditionalist American Knights of the Ku Klux Klan (TAKKKK) circulated a leaflet threatening "lethal force" against dissidents who they claimed to be "terrorists masquerading as 'peaceful protestors.'"[27] In response, Anonymous launched "Operation KKK," also known as "Operation Hoods Off,"[28] promising to publicly release the names and personal information of Klan members and affiliates. Reacting to Operation Hoods Off and Anonymous's Ferguson campaign in general, Frank Ancona, Grand Wizard of TAKKKK, chastised Anonymous for "hiding behind pathetic masks" and claimed to publicly reveal the names of two central Anonymous members, promising, "This is just the tip of the iceberg."[29] Over a year later, Anonymous was still engaged in this unmasking battle, threatening to release one thousand names of individuals they alleged were affiliated with the KKK, while arguing, "We feel confident that applying transparency to your organizational cells is the right, just, appropriate and only course of action" and "You are terrorists that hide your identities beneath sheets and infiltrate society on every level."[30] Here we have two masked social movements, each threatening to unmask the other, and each referring to the masks of the other group as evidence of their illegitimacy (to deem each other "terrorists"). Such a dynamic social drama highlights the fact that anonymous acts can take on contradictory meanings from different social standpoints, and that there is often a persistent tension between performances of anonymity and efforts to expose personal identities in the contemporary world.

Just as anonymity and pseudonymity shape an audience's perception of an action, expression, or product, the revelation of a previously obscured actor's personal identity causes such audiences to retrospectively and critically reevaluate their definition of the situation in interesting ways. In other words, just as anonymous and pseudonymous actors work to create meaning, so do unmaskers. In many circumstances, actors and audiences alike are quite heavily invested in performances of anonymity, as we saw with the cases of Elena Ferrante, Banksy, and Q, as well as with confessions, anonymous communities and forums, and various acts of typification. In such cases, personalization radically alters the character of the relationship and the meanings of particular situations and contexts. Personalization stands as the antithesis of anonymity. It undoes the *someoneness, anyoneness, everyoneness,* and *no oneness* of anonymous and pseudonymous acts, further revealing how our lives and our experiences were impacted by the performance of hidden identities.

# Acknowledgments

This book was a very different journey than the last—one marked, and interrupted at times, by heavy administrative duties, the birth of my daughter, a global pandemic, and a host of various related issues and profound experiences. Throughout the process, I have been very fortunate to have had the support of family, friends, and colleagues.

I owe a special word of thanks to several people who read full drafts or large sections of the book and provided invaluable feedback. For their careful readings, brilliant comments, and consistent encouragement, I am indebted to Eviatar Zerubavel, Gary Alan Fine, Asia Friedman, Lynn Chancer, Jeffrey Alexander, Philip Smith, Donileen Loseke, Robert Zussman, and Jason Mast. I also benefited from an engaging conversation about this project with the participants of the Yale Center for Cultural Sociology Workshop. Over the past few years, I have also discussed this project in a variety of settings with many people. For their helpful comments and suggestions, I am very grateful to Richard Alba, Mike Owen Benediktsson, Kathleen Blee, Yael Bromberg, Julia Stein Dessauer, Andrew Friedman, Christine Galotti, Mark Halling, James M. Jasper, Marnia Lazreg, Jenny Wiley Legath, Howard Lune, James McMullen, Omar Montana, Richard Ocejo, Scott Perlo, Israel Posner, Barbara Katz Rothman, Iddo Tavory, Robin Wagner-Pacifici, Talya Wolf, and Yael Zerubavel.

This book also benefited tremendously from the careful work of several excellent research assistants. They helped me gather literature and information about cases when I was working a time-consuming three years of service as chair of the Hunter College Senate. I am grateful for the assistance of Josephine Barnett, Matthew Batson, Tommy Chung, Miriam Moster, Max Papadantonakis, Krutee Parikh, and Andrew Shapiro.

Elizabeth Branch Dyson was a fantastic editor. She saw the potential of this project from day one and provided invaluable feedback, editorial support, and guidance throughout the process of bringing this book to life. I am also indebted to the careful work of Mollie McFee, Erin DeWitt, and the rest of the Chicago team. Any author would be lucky to have such a brilliant group of editors and other publishing professionals in their corner.

Additionally, I am immensely grateful for the ongoing support of family through difficult times, with a special word of thanks to Sharon Posner and Spiro Trupos for allowing me to work in their home during the darkest days of pandemic lockdown, to Izzy and Randi Posner for their support, to Carol Graham for providing much needed clarity, and to my mother, Cathi DeGloma, for her consistent love and encouragement.

A special word of thanks also goes to Nelson Downend for countless talks about anonymity, film, and the joys and challenges of fatherhood, and to Jamil Shakoor for pushing me to go farther on the trails and for many conversations about existential philosophy, psychology, and the power of the human spirit.

Finally, and most importantly, I am forever grateful for the love and support of my wife, Lena, and our daughter, Juniper, who breathe life into my spirit through days dark and bright, and who always make me smile and know what is most important in this world. In addition to being a wonderful life partner, Lena has also been an insightful conversation partner as I was hashing out several of the ideas and cases I discuss in this book. I feel fortunate every day she is in my life.

Work on this book was supported in part by a sabbatical provided by Hunter College, by the Hunter College President's Office, and by a Book Completion Award provided by the CUNY Office of Research.

# Notes

## Chapter One

1. See Fryer (1972).
2. Bayer (1981). See 109–11 for a discussion of the 1972 panel.
3. Clendinen (2003).
4. The practice of "passing" (see Goffman 1963, 73–91), which entails obscuring part of one's personal characteristics in order to be accepted as a member of another group, "can allow for different modes of double living" (76).
5. See Bayer (1981, 110), who writes, "His attire not only seemed to protect his own identity, but perhaps more importantly was designed to stress that he spoke not only for himself but for all homosexual psychiatrists. He informed his audience that there were more than two hundred homosexual psychiatrists attending the convention."
6. Lyons (1973). See also Bayer (1981).
7. Goffman (1963, 56). See also Zerubavel (1982). On one's unique position at the intersection of multiple networks of social affiliations, see Simmel ([1955] 1964). As Mauss ([1938] 1985) argued, the idea of the "person" as we know it has classical Roman roots and has evolved through several historical epochs.
8. Goffman (1963, 56, 57); see also Goffman's mention of the "identity document" (60). See also Marx (1999, 100) on "seven types of identity knowledge" and Marx (2016, 86–111) on the varieties of personal information, including private and public, and on the "unique and core identity" (102–3).
9. See Brazier et al. (2004) for a discussion of "software agents" and "anonymisation technology" (143). See 140–41 on the "technical measures" employed for the purpose of protecting personal information in online transactions and communications. See also Linder and Xiao (2020).
10. Wallace (1999, 23, 25). See also Nissenbaum (1999, 142). Goffman (1963, 63) was perhaps the first to directly articulate this social logic of "informational connectedness" and personal identity. See also Marx (2016, 103) on de-linking unique identifiers from one's "core identity," and Moore (2018) on the notions of "connectedness" and "traceability."
11. Ponesse (2013, 333, 331). See also Ponesse (2014); Karp (1973, 447).
12. Marx (1999) provides an illuminating and early call for a broad sociology of anonymity. In this brief but cogent and widely applicable piece, Marx lists a great many "socially sanctioned contexts of concealment and revelation" (102–9), which include references to many of the types of cases I explore throughout this book. Marx's paper is a visionary statement about the importance of this underexplored topic in sociol-

ogy. See also Wallace (1999) and Ponesse (2013, 2014) for illuminating philosophical discussions. Both Wallace and Ponesse raise several general examples of the types that I also explore here, including many related to my discussion of protective anonymity in chapter 2 (see especially Ponesse 2013, 321; 2014, 306–9). Many others have also contributed to this area of inquiry with their analyses of particular cases. I build on these and other important contributions throughout this book.

13. Other scholars have, in their various ways, conceptualized anonymity as social performance. In his study of how individuals hide in pornographic bookstores, Karp (1973) advanced a perspective in line with my approach, illuminating active processes of "fostering anonymity" (433) and arguing that "persons must work to maintain anonymity, and that work is of a highly social nature" (446). In their more recent study, Scott and Orlikowski (2014) discuss "performing anonymity" (885) and focus on anonymity as "an ongoing sociomaterial enactment" with regard to different types of hotel evaluations, each of which, according to the authors, involves "particular performative outcomes" (882). In another illuminating study, Curlew (2019) analyzes anonymity on a social media platform as "undisciplined performativity" and anonymous posts as "performative, digital acts mediated through a community of anonymous users" (1). See also Wallace (1999) for an early discussion of being "anonymous *qua* agent" (26) and anonymity as "some trait which is known" as "an action of some agent(s)" that "cannot be coordinated with other traits of the agent(s), so that the identity of the agent(s) is unknown to others except as performer(s) of the act or possessor(s) of the trait" (31). Marx (1999, 100) also recognized that "anonymity is fundamentally social" and "requires an audience of at least one person." See also Brennan and Pettit (2008), who distinguish between performer and audience in their cogent discussion of anonymity and pseudonymity with regard to reputation and esteem. Ponesse uses the phrase "acts of anonymity" (2013, 328) and recognizes that "anonymity is characteristically interpersonal" (2013, 333; see also 2014, 314–15) while grappling with the question of "how . . . the unknowability involved with anonymity [is] standardly accomplished" (2013, 322). Finally, several who have discussed anonymous and pseudonymous literature have, in the words Mullan (2007, 28) used to describe the work of Sir Walter Scott, understood anonymity to be an "act of creative self-dispossession."

14. See also Ponesse (2013, 329; 2014, 314–15); Wallace (1999).

15. Plato ([~380 BCE] 1956, 157–58).

16. See also Wallace (1999, 24).

17. Brennan and Pettit (2008, 189–91). See also Goffman (1963, 66–68) on the distinction "between the knowing and the unknowing" with regard to personal identity. Cf. Karp (1973, 432–33).

18. See Frois (2009a, 9) on the "relative and circumstantial" character of anonymity in twelve-step programs. See also Frois (2009b, 88). See Nissenbaum (1998; 2004) on the notion of "contextual integrity."

19. See, for example, Tverdek (2008); Ohm (2010); Savage (2016).

20. Alexander and Smith (2003); Alexander (2004; 2017); Smith (2005); Alexander and Mast (2006). See also Loseke (2009; 2019).

21. Zerubavel (1980; 2007; 2021); Brekhus (2007); DeGloma and Papadantonakis (2020). On "multi-area formal theory," see also Glaser and Strauss ([1967] 2008, 82–89). See also Prus (1987); Vaughan (1992); Marx (2016, 143); Jutel (2019). Cf. Turner (1982, 20–60) on "comparative symbology," which involves the analysis of symbols

across different *"cultural genres* or *subsystems* of expressive culture" (21; emphasis in original).

22. Zerubavel (2007, 131).

23. Cf. Weber ([1915] 1946) on "spheres of values."

24. Because opportunities to obscure our personal identities have become more common in the digital age, and because anonymity and pseudonymity are quite easy to achieve when we are disembodied in our online interactions, a great deal of recent scholarship addressing anonymity has focused on computer-mediated communications and behavior in online environments. However, the general characteristics of anonymity are not particularly unique to computer-mediated interactions. Furthermore, while computer and internet technology might facilitate anonymity, it certainly does not guarantee it. For various discussions related to computer-mediated anonymity, see, for example, Nicoll (2003); Christopherson (2007); Scott and Orlikowski (2014); Curlew (2019). See also Froomkin (1995; 2003); Nicoll, Prins, and van Dellen (2003); Brazier et al. (2004); Levmore and Nussbaum (2010); Levmore (2010); Ohm (2010); Moore (2018); Linder and Xiao (2020).

25. See Zerubavel (2007, 140) on "a *theme-driven* . . . style of inquiry . . ." (emphasis in original). See also DeGloma and Papadantonakis (2020) on thematic analysis.

26. Glaser and Strauss ([1967] 2008, 65). This approach facilitates "a multi-faceted investigation, in which there are no limits to the techniques of data collection, the way they are used, or the types of data acquired."

27. On sociomental boundaries, see Zerubavel (1991). On personification, see Napier (1986, 10).

28. Berger and Luckmann (1966, 152).

29. The etymological root of the word "incognito," which means to be disguised or to act "with concealed identity," shows a linguistic link between identification, cognition, and knowledge. To be incognito is to block or restrict social perception (cognition) or knowledge of one's identifying characteristics. Like the word "cognition," the word "incognito" derives from the word "cognizance," which stems "from [an] assimilated form of com 'together' (see co-) + gnoscere 'to know,' from PIE [Proto-Indo-European] root *gno- 'to know.'" Online Etymology Dictionary, https://www.etymonline.com.

30. See Mullan (2007, 296). See also Ponesse (2013, 325n13).

31. Ponesse (2013, 326; emphasis in original). See also Wallace (1999, 23).

32. Wallace (1999, 23). See also Nissenbaum (1999).

33. See Ponesse (2013, 324–29) for a discussion of the distinctions between anonymity and various forms of "unknowability" and "concealment."

34. Brissett and Edgley (1990, 19).

35. See Goffman (1963, 62–72) on the biographical foundations of personal identity. See Searle (1969, 172–73) on proper names as "pegs on which to hang descriptions" and with which to establish "spatio-temporal continuity." See Zerubavel (2003) on historical continuity with regard to biography. See Schutz (1962, 60) on the "biographically determined circumstances" of the individual and Giddens (1991, 70–108) on "the trajectory of the self." See also Frank (1995); DeGloma (2014a); Zerubavel (1982).

36. Somers (1994, 617). See also DeGloma and Johnston (2019).

37. Goffman (1963, 57).

38. Ricoeur (1991, 75). On the social attribution of motive, see Mills (1940); Burke ([1945] 1969); Schutz ([1932] 1967, 171–72); Brissett and Edgley (1990, 22–23). On the link between identifiability and accountability, see Marx (1999, 105–6). On these issues as they pertain to personal reputation, see Fine (2019).

39. See Goffman (1963, 67), where he mentions the link between anonymity and biography. See DeGloma (2014a, 64–95) on the general relevance of negating auto-biographical memory.

40. Fine (2019, 248).

41. This concept of the *impersonal front* builds on Goffman's (1959, 23–24) notion of the "personal front."

42. Consider the common metaphors and idioms that involve our concept of "face," such as the phrase "take it at face value," which means that something *is* what it *seems*, in contrast to the metaphoric use of the term "mask," as in "she masked her true intent." In this regard, consider also the legal term "prima facie evidence" (see Napier, 1986, 4–10). Consider also the meanings of the words *efface* ("to wipe out," "to erase, or obliterate") and *deface* ("to mar the surface or appearance of . . . as to make illegible or invalid"), both of which are generally about something's state of being or existence and thus reveal the strong cultural and linguistic link between the "face" of a thing and its ontological status (https://www.dictionary.com).

43. Napier (1986, 3). See also Honigmann (1977, 275).

44. Brissett and Edgley (1990, 21).

45. See Froomkin (1995, especially par. 17) and Brazier et al. (2004, 154) on software systems as third-party agents. Marx (1999, 103) mentions adoption agencies, and Griffin (1999, 885) and Mullan (2007, 32, 38–40) discuss publishers as third parties who represent anonymous and pseudonymous authors.

46. See Moore (2018, 176) on durability as a central dimension of anonymity and pseudonymity.

47. See Ponesse (2013, 328) on the distinction between "deceptive and nondeceptive forms" of anonymity.

48. Cf. Goffman (1969, 14) on the "covering move."

49. Scott and Orlikowski (2014, 876, 889). See also Marx (2016, 103). On the concept of traceability and the distinction between anonymity and pseudonymity with regard to reputation, see Froomkin (1995, par. 2; 1999, 114; 2003, 9). See also Brazier et al. (2004); Wright et al. (2005, 16–18); Brennan and Pettit (2008); Knuttila (2011); Jones and Hannem (2018, 493); Curlew (2019, 10). See also Moore's (2018) conception of "durability" as a measure of pseudonymity. On reputations and reputation management in general, see Fine (2001; 2019).

50. See Ellsworth-Jones (2012, 1) on Banksy as "famous but unknown."

51. Brennan and Pettit (2008, 192). See also Fine (2019) on "reputation work." In certain cases, a reputation can be achieved without a cover name by explicitly linking multiple anonymous acts together. For example, publishers extend such a reputation to authors when they advertise an anonymous book as "by the author of" a previous anonymous book, which "creates the relation of filiation without needing a name to do so" Griffin (1999, 882).

52. Easley (2004, 127). See also Brennan and Pettit (2008, 192).

53. Cases in which pseudonyms are *not* known to be a disguise, and therefore mislead observers and audiences into believing that the cover representation is an authentic personal identity, are more in line with what Goffman (1959, 59) refers to as

a "false front" and Marx (2016, 158) refers to as "masking moves." I am less interested in particular cases of deception and more interested in cases in which the pseudonym is known or discovered to be a cover while personal identity remains concealed. See also Marx (1999, 101, 108–9) on some ethical questions raised by pseudonymity.

54. Cusk (2015; emphasis added).

55. Mullan (2007, 6).

56. Simmel ([1903] 1950) was the first to note that freedom is a characteristic of the anonymity that marks life in large cities. See also Grazian (2008, 5–13).

57. Zimbardo (1969, 248).

58. Ponesse (2014, 312; emphasis in original). See also Brennan and Pettit (2008, 185, 192); Curlew (2019).

59. Homer, *The Odyssey*, Book IX. In a similar fashion, one well-known early internet troll took the name "Netochka Nezvanova" from a Dostoyevsky novel, a name that "means 'nameless nobody'" (Coleman 2014, 39).

60. See, for example, the blog *Anonymous Love Letters*, which contains several examples of different types (https://anonymousloveletters.wordpress.com/). On anonymous letters conveying various threats, see Thompson ([1975] 2011).

61. Cooley (1902); Mead ([1934] 2015). See also Perinbanayagam (1991); Athens (1994); Wiley (1994); Ruiz-Junco (2017).

62. Schutz ([1932] 1967, 170). See also Schwalbe ([2008] 2015) and Schwalbe and Mischke (2021) on "nets of accountability." See also Zimbardo's (1969) work linking anonymity to "deindividuation." See also Wallace (1999, 31), who argues that "anonymity always raises the issue of accountability," and Ponesse (2013), who comments that anonymity makes it "easier to detach ourselves from prevailing social bonds" (342) and that some anonymous actors seek to "avoid . . . the accountability that would normally lead a person to feel ashamed" (322n6). See also Kiesler, Siegel, and McGuire (1984, 1126), who were among the first to explore deindividuation in computer-mediated communications.

63. Curlew (2019, 6, 7). In his discussion of secrets and secret societies, Simmel (1950c, 374) points out that "the disguise of the person suspends all responsibility."

64. Curlew (2019, 3, 8).

65. Stein (2019, 137). See also Marx (1999, 105).

66. Goffman (1963, 100).

67. Cf. Curlew (2019, 11–12).

68. Goffman (1959, 79, 77–105).

69. Cf. Wallace (1999, 24) on sustainability. See Moore (2018, 176–77) on durability.

70. See also Marx (1999, 101).

71. Moore (2018, 176). See also Brennan and Pettit (2008).

72. Brennan and Pettit (2008, 177).

73. On information control, see Goffman (1959, 1963, 1969); Karp (1973); Zerubavel (1982). See also Marx (1999, 100); Ponesse (2013, 324–27).

74. Ponesse (2013, 323).

75. Boxer (2005).

76. See also Moore's (2018, 181) discussion where he recognizes "the value of anonymity" not just "as a means to privacy" but also "as a means to publicity." On the distinction between anonymity and privacy, see also Ponesse (2013, 329–32; 2014, 310–12), where she argues against a "reductionist view" posited by those "who aim to

reduce anonymity to other concepts" such as "privacy, liberty and autonomy, security and protection, and secrecy" (2014, 305).

77. This information slippage is related to a phenomenon that Goffman (1959) refers to as "giving off" an impression that one may not intend to give. See also Marx (1999, 101) on "the uncontrollable leakage of some information" that he sees as "a condition of physical and social existence." The view that guarded individuals unconsciously communicate sensitive information is also an essential feature of psychoanalysis.

78. Parsons (2005, 825; 2015, 91); Fry ([1975] 2001, 133–34).

79. Johnson (2011, loc. 3835).

80. The process of using an IP address to reveal the personal identity of a computer user illustrates the dimension of "traceability" discussed by Moore (2018, 175), and originally by Froomkin (1995; 2003, 9–15), in relation to anonymity and pseudonymity online. For interesting cases, see Knibbs (2015); Grygiel (2014). See also Harcourt (2015, 273) for a case in which the FBI obtained the IP addresses of individuals using Tor, a supposedly anonymous web browser. See also Newman (2014).

81. Marx (2016, 104).

82. Wolf (2017).

83. See Luke 24:13–35 (New International Version).

84. Wiedeman (2018); Hauser and Zraick (2019).

85. See Adut (2018, 150) on "spectatorship" and the calling of the *flâneur*. The practice of enshrouding theater audiences in darkness (first introduced by Richard Wagner), or providing audience members with masks (as in the contemporary theatrical production *Sleep No More*), also creates this effect.

86. Cf. Harcourt (2015, 117, 129); Peterson (2012).

87. Goffman (1963, 84).

88. Foucault ([1975] 1995, 202). See also Frois (2009a, 155).

89. Brennan and Pettit (2008, 189–91). See also Nicoll (2003, 100); Goffman (1963, 66–68).

90. Brennan and Pettit (2008, 189).

91. See Ellsworth-Jones (2012, 155–80) on "team Banksy."

92. Mullan (2007, 11).

93. See Taylor (2022) on audience agency with regard to social performance. The synonymous notions of some*body*, any*body*, every*body*, and no*body* call our attention to the fact that anonymity often involves disembodiment, or a masking of the corporal indicators of personal identity.

94. With regard to secrecy, Simmel (1950c, 333) comments that we often feel that "everything mysterious is something important and essential," and we tend "to intensify the unknown through imagination, and to pay attention to it with an emphasis that is not usually accorded to patent reality."

95. Pearson (2009). See also Rohter (1990).

96. See http://www.toynbeeidea.com/. See also Kilgannon (1999).

97. Anonymous (2019). Note that the word "Anonymous" is boldly and strikingly printed on the cover, as if the anonymity of the exposé gives it weight or informative value that would otherwise not be present. On October 28, 2020, Miles Taylor, former chief of staff to Trump's secretary of Homeland Security, Kirstjen Nielsen, revealed himself to be the author of *A Warning*.

98. Tverdek (2008, 205). Some scholars argue that voting is a form of anonymous speech in the United States. Voting actually blends aspects of anonymity and secrecy. We are protected in that others will not know *how* we voted (or for *whom* we voted), but that we, personally and legally, voted (or not) is a matter of public record.

99. See Churchill and Vander Wall (1990); Glick (1989).

100. Thompson ([1975] 2011).

101. The terrorist deemed the "Unabomber" was eventually exposed to be Theodore "Ted" Kaczynski.

102. Scott (1990, 149). See also Ponesse (2014, 313–16) for a discussion of anonymity in relation to secrecy, deception, and concealment.

103. According to the recollections of those who were present at the time King received the anonymous letter reproduced in fig. 2, there was a general speculation that the letter must have been sent by the FBI. Of course, because the letter was anonymous, its source could not be proven at the time. See Gage (2014).

104. Simmel (1950c, 352–54). See also Auerbach (2015b) on the significance of written discourse for anonymity in online forums.

105. Foucault ([1969] 1977, 127).

106. In a prescient early analysis of the social psychological impact of computer-mediated communication, Kiesler. Siegel, and McGuire (1984, 1126) note that the impersonal character of "communication via computer" prompts users to "redirect attention away from others and toward the message itself."

107. Both Simmel ([1903] 1950; 1950b) and Weber ([1922] 1978) explicitly highlighted such impersonality and interchangeability as a key characteristic of modern social relations, especially with regard to modern market economies and bureaucracies. See also Parsons ([1951] 1991, 38–44) on the particularism of expressive relations and the universalism of instrumental relations. See also Zerubavel (forthcoming) on impersonality and interchangeability.

108. Ponesse (2013, 331, 332).

109. Natanson (1986, 140).

110. See Coleman (2014, 46–49) on anonymity as a counter to celebrity with regard to the ethic of the hacker network Anonymous. As Goffman (1963, 69) notes, for the famous individual "a widened range of acts become assimilated to biography as newsworthy events."

111. Johnson (2011, loc. 947–78) reports that "masked heads of state" traveled "'incognito' with their immense masked entourages" in eighteenth-century Venice. The eighth-/ninth-century caliph Harun al-Rashid was depicted as going incognito among the commoners of Baghdad in a popular story in the collection titled *Arabian Nights, or One Thousand and One Nights*.

112. See Schutz ([1932] 1967, 185); Natanson (1986, 21).

113. See DeGloma (2014a, 127–49).

114. Sennett (1974, 264, 265).

115. Moore (2018, 183).

116. Woolf ([1940] 1979, 382).

117. Thompson ([1975] 2011, 273).

118. Eisen (2013, 115–16).

119. Authorship was later credited to be Joseph S. Benner.

120. Anonymous (2007). See also Coleman (2014, 1).

121. See season 1, episode 1 of HBO's *Watchmen*. See also Moore and Gibbons (1986).

122. Olesen (2005, 118).

123. Zimbardo (1969). See also Zerubavel (forthcoming) on anonymization, "envisioned groupness," and the loss of "embodied individuality."

124. Ponesse (2013, 341).

125. Foucault ([1978] 1990, 95).

126. Bauman (1989, 102-3).

127. See Goffman (1959) on impression management.

128. Goffman (1959, 22).

129. Shang, Chen, and Huang (2012). See also Gottschalk (2010); Li and Tian (2022).

130. Alexander (2004; 2017); Turner (1982); Schechner ([1977] 2003). See Alexander and Mast (2006, 3) on the need to move beyond "interactional context" to consider "cultural context." See also Loseke (2019) on the need to consider both the cognitive and emotional dimensions of meaning.

131. Marcos has described his balaclava as a "mirror" that symbolizes the struggles of different oppressed communities around the world. See Klein (2002, 3); Olesen (2005, 116); Ruiz (2013, 275).

132. Alexander and Mast (2006, 5) write, "Revolutionary guerrilla groups, like the Zapatista rebels . . . present their collective force via highly staged photo-marches, and their leaders, like subcommander Marcos, enter figuratively into the public sphere, as iconic representations of established cultural forms." See also Olesen (2005, 112, 116-18).

133. Ruiz (2013, 267-68). See also "An Examination of the History of Use of Masks and Why the Zapatistas Cover Their Faces." http://schoolsforchiapas.org/wp -content/uploads/2014/04/Whats-behind-the-mask_.pdf.

134. See also Frois (2009a,b).

135. See Goffman's (1963, 41-42) *Stigma* on "the discredited and the discreditable."

## Chapter Two

1. Anonymous ([1954] 2000, 75).

2. Enzensberger (2000, x).

3. Beevor (2000, xv). See also Harding (2003); Connerton (2008, 69).

4. Max Färberböck's 2008 film, *Anonyma: Eine Frau in Berlin* (English release, *A Woman in Berlin*), clearly portrays Hillers's German patriotism under the Third Reich as her anonymous character proclaims, "We were convinced we were right. We all breathed the same air and it was intoxicating" (English subtitles to the German language film).

5. Enzensberger (2000, xi). See also Beevor (2000, xxi). See Zerubavel (2006) on the social foundations of denial.

6. See also Marx (1999, 102-5) and Ponesse (2013, 321), who list different situations in which individuals use anonymity for protection, many of which I discuss in this chapter.

7. See Goffman (1963) on "the discredited and the discreditable" (41-42) and on stigma as a reason to conceal personal identity (65). Cf. Simmel (1950c, 331) on secrecy and immorality.

8. Norma McCorvey publicly admitted to being "Jane Roe" shortly after the *Roe v. Wade* case concluded. Former associate director of the FBI Mark Felt was exposed as Deep Throat in 2005. William Wilson and Dr. Robert Smith established the tradition of using nonspecific first names in Alcoholics Anonymous.

9. At this time of this writing, only some US states allow lottery winners to remain anonymous, and the issue of winner anonymity is contentious. See Blinder (2015).

10. See Jospeh (2021). See also https://shbb.org/.

11. See also Marx (1999, 102). The now-anachronistic phrase to "drop a dime" on someone refers to the act of using a public pay phone to inform police authorities of another's criminal activities. Public pay phones offer a protective anonymity not afforded by account-based landlines and mobile phones. Today, it is both less common and more difficult to make an anonymous phone call. However, various products and services can be used to make calls less easily linkable to the personal identity of the caller. See also Marx (2016, 156).

12. See Linder and Xiao (2020, 8).

13. Marx (1999, 103). As Marx (1999, 110–11n21) notes, this sometimes occurred with trials of the Sendero Luminoso and Tupac Amaru in Peru in the 1990s. Wallace (1999, 32n35) notes that some juries were anonymized in trials of Colombian drug dealers in the 1980s.

14. See "Mission for Masks: On the Front Lines of COVID-19" (https://docs .google.com/forms/d/e/1FAIpQLScqX7mNJv4cZtJTAsyb9ZEf-9VOxlXk9xwVe hO8sy0h5XKbbg/viewform). See also Lee (2020).

15. Donegan (2018); Peiser (2018).

16. See O'Sullivan (2016).

17. See also Simmel (1950c, 332). Mullan (2007, 31) recognizes this as a factor in the popularity of the anonymous 1996 novel *Primary Colors*, commenting, "It was as if the author . . . was breaking confidences and passing on secrets."

18. Anonymous (2013b).

19. Dante (2010).

20. Gioia (2017).

21. Shpitzle Shtrimpkind later revealed herself to be Frieda Vizel. See Vizel (2012), where she writes, "On the Internet, I was anonymous. . . . I was whoever I wanted to be, and I could say whatever I wanted to say without fear." See also Shpitzle Shtrimpkind's former blog at https://shtrimpkind.blogspot.com/.

22. See Strachan (2018).

23. See Levmore and Nussbaum (2010); Ponesse (2014, 307–8). As we can see from Easley's (2004, 131–35) discussion of the "signature wars" of the 1860s, contemporary debates concerning anonymity and speech follow lines that are very similar to the debates of previous eras.

24. *Talley v. California*, 362 U.S. 60 (1960). *McIntyre v. Ohio Elections Commission*, 514 U.S. 334 (1995). See also Constantine (1996).

25. 514 U.S. 335 (1995), 357.

26. Ponesse (2014, 308).

27. Dubrovsky, Kiesler, and Sethna (1991); Christopherson (2007, 3045–47). See also Kiesler, Siegel, and McGuire (1984, 1129), who found early evidence that computer-mediated communication decreases "inequality of participation" and allows for more "uninhibited interpersonal behavior." See also Froomkin (2003, 8);

De Hert (2003, 73); Moore (2018). See Wright et al. (2005, 7) for a technical treatise that addresses anonymity as "a useful and effective method for protection of the user" in computer-mediated interactions.

28. See Froomkin (1995, pars. 29, 44–52; 2003, 7); Curlew (2019).

29. 514 U.S. 334 (1995), 383, 385. See also Constantine (1996, 469–70).

30. See De Hert (2003) for a discussion of the history of this view in Western philosophy and his presentation of various positions. See also Levmore (2010, 54–55).

31. Moore (2018, 169).

32. Griffin (1999, 885).

33. Mullan (2007, 93).

34. Mullan (2007, 103).

35. Griffin (1999, 889).

36. Anonymous ([1554] 1908). Sir Clements Markham, the translator of this version of the book, attributes authorship to the poet and writer Diego Hurtado De Mendoza, "a scion of one of the noblest families of Spain" (xv), though this remains speculative.

37. Leys (2011).

38. Feldman (2002). Feldman notes that in the romantic era, "poetry had much higher literary status than novels," and "as a result, an author might be more given to claim a book of poetry than a novel" (282).

39. Brennan and Pettit (2008, 183, 184).

40. See Gioia (2017).

41. Brennan and Pettit (2008, 184).

42. Foucault ([1969] 1977).

43. Foucault ([1969] 1997, 124, 126).

44. Foucault ([1969] 1977, 138). See also Griffin (1999) for a critical discussion.

45. Wood (2013).

46. Ferri and Ferri (2015, 222). These are Ferrante's words quoted directly from an interview conducted by her publishers, Sandro and Sandra Ferri.

47. Easley (2004, 127).

48. Ferri and Ferri (2015, 222; emphasis in original).

49. Mullan (2007, 93, 100; see also 96–99).

50. See Schappell (2015). Here we see an additional commonality with Charlotte Brontë, whose "pseudonym was . . . an escape from herself" (Mullan 2007, 99).

51. Ferri and Ferri (2015, 223).

52. Schwartz (2016).

53. Mullan (2007, 27–28). This echoes a point made by Virginia Woolf ([1940] 1979, 397) that in an era before modern authorship, "anonymity . . . gave the early writing an impersonality, a generality."

54. Ferri and Ferri (2015, 226); Schappell (2015) on the notion of "erasure."

55. Ferrante (2016, 15). Also quoted in Wood (2013) and elsewhere.

56. See, for example, Gatti (2016); Appignanesi (2016); Geue (2016); Kirchgaessner (2016).

57. Ferri and Ferri (2015, 212).

58. Goffman (1963, 72). See also Marx (1999, 103).

59. Mishnah Torah, Book of Seeds, Matnot Aniyim, Chapter 10: 7–14, https://www .chabad.org/library/article_cdo/aid/986711/jewish/Matnot-Aniyim-Chapter-10 .htm.

60. Matt. 6:1–4 (New International Version).

61. Quran 2:271 (quran.com/2).

62. Simmel (1950c, 331).

63. Arendt (1958, 74, 75). See also Adut (2018, 175n13).

64. Marx (1999, 103).

65. See Oppenheimer (2013).

66. Peacey and Sanders (2014).

67. See Ubelacker (2018).

68. Wanshel (2016).

69. See Grow (2016).

70. Glazer and Konrad (1996).

71. Steve Hartman, *CBS Evening News*, December 14, 2018, https://www.youtube
.com/watch?v=DG94Txqnz7I.

72. Hoffman, Hilbe, and Nowak (2018); Gallagher (2018). See also Peacey and
Sanders (2014).

73. Matt. 6:1–4 (New International Version).

74. Quran 2:271 (quran.com/2).

75. Bossy (1975, 22).

76. Bossy (1975, 21, 22).

77. Bossy (1975, 29–30); Cornwell (2014).

78. Coughlin (2001, 10).

79. Online Etymology Dictionary, https://www.etymonline.com.

80. Catholic Church Code of Canon Law (1983, 964 §2), states that churches must
provide "confessionals with a fixed grate between the penitent and the confessor in an
open place so that the faithful who wish to can use them freely" (http://www.vatican
.va/archive/ENG1104/_P3F.HTM). See also the mandate by the United States Conference of Catholic Bishops http://www.usccb.org/beliefs-and-teachings/what-we
-believe/canon-law/complementary-norms/canon-964-2-the-confessional.cfm).

81. See Coughlin (2001) on all these points.

82. Coughlin (2001, 9). On the authority of the one who hears confession, including that individual's power to interpret the truth and meaning of transgression, see
also Foucault ([1978] 1990, 61–62, 66–67).

83. Such a depersonalized authority was also a characteristic of the "extraordinary
confessors" who traveled into a community on occasion to hear confessions without
the biases and judgments that might stem from locally rooted personal relationships.
See Simmonds (2000, 268).

84. Simmonds (2000, 268–70). See also Fantz (2008).

85. See Absolution Online, http://www.absolution-online.com/.

86. See https://postsecret.com/. There are several other examples of confessional
websites, some of which have ceased to operate but keep accessible archives. See
O'Connell (1998); Boxer (2005) for commentary. On confession and anonymous authorship, see Mullan (2007, 254–85).

87. Poletti (2011).

88. Warren (2007). Frank Warren started the PostSecret project in 2004 when he
distributed postcards asking people to anonymously mail him personal secrets that
he would post on a public blog. The project quickly grew and is still active as of this
writing. The Subway Therapy project, initiated by Matthew "Levee" Chavez, adopted
a similar format to allow individuals an expressive outlet following the 2016 presiden-

tial election. See http://www.subwaytherapy.com/home. See also the Clothesline Project, in which participants use shirts and clothing to anonymously expose various forms of interpersonal violence and abuse (http://www.clotheslineproject.info/.

89. Boxer (2005).

90. See also Foucault ([1978] 1990, 58–67).

91. Bakhtin ([1965] 1984, 10). See also Tseëlon (2001b, 27–29).

92. Tseëlon (2001a, 1). See also Napier (1986).

93. *Romeo and Juliet*, act I, scene V.

94. Soon after this encounter, Juliet ponders Romeo as separate from his personal identity and family affiliation when she utters the famous line, "What's in a name? That which we call a rose by any other name would smell as sweet." *Romeo and Juliet*, act II, scene II.

95. We see a very different expression of such social leveling in Edgar Allan Poe's (1842) "The Masque of the Red Death." In this short story, Prince Prospero (note the clear class connotations of both title and name) sealed himself and a thousand upper-class friends in a castle to avoid a vicious plague. While sheltered in luxury and totally indifferent to the suffering of the masses, the prince threw an extravagant masquerade party at which a mysterious figure dressed as the corpse of a plague victim showed up, made rounds through the crowd, and ultimately infected and killed all who were present. Using the masquerade as his setting, one that obscured the personal identities of its guests, Poe shows how "the Red Death held illimitable dominion over all."

96. Johnson (2011, loc. 3803).

97. Johnson (2011, loc. 978–79).

98. See Turner (1982, 20–60) on liminoid zones. See also Bakhtin ([1965] 1984, 11) on the "second world of folk culture" established by carnival.

99. See also Ponesse (2013, 334–35).

100. See also Marx (1999, 103) on depersonalized "judgements and decision making." See Parsons ([1951] 1991) on pattern variables and the distinction between ascription and achievement. See also Linton (1936).

101. See Goldin and Rouse (2000). See also Gladwell (2005, 245–54) on "listening with your eyes."

102. See Griffin (1999, 884); Wrigley (1983). See also Saks and Ostrom (1973) on anonymous letters to the editor. See also Ponesse (2014, 312).

103. See Scott and Orlikowski (2014).

104. See Goffman (1967) on the concept of "face." An example of inappropriate praise occurs when an anonymous student admires a professor's physical appearance on the Rate My Professor platform.

105. There is some evidence that this practice leads to greater diversity of author representation. See Budden et al. (2008). See also Ponesse (2014, 308).

106. Li (2011, 609).

107. See Li (2011, 605–6).

108. Afonso et al. (2005, 46). See also Cheong (1979).

109. See, for example, Riniolo et al. (2006); Stark (2013); Patton (2015); Mengel, Sauermann, and Zölitz (2019). For a critical discussion of anonymous workplace evaluations, see Cancialosi (2015).

110. Walker (2017).

111. See, for example, Samarati and Sweeney (1998); Sweeney (2002); de Montjoye et al. (2013); Savage (2016); Walker (2017).

112. See Walford (2018). See also Saunders, Kitzinger, and Kitzinger (2015); Reyes (2018); Jerolmack and Murphy (2019).

113. Crow and Wiles (2008). See also Scheper-Hughes (2000); Reyes (2018, 210); Jerolmack and Murphy (2019, 805).

114. Nespor (2000, 548).

115. Saunders, Kitzinger, and Kitzinger (2015, 125–26). See also Walford (2018, 518–19).

116. Walford (2018, 519). For reasons and justifications as to why a researcher might take these and other relatively extreme measures, see Saunders, Kitzinger, and Kitzinger (2015).

117. Jerolmack and Murphy (2019, 805).

118. Frois (2009a, 14–15).

119. Goffman (2014). See Neyfakh (2015) for more detail.

120. Contreras (2019).

121. Walford (2018, 519); Jerolmack and Murphy (2019, 805).

122. See Khan's (2019) discussion of his experience when his ethnographic data was subpoenaed in a civil suit.

123. Nespor (2000, 549). See also Walford (2018, 522).

124. See also Jerolmack and Murphy (2019, 803).

125. Bosk ([1979] 2003, 217).

126. Bosk ([1979] 2003, 218).

127. Bosk ([1979] 2003, 219).

128. Bosk ([1979] 2003, 220).

129. Bosk ([1979] 2003, 221, 222–23).

130. See Duclos (2019, 179). See also Scheper-Hughes's (2000, 119, 128) discussion. See also Jerolmack and Murphy (2019, 807).

131. Scheper-Hughes (2000, 128).

132. Nespor (2000, 550). See also Bosk ([1979] 2003, xvi–xviii); Jerolmack and Murphy (2019, 809–13). See also Krause (2021) on "model cases" more generally.

133. As Reyes (2018, 212) points out, because of this genericity, "pseudonyms in research are able to provide *plausible deniability*" (emphasis in original). See also Duclos (2019, 178) for a case in which such generalizations were inappropriate.

134. Knuttila (2011) uses the term "culture of anonymity" in reference to the anonymous internet imageboard 4chan. See also Coleman (2014, 41); Auerbach (2015b). See Frois (2009a) on "reciprocity in a context of anonymity" (153), on anonymity as "relational" (156, 173), and on focus and attention in twelve-step recovery groups (2009a, 159–61; 2009b, 93–94). See also Denzin (1987, 102, 113–21) on Alcoholics Anonymous as "a shared universe of discourse" and Karp's (1973, 447) comments about "the anonymous situation." On "informational norms," see Nissenbaum (2004, 138). On the "idiocultures" of small groups, see Fine (2012; 2021). On attentional norms, see Zerubavel (2015, 9–10, 59–69).

135. See Ponesse (2013, 322) on "shame-free zones." See Marx (2016, 150) on "safety zones, safe havens, and sanctuaries" as protective areas that allow for the avoidance of surveillance.

136. See Scott (2011, 30, 49–52; 2015, 178–80) on "performative regulation."

137. Turner (1982, 55). On the concept of the "lifeworld," see Habermas (1987). See also Schutz and Luckmann (1973); Berger and Luckmann (1966).

138. Turner (1982, 54, 33, 83). See also Knuttila (2011) on "the push of alterity through the contingent encounter of anonymity" in 4chan.

139. Cf. Turner (1982, 57) on "*loss of ego*" in liminoid spaces. See also Denzin (1987, 206, 187) on Alcoholics Anonymous as "a culture structure that stands to the side, if not outside, the mainstream of modern group life," and on the "loss of ego" that occurs in Alcoholics Anonymous.

140. Scott (2015, 177).

141. See also Goffman (1963, 20). See Curlew (2019) on therapeutic/supportive comments made via the anonymous app Yik Yak.

142. See Irvine (1999).

143. See the websites of Co-Dependents Anonymous (https://coda.org/), Sex Workers Anonymous (https://www.sexworkersanonymous.net/), Debtors Anonymous (https://debtorsanonymous.org/), and Racists Anonymous (http://rainternational .org/).

144. See DeGloma (2007, 2014a,b).

145. Christopherson (2007, 3052). See Spears et al. (2002, 572) on some implications of social support via computer-mediated communication, particularly as a means "to foster collective resistance" to powerful forces.

146. Adut (2018, 67).

147. Denzin (1987, 11 and throughout). See also Frois (2009a,b). My discussion of Alcoholics Anonymous draws heavily from this work.

148. See Alcoholics Anonymous ([1981] 2011, 5) for an explicit statement of this principle.

149. Denzin (1987, 115). See also Frois (2009a, 150–51).

150. See Denzin (1987, 64). See also Frois (2009a, 158).

151. AA was founded in 1935 by "Bill W." and "Dr. Bob," which are pseudonyms insofar as they obscure enough of each individual's name to mask his personal identity. Although the personal identities of both men are widely known today (they are William Wilson and Dr. Robert Smith), their pseudonyms are still commonly used out of respect for the tradition and practice of anonymity in the community.

152. See Bar-On (1989, 328) on the "double wall" of silence. See also Zerubavel (2006).

153. See Frois (2009a, 161–71; 2009b, 99–101) on the boundaries that separate the group from the outside world. If and when group members encounter one another in public, they may pretend a mutual lack of recognition. When AA members have relationships outside of the protective AA venues, they commonly avoid any information gleaned in anonymous spaces while in the presence of people who are not participants in the group.

154. This generic label for those who participate in Alcoholics Anonymous also appears in the collective's primary publication, *Alcoholic Anonymous* (2001), which is widely known as the "Big Book." See, for example, "Foreword to Fourth Edition" (xxiv).

155. See Denzin (1987, 18) on the alcoholic in treatment becoming "a *universal singular*," or an "instance of a process" that is shared by others in treatment or recovery (see also 31, 38–39, 54, 93, 102, 105). See also Frois (2009a,b); Wolf (2019).

156. See Denzin (1987, 122). See also Frois (2009b, 104; 2009a, 156).

157. Holstein and Gubrium (2000, 182). On formulaic storytelling in AA, see Denzin (1987, 31, 39, 98, 110, 167–70, 197); Rappaport (1993); Pollner and Stein (1996); Holstein and Gubrium (2000, 176–86); Frois (2009a, 70–79).

158. Scott (2011, 30–53; 2015, 177–204). See also Gubrium and Holstein (2000). See also Denzin (1987, 155–93) on "The Recovery of Self," and Frois (2009a, 178–79; 2009b, 90).

159. Wolf (2019).

160. Alcoholics Anonymous ([1953] 2017, 184).

161. Alcoholics Anonymous ([1953] 2017, 187). As Holstein and Gubrium (2000, 179) point out, these steps and traditions provide "a veritable set of rules for self characterization."

162. See Auerbach (2015b). Baizerman (1974, 300) discusses anonymity "as a social value and as a social norm" with regard to telephone hotlines.

163. This term comes from Fraser's discussion (1990, 67) of "*subaltern counterpublics*" as "parallel discursive arenas" (emphasis in original).

164. Moore (2018, 174). See also Poletti (2011, 26) on the PostSecret project "as an intimate public." See Auerbach (2015b) on 4chan and Dias (2003, 31) on pro-anorexia websites as a "sanctuary" that offers a way for disembodied participants to escape "relentless surveillance in the public sphere."

165. Knuttila (2011; emphasis in original). See also Coleman (2014, 42–43).

166. See Girgis (2014).

167. See, for example, Sociology Job Market Rumors, https://www.socjobrumors.com/.

168. https://www.4chan.org/advertise.

169. https://www.redditinc.com.

170. See Auerbach (2015a). See Hipp et al. (2017) for analysis of a Reddit thread in which users anonymously shared accounts about perpetrating sexual assault.

171. See Farrall (2012); Bartlett (2014); Linder, Pryciak, and Elsner (2020); Linder and Xiao (2020).

172. Martin (2014). Martin (2014, 356) points out that, at the time of his research, he easily located "links to more than 100 different cryptomarkets offering a range of illicit goods and services including, but not limited to: stolen credit card information; forged identity documents; plagiarized university essays; hacking/cracking services; money laundering; child pornography; illegal firearms and ammunition; and even contract killing." See also Foley, Karlsen, and Putniņš (2019); Linder, Pryciak, and Elsner (2020, 7–8).

173. Auerbach (2015a,b). See also Knuttila (2011).

174. Auerbach (2015b; emphasis in original).

175. Curlew (2019, 6, 8).

176. Auerbach (2015b). See also Knuttila (2011) on the "alterity" of 4chan.

177. Auerbach (2015b).

178. Veblen ([1899] 1918, 75).

179. See Young et al. (2017).

180. See *Tattered Cover, Inc. v. City of Thornton*, 44 P.3d 1044 (2002), Supreme Court of Colorado, En Banc (https://law.justia.com/cases/colorado/supreme-court/2002/01sa205-0.html).

181. See Karp (1973, 438–39) on "institutionalized shields" and on normative pressures to avoid others when visiting pornographic businesses (435, 439–44, 447–48n1).

182. See also Karp (1973, 439). This is an example of "blocking," one of twelve "neutralization moves" discussed by Marx (2016, 155).

183. See, for example, Jones and Hannem's (2018, 492) discussion of "online erotic review boards." See also Auerbach (2015a) on 4chan and pornography and Martin (2014) on anonymous online "cryptomarkets."

184. See also Marx (1999, 103).

185. See Simmel ([1978] 2011, 321). See also Agnew (1986, 9).

186. Simmel ([1903] 1950; [1978] 2011) associated the growing impersonality of exchange with modernity more generally.

187. Researchers have developed techniques to derive "Bitcoin address-to-IP mappings" that can potentially expose the personal identities of a significant number of users. Koshy, Koshy, and McDaniel (2014, 2, 6–14). Authorities have also adapted techniques to surveil and identify illegal activities involving cryptocurrencies. See Foley, Karlsen, and Putniņš (2019, 1807–8). For early discussions of digital cash, see Froomkin (1995, 2003).

188. See Brazier et al. (2004, 154); Froomkin (1995, especially par. 17).

189. Nicoll (2003, 114–16).

190. *Tattered Cover, Inc. v. City of Thornton*, 44 P.3d 1044 (2002). See also Garner (2012).

191. Levmore and Nussbaum (2010, 3). See also Levmore (2010, 55).

192. See Scott and Orlikowski (2014, 884–85) for a discussion of deceptive reviews posted to the travel industry website TripAdvisor.

193. See, for example, Fish (2010).

194. See Froomkin (1995, pars. 64–65) on *Griset v. Fair Political Practices Commission* (California, 1994).

195. See George Seaton's 1962 film, *The Counterfeit Traitor*, for a fictional portrayal of such a case.

196. See Baizerman (1974, 304) on "the masturbator."

## Chapter Three

1. ABC News (2020).

2. Q post of March 4, 2018. Retrieved December 2020 (https://qanon.pub/index2 .html).

3. "Q clearance" is a legitimate security clearance level at the US Department of Energy given to those who require access to top secret information.

4. See Q posts of October 29, 2017, and May 10, 2018 (https://qanon.pub/index2 .html).

5. Q posts of October 29 and November 5, 2017 (https://qanon.pub/index2.html).

6. All posts attributed to Q are, as of this writing, archived on the site https:// qanon.pub/. Forensic linguists have pointed to outspoken QAnon supporters Paul Furber and Ron Watkins as the actors who likely posted in the name of Q. See Kirkpatrick (2022). Both deny the accusation.

7. See, for example, Campbell (2018); LaFrance (2020).

8. Some of these followers and interpreters of Q also act anonymously or pseudonymously online, masking personal information that might otherwise undermine their claims.

9. See Francescani (2020); Griffin (2020); Roose (2020). See also Cooper (2021).

10. See LaFrance (2020).

11. See, for example, Q posts of October 29, 2017, July 8, 2019, and March 28, 2020 (https://qanon.pub/index2.html). See also Francescani (2020); LaFrance (2020). The start of the Biden presidency threw QAnon followers into disarray, with some adjusting their conspiratorial beliefs to suit new circumstances and others wondering if they were "played" (Brewster 2021).

12. LaFrance (2020).

13. See ABC News (2020).

14. In addition to other violent and illegal acts, QAnon was a motivating factor for some who stormed the US Capitol, disrupted Congress, and interfered with the congressional certification of President Joe Biden's victory on January 6, 2021.

15. Cf. Wallace (1999, 29).

16. Zimbardo (1969). See also Le Bon ([1895] 2002, 6); Diener (1976).

17. Zimbardo (1969, 251).

18. Zimbardo (1969). In the case of Stanley Milgram's (1963) famous shock experiment, the "teacher" (the naive subject of the experiment) and the "learner" (an accomplice to the experiment, the person supposedly receiving the shocks) initially met face-to-face, but were then segregated so that the "learner" was in another room and therefore out of visual range to the subject administering the shocks. In subsequent experiments, Milgram (1965, 1974, 33–36) found that the more remote the victim was from the subject, the more likely the subject was to obey an experimenter's order to shock the other person and to do so at higher levels of severity. Zimbardo and Milgram obscured personal identity in different ways to show that increased anonymity can lead to greater willingness to perpetrate harm.

19. Zimbardo (1969, 282).

20. Zimbardo (1969, 237, 240).

21. Reicher, Spears, and Postmes (1995, 168).

22. Reicher, Spears, and Postmes (1995, 163). See also Spears and Lea (1992).

23. See Lea and Spears (1991); Spears and Lea (1994); Reicher, Spears, and Postmes (1995); Postmes, Spears, and Lea (1999); Lea, Spears, and Watt (2007); Spears et al. (2014); Spears and Postmes (2015).

24. Spears and Lea (1994, 444). See also Reicher (1984); Postmes and Spears (1998, 254).

25. Reicher, Spears, and Postmes (1995, 173, 175). See also Postmes, Spears, and Lea (1999).

26. See Spears and Lea (1994); Reicher, Spears, and Postmes (1995, 187–91); Spears et al. (2002); Christopherson (2007, 3045, 3048–49); Spears et al. (2014, 30–34).

27. Postmes and Spears (1998, 242). See also Kim, Lee, and Lee (2019) for such a perspective.

28. Nussbaum (2010, 79). See also Rodriguez (2015, 29) on graffiti that facilitates "sexist, racist, and homophobic speech." See also Cole (1991, 402).

29. Nussbaum (2010, 85). See also Moore (2018, 178).

30. See Bakhtin ([1965] 1984); Wiles (2000, 153). For a fictional portrayal of a sexually subversive masquerade ritual, see Stanley Kubrick's 1999 film, *Eyes Wide Shut*.

31. Schutz ([1932] 1967, 181) calls our attention to "artifacts of any kind which bear witness to the subjective meaning-context of some unknown person." Foucault

([1969] 1977, 127) writes, "Modern criticism, in its desire to 'recover' the author from a work, employs devices strongly reminiscent of Christian exegesis when it wished to prove the value of a text by ascertaining the holiness of its author."

32. Ezell (2003, 76).

33. Mullan (2007, 78).

34. Mullan (2007, 82).

35. Easley (2004, 124).

36. Easley (2004, 117, 125, 128–29). In this regard, contemporary female music composers have sometimes adopted gender-ambiguous or male pseudonyms to avoid discrimination in their male-dominated field. See Bennett et al. (2019).

37. Mullan (2007, 104).

38. Ciuraru (2011, 39).

39. Baena (2015); van den Berg (2011).

40. Some artists and scholars distinguish between different types of illicit street art. Here, I use the terms "graffiti" and "street art" in the most general way, lumping various potentially distinguishable forms together.

41. Barnett (2016).

42. See Meade (2015) on "latrinalia."

43. Lovata and Olton (2015, 139–40); Pozorski and Pozorski (2015); Beck, Falvey, and Drollinger (2015).

44. See Lovata (2015) on "arborglyphs."

45. Baudrillard ([1976] 1993, 96–97). See also Bush (2013); Olton and Lovata (2015, 12–13); Barnett (2016).

46. See Kukla (2020) on this connection.

47. Lennon (2015).

48. Thompson (1975] 2011, 281).

49. Kukla (2020).

50. Mikael-Debass (2017).

51. Rodriguez (2015, 25–26); Starr (1990). See also Cole (1991).

52. Cole (1991, 401).

53. Olton and Lovata (2015, 14). See also Bush (2013).

54. Kukla (2020).

55. Burrows (2020).

56. See https://www.dedebandaid.com/site-specific-dede.

57. Kukla (2020; emphasis in original).

58. See also Banksy (2006, 168–85); Ellsworth-Jones (2012, 9–21).

59. Ellsworth-Jones (2012, 297)

60. See also Ellsworth-Jones (2012, 20–21).

61. Ellsworth-Jones (2012, 103).

62. See https://www.guerrillagirls.com/.

63. Maniak (2018, 87).

64. Interview with Guerrilla Girl using the pseudonym Frida Kahlo. Smithsonian Archives of American Art (2008a).

65. Guerrilla Girls (2021). See also Maniak (2018, 88).

66. Olton and Lovata (2015, 15).

67. Interview with Guerrilla Girl using the pseudonym Alma Thomas. Smithsonian Archives of American Art (2008b).

68. Guerrilla Girls (2021).

69. Interview with Guerrilla Girl using the pseudonym Alice Neel. Smithsonian Archives of American Art (2007).

70. Interview with Guerrilla Girl using the pseudonym Kathe Kollwitz. Smithsonian Archives of American Art (2008a).

71. Thompson (1974, 398–400). The third characteristic was "swift direct action" (401). All three are characteristics of the movements I study in this chapter. See also Thompson ([1975] 2011).

72. Scott (1990, 136).

73. Scott (1990, 151–52).

74. Ruiz (2013, 264).

75. Markman and Markman (1989, 66). See Andrew (2014, 215) with regard to the rituals of various African communities. See also Lévi-Strauss (1963, 264), who comments that in certain cultures, "masks also represent ancestors, and by wearing the mask the actor incarnates the ancestor."

76. Kobayashi (1981, 7; emphasis added). This study is based on modern manifestations of ancient rites. Similarly, Napier (1986, 22) points out, men of the North American Kwakiutl Indian communities "acquire their supernatural masks in initiations held only in winter, only at night."

77. On masking practices and symbolism in such religious rituals, see Lévi-Strauss (1963, 261–66; [1975] 1988); Napier (1986); Wiles (2000). In *The Elementary Forms of Religious Life*, Émile Durkheim ([1912] 1995) shows how the power attributed to sacred items and totemic figures stems from the collective energy and sentiment coordinated and expressed in ritual.

78. See Alexander's (2004, 540–47) important discussion of the rise of Greek drama, which has significantly shaped my perspective and analysis in this section. See also Alexander (2017, 4–6); Turner (1982). Cf. Schechner ([1977] 2003, 152). See also Calame's (1986, 137) brief discussion of "the civic value of Greek tragedy" and Napier's (1986, 35) comment about "a *dramatis persona*'s very special role in commenting on real events."

79. See Alexander (2004) on the concept of performative fusion. See also Calame (1986, 127, 135); Turner (1982, 18).

80. Alexander (2017, 5).

81. Wiles (2000, 151). See also Tseëlon (2001b, 24).

82. Rehm (1992, 41). See also Johnson (1992, 24).

83. "A Greek Theatre Mask," British Museum, http://www.teachinghistory100 .org/objects/about_the_object/greek_theatre_mask.

84. As Napier (1986, 8) points out, "The Greek word *prosōpon* was, as was the Latin word *persona*, used to designate a mask." Moreover, "the word *prosōpon* could mean the mask, the dramatic part, the person, and the face; likewise, *persona* . . . could also refer to one who plays a part or to characters acted."

85. We can also consider the emergence of Noh and Kuōgen theater centuries later in Japan. Noh theater was initially designed around Buddhist principles during the fourteenth century, but evolved (in form and content) from much earlier religious rites and ceremonial folk festivals, both indigenous to Japan and foreign. See Tyler (1987); Ortolani (1990). Noh theater was not directly critical of authority like its Greek counterpart. However, Noh was certainly socially reflexive. Actors used its masks, robes, and other elements of costume to animate culturally and emotionally coded character-symbols and convey meaningful stories that carried deep-seated mor-

als and rich sentiments about Japanese customs, values, and traditions. See Udaka (2010) on the symbolism of Noh masks.

86. Tertullian (~197–202, chap. 20). See also Barish (1981, 44–52).

87. Brandon (2013, 18). See also Tertullian (~197–202, chap. 23); Barish (1986, 44–52).

88. See Augustine ([397–98] 1961). See also Barish (1981, 52–65).

89. Napier (1986, 6). See also Nixey (2017, 201–9).

90. See Napier (1986, 11–15). See also Tseëlon (2001a, 4).

91. Wiles (2000, 151).

92. Mauss ([1938] 1985, 19, 22). See also Agnew (1986, 101–48); Napier (1986, 4–10).

93. Turner (1982, 38–39) notes how the English Puritans further attacked and outlawed the dramatic arts, including "theatrical productions, masques, pageants, musical performances, and, of course, the popular genres of carnivals, festivals, charivaris, ballad singing, and miracle plays." See also Agnew (1986).

94. Tseëlon (2001b, 20–21).

95. Bakhtin ([1965] 1984, 6).

96. See Kinser (1990, 5). See also Tseëlon (2001a, 11) on masking as a "device for destabilising categories" and "subverting established meanings."

97. Bakhtin ([1965] 1984, 6, 9, 10).

98. Holquist (1985, xxi). On subversive inversions as they pertain to carnival, see also Scott (1990, 172–82). Scott (1990, 181) notes that "actual rebels mimic carnival" because "Carnival, in its ritual structure and anonymity, gives a privileged place to normally suppressed speech and aggression."

99. Bakhtin ([1965] 1984, 7).

100. Honigmann (1977, 278). Masking and costume remain central to contemporary carnival events and experiences, including various popular folk festivals and holidays such as Halloween and related rituals in various parts of the world, Día de los Muertos in Mexico, Guy Fawkes Day in Britain, the Philadelphia Mummers Parade, Mardi Gras in New Orleans, and the Burning Man festival in the Nevada desert.

101. Shalev (2003, 172, 165, 167). This general point was first made by Karl Marx ([1851–52] 1968, 96–97) when he discussed the fact that the French revolutionaries "performed the task of their time in Roman costume and with Roman phrases" (96).

102. Alexander (2004, 546).

103. See De Hert (2003). Marx ([1851–52] 1968, 97) also addressed this phenomenon when he recognized that after the revolutions of this era were securely won, "bourgeois society . . . no longer comprehended that ghosts from the days of Rome had watched over its cradle."

104. Johnson (2001, 90).

105. Mill (1859, 47). See also Adut (2018, 91).

106. See De Hert (2003, 56). See Moore (2018) for an alternative take on this principle.

107. Gardner (2011, 929).

108. Simmel (1950c, 373).

109. See also Marx (1999, 102).

110. See Coleman (2014, 46–51) on the "collectivist, anti-celebrity ethic" of Anonymous and "the self-effacement of the individual" (47). See Nail (2013, 36) on the Zapatista "practice of collective masking," which "creates a visual equality between

subjects, without leaders" and expresses the notion that the movement is "open to anyone."

111. Cf. Coleman (2014, 395) on "Anonymous Everywhere."

112. See Nail (2013, 33–34), who argues that the use of masks by movements in the late modern era expresses an "anti-authoritarian horizontalism" and "indistinguishable anonymity" that "creates a group subjectivity" that undermines more traditional liberal forms of representation by the state or other authorities. See also Koch (2014, 449, 453–54, 462); Spiegel (2015); Boyd and Field (2016, 356); Eyerman (2006, 209).

113. Coleman (2014, 399). See also Ruiz (2013, 266). Simultaneously, masks can also obscure the diversity of movement participants.

114. See also Spiegel (2015).

115. Miller (2017; emphasis added).

116. Spiegel (2015, 790–91).

117. Spiegel (2015, 787–88).

118. See Alexander (2004, 530) on "the deep background of collective representations for social performance." See also Turner (1967, 20; 1982, 22); Tseëlon (2001b, 19).

119. See Alexander (2004, 530) on the symbolic "foreground" of social performance. In such cases, anonymity is a central characteristic of all four technical aspects of social movement dramaturgy identified by Benford and Hunt (1992): "scripting, staging, performing and interpreting" (36).

120. See Benford and Hunt (1992) on social movements' uses of "dramatic techniques" to "construct and communicate power" (36).

121. Linda Gordon (2017, 88) describes the Klan of the 1920s as "a pan-Protestant evangelical movement." See also Fossett (1997, 36); Bouie (2015).

122. Mahboob (2017). See also Gordon (2017, 26–28, 202) on the "nativism" of the Klan and the idea of "undiluted Anglo-Saxon heritage," as well as her description of the standard Prussian cross insignia on Klan robes of the early twentieth century (71). On ancestral and historical continuity, see Zerubavel (2003, 2012).

123. The original "Ku Klux Kreed" (Ku Klux Klan 1917) professes dedication to "the sublime principles of a pure Americanism." See also Gordon (2017, 34, 56).

124. Dixon (1905). This was the second installment of a trilogy, which also included *The Leopard's Spots* (1902) and *The Traitor* (1907). See Fossett (1997) for an important discussion.

125. Dixon (1905, 326). The illustrator was Arthur I. Keller.

126. See also Simcovitch (1972). The film inspired the revitalization of the Klan and the organization, in turn, "relied a great deal on the film as a major source of propaganda" (52).

127. See especially Blee and McDowell (2013); Gordon (2017).

128. Gordon (2017, 2, 79, 81–88). See also Blee and McDowell (2013, 258–60) on the Klan's "public spectacles."

129. Gordon (2017, 31, 71–77).

130. Gordon (2017, 93–107).

131. Blee and McDowell (2013, 250); Gordon (2017). Gordon notes that "the Klan also claimed the Boston Tea Party as an honored ancestor, naming it the first recorded Klan meeting" (218n8).

132. Parsons (2005; 2015). See especially (2005, 819, 823; 2015, 88) on "folk serenading."

133. Parsons (2005, 811, 812, 818; 2015, 78); Silver (2000, 356). European carnival

practices influenced nineteenth- and twentieth-century American practices. European antecedents included "abundant street masking" along with "raucous orchestras on foot," where "mannequins . . . were burned," and satire and "sharp-tongued insults" were common (Kinser 1990, 8, 9). Moreover, American Mardi Gras folk troops often referred to themselves as "Knights," as in the "Knights of Revelry" (Kinser 1990, 13). This is a feudal-Christian influence that had previously been adopted by the Knights of the Ku Klux Klan. In fact, "the legitimation of New Orleans carnival generally paralleled the incorporation of the Klan and its ideas into mainstream culture" (Parsons 2005, 834).

134. See Parsons (2005, 812, 813, 819, 821, 823, 824–26; 2015, 41–44, 76–96). See also Silver (2000, 342); Fossett (1997).

135. Silver (2000, 345); Parsons (2015, 81–84).

136. Napier (1986, 18–19).

137. Calame (1986, 139–40).

138. Calame (1986, 140).

139. Parsons (2005, 820). See also Parsons (2015, 81); Silver (2000, 345); Fry ([1975] 2001). With the revival of the Klan in the early twentieth century, the order was dedicated to "the valiant, venerated Dead" (Ku Klux Klan 1917).

140. Fry ([1975] 2001, 53, 56).

141. See Parsons (2015, 2, 117). See also Silver (2000).

142. Fry ([1975] 2001, 54).

143. Ku Klux Klan (1868). Capitalizations in the original text. In his publication *K.K.K. Sketches*, Beard (1877, 82) writes, "The raiding force always moved in the night season, and members of the Order never exhibited themselves in the Ku-Klux role in the daytime."

144. Forrest (1868). See Parsons (2015, 111–43) on the "postwar racial order."

145. Forrest (1868).

146. Ku Klux Klan (1917).

147. See Parsons (2005, 813–14; 2015). Parsons (2015, 126) comments, "The Ku-klux attack was, above all, a ritual of exclusion, in which the subject was excised from the body politic."

148. Coleman (2014, 3). Notably, a "commitment to the maintenance of anonymity," which involves blocking vital identifying information, and "a broad dedication to the free flow of information" might be seen as contradictory.

149. Coleman (2014, 75, 106). See also Klein (2002, 8), who describes the contemporary global movement against neoliberalism and capitalism as "multiheaded, impossible to decapitate."

150. Knuttila (2011).

151. The term "hacktivist" stems from a combination of the words "hacker" and "activist." The *United States Cybersecurity Magazine*, an online resource, defines hacktivism simply and broadly as "hacking for political and social change." See Putman (n.d.). As Gary Alan Fine (2015, 20) describes with regard to the world of chess, hacktivism "is both a subculture, spread widely, and an idioculture—a shared culture found in tight-knit groups." The broadening appeal of hacktivist subculture in the twenty-first century became evident with the popularity of films (such as The Matrix trilogy), television programs (such as the USA Network's *Mr. Robot*), and literature (such as Stieg Larsson's Millennium series), which portray hacktivism and hactivist protagonists in various positive ways.

152. Coleman (2014, 46).

153. Koch (2014, 457).

154. See Sharpe (2005).

155. The global Occupy movement began in 2011 with the Occupy Wall Street encampment in Zuccotti Park, New York. David Lloyd, the illustrator of *V for Vendetta*, comments, "The Guy Fawkes mask has now become a common brand and a convenient placard to use in protest against tyranny—and I'm happy with people using it, it seems quite unique, an icon of popular culture being used this way." Reported in Waites (2011).

156. See especially Koch's (2014) fascinating analysis of "the Guy Fawkes mask as political icon."

157. Olesen (2005, 108–9, 110). See also Olesen (2005, 9–10, 102–26) for a broader discussion.

158. See Olesen (2005) on all of these points. See also Nail (2013, 21, 33–37), who discusses "the political use of masks" as an important dimension that shows the influence of the Zapatistas on the Occupy movement. See also Klein (2002, 4); Ruiz (2013, 267–68); Spiegel (2015, 795).

159. My argument here is in line with Eyerman's (2006, 204–5) point about "the current anti-globalization movement."

160. Prior to the Zapatistas, masks became common garb for various anarchistic-influenced groups practicing "black bloc" tactics, which began with the Italian and especially German Autonomous movements of the 1970s and '80s. These *Autonomen* [were] dressed in black with their faces covered by motorcycle helmets, balaclavas, or other masks to create a uniform, anonymous mass of revolutionaries prepared to carry out militant actions" (Bray 2017, 52; emphasis in original). See also Gilligan 2017. Such tactics are often practiced under the banner of Antifa (short for "anti-fascist") today, a broadening, increasingly visible, and controversial network of activists who often merge their notion of anti-fascism directly with "antiracist organizing" and a transnational "anti-imperialism" (Bray 2017, xvii, 67, 87). When Antifa activists mask themselves with scarves or bandannas at political rallies, this masking is also a performance of a shared subversive identity rooted in political solidarity with the diverse rebel communities of the world, as much as it is a means of self-protection.

161. In late 2006, before the Fawkes mask was adopted in the name of activism, it was used as a meme character known as "Epic Fail Guy" in the 4chan forum. Epic Fail Guy, like the real Guy Fawkes, is primarily known for failure.

162. When engaging in physical public protest for the first time in 2008, Anonymous established a "code of conduct" that urged its affiliates to "use scarves, hats, and sunglasses" to cover their faces while protesting. Many chose to don the Guy Fawkes mask (instead of a scarf) because it symbolized the political ethic expressed in the film *V for Vendetta*. See Coleman (2014, 64–65).

163. See Koch (2014, 472–75) on "the Guy Fawkes mask as a transnational phenomenon" (472), which is "influenced by local structures" (473) when and where activists use it. Cf. Nail (2013, 35–37) for a related discussion.

164. See, for example, Anonymous (2012b); Anonymous (2013a); Anonymous (2019).

165. Benford and Hare (2015, 646). See also Gottschalk and Whitmer (2013); Markham (2013).

166. Anonymous (2012a). See also Anonymous (2014a), in which the spokesperson

portrays Anonymous as the universal "we" with comments such as "We, as in you and us. We, as in everything and everyone. . . . We are you. We are your neighbors. . . . We are them and they are us." See also Koch (2014, 461).

167. Coleman (2014, 48–49).

168. Anonymous (2019). See also Anonymous (2008).

169. Anonymous (2017). Around this time, a wave of similar videos appeared under the banner of Anonymous.

170. See also Coleman (2014, 49); Woolf (2016). Similarly, some originators of the Ku Klux Klan would question the legitimacy of other actors who donned the cover representation. See Parsons (2005, 815–16; 2015, 68–69).

171. Ku Klux Klan (1917).

172. Parsons (2015, 9, 10; emphasis added).

173. Parsons (2015, 75).

174. The phrase "you can kill a man, but you can't kill an idea" is attributed to civil rights leader Medgar Evers. However, this sentiment was also expressed in the film *V for Vendetta*. When, toward the end of the film, V is asked by Peter Creedy, the director of the secret police, "Why won't you die?" he responds, "Beneath this mask there is more than flesh. Beneath this mask there is an idea . . . and ideas are bulletproof." See also Coleman (2014, 16).

175. Anonymous (2014a).

176. Silver (2000, 340, 342).

177. Silver (2000, 342). See also Parsons (2005, 824).

178. Silver (2000, 342).

179. Coleman (2014, 31). See also where Coleman defines "the lulz" as "a deviant style of humor and a quasi-mystical state of being" (2). See also Auerbach (2015a,b). Such "mischief," as John Mullan (2007, 9–40) shows, was also a key motivation for some authors of various eras to remain anonymous.

180. Bakhtin ([1965] 1984, 88). See also Thompson (1974, 400–401), who shows that theatrical and comedic performances, as well as satirical music, were also common in popular English protests targeting the ruling elite. See also Auerbach (2015b) and Moore (2018, 185) on play as a feature of anonymous online spaces, such as 4chan.

181. Coleman (2014, 2).

182. Serracino-Inglott (2013, 217, 228–33).

183. Koch (2014, 457).

184. On historical analogies and mnemonic bridging, see Zerubavel (2003); De-Gloma (2015).

185. See Schafer and Dickens (2016) on the mnemonic battle over the legacy of Emiliano Zapata. See also Olesen (2005, 117–18) on the "melding" of Zapata with "local indigenous myths" to create "the figure of Votán Zapata."

186. Ku Klux Klan (1917).

187. Marx ([1851–52] 1968, 96). See also Alexander (2004, 530).

188. Ku Klux Klan (1917).

189. FBI directive, August 25, 1967. Reprinted in Glick (1989, 77). The directive quoted was specifically written to address the case of Black Nationalist groups in the United States but also exemplifies the general purposes of COINTELPRO.

190. Churchill and Vander Wall (1990, 57–60). Churchill and Vander Wall's *The COINTELPRO Papers* is one of the most comprehensive collections of official FBI documents issued in conjunction with this program and an essential source of infor-

mation. The FBI also maintains a comprehensive online database of COINTELPRO documents. See https://vault.fbi.gov/cointel-pro.

191. Churchill and Vander Wall (1990).

192. Johnson (2001, 96; emphasis in original). See also Ruiz (2013, 266).

193. Goffman (1959, 59). See also Goffman (1969, 9, 10, 13, 71).

194. Simmel (1950b, 162). See also Goffman (1969, 73–77) for a discussion of triadic dynamics of information control.

195. See "FBI Records: The Vault: Puerto Rican Groups" for a comprehensive record of documents. https://vault.fbi.gov/cointel-pro/puerto-rican-groups. See also Churchill and Vander Wall (1990, 63–90).

196. FBI memorandum from Special Agent in Charge of the San Juan FBI Field Office to FBI Director, November 13, 1967. Quoted in Churchill and Vander Wall (1990, 74).

197. Churchill and Vander Wall (1990, 77).

198. FBI memorandum from FBI Director to Special Agent in Charge, San Juan Field Office, May 11, 1967. Reprinted in Churchill and Vander Wall (1990, 81).

199. Churchill and Vander Wall (1990, 76).

200. On the "back region," see Goffman (1959, 112). On the "performance team," see Goffman (1959, 79, 77–105).

## Chapter Four

1. Steinbeck (1939, 40).

2. Peterson and Harvey (2015, 207).

3. Steinbeck (1939, 38).

4. Some have more power to direct these institutional forces than others and, as Spears and Lea (1994, 448) recognize, "the anonymity of people in powerful or high-status positions may give them the freedom to express and wield the power owing to their position." Furthermore, we often face pressures not to look for powerful operatives behind systems, as expressed in the famous line from Victor Fleming's 1939 film, *The Wizard of Oz*, "Pay no attention to that man behind the curtain."

5. Smith ([1776] 2003, 572). See also Smith ([1759] 2010, 165).

6. Bauman (1989, 102–6, 135–49).

7. Weber ([1922] 1978; [1930] 1992). See Parsons ([1951] 1991) on pattern variables and the distinction between "universalism" and "particularism." See also Wallace (1999, 24) who mentions "natural or social anonymity that is the byproduct of complex social forces and arrangements."

8. Weber ([1922] 1978, 86). See also Simmel ([1978] 2011, 481) on "the calculating character of modern times."

9. Habermas (1987). The anonymity of social systems is countered by the intimacy of small communities and local place. On the latter, see Fine (2012); Gould (1995). However, while small group relations are typically personal and intimate, groups such as families, teams, and social movement communities can also serve as collective fronts that obscure the individual identities of their members when viewed from the outside.

10. See Simmel (1950b) on replaceability as a characteristic that distinguishes the triad from the dyad and, by extension, a feature of large groups in general. As Thompson (1980, 909) argues, "In organizations persons often are fungible," providing a foun-

dation for "causal excuses" like the one given by Steinbeck's driver when he justifies his actions by claiming that if he does not demolish the house, someone else will. As Thompson points out, "If the excuse is valid, no one is responsible."

11. Simmel ([1903] 1950). See also Wirth (1938); Grazian (2008, 5–13).

12. See also Simmel (1950b; [1978] 2011). See also Auerbach (2015b) and Moore (2018, 184–85) on such freedom as a characteristic of anonymous and pseudonymous spaces online.

13. Adut (2018).

14. Douglas, Rasmussen, and Flanagan (1977).

15. Singh (2017, 145).

16. See Darley and Latané (1968) for a classic psychological study that shows the diffusion of responsibility in crowds to be a primary factor inhibiting bystander responses to emergency situations. See also Diener et al. (1976).

17. Schweingruber and Wohlstein (2005, 139–40).

18. Simmel (1898, 664).

19. See Olesen (2019, 286–87)

20. Thompson (1980, 907).

21. Simmel (1950c, 375).

22. Schutz ([1932] 1967, 199). See also Fine (1991, 171; 2021, 13–14).

23. Schutz ([1932] 1967, 198–99). Likewise, Fine (1991, 171) mentions "the government, the police, the schools, the corporation, the stock market, the networks."

24. In line with this argument, Max Weber ([1922] 1978, 14) writes, "For sociological purposes there is no such thing as a collective personality which 'acts.' When reference is made in a sociological context to a state, a nation, a corporation, a family, or an army corps, or to similar collectivities, what is meant is, on the contrary, *only* a certain kind of development of actual or possible social actions of individual persons."

25. Freud ([1930] 1961).

26. Cf. Snow, Zurcher, and Peters (1981, 31–32) on "the *main task activity*" and "*subordinate task activities*" in crowds (emphasis in original).

27. See also Ponesse (2013, 341).

28. Olesen (2019, 292).

29. Eren (2017, 1).

30. Many of these institutions are part of the "shadow banking" system, which means that they are not subject to governmental (public) banking regulations and oversight. See Friedrichs (2013, 16) on "financial industry practices as crimes."

31. Pitesa (2015, 358, 360).

32. Boyd and Field (2016, 338).

33. See also Ansart and Monvoisin (2015).

34. Peterson and Harvey (2015, 201).

35. Peterson and Harvey (2015, 204–5).

36. See Kiel (2012, 9).

37. Cf. Eren (2017) on Bernie Madoff as a personalized villain (face) of bank malfeasance. Eren argues that Madoff's "guilt came to represent the guilt of an entire system" in "a culture that seeks individualist explanations for social problems" (15). This involves "displacing blame for systemic problems onto individuals" and "the use of punishment as panacea for systemic issues" (149). In line with my argument, the social focus on Madoff's arrest, trial, and harsh sentence may have actually helped to reinforce the anonymity of other actors who were shielded by the fact that he took

the blame for problems they helped to create. Such a case raises the notion of the "fall guy" or "scapegoat" as providing a single personal face to broader social problems. Likewise, when corporations bear the names of their founders or owners, those individuals often become the public front for corporate activity, even when they are no longer personally responsible for the activities of the company. Moreover, when a CEO becomes the public face of a company or its product (as, for example, Lee Iaccoca was to Chrysler in the 1980s, Phil Knight was to Nike in the 1990s and 2000s, and Mark Zuckerberg is to Facebook as of this writing) that individual personifies the product and brand while the vast majority of others engaged in the production process, holding seats of the board of directors, or otherwise affiliated with the corporate enterprise remain relatively anonymous to consumers and to the public at large.

38. Zuckerman (2010). See Thompson (1980, 907–8) on the "collective responsibility" framework.

39. Bianco (2008, 18, 20).

40. Friedrichs (2013, 6). See also Eren (2017).

41. See Nicol (2016). See also, for example, Dunbar and Donald (2009). While some—for example, *Time* (2009); Wallison (2011)—did name and blame particular individuals (including financial industry CEOs; bureaucrats such as Alan Greenspan, who chaired the Federal Reserve until 2006; and politicians such as Massachusetts congressional representative Barney Frank, who championed liberal housing initiatives), the institutions they represent (corporate or governmental) received the brunt of public blame.

42. Holland (2012). See also, for example, Brooks (2010).

43. Arnold (2010).

44. Kiel (2012).

45. See Milkman, Luce, and Lewis (2013, 23). See also Eren (2017, 151).

46. Ansart and Monvoisin (2015, 285, 287).

47. Lau (2019).

48. Dowling and Wichowsky (2013, 969, 985).

49. See also Boyd and Field (2016, 353–54).

50. Dowling and Wichowsky (2013); Ridout, Franz, and Fowler (2014).

51. Boyd and Field (2016, 354).

52. See Harcourt (2015, 2–3) for an introductory discussion.

53. Lyon (2014).

54. Lyon (2014, 4, 6).

55. See Harcourt (2015, 13–14, 19, 129). See also Bauman et al. (2014, 137–40). One form of data we share is the information we generate when we watch others online. As Marx (2016, 141) notes, surveillance can "involve horizontal rather than vertical ties, and share, merge, or blur the roles of watcher and watched." Such an astute analysis of the complex structure of surveillance in our late modern world fits nicely with Adut's (2018) discussion of spectatorship and the public sphere. By democratizing acts of surveillance, people become increasingly aware of the fact that they are potentially being watched, always and by anyone or everyone.

56. See especially Olesen (2019, 283–85). See also Elliston (1982, 168); Marx (2016, 166).

57. Olesen (2019, 282, 284).

58. Doyle and Veranas (2014, 215). See also Spiegel (2015, 792), who addresses "the asymmetrical logic of coding and surveilling individuals while *obscuring* the actions of

public forces that, in principle, serve and answer to these same individuals" (emphasis in original).

59. Foucault ([1975] 1995). Notably, the original French title of Foucault's *Discipline and Punish* is *Surveiller et Punir*, to monitor/surveil and punish.

60. Foucault ([1975] 1995, 201, 202).

61. Douglass (1845, 60, 61).

62. Olesen (2019, 287).

63. See also Lyon (2014, 7). Harcourt (2015, 54–58) notes that there are three main views of the "surveillance state"—one takes the state as a benevolent protector, another as a deceptive monster, and a third as a necessary and efficient administrator.

64. Bauman et al. (2014, 142) identify familiarity, fear (associated with the threat of terrorism), and fulfillment provided by relationships as factors that render surveillance "publicly acceptable to many."

65. Linder and Xiao (2020). The Onion Router (Tor) is a free web browser that encrypts and relays a user's web-browsing activity through a complex network of third-party computers, making it very difficult to determine a user's unique IP address, effectively anonymizing them as they engage in online activity. See https://www.torproject.org/. While "Tor has vulnerabilities [that] have been exploited by hackers and law enforcement alike to expose users in the past," Linder and Xiao (2020, 5) explain, "it remains one of the more secure means of masking one's identity online." See also Harcourt (2015, 271–74).

66. Preibusch (2015, 55). See also Bauman et al. (2014, 143).

67. Marx (2016, 57).

68. Bauman et al. (2014, 140). See also Lyon (2014, 7–8).

69. Giddens (1990, 145).

70. Gusterson (2014, 193).

71. Sluka (2013, 172).

72. With regard to both war and terrorism, the commemorative practice of listing the names of those who have died (as with the Washington, DC, Vietnam Veterans Memorial and the New York City 9/11 Memorial) serves to personalize such mass acts of violence. See Wagner-Pacifici and Schwartz (1991); Simko (2015).

73. See Colonomos (2016) for a critical engagement on this point. See Brunstetter and Braun (2011) for an overview of central ethical issues.

74. Whitehead and Finnström (2013, 2). See also Brunstetter and Braun (2011, 352–55).

75. Gusterson (2014, 197). Distance does not appear to mitigate the psychological impact and moral burden of killing. Drone operators suffer similarly from posttraumatic stress disorder compared to other military combat personnel. See Dao (2013).

76. Sluka (2013, 175). Even though this critical scholar explicitly acknowledges and discusses the situation of drone operators, the term shows a broader cultural norm of referring to drones as agents.

77. Baker (2015; emphasis added).

78. See, for example, Sonia Kennebeck's 2016 documentary film, *National Bird*.

79. Ackerman (2016). See Gusterson (2014, 194) on this distinction. The italics in the terms are mine.

80. Brunstetter and Braun (2011, 348, 351).

81. Shane (2015).

82. See, for example, *Ahmed Salem Bin Ali Jaber and Esam Abdullah Abdulmah-moud Bin Ali Jaber v. The United States of America, Barack Obama, Leon Panetta, David Petraeus, Unknown Defendant One, Unknown Defendant Two, and Unknown Defendant Three*, Complaint in Civil Action No. 1:15-cv-840, United States District Court, District of Columbia (filed June 7, 2015).

83. Sluka (2013, 186; see 182–88). See also Kilcullen and Exum (2009).

84. Gusterson (2014, 194). See also Watson (2012).

85. See Monbiot (2012).

86. See Aikins and Rubin (2021); Levenson (2021).

87. See "Drone Wars: The Constitutional and Counterterrorism Implications of Targeted Killing," Hearing before the Subcommittee on the Constitution, Civil Rights and Human Rights of the Committee on the Judiciary, United States Senate, April 23, 2013, https://www.govinfo.gov/content/pkg/CHRG-113shrg26147/html/CHRG-113shrg26147.htm.

88. Walzer (2016, 16). See also the 2012 report of the International Human Rights and Conflict Resolution Clinic at Stanford Law School and the Global Justice Clinic at NYU School of Law, "Living under Drones: Death, Injury, and Trauma to Civilians from US Drone Practices in Pakistan," 80–88 (https://law.stanford.edu/projects/living-under-drones/). Also cited by Walzer (2016). As Walzer notes, when drones are seen and heard, it may be by design, not unlike the case of Mr. Covey addressed previously. See also Gusterson (2014, 195).

89. See especially the 2012 report of the International Human Rights and Conflict Resolution Clinic at Stanford Law School and the Global Justice Clinic at NYU School of Law, "Living under Drones: Death, Injury, and Trauma to Civilians from US Drone Practices in Pakistan."

90. This video, along with ample media commentary, can be found with a simple search and viewed online as of this writing.

91. Vasquez (2008, 96; see also 98). See also Brunstetter and Braun (2011); Robben (2013). Viewing real people as images on a screen also facilitates their dehumanization, as is evident in slang terms used by drone operators, such as "squirters" (people seen on a screen scattering for cover) or "bug splat" (a person whose body is annihilated by a strike). See Mayer (2009); Hastings (2012).

92. Torpey and Hooiveld (2016, 3, 11). See also Benjamin (2013).

93. See Horowitz (2016) on "lethal autonomous weapon systems." The distinguishing feature of such weapons "is that the weapon system, not a person, selects and engages targets" (26). Of course, real people would program, initiate, and maintain these systems if used in warfare, people who would remain anonymous behind the technical system in the act of killing.

94. Arie (2011, 1286). See also Davidson and Barajas (2014, 84).

95. Roko (2007, 2808–11). As Roko points out, "Prison officials have voiced concerns that identifying the execution team members would make it difficult to find anyone willing to take on the job" (2800). See also Japenga (1989), who interviewed an anonymous Washington State hangman and reports that while he is not conflicted about his work, he is disturbed by the possibility of people identifying him as the executioner.

96. See Davidson and Barajas (2014, esp. 51–52, 68, 76–84). For the Missouri statute (MO Rev Stat § 546.720), see https://law.justia.com/codes/missouri/2011/title xxxvii/chapter546/section546720/.

97. Lofland (1975, esp. 284–87). As Lofland points out, the routine strategies of concealment practiced in the modern era not only serve to remove the act of killing from public view, but to "impersonalize" the process for those involved (281, 287, 290). See also Bessler (1997); LeGraw and Grodin (2002); Roko (2007); Garland (2010, 268–72); Davidson and Barajas (2014). As of June 2020, twenty-eight US states have the death penalty. Of those, most have legislation protecting the identities of individuals who participate in the execution process (typically referred to as the "execution team"). Three states (California, Oregon, and Pennsylvania) have moratoriums on state executions. Since 1976 in the United States, 1,338 executions have been carried out by lethal injection, 163 by electrocution, 11 by gas, 3 by hanging, and 3 by firing squad. See the Death Penalty Information Center, https://deathpenaltyinfo.org/state-and -federal-info/state-by-state and https://deathpenaltyinfo.org/executions/methods -of-execution. For information on state laws protecting the identities of executioners and execution team members, see https://deathpenaltyinfo.org/executions/lethal -injection/state-by-state-lethal-injection-protocols.

98. Strong (2021); Gill (2020).

99. Lofland (1975, 272, 293). See also Hornum (1968, 331–32); Foucault ([1975] 1995); Sarat (1999, 154–59); Smith (2008, 34–56). The convention in the literature has been to contrast modern methods of punishment in the West with premodern and early modern European practices. However, public executions are neither exclusively premodern nor are they unique to European history. As Garland (2010, 27–32) details, "spectacle lynchings" were common across the southern United States over the course of the late nineteenth and first half of the twentieth centuries. These public executions were carried out by mobs of white vigilantes who tortured and killed accused Black individuals, often in a communal and celebratory manner. Garland argues that "the specter of these lynchings has long haunted the American legal system and played a crucial role in shaping the reinvented death penalty that emerged at the end of the twentieth century" (33).

100. Hornum (1968, 128).

101. Lofland (1975, 284, 285).

102. Kinney (2016, 32). Although the anonymity of the feudal executioner is largely mythical, there is some evidence that executioners "kept their distance from the lay-people in the community" (Hornum 1968, 135), and thus must have carried a mysterious allure. Furthermore, there is some evidence that professional executioners justified their actions with a rationalized "professional detachment" from the act of killing itself, from their personal feelings about the condemned, and from the competing sides to debates about the moral and political character of state execution. See Applbaum (1995, esp. 483). Such a mechanism of detachment or compartmentalization, which is likely strengthened by anonymity in our late modern era, may also allow some doctors and nurses to engage in these killing acts today despite the fact that their actions conflict in many ways with their professional medical roles. See Lifton ([1986] 2000, 418–29) on the psychosocial character of splitting or doubling. See also Ponesse (2013, 342–43) for a related discussion about "segregated identities."

103. See especially *Furman v. Georgia* (408 U.S. 238, 1972) and *Gregg v. Georgia* (428 U.S. 153, 1976), which bookended a four-year national cessation of executions. See Garland (2010), who argues that the *Gregg* decision "inaugurated a whole new capital punishment complex—America's death penalty in a late-modern mode" (261).

104. Garland (2009, 264).

105. See Sanburn (2014) for an interview with Chapman.

106. See Applbaum (1995, 460, 463, 472–73). As some have also pointed out, "The Nazis used the imagery of medicine to justify killing" (Groner 2002, 1028). See also Lifton ([1986] 2000).

107. Gawande (2006, 1222).

108. See Roko (2007) for a review of several legal challenges. See LeGraw and Grodin (2002, 419) for an argument that "the use of a medical procedure to execute human beings is, by itself, a violation of medical ethics and human rights."

109. See Emanuel and Bienen (2001); LeGraw and Grodin (2002); Gawande (2006); Roko (2007); Davidson and Barajas (2014).

110. In a particularly notable case, one anonymous doctor "supervised the lethal injections of fifty-four inmates in Missouri over a decade" (Roko 2007, 2791). Because he was called to testify during a federal lawsuit against the state (*Tylor v. Crawford*, 2007), which he was allowed to do anonymously (as "John Doe I"), it was revealed that he had "been sued for malpractice more than 20 times," was denied privileges at two local hospitals due to ethical concerns, was publicly reprimanded by the state for failure to disclose information pertinent to his practice of medicine, and personally altered the state's lethal injection protocol (Kohler 2006). Following a subsequent investigation by journalists working for the *St. Louis Post-Dispatch*, the executioner was revealed to be Dr. Alan Doerhoff. Kohler (2006) reports that both the State Attorney General's office and the State Department of Corrections worked to preserve Dr. Doerhoff's anonymity.

111. LeGraw and Grodin (2002, 410–11, 385) argue that "because lethal injection utilizes medical skills and procedures to sanitize and legitimize the death penalty," the medical profession as a whole is complicit in what ultimately amounts to a human rights violation and "judicial homicide."

112. On the importance of meaning with regard to the death penalty, I build on the important work of Philip Smith (2003, 2008) and David Garland (2006; 2010). As Garland (2006, 428) states, such a focus on meaning serves to "enhance our understanding of penal power, penal violence, penal techniques and penal resources, not inhibit or displace it."

113. See Farber et al. (2001); Gawande (2006). In general, "The anonymous executioner is, at once, a stand-in for the community in whose name the execution was carried out" (Sarat 1999, 157n24).

114. Garland (2010, 271).

115. Groner (2002, 1027, 1026).

116. Gawande (2006).

117. Emanuel and Bienen (2016, 922). See also Gawande (2006) on this point.

118. AMA Code of Medical Ethics Opinion 9.7.3, https://www.ama-assn.org /delivering-care/ethics/capital-punishment. See also LeGraw and Grodin (2002, 407–12). Arie (2011, 1286) reports that "when medical bodies have attempted to strike off or discipline physicians who have participated in executions, they have been overruled by courts in the states concerned."

119. See, for example, the position of the American Society of Anesthesiologists, https://www.asahq.org/standards-and-guidelines/statement-on-physician -nonparticipation-in-legally-authorized-executions. See also the position of the

American Nurses Association, https://www.nursingworld.org/practice-policy/nursing-excellence/official-position-statements/id/capital-punishment-and-nurse-participation-in-capital-punishment/.

120. Milgram (1965, 63). See also Bauman (1989, 104, 151–68) on "the role of bureaucracy" and on the relevance of Milgram's findings to understanding the Holocaust.

121. Milgram (1965, 65).

122. Milgram (1965, 69–71).

123. Milgram (1965, 73). See also Bauman (1989, 154, 156–57, 164).

124. Bauman (1989, 159).

125. See Milgram (1974, 132–34); Bauman (1989, 162–63).

126. Bauman (1989, 163; italics removed). See also Zerubavel (forthcoming) on impersonality and dehumanization.

127. See Daniels (1987); DeVault (1994).

128. Poster, Crain, and Cherry (2016, 3).

129. Marx ([1845–46] 1978, 158–63). See also Zerubavel's (forthcoming) discussion of the impersonal character of capitalism.

130. Schutz ([1932] 1967, 201). See also Simmel ([1903] 1950, 411–12).

131. Marx ([1867] 1978, 321).

132. Marx ([1867] 1978, 322).

133. See also Natanson (1979, 538), who argues that when an "act is taken on its own, as autonomous, then . . . the actor becomes anonymous."

134. On the marked and unmarked, see Brekhus (1996; 1998; 2003) and Zerubavel (2015; 2018).

135. See Zweig (2014, 39–40). See Price (2003) for a fascinating discussion of the history, as well as the gendered and class dynamics, of ghostwriting. See Scott (2017) on art restoration.

136. See Price (2003, 228).

137. Price (2003, 214, 215).

138. Anonymous (2014b).

139. Journal practices of listing the names of all reviewers in one issue per year, or newer practices such as the Open Research and Contributor ID (ORCID) system, acknowledge this issue by providing some measure of individual reviewer recognition while maintaining reviewer anonymity with regard to each particular review process.

140. Rubenstein ([2005] 2019, 1; emphasis in original). See also Rubenstein (2003, 4).

141. Rubenstein ([2005] 2019, 1).

142. Eisen (2013, 7, 99–138).

143. Rubenstein ([2005] 2019, 5). See also Rubenstein (2003); Moster (2018).

144. See Boyarin ([2005] 2019, 238). See also Rubenstein (2003, 159–60); Moster (2018).

145. Rubenstein (2003, 16).

146. Rubenstein (2003, 2, 22–23).

147. Eisen (2013, 110).

148. Rubenstein (2003, 143).

149. Aneesh (2006, 5, 67–99).

150. Aneesh (2006, 9).

151. See https://www.gapinc.com/en-us/values/sustainability/people/supply-chain-working-conditions/supplier-partnerships for detailed information about

factory locations and the efforts of Gap, Inc., to monitor and improve working conditions.

152. For an in-depth discussion, see Aneesh (2006, 13, 133–52).

153. Brooks (2007, 151).

154. Wirth (1938, 13).

155. See also Zerubavel (forthcoming) on impersonality and dehumanization.

156. Mills ([1951] 2002, 224–38, 324–32).

## Chapter Five

1. Du Bois ([1903] 1995, 44, 45).

2. Schutz (1962; 1970, 111–22). See also McKinney (1969); Natanson (1979; 1986).

3. Schutz (1970, 120).

4. See Goffman (1963, 1–40, 55–62) on the difference between "social identity" and "personal identity." See also Snow and Anderson (1987, 1347).

5. See Natanson (1986, 52) on "acts of typification." See also Scheff (1975; 1984) on labeling.

6. Schutz ([1932] 1967, 195; 1970, 228). To add further precision to Schutz's view, such typifications fall somewhere in between anonymity and pseudonymity in terms of their degree of generality and specificity. The categorical cover is shared by many but the type is also identified as separate from other types.

7. Berger and Luckmann (1966, 32, 31). See also Schutz and Luckmann (1973, 79–84); Natanson (1986).

8. Simmel ([1908] 1950, 407, 405; emphasis added). See Alexander (2013, 78–98) for an important critical development of Simmel's contribution. See also Marx (1999, 105), who mentions that "a degree of de facto anonymity exists . . . in being away from home—whether as a tourist, traveler, or expatriate," where one is lumped into "the broad class of foreigner."

9. Simmel ([1908] 1950, 402).

10. See Simmel ([1955] 1964). See also Brekhus (2003, 74–94) on identity "integrators."

11. See McKinney (1969, 3). On the sociocognitive processes of marking and "mental coloring," see Brekhus (1996). See also Mullaney (1999) on "mental weighing"; Friedman (2013); Zerubavel (2018). See also Papadantonakis (2020) on the interpersonal dynamics of racialization.

12. Schutz ([1932] 1967, 184).

13. See also Bhatia (2005); Ivie (2005) on "the politics of naming."

14. Zerubavel (2018, 50). See also Brekhus (1996). See Zerubavel (forthcoming) on the impersonality of "social *quotas*" (emphasis in original).

15. Adut (2018, 128; see also 123–25, 129–31, 137).

16. See Zerubavel (2016) on essentialism.

17. See Simmel ([1978] 2011, 322) on "the interchangeability of persons." See also Simmel (1898, 672–73) on the replaceability of feudal leadership, where he discusses the phrase "The king never dies." Weber (1948) noted a similar characteristic of modern instrumental legal authority that regards the political office to be more important than the particular individual who occupies it. See also Parsons ([1951] 1991, 180–200) on "universalistic" and "particularistic" logics of social value and action.

18. See also Zerubavel (forthcoming) on interchangeability.

19. See Zerubavel (1991) on lumping and splitting in general.

20. Natanson (1970, 14).

21. Collins ([1990] 2000, 18).

22. See Christopherson (2007, 3045–47) on the "equalization hypothesis" regarding anonymity in computer-mediated communication. Even in anonymized computer-mediated social interactions, "cues to social category membership . . . often seep through," leading participants to typify one another and accentuate "intergroup differences" (Spears et al. 2002, 557–58).

23. See Friedman (2013) on the social perception of sexed and gendered bodies.

24. See Aneesh (2015) for a study of how call center workers in India "neutralize" their accents to manage vocal typification. See also Marx (2016, 159). See Spike Lee's 2018 film, *BlacKkKlansman*, for a fictional case in which the definition of a situation is shaped by vocal typification.

25. Alexander and Mast (2006, 4).

26. See Schutz (1962, 19). Cf. Zimbardo's (1969, 299–303) discussion of deindividuation as "imposed or chosen."

27. Natanson (1986, 24).

28. Schutz ([1932] 1967, 202).

29. Adut (2018, 36). See also Wirth (1938, 17–18).

30. Schutz ([1932] 1962, 60). See also Natanson (1986, 29).

31. See Schutz ([1932] 1962, 11–19).

32. Ezell (2003, 74, 75).

33. See Goldenberg and Addley (2011).

34. See Moran (2021).

35. Burrowes (2021).

36. See Oswell (2015). See also Gilbert (2017) on men who publish crime dramas under female or gender-neutral pseudonyms.

37. Froomkin (2003, 9). See also Kang (2000), to whom Froomkin refers. While actors who perform in "blackface" may not actually obscure their personal identities, they are engaging in discriminatory acts of typification. In addition to its history as a tool of ridicule and justification for racial hierarchy and oppression, a more general reason blackface is so offensive is that actors who wear it do not do so (or do not only do so) to become other individuals; they wear it to perform "black" as a type and to define blackness from an illegitimate standpoint.

38. Tavory (2009, 56, 57).

39. Tavory (2009, 57).

40. Tavory (2009, 62; see also 53n17, 66).

41. Schutz (1962, 19).

42. See also Reicher, Spears, and Lea (1995, 177).

43. Polletta (2020, 17).

44. See also Zimbardo (1969, 296); Zerubavel (forthcoming) on impersonality and dehumanization.

45. Zimbardo et al. (1971); Zimbardo (2021).

46. Zimbardo et al. (1971, 4). Zhong, Bohns, and Gino (2010) have explored how sunglasses provide people with a feeling of anonymity that can shape their behavior.

47. Zimbardo et al. (1971, 3, 4).

48. Bauman (1989, 166).

49. Zimbardo et al. (1971, 14).

50. Said (1978). See also Alexander (2013, 87-88).

51. Said (1978, 5, 7). See also Gordon (1997, 70), who comments with regard to racism that "the inferior Other becomes a fundamental project for the establishment of the Superior Self."

52. The term "Charlie" is derived from the International Radiotelephony Spelling Alphabet communication "Victor Charlie" used for "VC" or Viet Cong, which is derived from the Vietnamese term for "Vietnamese Communist."

53. The term "gook" is a US military slang term used in different wars to classify different foreign enemies, eventually taking on meaning as a derogatory term for people of Asian appearance during the Vietnam War. See https://www.etymonline .com/search?q=gook.

54. Comments quoted from testimony shown in the 1974 documentary film *Hearts and Minds*, directed by Peter Davis.

55. *Hearts and Minds* (1974).

56. See Said (1978, 284-325); Bhatia (2005).

57. See Ivie (2005).

58. Bhatia (2005, 19).

59. See Butler (2009). See also Archer (2014).

60. Bhatia (2005, 6, 13).

61. The literature addressing power as an intersectional phenomenon is vast, stemming from foundational work by Collins ([1990] 2000), Crenshaw (1991), and others. For a recent theoretical statement, see Collins (2019).

62. Schutz (1970, 120) comments, "By living up to his role" an actor "typifies himself; that is, he resolves to act in the typical way defined by the social role he has assumed."

63. Adut (2018, 31).

64. See Butler (1990) on "performative subversions" of established binary types with regard to sex and gender.

65. See a reprint of the 1946 *Fortune* piece in Zander (2016, 20-21). See also Ryder (2016). The text that accompanied the photos of *Labor Anonymous* marvels at the diversity and "self-possession" of the subjects while simultaneously framing all as "American labor" with collective strength and character.

66. Evans photographed several women, but left those shots out of the published spread. See Zander (2016).

67. Thompson (2016, 7).

68. See West and Fenstermaker (1995, 26-27) on such an accountability.

69. Schutz ([1932] 1967, 185).

70. Natanson (1986, 21).

71. See Weingarten (2007).

72. Genesis 42.

73. See Burke ([1945] 1969, 506-11) on metonymy and synecdoche.

74. Online Etymology Dictionary, https://www.etymonline.com/word/cop #etymonline_v_19052.

75. See, for example, Almasy (2020).

76. See "'Right to Know' Act Begins in New York City for NYPD," *Eyewitness News*, October 20, 2018, https://abc7ny.com/right-to-know-act-officer-information /4515782/.

77. See Snow and Anderson (1987, 1339-40).

78. See Langegger and Koester (2016, 1030–31). For these scholars, policies that prevent homeless people from meeting their basic personal needs in marginal public spaces—those that disrupt their social mobility and "regimes of personal hygiene" (1035)—can inhibit the ability of these individuals to be generally anonymous and invisible in cities while increasing their visibility *as homeless*.

79. Wasserman, Clair, and Platt (2012).

80. See discussion in Wasserman, Clair, and Platt (2012, 344–47).

81. Snow and Anderson (1987).

82. See, for example, Jones and Hannem (2018, 499).

83. Humphreys ([1970] 2017).

84. See Humphreys ([1970] 2017, 13–14, 18).

85. See Humphreys ([1970] 2017, 65, 67–68, 149).

86. There are many varieties of sex work and a vast literature that addresses this topic, highlighting a diverse array of issues. I focus my limited discussion here on the ways that sex work can, but does not always, involve anonymity or pseudonymity that stems from typification.

87. Simmel ([1978] 2011, 408, 407).

88. Quoted in Hubbard (2002, 376; emphasis added).

89. Quoted in Bernstein (2007, 132; emphasis added).

90. See especially Bernstein (2007) on "bounded authenticity"; Sanders (2008); Jones and Hannem (2018, 494, 507) on "bounded intimacy."

91. See Sanders (2008); Jones and Hannem (2018, esp. 496–99).

92. Jones and Hannem (2018).

93. Sanders (2008, 400).

94. Bernstein (2007, 126–30)

95. Bernstein (2007, 127).

96. Jones and Hannem (2018, 500).

97. Avery (2016, 171; emphasis added).

98. Avery (2016, 171, 175).

99. Hubbard (2002, 374–78).

100. See Bernstein (2007, 75–111).

101. See Liao (unpublished).

102. See discussions in Hubbard (2002); Bernstein (2007).

103. See Bernstein (2007, 139).

104. Omi and Winant (1994, 55).

105. See West and Fenstermaker (1995); Papadantonakis (2020).

106. West and Fenstermaker (1995, 26; emphasis in original).

107. West and Fenstermaker (1995, 23–24).

108. Omi and Winant (1994, 60).

109. Gordon (1997, 74, 75).

110. To this point, Omi and Winant (1994, 66) write that European colonial "conquest created the 'native' where once there had been Pequot, Iroquois, or Tutelo" and "created the 'black' where once there had been Asante or Ovimbundu, Yoruba or Bakongo."

111. Gordon (1997, 75; emphasis in original; 1995, 41).

112. Ellison ([1952] 1995).

113. Gordon (1995, 58; emphasis in original).

114. Fanon ([1952] 2008, 95). See also Gordon (1997, 73).

115. Anderson (1990, 208). See also discussion in Alexander (2013, 90); Papadan-tonakis (2020); and Ahmed's (2007) discussion of whiteness.

116. Harris (1999).

117. Harris (1999).

118. Harris (1999).

119. NYCLU (2019, 9). See also NYCLU (2011).

120. NYCLU (2019, 7).

121. Regarding traffic stops, the US Supreme Court has ruled that "the temporary detention of a motorist upon probable cause to believe that he has violated the traffic laws does not violate the Fourth Amendment's prohibition against unreasonable sei-zures, even if a reasonable officer would not have stopped the motorist absent some additional law enforcement objective." *Whren v. United States*, 517 U.S. 806 (1996, 806). In other words, police officers can use the pretext of a traffic stop if their ultimate objective is to search for drugs or evidence of some other crime, regardless of the fact that they lack such evidence before the stop.

122. Harris (1999).

123. See Ahmed's (2007, 161–63) important discussion of a racial "politics of mo-bility" (162).

124. Gladwell (2005, 197, 222).

125. Gladwell (2005, 243).

126. See Mack (2015a,b); Neuman (2015).

127. See also African American Policy Forum (2015, 4, 36–37n3).

128. As quoted in Mack (2015a), where the words "the cop" also appear in brackets.

129. One white teenage girl, fourteen-year-old Grace Stone, who vocally con-fronted local residents for making racist comments to her friends, was handcuffed only after she insisted on explaining the situation to police officers in defense of her Black friends. See Mack (2015b).

130. See Goffman ([1974] 1986, 201–46) on "out-of-frame activity."

131. African American Policy Forum (2015).

132. The documentary is titled *Say Her Name: The Life and Death of Sandra Bland*.

133. See, for example, African American Policy Forum (2015). See also theirnames .org. Using a similar logic to identify police officers and hold them personally ac-countable for their professional actions, New York governor Andrew Cuomo pushed a multifaceted initiative titled "Say Their Name."

134. See the *New Yorker*, June 22, 2020, https://www.newyorker.com/culture/cover -story/cover-story-2020-06-22.

135. Napier (1986, 8; emphasis in original).

136. See, for example, Garfinkel (1967); Kessler and McKenna (1978); West and Zimmerman (1987); Butler (1990); Ridgeway and Correll (2004); Ridgeway (2009); Friedman (2013).

137. See, for example, Cavanagh (2010, 8, 12–13, 53–54) on "cissexist cultures" and "cissexual privilege"; Sumerau, Cragun, and Mathers (2016) on "cisgendering reality"; and Mathers (2017) on "cisgendering interactions." See Friedman (2013, 2) on the ways that "social norms of selective perception," which involve "selective attention to sex differences and selective *inattention* to sex similarities," shape the classification of bodies into opposed male and female types (emphasis in original).

138. See Garfinkel (1967, 116); Kessler and McKenna (1978, 1–12, 113–14); Ridgeway and Correll (2004).

139. See Ridgeway and Correll (2004) on "social relational contexts" as "the arenas in which" cultural norms of sex/gender classification "are brought to bear on the behavior and evaluations of individuals" (514). See also Ridgeway (2009).

140. Mathers (2017, 300).

141. Kessler and McKenna (1978, 3; emphasis in original). See also Westbrook and Schilt (2014) on "determining gender."

142. West and Fenstermaker (1995, 22).

143. The belief that sex is the biological foundation for gender, and for polar distinctions between maleness and femaleness, arose as a "strategy of the Enlightenment" and was "intrinsic to" the profound social, political, and economic changes of the new modern world order (Laqueur 1990, 8, 11; see also 149–54).

144. West and Fenstermaker (1995, 21). See also Kessler and McKenna (1978, 58–59) on "genitals and gender attribution." See also West and Zimmerman (1987, 134–37).

145. There is an entire industry supporting these associations. See, for example, "35 Gender Reveal Ideas We Love," https://www.thebump.com/a/creative-baby-gender-reveal-ideas; or "25 Gender Reveal Ideas to Celebrate Your Exciting News," https://www.happiestbaby.com/blogs/pregnancy/gender-reveal-ideas.

146. West and Fenstermaker (1995, 20). See also West and Zimmerman (1987); Butler (1990; 1991); Ridgeway and Correll (2004, 514–15); Friedman (2013).

147. Kessler and McKenna (1978, 153, 154). See also Garfinkel (1967, 123).

148. Friedman (2013, 73–78); Schilt (2010, 65–66).

149. See, for example, Kralik (2019) for a legislative guide. While most of these efforts have thus far failed, the issue of restroom segregation remains a prominent political controversy. As Westbrook and Schilt (2014, 45, 49) point out, proponents often argue that these laws are necessary to protect women and girls from encountering "people with penises," which shows how sexuality is also a key factor in cisgender normativity. On this point, see also Cavanagh (2010).

150. See Fausset (2017).

151. Following Cavanagh (2010, 16), I use "the designation 'trans' or 'transgender' . . . as an overarching, and necessarily imprecise way to denote those whose gender identities are, in some way, at odds with conventional sex/gender systems." Thus, the term "transgender" is itself both a popular and an analytic typification (see next section) that requires this qualification. Readers should keep in mind that "the danger of using an umbrella term is that it posits a uniform collectivity and cannot do justice to the myriad differences subsumed into the category" (17). See also Friedman (2013, 8–10).

152. See Platt and Milam (2018) on this "oppressive bind."

153. Platt and Milam (2018). See Herman (2013, 65) for a study of transgender experiences in which "seventy percent of survey respondents reported being denied access, verbally harassed, or physically assaulted in public restrooms." In the midst of this climate, many other states and municipalities have passed laws prohibiting discrimination against trans individuals, explicitly allowing all people to use public facilities consistent with their gender identities.

154. See Cavanagh (2010, 69–78) and Bender-Baird (2016) on such policing in restrooms.

155. See Sumerau, Cragun, and Mathers (2016) on "erasing," "marking," and "punishing" transgender individuals and experiences. See also Cavanagh (2010); West-

brook and Schilt (2014); Bender-Baird (2016); Mathers (2017). See also Kessler and McKenna (1978, 3), who point out that those "who were in the process of changing from one gender to the other" report that some people feel "uneasy" when unable to define them as a normative cisgender type, even asking, "'What are you?'"

156. Sumerau, Cragun, and Mathers (2016); Mathers (2017).

157. Schutz (1962, 41).

158. Schutz (1962, 255; emphasis in original).

159. Schutz (1962, 40); Natanson (1986, 63–64).

160. Weber ([1903–17] 1949, 90; emphasis in original).

161. See also Coser (1971, 223).

162. Simmel (1950a, 23); [1908] 1950, 403). See also Coser (1971, 182–83); Zerubavel (2007; 2021); DeGloma (2014a, 18–19); DeGloma and Papadantonakis (2020, 98–99).

163. Coser (1971, 182).

164. Cf. Coser (1971, 182).

165. Schutz (1970, 273). See also Schutz ([1932] 1967, 205–6). See McKinney (1969) on the distinction between "existential" and "constructed" types. Clifford Geertz (1973, 9) also recognized "that what we call our data are really our own constructions of other people's constructions." See also Reed (2017, 29–31); DeGloma and Wiest (2022, 16n4).

166. Natanson (1986, 87).

167. Simmel ([1908] 1950, 407; emphasis in original).

168. Bourdieu (1984).

169. See Marx ([1847] 1955, ch. 2, part 5).

## Chapter Six

1. Johnson (2011, loc. 3853).

2. Mullan (2007, 5, 76–113).

3. Mullan (2007, 13).

4. The controversy concerning this phone call centers on Trump's implied threat to withhold US financial aid to Ukraine unless and until Ukrainian officials publicly announced an investigation into the financial affairs of Hunter Biden, son of Joe Biden, who was the leading Democratic Party presidential contender during the time of Trump's phone call with Zelenskyy.

5. See Lam (2019). See also Spiegel (2015); Boyd and Field (2016, 354–58).

6. See "H.R.6054—Unmasking Antifa Act of 2018," https://www.congress.gov /bill/115th-congress/house-bill/6054/text.

7. See Foley, Karlsen, and Putniņš (2019, 1807–8).

8. See "Mexico Unmasks Guerrilla Commander Subcomandante Marcos Really Is Well-Educated Son of Furniture-Store Owner," *Spokesman Review*, February 11, 1995, https://www.spokesman.com/stories/1995/feb/11/mexico-unmasks-guerrilla -commander-subcomandante/.

9. Kirkpatrick (2022).

10. See also Frois (2009a, 163–66; 2009b, 96–99) on "breaking anonymity" with regard to recovery groups. See also Colman (2011).

11. Leipholtz (2016).

12. Miller (2019, 2).

13. See also Miller's short film *I Am with You.*

14. African American Policy Forum (2015).

15. See Henderson (2018); Sodaro (forthcoming). See also https://eji.org/.

16. Aizenman (2015); Wong (2020).

17. See also Zerubavel (forthcoming) on *"personalization* efforts" (emphasis in original).

18. See Whitlinger (2020).

19. Arendt (1958, 74, 75).

20. Brennan and Pettit (2008, 193). See also Gioia (2017).

21. See Scammell (2016).

22. Gatti (2016).

23. Ferrante (2016).

24. See, for example, Orr (2016); Schwartz (2016).

25. Appignanesi (2016).

26. Rogers (2014).

27. Speri (2014).

28. See Woolf (2015b).

29. Ancona (2014). See also Gilbert (2014).

30. Bennett (2015); Schuppe (2015); Woolf (2015a,b). The original statement by Anonymous appears to no longer be available.

# References

ABC News. 2020. "Unfounded 'QAnon' Conspiracy Theory Gains Traction in Politics: Part 1." September 22, 2020. Video. https://abcnews.go.com/Politics/men-qanon/story?id=73046374.

Ackerman, Spencer. 2016. "Obama Claims US Drones Strikes Have Killed Up to 116 Civilians." *The Guardian*, July 1, 2016. https://www.theguardian.com/us-news/2016/jul/01/obama-drones-strikes-civilian-deaths.

Ancona, Frank. 2014. "Klu Klux Klan, a message to #Ferguson and #Anonymous." https://pastebin.com/3PuA4eS5.

Adut, Ari. 2018. *Reign of Appearances: The Misery and Splendor of the Public Sphere.* New York: Cambridge University Press.

Afonso, Nelia M., Lavoisier J. Cardoza, Oswald A. J. Mascarenhas, Anil N. F. Aranha, and Chirag Shah. 2005. "Are Anonymous Evaluations a Better Assessment of Faculty Teaching Performance? A Comparative Analysis of Open and Anonymous Evaluation Processes." *Family Medicine* 37 (1): 43–47.

African American Policy Forum. 2015. "Say Her Name: Resisting Police Brutality against Black Women." https://www.aapf.org/sayhername.

Agnew, Jean-Christophe. 1986. *Worlds Apart: The Market and the Theater in Anglo-American Thought, 1550–1750.* Cambridge: Cambridge University Press.

Ahmed, Sara. 2007. "A Phenomenology of Whiteness." *Feminist Theory* 8 (2): 149–68.

Aikins, Matthieu, and Alissa J. Rubin. 2021. "First Tied to ISIS, Then to U.S.: Family in Drone Strike Is Tarnished Twice." *New York Times*, September 18, 2021. https://www.nytimes.com/2021/09/18/world/asia/afghanistan-drone-strike-reaction.html.

Aizenman, Nurith. 2015. "An Artist's Brainstorm: Put Photos on Those Faceless Ebola Suits." *National Public Radio*, April 9, 2015. https://www.npr.org/sections/goatsandsoda/2015/04/09/397853271/an-artists-brainstorm-put-photos-on-those-faceless-ebola-suits.

Alcoholics Anonymous. (1953) 2017. *Twelve Steps and Twelve Traditions.* New York: Alcoholics Anonymous World Services.

Alcoholics Anonymous. (1981) 2011. *Understanding Anonymity.* New York: Alcoholics Anonymous World Services.

Alcoholics Anonymous. 2001. *Alcoholics Anonymous: The Story of How Many Thousands of Men and Women Have Recovered from Alcoholism.* New York: Alcoholics Anonymous World Services.

Alexander, Jeffrey C. 2004. "Cultural Pragmatics: Social Performance between Ritual and Strategy." *Sociological Theory* 22 (4): 527–73.

Alexander, Jeffrey C. 2013. *The Dark Side of Modernity*. Cambridge: Polity Press.

Alexander, Jeffrey C. 2017. *The Drama of Social Life*. Cambridge: Polity Press.

Alexander, Jeffrey C., and Jason L. Mast. 2006. "Introduction: Symbolic Action in Theory and Practice: The Cultural Pragmatics of Symbolic Action." In *Social Performance: Symbolic Action, Cultural Pragmatics, and Ritual*, edited by Jeffrey C. Alexander, Bernhard Giesen, and Jason L. Mast, 1–28. Cambridge: Cambridge University Press.

Alexander, Jeffrey C., and Philip Smith. 2003. "The Strong Program in Cultural Sociology: Elements of a Structural Hermeneutics." In *The Meanings of Social Life: A Cultural Sociology*, 11–26. Oxford: Oxford University Press.

Almasy, Steve. 2020. "Some Law Enforcement Officers at Protests Have No Badges and Some Have Covered Them. City Officials Say That Is Unacceptable." CNN, June 5, 2020. https://www.cnn.com/2020/06/05/politics/law-enforcement -badges-protests/index.html.

Anderson, Elijah. 1990. *Streetwise: Race, Class, and Change in an Urban Community*. Chicago: University of Chicago Press.

Andrew, Esekong H. 2014. "Configurations of the African Mask: Forms, Functions and the Transcendental." *Cross-Cultural Communication* 10 (4): 211–16.

Aneesh, A. 2006. *Virtual Migration: The Programming of Globalization*. Durham, NC: Duke University Press.

Aneesh, A. 2015. *Neutral Accent: How Language, Labor, and Life Become Global*. Durham, NC: Duke University Press.

Anonymous. (1554) 1908. *The Life of Lazarillo de Tormes: His Fortunes and Adversities*. London: Adam and Charles Black. https://www.gutenberg.org/files/53489 /53489-h/53489-h.htm.

Anonymous. (1954) 2000. *A Woman in Berlin: Eight Weeks in the Conquered City*. New York: Picador.

Anonymous. 2007. "Dear Fox News." YouTube. https://www.youtube.com/watch ?v=RFjU8bZR19A.

Anonymous. 2008. "Message to Scientology." YouTube. https://www.youtube.com /watch?v=JCbKv9yiLiQ.

Anonymous. 2012a. "Anonymous November 5th Defend Your Freedom Worldwide Protests 360p." YouTube. https://www.youtube.com/watch?v=s6l8rDDKJXg.

Anonymous. 2012b. "Message to the Federal Reserve System." YouTube. https:// www.youtube.com/watch?v=6p__MgUPUDQ.

Anonymous. 2013a. "A Message to the LAPD." YouTube. https://www.youtube.com /watch?v=DeYA7PiiGYw.

Anonymous. 2013b. "The Sexual Fantasy Lives of Men: An All-Access Pass to Four Men's Inner Thoughts." *Elle*, March 22, 2013. https://www.elle.com/life-love /sex-relationships/advice/a2456/they-like-it-like-that-why-every-woman-is -desirable-455616/.

Anonymous. 2014a. "Anonymous—The Final Resistance." YouTube. https://www .youtube.com/watch?v=ghoeYzE5Vjc.

Anonymous. 2014b. "The Anonymous Men Who Built Central Park." *Ephemeral New York*, July 7, 2014. https://ephemeralnewyork.wordpress.com/2014/07/14 /the-anonymous-men-who-built-central-park/.

Anonymous. 2014c. "Anonymous—Operation NSA Campus 2014." YouTube. https://www.youtube.com/watch?v=Z40_oAnK-fk.

Anonymous. 2017. "Message to the President of the United States (Donald Trump)." YouTube. https://www.youtube.com/watch?v=qt0o3Cx2nOI.

Anonymous. 2019. "Anonymous Message to Tom Cruise and Scientology." YouTube. https://www.youtube.com/watch?v=VTXAB-RjVaw.

Anonymous (A Senior Trump Administration Official). 2019. *A Warning*. New York: Twelve (Hachette).

Ansart, Sandrine, and Virginie Monvoisin. 2015. "The Bank, Its Societal Functions and Its Practices: Conflictual Relationships between and Economic Agent and Democracy." In *The Philosophy, Politics and Economics of Finance in the 21st Century*, edited by Patrick O'Sullivan, Nigel F. B. Allington, and Mark Esposito, 283–99. London: Routledge.

Appignanesi, Lisa. 2016. "Frantumaglia: *A Writer's Journey* by Elena Ferrante Review—Astute, Revelatory Ruminations." *The Guardian*, October 29, 2016. https://www.theguardian.com/books/2016/oct/29/frantumaglia-a-writers-journey-elena-ferrante-review.

Applbaum, Arthur Isak. 1995. "Professional Detachment: The Executioner of Paris." *Harvard Law Review* 109 (2): 458–86.

Archer, Nicole. 2014. "Security Blankets: Uniforms, Hoods, and the Textures of Terror." *Women and Performance* 24 (2–3): 186–202.

Arendt, Hannah. 1958. *The Human Condition*. 2nd ed. Chicago: University of Chicago Press.

Arie, Sophie. 2011. "Unwilling Executioners? Where and Why Do Some Doctors Still Help Carry Out the Death Penalty?" *BMJ: British Medical Journal* 342 (7810): 1286–87.

Arnold, Chris. 2010. "A Mistake That Stole Christmas? A Foreclosure Story." NPR, December 3, 2010. https://www.npr.org/2010/12/23/132285516/a-mistake-that-stole-christmas-a-foreclosure-story.

Athens, Lonnie. 1994. "The Self as a Soliloquy." *Sociological Quarterly* 35 (3): 521–32.

Auerbach, David. 2015a. "Anonymity as Culture: Case Studies." *Triple Canopy*. https://www.canopycanopycanopy.com/issues/15/contents/anonymity_as_culture__case_studies.

Auerbach, David. 2015b. "Anonymity as Culture: Treatise." *Triple Canopy*. https://www.canopycanopycanopy.com/contents/anonymity_as_culture__treatise.

Augustine. (397–98) 1961. *Confessions*. London: Penguin Books.

Avery, Dianne. 2016. "The Female Breast as Brand: The Aesthetic Labor of Breastaurant Servers." In *Invisible Labor: Hidden Work in the Contemporary World*, edited by Marion G. Crain, Winifred R. Poster, and Miriam A. Cherry, 171–92. Oakland: University of California Press.

Baena, Victoria. 2015. "The Greatest Literary Impostor of All Time Deserves to Be Remembered." *Tablet*, December 1, 2015. https://www.tabletmag.com/sections/arts-letters/articles/romain-gary-literary-impostor.

Baizerman, Michael. 1974. "Toward Analysis of the Relations among the Youth Counterculture, Telephone Hotlines, and Anonymity." *Journal of Youth and Adolescence* 3 (4): 293–306.

Baker, Peter. 2015. "Obama Apologizes after Drone Kills American and Italian Held by Al Qaeda." *New York Times*, April 23, 2015. https://www.nytimes.com/2015 /04/24/world/asia/2-qaeda-hostages-were-accidentally-killed-in-us-raid -white-house-says.html.

Bakhtin, Mikhail. (1965) 1984. *Rabelais and His World*. Bloomington: Indiana University Press.

Banksy. 2006. *Wall and Piece*. London: Century.

Barish, Jonas. 1981. *The Anti-Theatrical Prejudice*. Berkeley: University of California Press.

Barnett, Jo. 2016. "Painting a Voice." International Visual Sociological Association Showcase. https://visualsociology.org/?p=1263.

Bar-On, Dan. 1989. *Legacy of Silence: Encounters with Children of the Third Reich*. Cambridge, MA: Harvard University Press.

Bartlett, Jamie. 2014. *The Dark Net: Inside the Digital Underworld*. New York: Melville Publishing.

Baudrillard, Jean. (1976) 1993. *Symbolic Exchange and Death*. London: Sage.

Bauman, Zygmunt. 1989. *Modernity and the Holocaust*. Ithaca, NY: Cornell University Press.

Bauman, Zygmunt, Didier Bigo, Paulo Esteves. Elspeth Guild, Vivienne Jabri, David Lyon, and R. B. J. Walker. 2014. "After Snowden: Rethinking the Impact of Surveillance." *International Political Sociology* 8 (2): 121–44.

Bayer, Ronald. 1981. *Homosexuality and American Psychiatry: The Politics of Diagnosis*. New York: Basic Books.

Beard, James Melville. 1877. *K.K.K. Sketches*. Philadelphia: Claxton, Remsen, and Haffelfinger.

Beck, Colleen M., Lauren W. Falvey, and Harold Drollinger. 2015. "Inside the Tunnels, Inside the Protests: The Artistic Legacy of Anti-Nuclear Activists at a Nevada Peace Camp." In *Understanding Graffiti: Multidisciplinary Studies from Prehistory to Present*, edited by Troy Lovata and Elizabeth Olton, 177–91. Abington, UK: Routledge.

Beevor, Antony. 2000. Introduction to *A Woman in Berlin: Eight Weeks in the Conquered City*. New York: Picador.

Bender-Baird, Kyla. 2016. "Peeing under Surveillance: Bathrooms, Gender Policing, and Hate Violence." *Gender, Place and Culture* 23 (7): 983–88.

Benford, Robert A., and A. Paul Hare. 2015. "Dramaturgical Analysis." In *International Encyclopedia of the Social & Behavioral Sciences*. 2nd ed. Vol. 6, 646–50. Oxford: Elsevier.

Benford, Robert D., and Scott A. Hunt. 1992. "Dramaturgy and Social Movements: The Social Construction and Communication of Power." *Sociological Inquiry* 62 (1): 36–55.

Benjamin, Medea. 2013. *Drone Warfare: Killing by Remote Control*. London: Verso.

Bennett, Cory. 2015. "Anonymous Threatens to Unmask Alleged KKK Members." *The Hill*, October 31, 2015. https://thehill.com/policy/cybersecurity/258721 -anonymous-threatens-to-unmask-alleged-kkk-members.

Bennett, Dawn, Sophie Hennekam, Sally Macarthur, Cat Hope, and Talisha Goh. 2019. "Hiding Gender: How Female Composers Manage Gender Identity." *Journal of Vocational Behavior* 113:20–32.

Bentham, Jeremy. 1843. "An Essay on Political Tactics." In *The Works of Jeremy Bentham*. Vol. 2, 299–373. Edinburgh: William Tait.

Berger, Peter L., and Thomas Luckmann. 1966. *The Social Construction of Reality: A Treatise in the Sociology of Knowledge*. New York: Doubleday.

Bernstein, Elizabeth. 2007. *Temporarily Yours: Intimacy, Authenticity, and the Commerce of Sex*. Chicago: University of Chicago Press.

Bessler, John D. 1997. *Death in the Dark: Midnight Executions in America*. Boston: Northeastern University Press.

Bhatia, Michael V. 2005. "Fighting Words: Naming Terrorists, Bandits, Rebels, and Other Violent Actors." *Third World Quarterly* 26 (1): 5–22.

Bianco, Katalina M. 2008. "The Subprime Lending Crisis: Causes and Effects of the Mortgage Meltdown." CCH. https://business.cch.com/images/banner/subprime.pdf.

Blee, Kathleen, and Amy McDowell. 2013. "The Duality of Spectacle and Secrecy: A Case Study of Fraternalism in the 1920s US Ku Klux Klan." *Ethnic and Racial Studies* 36 (2): 249–65.

Blinder, Alan. 2015. "States Consider Awarding Lottery Winners Something Else: Anonymity." *New York Times*, March 26, 2015. https://www.nytimes.com/2015/03/26/us/states-consider-awarding-lottery-winners-something-else-anonymity.html.

Bosk, Charles L. (1979) 2003. *Forgive and Remember: Managing Medical Failure*. 2nd ed. Chicago: University of Chicago Press.

Bossy, John. 1975. "The Social History of Confession in the Age of Reformation." *Transaction of the Royal Historical Society* 25:21–38.

Bouie, Jamelle. 2015. "Christian Soldiers." *Slate*, February 10, 2015. https://slate.com/news-and-politics/2015/02/jim-crow-souths-lynching-of-blacks-and-christianity-the-terror-inflicted-by-whites-was-considered-a-religious-ritual.html.

Bourdieu, Pierre. 1984. *Distinction: A Social Critique of the Judgement of Taste*. Cambridge, MA: Harvard University Press.

Boxer, Sarah. 2005. "Bless Me, Blog, for I've Sinned." *New York Times*, May 31, 2005. https://www.nytimes.com/2005/05/31/arts/design/bless-me-blog-for-ive-sinned.html.

Boyarin, Daniel. (2005) 2019. "The Yavneh-Cycle of the Stammaim and the Invention of the Rabbis." In *Creation and Composition: The Contribution of the Bavli Redactors (Stammaim) to the Aggada*, edited by Jeffrey L. Rubenstein, 237–89. Tübingen: Mohr Siebeck.

Boyd, Richard, and Laura K. Field. 2016. "Blind Injustice: Theorizing Anonymity and Accountability in Modern Democracies." *Polity* 48 (3): 332–58.

Brandon, Kathleen J. 2013. "A Grounded Theory Study of Contemporary Christian Attitudes to Theatre." PhD diss., Wayne State University.

Bray, Mark. 2017. *Antifa: The Anti-Fascist Handbook*. Brooklyn: Melville House.

Brazier, Frances, Anja Oskamp, Corien Prins, Maurice Schellekens, and Niek Wijngaards. 2004. "Anonymity and Software Agents: An Interdisciplinary Challenge." *Artificial Intelligence and Law* 12:137–57.

Brekhus, Wayne H. 1996. "Social Marking and the Mental Coloring of Identity: Sexual Identity Construction and Maintenance in the United States." *Sociological Forum* 11:497–522.

Brekhus, Wayne H. 1998. "A Sociology of the Unmarked: Redirecting Our Focus." *Sociological Theory* 16 (1): 34–51.

Brekhus, Wayne H. 2003. *Peacocks, Chameleons, Centaurs: Gay Suburbia and the Grammar of Social Identity*. Chicago: University of Chicago Press.

Brekhus, Wayne H. 2007. "The Rutgers School: A Zerubavelian Culturalist Cognitive Sociology." *European Journal of Social Theory* 10 (3): 448–64.

Brennan, Geoffrey, and Philip Pettit. 2008. "Esteem, Identifiability, and the Internet." In *Information Technology and Moral Philosophy*, edited by Jeroen van den Hoven and John Weckert, 175–94. Cambridge, UK: Cambridge University Press.

Brewster, Jack. 2021. "'We All Got Played': QAnon Followers Implode after Big Moment Never Comes." *Forbes*, January 20, 2021. https://www.forbes.com/sites /jackbrewster/2021/01/20/we-all-got-played-qanon-followers-implode-after -big-moment-never-comes/.

Brissett, Dennis, and Charles Edgley. 1990. "The Dramaturgical Perspective." In *Life as Theater: A Dramaturgical Source Book*, edited by Dennis Brissett and Charles Edgley, 1–50. New York: Aldine de Gruyter.

Brooks, Anthony. 2010. "Housing Nightmare Upends Family, Enriches Investor." NPR, December 12, 2010. https://www.npr.org/2010/12/20/132146568 /housing-nightmare-upends-family-enriches-investor.

Brooks, Ethel C. 2007. *Unraveling the Garment Industry: Transnational Organizing and Women's Work*. Minneapolis: University of Minnesota Press.

Brunstetter, Daniel, and Megan Braun. 2011. "The Implications of Drones on the Just War Tradition." *Ethics & International Affairs* 25 (3): 337–58.

Budden, Amber E., Tom Tregenza, Lonnie W. Aarssen, Julia Koricheva, Roosa Leimu, and Christopher J. Lortie. 2008. "Double-Blind Review Favours Increased Representation of Female Authors." *Trends in Ecology and Evolution* 23 (1): 4–6.

Burke, Kenneth. (1945) 1969. *A Grammar of Motives*. Berkeley: University of California Press.

Burrowes, G. Delano. 2021. "My White Teacher Used a POC Pen Name to Sell Her Book. Should I Have Outed Her?" *HuffPost*, November 2, 2021. https://www .huffpost.com/entry/teacher-black-student-book-racism_n_617feafde4b 09314321ac0e3.

Burrows, Sara. 2020. "'Guerilla Grafters' Secretly Graft Fruit-Bearing Branches onto Sterile City Trees." *Return to Now*, March 30, 2020. https://returntonow .net/2020/05/30/guerilla-grafters-secretly-graft-fruit-bearing-branches-onto -sterile-city-trees/.

Bush, Kenneth. 2013. "The Politics of Post-Conflict Space: The Mysterious Case of Missing Graffiti in 'Post-Troubles' Northern Ireland." *Contemporary Politics* 19 (2): 167–89.

Butler, Judith. 1990. *Gender Trouble: Feminism and the Subversion of Identity*. New York: Routledge.

Butler, Judith. 1991. "Imitation and Gender Insubordination." In *Inside/Out: Lesbian Theories, Gay Theories*, edited by Diana Fuss, 13–31. New York: Routledge.

Butler, Judith. 2009. *Frames of War: When Is Life Grievable?* London: Verso.

Calame, Claude. 1986. "Facing Otherness: The Tragic Mask in Ancient Greece." *History of Religions* 26 (2): 125–42.

Campbell, Andy. 2018. "The QAnon Conspiracy Has Stumbled into Real Life, and It's Not Going to End Well." *HuffPost*, July 24, 2018. https://www.huffpost.com /entry/qanon-conspiracy-real-life_n_5b54bbafe4b0b15aba8fe484.

Cancialosi, Chris. 2015. "Is Your Anonymous Employee Survey Doing More Harm than Good?" *Forbes*, January 12, 2015. https://www.forbes.com/sites/chris cancialosi/2015/01/12/is-your-anonymous-employee-survey-doing-more -harm-than-good/.

Carter, Jane Burr. 1987. "The Masks of Ortheia." *American Journal of Archeology* 91 (3): 355–83.

Cavanagh, Sheila L. 2010. *Queering Bathrooms: Gender, Sexuality, and the Hygienic Imagination*. Toronto: University of Toronto Press.

Chand, Daniel E. 2017. "'Dark Money' and 'Dirty Politics': Are Anonymous Ads More Negative?" *Business and Politics* 19 (3): 454–81.

Cheong, George S. C. 1979. "Students' Evaluations of Instructors: Before and After the Examination, Names Identified *versus* Anonymous." *Canadian Journal of Higher Education* 9 (1): 80–86.

Christopherson, Kimberly M. 2007. "The Positive and Negative Implications of Anonymity in Internet Social Interactions: 'On the Internet, Nobody Knows You're a Dog.'" *Computers in Human Behavior* 23 (6): 3038–56.

Churchill, Ward, and Jim Vander Wall. 1990. *The COINTELPRO Papers: Documents from the FBI's Secret Wars against Dissent in the United States*. Cambridge, MA: South End Press.

Ciuraru, Carmela. 2011. *Nom De Plume: A (Secret) History of Pseudonyms*. New York: HarperCollins.

Clendinen, Dudley. 2003. "Dr. John Fryer, 65, Psychiatrist Who Said in 1972 He Was Gay." Obituary. *New York Times*, March 5, 2003. https://www.nytimes.com /2003/03/05/us/dr-john-fryer-65-psychiatrist-who-said-in-1972-he-was-gay .html.

Cole, Caroline M. 1991. "'Oh Wise Women of the Stalls . . .'" *Discourse & Society* 2 (4): 401–11.

Coleman, Gabriella. 2014. *Hacker, Hoaxer, Whistleblower, Spy: The Many Faces of Anonymous*. London: Verso.

Collins, Patricia Hill. (1990) 2000. *Black Feminist Thought: Knowledge, Consciousness, and the Politics of Empowerment*. London: Routledge.

Collins, Patricia Hill. 2019. *Intersectionality as Critical Social Theory*. Durham, NC: Duke University Press.

Colman, David. 2011. "Challenging the Second 'A' in A.A." *New York Times*, May 6, 2011. https://www.nytimes.com/2011/05/08/fashion/08anon.html.

Colonomos, Ariel. 2016. "Precision Warfare and the Case for Symmetry: Targeted Killings and Hostage Taking." In *Transformations of Warfare in the Contemporary World*, edited by John C. Torpey and David Jacobson, 134–52. Philadelphia: Temple University Press.

Connerton, Paul. 2008. "Seven Types of Forgetting." *Memory Studies* 1 (1): 59–71.

Constantine, Amy. 1996. "What's in a Name? McIntyre v. Ohio Elections Commission: An Examination of the Protection Afforded to Anonymous Political Speech." *Connecticut Law Review* 29:459–83.

Contreras, Randol. 2019. "Transparency and Unmasking Issues in Ethnographic Crime Research: Methodologic Considerations." *Sociological Forum* 34 (2): 293–312.

Cooley, Charles Horton. 1902. *Human Nature and the Social Order*. New York: Charles Scribner's Sons.

Cooper, Anderson. 2021. "Former QAnon Supporter to Cooper: I Apologize for Thinking You Ate Babies." CNN, January 30, 2021. https://www.cnn.com /videos/us/2021/01/30/anderson-cooper-former-qanon-supporter-special -report-sot-ac360-vpx.cnn.

Cornwell, John. 2014. *The Dark Box: A Secret History of Confession*. New York: Basic Books.

Coser, Lewis A. 1971. *Masters of Sociological Thought: Ideas in Historical and Social Context*. New York: Harcourt Brace Jovanovich.

Coughlin, John J. 2011. "The Perennial Value of the Traditional Confessional." *Sacred Architecture* 20:9–10.

Crenshaw, Kimberle. 1991. "Mapping the Margins: Intersectionality, Identity Politics, and Violence against Women of Color." *Stanford Law Review* 43 (6): 1241–99.

Crow, Graham, and Rose Wiles. 2008. "Managing Anonymity and Confidentiality in Social Research: The Case of Visual Data in Community Research." *ESRC National Centre for Research Methods*. NCRM Working Paper Series. http://eprints .ncrm.ac.uk/459/.

Curlew, Abigail E. 2019. "Undisciplined Performativity: A Sociological Approach to Anonymity." *Social Media + Society* 5 (1): 1–14. https://doi.org/10.1177/2056 305119829843.

Cusk, Rachel. 2015. "'The Story of the Lost Child,' by Elena Ferrante." *New York Times Book Review*, August 30, 2015. https://www.nytimes.com/2015/08/30 /books/review/the-story-of-the-lost-child-by-elena-ferrante.html.

Daniels, Arlene. 1987. "Invisible Work." *Social Problems* 34 (5): 403–15.

Dante, Ed. 2010. "The Shadow Scholar." *Chronicle Review*, November 12, 2010. https://www.chronicle.com/article/The-Shadow-Scholar/125329.

Dao, James. 2013. "Drone Pilots Are Found to Get Stress Disorders Much as Those in Combat Do." *New York Times*, February 22, 2013. https://www.nytimes.com /2013/02/23/us/drone-pilots-found-to-get-stress-disorders-much-as-those-in -combat-do.html.

Darley, John M., and Bibb Latané. 1968. "Bystander Intervention in Emergencies: Diffusion of Responsibility." *Journal of Personality and Social Psychology* 8 (4): 377–83.

Davidson, Sandra, and Michael Barajas. 2014. "Masking the Executioner and the Source of Execution Drugs." *Saint Louis University Law Journal* 59 (1): 45–95.

DeGloma, Thomas. 2004. "'Safe Space' and Contested Memories: Survivor Movements and the Foundation of Alternative Mnemonic Traditions." Paper presented at the Spaces of Memory, Spaces of Violence conference, New School University, New York, April 2004.

DeGloma, Thomas. 2007. "The Social Logic of 'False Memories': Symbolic Awakenings and Symbolic Worlds in Survivor and Retractor Narratives." *Symbolic Interaction* 30 (4): 543–65.

DeGloma, Thomas. 2014a. *Seeing the Light: The Social Logic of Personal Discovery*. Chicago: University of Chicago Press.

DeGloma, Thomas. 2014b. "The Unconscious in Cultural Dispute: On the Ethics of Psychosocial Discovery." In *The Unhappy Divorce of Psychoanalysis and Sociology: Diverse Perspectives on the Psychosocial*, edited by Lynn Chancer and John Andrews, 77–98. London: Palgrave Macmillan.

DeGloma, Thomas. 2015. "The Strategies of Mnemonic Battle: On the Alignment of Autobiographical and Collective Memories in Conflicts over the Past." *American Journal of Cultural Sociology* 3 (1): 156–90.

DeGloma, Thomas, and Erin F. Johnston. 2019. "Cognitive Migrations: A Cultural and Cognitive Sociology of Personal Transformation." In *Oxford Handbook of Cognitive Sociology*, edited by Wayne H. Brekhus and Gabe Ignatow, 623–42. Oxford: Oxford University Press.

DeGloma, Thomas, and Max Papadantonakis. 2020. "The Thematic Lens: A Formal and Cultural Framework for Comparative Ethnographic Analysis." In *Comparative Ethnography*, edited by Corey M. Abramson and Neil Gong, 88–110. New York: Oxford University Press.

DeGloma, Thomas, and Julie B. Wiest. 2022. "On the Multidimensional Foundations of Meaning in Social Life: An Invitation to the Series *Interpretive Lenses in Sociology*." Open Access. Bristol, UK: Bristol University Press. https://bristol universitypress.co.uk/asset/11003/de-gloma-wiest-series-editors-article .pdf.

De Hert, Paul. 2003. "The Case of Anonymity in Western Political Philosophy: Benjamin Constant's Refutation of Republican and Utilitarian Arguments against Anonymity." In *Digital Anonymity and the Law: Tensions and Dimensions*, edited by C. Nicoll, J. E. J. Prins, and M. J. M. van Dellen, 47–97. The Hague: Asser Press.

de Montjoye, Yves-Alexandre, César A. Hidalgo, Michel Verleysen, and Vincent D. Blondel. 2013. "Unique in the Crowd: The Privacy Bounds of Human Mobility." *Scientific Reports* 3:1376. https://www.nature.com/articles/srep01376#Sec6.

Denzin, Norman K. 1987. *The Recovering Alcoholic*. Newbury Park, CA: Sage.

DeVault, Marjorie L. 1994. *Feeding the Family: The Social Organization of Caring as Gendered Work*. Chicago: University of Chicago Press.

Dias, Karen. 2003. "The Ana Sanctuary: Women's Pro-Anorexia Narratives in Cyberspace." *Journal of International Women's Studies* 4 (2): 31–45.

Diener, Edward. 1976. "Effects of Prior Destructive Behavior, Anonymity, and Group Presence on Deindividuation and Aggression." *Journal of Personality and Social Psychology* 33 (5): 497–507.

Diener, Edward, Scott C. Fraser, Arthur L. Beaman, and Roger T. Kelem. 1976. "Effects of Deindividuation Variables on Stealing among Halloween Trick-or-Treaters." *Journal of Personality and Social Psychology* 33 (2): 178–83.

Dixon, Thomas, Jr. 1905. *The Clansman: An Historical Romance of the Ku Klux Klan*. New York: Doubleday, Page & Company. https://archive.org/details/clansman historic00dixouoft/mode/2up?ref=ol&view=theater.

Dixon, Thomas, Jr. 1907. *The Traitor: The Story of the Fall of the Invisible Empire*. New York: Doubleday, Page and Company. https://www.gutenberg.org/files /54766/54766-h/54766-h.htm.

Donegan, Moira. 2018. "I Started the Media Men List: My Name Is Moira Donegan." *The Cut*, January 10, 2018. https://www.thecut.com/2018/01/moira -donegan-i-started-the-media-men-list.html.

Douglas, Jack D., Paul K. Rasmussen, and Carol Ann Flanagan. 1977. *The Nude Beach*. Beverly Hills, CA: Sage.

Douglass, Frederick. 1845. *Narrative of the Life of Frederick Douglass, an American Slave*. Boston: The Anti-Slavery Office. https://docsouth.unc.edu/neh/douglass /douglass.html.

Dowling, Conor M., and Amber Wichowsky. 2013. "Does It Matter Who's Behind the Curtain? Anonymity in Political Advertising and the Effects of Campaign Finance Disclosure." *American Politics Research* 41 (6): 965–96.

Doyle, Tony, and Judy Veranas. 2014. "Public Anonymity and the Connected World." *Ethics and Information Technology* 16 (3): 207–18.

Du Bois, W. E. B. (1903) 1995. *The Souls of Black Folk*. New York: Penguin Books.

Dubrovsky, Vitaly J., Sara Kiesler, and Beheruz N. Sethna. 1991. "The Equalization Phenomenon: Status Effects in Computer-Mediated and Face-to-Face Decision-Making Groups." *Human-Computer Interaction* 6 (2): 119–46.

Duclos, Diane. 2019. "When Ethnography Does Not Rhyme with Anonymity: Reflections on Name Disclosure, Self-Censorship, and Storytelling." *Ethnography* 20 (2): 175–83.

Dunbar, John, and David Donald. 2009. "The Roots of the Financial Crisis: Who Is to Blame?" The Center for Public Integrity, May 6, 2009. https://www.public integrity.org/2009/05/06/5449/roots-financial-crisis-who-blame.

Durkheim, Émile. (1912) 1995. *The Elementary Forms of Religious Life*. New York: Free Press.

Easley, Alexis. 2004. *First-Person Anonymous: Women Writers and Victorian Print Media, 1830–70*. Aldershot, UK: Ashgate.

Eisen, Joshua Evan. 2013. "Stammaitic Activity versus Stammaitic Chronology: Anonymity's Impact on the Legal Narrative of the Babylonian Talmud." PhD diss., Columbia University.

Eliasoph, Nina, and Paul Lichterman. 2003. "Culture in Interaction." *American Journal of Sociology* 108 (4): 735–94.

Ellison, Ralph. (1952) 1995. *Invisible Man*. New York: Vintage International.

Elliston, Frederick A. 1982. "Anonymity and Whistleblowing." *Journal of Business Ethics* 1 (3): 167–77.

Ellsworth-Jones, Will. 2012. *Banksy: The Man Behind the Wall*. London: Aurum Press.

Emanuel, Linda L., and Leigh B. Bienen. 2016. "Physician Participation in Executions: Time to Eliminate Anonymity Provisions and Protest the Practice." *Annals of Internal Medicine* 135 (10): 922–24.

Emerson, Joan P. 1970. "Behavior in Private Places: Sustaining Definitions of Reality in Gynecological Examinations." In *Recent Sociology No. 2: Patterns of Communicative Behavior*, edited by Hans-Peter Dreitzel, 74–97. London: Macmillan.

Enzensberger, Hans Magnus. 2000. Foreword to *A Woman in Berlin: Eight Weeks in the Conquered City*. New York: Picador.

Eren, Colleen P. 2017. *Bernie Madoff and the Crisis: The Public Trial of Capitalism*. Stanford, CA: Stanford University Press.

Eyerman, Ron. 2006. "Performing Opposition or, How Social Movements Move." In *Social Performance: Symbolic Action, Cultural Pragmatics, and Ritual*, edited by Jeffrey C. Alexander, Bernhard Giesen, and Jason L. Mast, 193–217. Cambridge: Cambridge University Press.

Ezell, Margaret J. M. 2003. "'By a Lady': The Mask of the Feminine in Restoration, Early Eighteenth-Century Print Culture." In *The Faces of Anonymity: Anonymous and Pseudonymous Publication from the Sixteenth to the Twentieth Century*, edited by Robert J. Griffin, 63–79. New York: Palgrave Macmillan.

Fanon, Frantz. (1952) 2008. *Black Skin, White Masks*. New York: Grove Press.

Fantz, Ashley. 2008. "Forgive Us, Father; We'd Rather Go Online." CNN, March 13, 2008. http://edition.cnn.com/2008/LIVING/wayoflife/03/13/online .confessions/.

Farber, Neil J, Brian M. Aboff, Joan Weiner, Elizabeth B. Davis, E. Gil Boyer, and Peter A. Ubel. 2001. "Physicians' Willingness to Participate in the Process of Lethal Injection for Capital Punishment." *Annals of Internal Medicine* 135 (10): 884–88.

Farrall, Kenneth. 2012. "Online Collectivism, Individualism and Anonymity in East Asia." *Surveillance and Society* 9 (4): 424–40.

Fausset, Richard. 2017. "Bathroom Law Repeal Leaves Few Pleased in North Carolina." *New York Times*, March 30, 2017. https://www.nytimes.com/2017/03/30 /us/north-carolina-senate-acts-to-repeal-restrictive-bathroom-law.html.

Feldman, Paula R. 2002. "Women Poets and Anonymity in the Romantic Era." *New Literary History* 33 (2): 279–89.

Ferrante, Elena. 2016. *Frantumaglia: A Writer's Journey*. New York: Edizioni E/O.

Ferri, Sandro, and Sandra Ferri. 2015. "Elena Ferrante, Art of Fiction No. 228." *Paris Review* 212:210–32.

Fine, Gary Alan. 1991. "On the Macrofoundations of Microsociology: Constraint and the Exterior Reality of Structure." *Sociological Quarterly* 32 (2): 161–77.

Fine, Gary Alan. 2001. *Difficult Reputations: Collective Memories of the Evil, Inept, and Controversial*. Chicago: University of Chicago Press.

Fine, Gary Alan. 2012. *Tiny Publics: A Theory of Group Action and Culture*. New York: Russell Sage Foundation.

Fine, Gary Alan. 2015. *Player and Pawns: How Chess Builds Community and Culture*. Chicago: University of Chicago Press.

Fine, Gary Alan. 2019. "Moral Cultures, Reputation Work, and the Politics of Scandal." *Annual Review of Sociology* 45:247–64.

Fine, Gary Alan. 2021. *The Hinge: Civil Society, Group Cultures, and the Power of Local Communities*. Chicago: University of Chicago Press.

Fish, Stanley. 2010. "Student Evaluations, Part Two." *New York Times*, June 28, 2010. https://opinionator.blogs.nytimes.com/2010/06/28/student-evaluations-part -two/?_r=0.

Foley, Sean, Jonathan R. Karlsen, and Tālis J. Putniņš. 2019. "Sex, Drugs, and Bitcoin: How Much Illegal Activity Is Financed through Cryptocurrencies?" *Review of Financial Studies* 32 (5): 1798–853.

Forest, N. B. 1868. "An Interview with the Rebel Cavalryman—He Thinks He Could Raise 40,000 Men in Five Days—Half a Million Kuklux in the South." *New York Times*, September 3, 1868.

Fossett, Judith Jackson. 1997. "(K)Night Riders in (K)Night Gowns: The Ku Klux Klan, Race, and Constructions of Masculinity." In *Race Consciousness: African-American Studies for the New Century*, edited by Judith Jackson Fossett and Jeffrey A. Tucker, 35–49. New York: NYU Press.

Foucault, Michel. (1969) 1977. "What Is an Author?" In *Language, Counter-Memory, Practice*, 113–38. Ithaca, NY: Cornell University Press.

Foucault, Michel. (1975) 1995. *Discipline and Punish: The Birth of the Prison*. New York: Vintage Books.

Foucault, Michel. (1978) 1990. *The History of Sexuality*. Vol. 1. New York: Vintage Books.

Francescani, Chris. 2020. "The Men Behind Qanon." *ABC News*, December 22, 2020. https://abcnews.go.com/Politics/men-qanon/story?id=73046374.

Frank, Arthur W. 1995. *The Wounded Storyteller: Body, Illness, and Ethics*. Chicago: University of Chicago Press.

Fraser, Nancy. 1990. "Rethinking the Public Sphere: A Contribution to the Critique of Actually Existing Democracy." *Social Text* 25/26:56–80.

Freud, Sigmund. (1930) 1961. *Civilization and Its Discontents*. New York: W. W. Norton.

Friedman, Asia. 2013. *Blind to Sameness: Sexpectations and the Social Construction of Male and Female Bodies*. Chicago: University of Chicago Press.

Friedrichs, David O. 2013. "Wall Street: Crime Never Sleeps." In *How They Got Away with It: White Collar Criminals and the Financial Meltdown*, edited by Susan Will, Stephen Handelman, and David C. Brotherton, 3–25. New York: Columbia University Press.

Frois, Catarina. 2009a. *The Anonymous Society: Identity, Transformation, and Anonymity in 12 Step Associations*. Newcastle upon Tyne, UK: Cambridge Scholars Publishing.

Frois, Catarina. 2009b. "Anonymity in 12-Step Groups: An Anthropological Approach." In *Contours of Privacy*, edited by David Matheson, 85–105. Newcastle upon Tyne, UK: Cambridge Scholars Publishing.

Froomkin, A. Michael. 1995. "Anonymity and Its Enmities." 1 *Journal of Online Law*, art. 4. https://ssrn.com/abstract=2715621.

Froomkin, A. Michael. 1999. "Legal Issues in Anonymity and Pseudonymity." *The Information Society* 15 (2): 113–27.

Froomkin, A. Michael. 2003. "Anonymity in the Balance." In *Digital Anonymity and the Law: Tensions and Dimensions*, edited by C. Nicoll, J. E. J. Prins, and M. J. M. van Dellen, 5–46. The Hague: Asser Press.

Fry, Gladys-Marie. (1975) 2001. *Night Riders in Black Folk History*. Chapel Hill: University of North Carolina Press.

Fryer, John Ercel. 1972. "Speech of 'Dr. Henry Anonymous' [John Fryer] at the American Psychiatric Association 125th Annual Meeting." May 2, 1972. http://digitalhistory.hsp.org/pafrm/doc/speech-dr-henry-anonymous-john-fryer-american-psychiatric-association-125th-annual-meeting.

Gage, Beverly. 2014. "What an Uncensored Letter to M.L.K. Reveals." *New York Times Magazine*. https://www.nytimes.com/2014/11/16/magazine/what-an-uncensored-letter-to-mlk-reveals.html?auth=login-email&login=email.

Gallagher, Brian. 2018. "Larry David and the Game Theory of Anonymous Donations." *Nautilus*, June 8, 2018. http://nautil.us/blog/larry-david-and-the-game-theory-of-anonymous-donations.

Gardner, James A. 2011. "Anonymity and Democratic Citizenship." *William & Mary Bill of Rights Journal* 19:927–57.

Garfinkel, Harold. 1967. *Studies in Ethnomethodology*. Cambridge: Polity Press.

Garland, David. 2006. "Concepts of Culture in the Sociology of Punishment." *Theoretical Criminology* 10 (4): 419–47.

Garland, David. 2009. "A Cultural Theory of Punishment?" *Punishment and Society* 11 (2): 259–68.

Garland, David. 2010. *Peculiar Institution: America's Death Penalty in an Age of Abolition*. Cambridge, MA: Harvard University Press.

Garner, Martin L. 2012. "For the Sake of One Child: Privacy, Anonymity, and Confidentiality in Libraries." *Journal of Information Ethics* 21 (1): 12–20.

Gatti, Claudio. 2016. "Elena Ferrante: An Answer?" *New York Review of Books*, October 2, 2016. https://www.nybooks.com/daily/2016/10/02/elena-ferrante-an-answer/.

Gawande, Atul. 2006. "When Law and Ethics Collide—Why Physicians Participate in Executions." *New England Journal of Medicine* 354 (12): 1221–29.

Geertz, Clifford. 1973. "Thick Description: Toward an Interpretive Theory of Culture." In *The Interpretation of Cultures*, 3–30. New York: Basic Books.

Geue, Tom. 2016. "Elena Ferrante Has Her Reasons for Anonymity—We Should Respect Them." *The Conversation*, October 3, 2016. https://theconversation.com/elena-ferrante-has-her-reasons-for-anonymity-we-should-respect-them-66436.

Giddens, Anthony. 1990. *The Consequences of Modernity*. Stanford, CA: Stanford University Press.

Giddens, Anthony. 1991. *Modernity and Self-Identity: Self and Society in the Late Modern Age*. Stanford, CA: Stanford University Press.

Gilbert, David. 2014. "Anonymous: Ferguson Killer Cop Darren Wilson 'Linked to KKK Ghoul Squad.'" *International Business Times*, November 21, 2014. https://www.ibtimes.co.uk/anonymous-ferguson-killer-cop-darren-wilson-linked-kkk-ghoul-squad-1475953.

Gilbert, Sophie. 2017. "Why Men Pretend to Be Women to Sell Thrillers." *The Atlantic*, August 3, 2017. https://www.theatlantic.com/entertainment/archive/2017/08/men-are-pretending-to-be-women-to-write-books/535671/.

Gill, Lauren. 2020. "Alabama Executes Nathaniel Woods Despite Claims That He Was an 'Innocent Man.'" *The Appeal*, March 6, 2020. https://theappeal.org/alabama-executes-nathaniel-woods-despite-claims-that-he-was-an-innocent-man/.

Gilligan, Heather. 2017. "The Black Bloc Protestors in Hoodies Started in Germany in the Late 1970s." *Timeline*, February 7, 2017. https://timeline.com/black-bloc-started-1980s-e228bf3981b4#.qi69bfpm0.

Gioia, Ted. 2017. "Banksy, Daft Punk, Elena Ferrante: The New Cult of the Anonymous Artist." *Daily Beast*. Updated April 13, 2017. https://www.thedailybeast.com/banksy-daft-punk-elena-ferrante-the-new-cult-of-the-anonymous-artist?ref=scroll.

Girgis, Linda. 2014. "The Value of Anonymity in Online Medical Crowdsourcing Communities." *MedCity News*, December 10, 2014. https://medcitynews.com/2014/12/value-anonymity-online-medical-crowdsourcing-communities/.

Gladwell, Malcolm. 2005. *Blink: The Power of Thinking without Thinking*. New York: Little, Brown.

Glaser, Barney G., and Anselm L. Strauss. (1967) 2008. *The Discovery of Grounded Theory: Strategies for Qualitative Research*. New Brunswick, NJ: Aldine Transaction.

Glazer, Amihai, and Kai A. Konrad. 1996. "A Signaling Explanation for Charity." *American Economic Review* 86 (4): 1019–28.

Glick, Brian. 1989. *War at Home: Covert Action against U.S. Activists and What We Can Do about It*. Cambridge, MA: South End Press.

Goffman, Alice. 2014. *On the Run: Fugitive Life in an American City*. Chicago: University of Chicago Press.

Goffman, Erving. 1959. *The Presentation of Self in Everyday Life*. New York: Anchor Books.

Goffman, Erving. 1961. *Asylums: Essays on the Social Situation of Mental Patients and Other Inmates*. New York: Anchor Books.

Goffman, Erving. 1963. *Stigma: Notes on the Management of a Spoiled Identity*. New York: Simon and Schuster.

Goffman, Erving. 1967. *Interaction Ritual*. New York. Doubleday.

Goffman, Erving. 1969. *Strategic Interaction*. Philadelphia: University of Pennsylvania Press.

Goffman, Erving. (1974) 1986. *Frame Analysis: An Essay on the Organization of Experience*. Boston: Northeastern University Press.

Goldenberg, Suzanne, and Esther Addley. 2011. "Outrage in US as 'Lesbian' Bloggers Revealed to Be Men." *The Guardian*, June 14, 2011. https://www.the guardian.com/world/2011/jun/14/lesbian-bloggers-revealed-men.

Goldin, Claudia, and Cecilia Rouse. 2000. "Orchestrating Impartiality: The Impact of 'Blind' Auditions on Female Musicians." *American Economic Review* 90 (4): 715–41.

Gordon, Lewis R. 1995. *Fanon and the Crisis of European Man: An Essay on Philosophy and the Human Sciences*. New York: Routledge.

Gordon, Lewis R. 1997. "Existential Dynamics of Theorizing Black Invisibility." In *Existence in Black: An Anthology of Black Existential Philosophy*, edited by Lewis R. Gordon, 69–79. New York: Routledge.

Gordon, Linda. 2017. *The Second Coming of the KKK: The Ku Klux Klan of the 1920s and the American Political Tradition*. New York: Liveright.

Gottschalk, Simon. 2010. "The Presentation of Avatars in Second Life: Self and Interaction in Social Virtual Spaces." *Symbolic Interaction* 33 (4): 501–25.

Gottschalk, Simon, and Jennifer Whitmer. 2013. "Hypermodern Dramaturgy in Online Encounters." In *The Drama of Social Life: A Dramaturgical Handbook*, edited by Charles Edgley, 309–34. Surrey, UK: Ashgate.

Gould, Roger V. 1995. *Insurgent Identities: Class, Community, and Protest in Paris from 1848 to the Commune*. Chicago: University of Chicago Press.

Grazian, David. 2008. *On the Make: The Hustle of Urban Nightlife*. Chicago: University of Chicago Press.

Griffin, Andrew. 2020. "What Is QAnon? The Origins of Bizarre Conspiracy Theory Spreading Online." *The Independent*, October 7, 2020. https://www.independent .co.uk/life-style/gadgets-and-tech/news/qanon-explained-what-trump-russia -investigation-pizzagate-a8845226.html.

Griffin, Robert J. 1999. "Anonymity and Authorship." *New Literary History* 30 (4): 877–95.

Groner, Jonathan I. 2002. "Lethal Injection: A Stain on the Face of Medicine." *British Medical Journal* 325 (2): 1026–28.

Grow, Kory. 2016. "Prince, the Secret Philanthropist: 'His Cause Was Humanity.'" *Rolling Stone*, April 25, 2016. https://www.rollingstone.com/culture/culture -news/prince-the-secret-philanthropist-his-cause-was-humanity-157700/.

Grygiel, Chris. 2014. "FBI Admits Agent Impersonated Reporter during Criminal

Investigation." *San Diego Union-Tribune*, November 6, 2014. Associated Press. https://www.sandiegouniontribune.com/sdut-fbi-admits-agent-impersonated-ap-reporter-2014nov06-story.html.

Gubrium, Jaber F., and James A. Holstein. 2000. "The Self in a World of Going Concerns." *Symbolic Interaction* 23 (2): 95–115.

Guerrilla Girls. 2021. "Guerrilla Girls: Reinventing the 'F' Word: Feminism." https://www.guerrillagirls.com/our-story.

Gusterson, Hugh. 2014. "Toward an Anthropology of Drones: Remaking Space, Time, and Valor in Combat." In *The American Way of Bombing: Changing Ethical and Legal Norms, from Flying Fortresses to Drones*, edited by Matthew Evangelista and Henry Shue, 191–206. Ithaca, NY: Cornell University Press.

Habermas, Jürgen. 1987. *The Theory of Communicative Action*. Vol. 2, *Lifeworld and System: A Critique of Functionalist Reason*. Boston: Beacon Press.

Hallett, Tim. 2007. "Between Difference and Distinction: Interaction Ritual through Symbolic Power in an Educational Institution." *Social Psychology Quarterly* 70 (2): 148–71.

Harcourt, Bernard E. 2015. *Exposed: Desire and Disobedience in the Digital Age*. Cambridge, MA: Harvard University Press.

Harding, Luke. 2003. "Row over Naming of Rape Author." *The Guardian*, October 4, 2003. https://www.theguardian.com/world/2003/oct/05/historybooks.germany.

Harris, David A. 1999. "Driving While Black: Racial Profiling on Our Nation's Highways." An American Civil Liberties Union Special Report, June 1999. https://www.aclu.org/report/driving-while-black-racial-profiling-our-nations-highways.

Hastings, Michael. 2012. "The Rise of the Killer Drones: How America Goes to War in Secret." *Rolling Stone*, April 16, 2012. https://www.rollingstone.com/politics/politics-news/the-rise-of-the-killer-drones-how-america-goes-to-war-in-secret-231297/.

Hauser, Christine, and Karen Zraick. 2019. "New Jersey Family Terrorized by 'The Watcher' Sells Home at a Loss." *New York Times*, August 9, 2019. https://www.nytimes.com/2019/08/09/nyregion/the-watcher-house-sold-new-jersey.html.

Henderson, Nia-Malika. 2018. "This New Lynching Memorial Rewrites American History." CNN, April 26, 2018. https://www.cnn.com/travel/article/lynching-memorial-montgomery-alabama/index.html?sr=fbCNN040918lynching-memorial-montgomery-alabama0948AMVODtopVideo.

Herman, Jody L. 2013. "Gendered Restrooms and Minority Stress: The Public Regulation of Gender and Its Impact on Transgender People's Lives." *Journal of Public Management & Social Policy* 19 (1): 65–80.

Hipp, Tracy N., Alexandra L. Bellis, Bradley L. Goodnight, Carolyn L. Brennan, Kevin M. Swartout, and Sarah L. Cook. 2017. "Justifying Sexual Assault: Anonymous Perpetrators Speak Online." *Psychology of Violence* 7 (1): 82–90.

Hoffman, Moshe, Christian Hilbe, and Martin A. Nowak. 2018. "The Signal-Burying Game Can Explain Why We Obscure Positive Traits and Good Deeds." *Nature Human Behaviour* 2:397–404.

Holland, Gale. 2012. "An Ugly Foreclosure Story, Starring Bank of America." *Los*

*Angeles Times*, April 13, 2012. https://www.latimes.com/local/la-xpm-2012-apr -13-la-me-holland-20120413-story.html.

Holquist, Michael. 1985. Prologue to *Rabelais and His World*, xiii–xxiii. Bloomington: Indiana University Press.

Holstein, James A., and Jaber F. Gubrium. 2000. *The Self We Live By: Narrative Identity in a Postmodern World*. New York: Oxford University Press.

Homer. (~800 BCE) 1994–2009. *The Odyssey*. Translated by Samuel Butler. Internet Classics Archive. http://classics.mit.edu/Homer/odyssey.html.

Honigmann, John J. 1977. "The Masked Face." *Ethos* 5 (3): 263–80.

Hornum, Finn. 1968. "The Executioner: His Role and Status in Scandinavian Society." In *Sociology and Everyday Life*, edited by Marcello Truzzi, 125–37. Englewood Cliffs, NJ: Prentice-Hall.

Horowitz, Michael C. 2016. "The Ethics and Morality of Robotic Warfare: Assessing the Debate over Autonomous Weapons." *Dædalus* 145 (4): 25–36.

Hubbard, Phil. 2002. "Sexing the Self: Geographies of Engagement and Encounter." *Social & Cultural Geography* 3 (4): 365–81.

Humphreys, Laud. (1970) 2017. *Tearoom Trade: Impersonal Sex in Public Places*. Abington, UK: Routledge.

Irvine, Leslie. 1999. *Codependent Forevermore: The Invention of Self in a Twelve Step Group*. Chicago: University of Chicago Press.

Ivie, Robert L. 2005. "Savagery in Democracy's Empire." *Third World Quarterly* 26 (1): 55–65.

Japenga, Ann. 1989. "Mystery Hangman Sets Off a Washington Controversy." *Los Angeles Times*, April 12, 1989. https://www.latimes.com/archives/la-xpm-1989 -04-12-vw-1826-story.html.

Jerolmack, Colin, and Alexandra K. Murphy. 2019. "The Ethical Dilemmas and Social Scientific Trade-Offs of Masking in Ethnography." *Sociological Methods and Research* 48 (4): 801–27.

Johnson, James H. 2001. "Versailles, Meet Les Halles: Masks, Carnival, and the French Revolution." *Representations* 73 (1): 89–116.

Johnson, James H. 2011. *Venice Incognito: Masks in the Serene Republic*. Berkeley: University of California Press. Kindle ed.

Johnson, Martha. 1992. "Reflections of Inner Life: Masks and Masked Acting in Ancient Greek Tragedy and Japanese Noh Drama." *Modern Drama* 35 (1): 20–34.

Jones, Zoey, and Stacey Hannem. 2018. "Escort Clients' Sexual Scripts and Constructions of Intimacy in Commodified Sexual Relationships." *Symbolic Interaction* 41 (4): 488–512.

Jospeh, Jisha. 2021. "Teen Spent over a Year Raising $10k for a Baby Drop-Off Box. So Far, 12 Babies Have Been Left Inside." *Upworthy*, October 29, 2021. https:// scoop.upworthy.com/indiana-teen-raised-ten-thousand-dollars-baby-drop-off -box-receives-first-newborn.

Jutel, Annemarie. 2019. "'The Expertness of His Healer': Diagnosis, Disclosure and the Power of a Profession." *Health: An Interdisciplinary Journal for the Social Study of Health, Illness and Medicine* 23 (3): 289–305.

Kang, Jerry. 2000. "Cyber-Race." *Harvard Law Review* 113 (5): 1130–1208.

Karp, David A. 1973. "Hiding in Pornographic Bookstores: A Reconsideration of the Nature of Urban Anonymity." *Urban Life and Culture* 1 (4): 427–51.

Katz, Emily Tess. 2015. "This Woman Was Catfished for 12 Years." *HuffPost.*
https://www.huffpost.com/entry/this-woman-was-catfished-for-12-years_n
_55b291b3e4b0224d88323be9.

Kessler, Suzanna J., and Wendy McKenna. 1978. *Gender: An Ethnomethodological
Approach.* Chicago: University of Chicago Press.

Khan, Shamus. 2019. "The Subpoena of Ethnographic Data." *Sociological Forum* 34
(1): 253–63.

Kiel, Paul. 2012. "The Great American Foreclosure Story: The Struggle for Justice
and a Place to Call Home." ProPublica, April 10, 2012. https://www.propublica
.org/article/the-great-american-foreclosure-story-the-struggle-for-justice-and
-a-place-t.

Kiesler, Sara, Jane Siegel, and Timothy W. McGuire. 1984. "Social Psychological
Aspects of Computer-Mediated Communication." *American Psychologist* 39 (10):
1123–34.

Kilcullen, David, and Andrew McDonald Exum. 2009. "Death from Above, Outrage
Down Below." *New York Times,* May 16, 2009. https://www.nytimes.com/2009
/05/17/opinion/17exum.html.

Kilgannon, Corey. 1999. "An Asphalt Mystery Examined." *New York Times.* April
25, 1999. https://archive.nytimes.com/www.nytimes.com/library/tech/99/04
/biztech/articles/25onli.html.

Kim, Kyung Kyu, Ae Ri Lee, and Un-Kon Lee. 2019. "Impact of Anonymity on
Roles of Personal and Group Identities in Online Communities." *Information &
Management* 56(1): 109–21.

Kinney, Alison. 2016. "Off with His Hood." *History Today.* June 2016: 28–35.

Kinser, Samuel. 1990. *Carnival, American Style: Mardi Gras at New Orleans and
Mobile.* Chicago: University of Chicago Press.

Kirchgaessner, Stephanie. 2016. "Elena Ferrante: Literary Storm as Italian Reporter
'Identifies' Author." *The Guardian,* October 2, 2016. https://www.theguardian
.com/world/2016/oct/02/elena-ferrante-literary-storm-as-italian-reporter
-identifies-author.

Kirkpatrick, David D. 2022. "Who Is Behind QAnon? Linguistic Detectives Find
Fingerprints." *New York Times,* February 19, 2022. https://www.nytimes.com
/2022/02/19/technology/qanon-messages-authors.html.

Klein, Naomi. 2002. "Farewell to 'The End of History': Organization and Vision in
Anti-Corporate Movements." *Socialist Register* 38:1–14.

Knibbs, Kate. 2015. "Asshole Gets Busted Because Yik Yak's Not Really Anonymous." Gizmodo, November 11, 2015. https://gizmodo.com/asshole-gets-busted
-because-yik-yaks-not-really-anonymo-1741931009.

Knuttila, Lee. 2011. "User Unknown: 4chan, Anonymity and Contingency." *First
Monday* 16 (10). https://firstmonday.org/ojs/index.php/fm/article/view/3665.

Kobayashi, Kazushige. 1981. "On the Meaning of Masked Dances in Kagura." Translated by Peter Knecht. *Asian Folklore Studies* 40 (1): 1–22.

Koch, Christina Marie. 2014. "Occupying Popular Culture: Anonymous, Occupy
Wall Street, and the Guy Fawkes Mask as a Political Icon." In *Towards a Post-
Exceptionalist American Studies,* edited by Winfried Fluck and Donald E. Pease,
445–82. Tübingen: Narr.

Kohler, Jeremy. 2006. "Behind the Mask of the Execution Doctor—Revelations
about Dr. Alan Doerhoff Follow Judge's Halt of Lethal Injections." *St. Louis Post-*

*Dispatch*, June 30, 2006. https://infoweb.newsbank.com/apps/news/document
-view?p=WORLDNEWS&docref=news/11335988E13BBC78.

Koshy, Philip, Diana Koshy, and Patrick McDaniel. 2014. "An Analysis of Anonym-
ity in Bitcoin Using P2P Network Traffic." In *Financial Cryptography and Data
Security*, edited by Nicolas Christin and Reihaneh Safavi-Naini, 469–85. Berlin:
Springer.

Kralik, Joellen. 2019. "'Bathroom Bill' Legislative Tracking." National Conference of
State Legislatures, October 24, 2019. https://www.ncsl.org/research/education
/-bathroom-bill-legislative-tracking635951130.aspx.

Krause, Monika. 2021. *Model Cases: On Canonical Research Objects and Sites*. Chicago: University of Chicago Press.

Kukla, Quill. 2020. "Street Art, Place-Making, and Anti-Capitalist Spatial Activism."
*Spectre*, July 22, 2020. https://spectrejournal.com/street-art-place-making-and
-anti-capitalist-spatial-activism/.

Ku Klux Klan. 1868. "Ku Klux Klan to Davie Jeems." Gilder Lehrman Collection
#GLC09090. Gilder Lehrman Institute of American History. https://www
.gilderlehrman.org/collection/glc09090.

Ku Klux Klan. 1917. "ABC of the Invisible Empire." Ku Klux Press. http://credo
.library.umass.edu/view/full/mums312-b009-i215. W. E. B. Du Bois Papers
(MS 312). Special Collections and University Archives, University of Massachusetts Amherst Libraries.

LaFrance, Adrienne. 2020. "The Prophecies of Q." *The Atlantic*, May 14, 2020.
https://www.theatlantic.com/magazine/archive/2020/06/qanon-nothing-can
-stop-what-is-coming/610567/.

Lam, Carrie. 2019. "Hong Kong: Face Mask Ban Prompts Thousands to Protest."
*BBC News*. https://www.bbc.com/news/world-asia-china-49939173.

Langegger, Sig, and Stephen Koester. 2016. "Invisible Homelessness: Anonymity,
Exposure, and the Right to the City." *Urban Geography* 37 (7): 1030–48.

Laqueur, Thomas. 1990. *Making Sex: Body and Gender from the Greeks to Freud*.
Cambridge, MA: Harvard University Press.

Lau, Tim. 2019. "Citizens United Explained." Brennan Center for Justice. December
12, 2019. https://www.brennancenter.org/our-work/research-reports/citizens
-united-explained.

Lea, Martin, and Russell Spears. 1991. "Computer-Mediated Communication,
De-Individuation and Group Decision-Making." *International Journal of Man-
Machine Studies* 34:283–301.

Lea, Martin, Russell Spears, and Susan E. Watt. 2007. "Visibility and Anonymity
Effects on Attraction and Group Cohesiveness." *European Journal of Social Psychology* 37 (4): 761–73.

Le Bon, Gustave. (1895) 2002. *The Crowd: A Study of the Popular Mind*. Mineola,
NY: Dover.

Lee, Edmund. 2020. "Nurses Share Coronavirus Stories Anonymously in an Online
Document." *New York Times*, March 25, 2020. https://www.nytimes.com/2020
/03/25/business/media/coronavirus-nurses-stories-anonymous.html.

LeGraw, Joan M., and Michael A. Grodin. 2002. "Health Professionals and Lethal
Injection Execution in the United States." *Human Rights Quarterly* 24 (2):
382–423.

Leipholtz, Beth. 2016. "6 Reasons to Break Anonymity in Sobriety." *HuffPost*, September 18, 2016. https://www.huffpost.com/entry/six-reasons-to-break-anon _b_8160670.

Lennon, John. 2015. "Writing with a Global Accent: Cairo and the Roots/Routes of Conflict Graffiti." In *Understanding Graffiti: Multidisciplinary Studies from Prehistory to Present*, edited by Troy Lovata and Elizabeth Olton, 59–72. Abington, UK: Routledge.

Levenson, Michael, 2021. "What to Know about the Civilian Casualty Files." *New York Times*, December 18, 2021. https://www.nytimes.com/2021/12/18/us /airstrikes-civilian-casualty-files-pentagon.html.

Lévi-Strauss, Claude. 1963. *Structural Anthropology*. New York: Basic Books.

Lévi-Strauss, Claude. (1975) 1988. *The Way of the Masks*. Seattle: University of Washington Press.

Levmore, Saul, 2010. "The Internet's Anonymity Problem." In *The Offensive Internet*, edited by Saul Levmore and Martha C. Nussbaum, 50–67. Cambridge, MA: Harvard University Press.

Levmore, Saul, and Martha C. Nussbaum. 2010. "Introduction." In *The Offensive Internet*, edited by Saul Levmore and Martha C. Nussbaum, 1–11. Cambridge, MA: Harvard University Press.

Leys, Simon. 2011. "The Intimate Orwell." *New York Review of Books*, May 26, 2011. https://www.nybooks.com/articles/2011/05/26/intimate-orwell/.

Li, Hongtao. 2011. "Anonymous Review as Strategic Ritual: Examining the Rise of Anonymous Review among Mainland Chinese Communication Journals." *Asian Journal of Communication* 21 (6): 595–612.

Li, Qian, and Xiaoli Tian. 2022. "The Presence, Performance, and Publics of Online Interactions." *Oxford Handbook of Symbolic Interactionism*, edited by Wayne H. Brekhus, Thomas DeGloma, and William Ryan Force. New York: Oxford University Press.

Liao, Yen-Chiao. Unpublished. *The Limitation of Helping Victims: The Ambivalent Model of Human Trafficking Intervention Courts*. PhD diss., Department of Sociology, The Graduate Center, City University of New York.

Lifton, Robert Jay. (1986) 2000. *The Nazi Doctors: Medical Killing and the Psychology of Genocide*. New York: Basic Books.

Lindner, Andrew M., Gina Pryciak, and Jamie Elsner. 2020. "Tor and the City: MSA-Level Correlates of Interest in Anonymous Web Browsing." SocArXiv. February 9, 2020. https://osf.io/preprints/socarxiv/3e2vq/.

Linder, Andrew M., and Tongtian Xiao. 2020. "Subverting Surveillance or Accessing the Dark Web? Interest in the Tor Anonymity Network in U.S. States, 2006–2015." *Social Currents* 7 (4): 352–70.

Linton, Ralph. 1936. *The Study of Man*. New York: Appleton-Century-Crofts.

Lofland, John. 1975. "Open and Concealed Dramaturgical Strategies: The Case of the State Execution." *Urban Life* 4 (3): 272–95.

Loseke, Donileen R. 2009. "Examining Emotion as Discourse: Emotion Codes and Presidential Speeches Justifying War." *Sociological Quarterly*, 50 (3): 497–524.

Loseke, Donileen R. 2019. *Narrative Productions of Meaning*. Lanham, MD: Lexington Books.

Lovata, Troy. 2015. "Marked Trees: Exploring the Context of Southern Rocky

Mountain Arborglyphs." In *Understanding Graffiti: Multidisciplinary Studies from Prehistory to Present*, edited by Troy Lovata and Elizabeth Olton, 91–104. Abington, UK: Routledge.

Lovata, Troy, and Elizabeth Olton, eds. 2015. *Understanding Graffiti: Multidisciplinary Studies from Prehistory to Present*. Abington, UK: Routledge.

Lyon, David. 2014. "Surveillance, Snowden, and Big Data: Capacities, Consequences, Critique." *Big Data & Society* 1 (2): 1–13.

Lyons, Richard D. 1973. "Psychiatrists, in a Shift, Declare Homosexuality No Mental Illness." *New York Times*, December 16, 1973. https://www.nytimes.com/1973/12/16/archives/psychiatrists-in-a-shift-declare-homosexuality-no-mental-illness.html.

Mack, David. 2015a. "Texas Police Officer on Administrative Leave after Pulling Weapon on Teens during Pool Party." *BuzzFeed News*, June 8, 2015. https://www.buzzfeednews.com/article/davidmack/texas-police-officer-suspended-after-pulling-weapon-on-teens#.mxLbPnWPM.

Mack, David. 2015b. "This Man Speaking Out about the McKinney Pool Party Isn't Telling the Full Story." *BuzzFeed News*, June 10, 2015. https://www.buzzfeednews.com/article/davidmack/what-caused-mckinneys-pool-to-boil-over.

Mahboob, Tahiat. 2017. "From the Pointed Hat to the Burning Cross: The Real Origins of Ku Klux Klan Symbols." December 8, 2017. https://www.cbc.ca/passionateeye/features/from-the-pointed-hat-to-the-burning-cross-the-real-origins-of-ku-klux-klan.

Maniak, Katarzyna. 2018. "Guerrilla Girls: Invisible Sex in the Field of Art." *Annales Universitatis Paedagogicae Cracoviensis. Studia de Arte et Educatione* 13:87–95.

Markham, Annette. 2013. "The Dramaturgy of Digital Experience." In *The Drama of Social Life: A Dramaturgical Handbook*, edited by Charles Edgley, 279–93. Surrey, UK: Ashgate.

Markman, Roberta H., and Peter T. Markman. 1989. *Masks of the Spirit: Image and Metaphor in Mesoamerica*. Berkeley: University of California Press.

Martin, James. 2014. "Lost on the Silk Road: Online Drug Distribution and the 'Cryptomarket.'" *Criminology and Criminal Justice* 14 (3): 351–67.

Marx, Gary T. 1999. "What's in a Name? Some Reflections on the Sociology of Anonymity." *The Information Society* 15 (2): 99–112.

Marx, Gary T. 2016. *Windows into the Soul: Surveillance and Society in an Age of High Technology*. Chicago: University of Chicago Press.

Marx, Karl. (1845–46) 1978. *The German Ideology: Part I*. In *The Marx-Engels Reader*, 2nd ed., edited by Robert C. Tucker, 146–200. New York: W. W. Norton.

Marx, Karl. (1847) 1955. *The Poverty of Philosophy*. Progress Publishers. Online version Marx/Engels Internet Archive (1999). https://www.marxists.org/archive/marx/works/1847/poverty-philosophy/.

Marx, Karl. (1851–52) 1968. "The Eighteenth Brumaire of Louis Bonaparte." In *Karl Marx and Frederick Engels: Selected Works*, 96–179. Moscow: Progress Publishers.

Marx, Karl. (1867) 1978. *Capital: A Critique of Political Economy*. Vol. 1. In *The Marx-Engels Reader*, 2nd ed., edited by Robert C. Tucker, 294–438. New York: W. W. Norton.

Mathers, Lain A. B. 2017. "Bathrooms, Boundaries, and Emotional Burdens: Cisgendering Interactions through the Interpretation of Transgender Experience." *Symbolic Interaction* 40 (3): 295–316.

Mauss, Marcel. (1938) 1985. "The Category of the Human Mind: The Notion of Person; the Notion of the Self." In *The Category of the Person: Anthropology, Philosophy, History*, edited by Michael Carrithers, Steven Collins, and Steven Lukes, 1–25. Cambridge: Cambridge University Press.

Mayer, Jane. 2009. "The Predator War." *New Yorker*, October 19, 2009. https://www.newyorker.com/magazine/2009/10/26/the-predator-war.

McKinney, John C. 1969. "Typification, Typologies, and Sociological Theory." *Social Forces* 48 (1): 1–12.

Mead, George Herbert. (1934) 2015. *Mind, Self, and Society*. Chicago: University of Chicago Press.

Meade, Melissa R. 2015. "Latrinalia in a Room of One's Own: Language, Gender, and Place." In *Understanding Graffiti: Multidisciplinary Studies from Prehistory to Present*, edited by Troy Lovata and Elizabeth Olton, 33–46. Abington, UK: Routledge.

Mengel, Friederike, Jan Sauermann, and Ulf Zölitz. 2019. "Gender Bias in Teaching Evaluations." *Journal of the European Economic Association* 17 (2): 535–66. https://doi.org/10.1093/jeea/jvx057.

Mikael-Debass, Milena. 2017. "These Anonymous Street Artists Want an Independent Puerto Rico." *Vice News*, June 14, 2017. https://www.vice.com/en/article/d3xjdw/these-anonymous-street-artists-want-an-independent-puerto-rico.

Milgram, Stanley. 1963. "Behavioral Study of Obedience." *Journal of Abnormal and Social Psychology* 67:371–78.

Milgram, Stanley. 1965. "Some Conditions of Obedience and Disobedience to Authority." *Human Relations* 18 (1): 57–76.

Milgram, Stanley. 1974. *Obedience to Authority: An Experimental View*. New York: HarperCollins.

Milkman, Ruth, Stephanie Luce, and Penny Lewis. 2013. *Changing the Subject: A Bottom-Up Account of Occupy Wall Street in New York City*. New York: The Murphy Institute, City University of New York.

Mill, John Stuart. 1859. "Thoughts on Parliamentary Reform." London: Savill and Edwards. Public domain. https://en.wikisource.org/wiki/Thoughts_on_Parliamentary_Reform.

Miller, Chanel. 2019. *Know My Name*. New York: Viking.

Miller, Michael E. 2017. "Antifa: Guardians against Fascism or Lawless Thrill-Seekers?" *Washington Post*, September 14, 2017. https://www.washingtonpost.com/local/antifa-guardians-against-fascism-or-lawless-thrill-seekers/2017/09/14/38db474c-93fe-11e7-89fa-bb822a46da5b_story.html.

Mills, C. Wright. 1940. "Situated Actions and Vocabularies of Motive." *American Sociological Review* 5 (6): 904–13.

Mills, C. Wright. (1951) 2002. *White Collar: The American Middle Classes*. Oxford: Oxford University Press.

Minford, Patrick. 2015. "Who Was Really Responsible for the Financial Crisis?" *World Economic Forum*, May 4, 2015. https://www.weforum.org/agenda/2015/05/who-was-really-responsible-for-the-financial-crisis/.

Monbiot, George. 2012. "In the US, Mass Child Killings Are Tragedies. In Pakistan,

Mere Bug Splats." *The Guardian*, December 17, 2012. https://www.theguardian
.com/commentisfree/2012/dec/17/us-killings-tragedies-pakistan-bug-splats.

Moore, Alan, and David Lloyd. (1982) 2005. *V for Vendetta*. New York: DC Comics.

Moore, Alan, and Dave Gibbons. 1986. *Watchmen*. Burbank, CA: DC Comics.

Moore, Alfred. 2018. "Anonymity, Pseudonymity, and Deliberation: Why Not
Everything Should Be Connected." *Journal of Political Philosophy* 26 (2): 169–92.

Moran, Lee. 2021. "Carmen Mola, Popular Spanish Female Thriller Author, Revealed to Be 3 Men." *HuffPost*, October 19, 2021. https://www.huffpost.com
/entry/spanish-author-carmen-mola-men_n_616e7d19e4b00cb3cbd7485c.

Moster, Miriam. 2018. "Jewish Education: A Cognitive Sociological Interrogation of
the Historical Narrative." Paper delivered at the Association for Jewish Studies
50th Annual Conference, Boston, MA, December 16–18, 2018.

Mullan, John. 2007. *Anonymity: A Secret History of English Literature*. London:
Faber and Faber.

Mullaney, Jamie L. 1999. "Making it 'Count': Mental Weighing and Identity Attribution." *Symbolic Interaction* 22 (3): 269–83.

Nail, Thomas. 2013. "Zapatismo and the Global Origins of Occupy." *Journal for
Cultural and Religious Theory* 12 (3): 20–38.

Napier, A. David. 1986. *Masks, Transformations, and Paradox*. Berkeley: University
of California Press.

Natanson, Maurice. 1970. "Phenomenology and Typification: A Study in the Philosophy of Alfred Schutz." *Social Research* 37 (1): 1–22.

Natanson, Maurice. 1979. "Phenomenology, Anonymity, and Alienation." *New Literary History* 10 (3): 533–46.

Natanson, Maurice. 1986. *Anonymity: A Study in the Philosophy of Alfred Schutz*.
Bloomington: Indiana University Press.

Nespor, Jan. 2000. "Anonymity and Place in Qualitative Inquiry." *Qualitative Inquiry*
6 (4): 546–69.

Neuman, Scott. 2015. "Video Shows Texas Police Officer Pulling Gun on Teens at
Pool Party." NPR, June 7, 2015. https://www.npr.org/sections/thetwo-way
/2015/06/07/412708943/video-shows-texas-police-officer-pulling-gun-on
-teens-at-pool-party.

Newman, Lily Hay. 2014. "Open Secrets: The New Wave of Anonymous Social Networks Is Neither New nor Anonymous." *Slate*, March 21, 2014. http://www.slate
.com/articles/technology/technology/2014/03/whisper_secret_yik_yak
_new_anonymous_social_networks_are_neither_new_nor.html.

Neyfakh, Leon. 2015. "The Ethics of Ethnography." *Slate*, June 18, 2015. https://
slate.com/news-and-politics/2015/06/alice-goffmans-on-the-run-is-the
-sociologist-to-blame-for-the-inconsistencies-in-her-book.html.

Nicol, Olivia. 2016. "The Blame Game for the Financial Crisis (2007–2010): A
Sociological Theory of Fields of Accusation." European University Institute
Working Papers: Max Weber Programme. http://cadmus.eui.eu/bitstream
/handle/1814/40728/MWP_2016_03.pdf?sequence=1.

Nicoll, Chris. 2003. "Concealing and Revealing Identity on the Internet." In *Digital
Anonymity and the Law: Tensions and Dimensions*, edited by C. Nicoll, J. E. J.
Prins, and M. J. M. van Dellen, 99–119. The Hague: Asser Press.

Nicoll, C., J. E. J. Prins, and M. J. M. van Dellen, eds. 2003. *Digital Anonymity and
the Law: Tensions and Dimensions*. The Hague: Asser Press.

Nissenbaum, Helen. 1998. "Protecting Privacy in an Information Age: The Problem of Privacy in Public." *Law and Philosophy* 17:559–96.

Nissenbaum, Helen. 1999. "The Meaning of Anonymity in an Information Age." *The Information Society* 15 (2): 141–44.

Nissenbaum, Helen. 2004. "Privacy as Contextual Integrity." *Washington Law Review* 79 (1): 119–57.

Nixey, Catherine. 2017. *The Darkening Age: The Christian Destruction of the Classical World*. Boston: Mariner Books.

Nussbaum, Martha C. 2010. "Objectification and Internet Misogyny." In *The Offensive Internet*, edited by Saul Levmore and Martha C. Nussbaum, 68–87. Cambridge, MA: Harvard University Press.

NYCLU. 2011. "Stop-and-Frisk 2011." An NYCLU Briefing. New York City Liberties Union. https://www.nyclu.org/sites/default/files/publications/NYCLU_2011 _Stop-and-Frisk_Report.pdf.

NYCLU. 2019. "Stop-and-Frisk in the de Blasio Era." New York City Liberties Union, March 2019. https://www.nyclu.org/sites/default/files/field _documents/20190314_nyclu_stopfrisk_singles.pdf.

O'Connell, Pamela LiCalzi. 1998. "Many Sites to Confess One's Sins." *New York Times*, September 3, 1998. https://archive.nytimes.com/www.nytimes.com /library/tech/98/09/circuits/articles/03conf.html.

Ohm, Paul. 2010. "Broken Promises of Privacy: Responding to the Surprising Failure of Anonymization." *UCLA Law Review* 57 (6): 1701–77.

Olesen, Thomas. 2005. *International Zapatismo: The Construction of Solidarity in the Age of Globalization*. London: Zed Books.

Olesen, Thomas. 2019. "The Politics of Whistleblowing in Digitalized Societies." *Politics & Society* 47 (2): 277–97.

Olton, Elizabeth, and Troy Lovata. 2015. "Introduction." In *Understanding Graffiti: Multidisciplinary Studies from Prehistory to Present*, edited by Troy Lovata and Elizabeth Olton, 11–16. Abington, UK: Routledge.

Omi, Michael, and Howard Winant. 1994. *Racial Formation in the United States: From the 1960s to the 1990s*. New York: Routledge.

Oppenheimer, Mark. 2013. "In Big-Dollar Philanthropy, (Your Name Here) vs. Anonymity." *New York Times*, May 10, 2013. https://www.nytimes.com/2013/05/11 /us/in-philanthropy-your-name-here-vs-anonymous-giving.html.

Orr, Deborah. 2016. "The Unmasking of Elena Ferrante Has Violated My Right Not to Know." *The Guardian*, October 3, 2016. https://www.theguardian.com/books /2016/oct/03/unmasking-elena-ferrante-italian-journalist-claudio-gatti.

Ortolani, Benito. 1990. *The Japanese Theater: From Shamanistic Ritual to Contemporary Pluralism*. Princeton, NJ: Princeton University Press.

O'Sullivan, Donie. 2016. "The Women Tweeting for Their Freedom in Saudi Arabia." CNN, September 16, 2016. https://www.cnn.com/2016/09/16/world/saudi -arabia-male-guardianship-campaign/index.html.

Oswell, Paul. 2015. "Meet the Male Writers Who Hide Their Gender to Attract Female Readers." *The Guardian*, July 31, 2015. https://www.theguardian.com /books/2015/jul/31/male-writers-hide-gender-sell-more-books.

Papadantonakis, Max. 2020. "Black Athenians: Making and Resisting Racialized Symbolic Boundaries in the Greek Street Market." *Journal of Contemporary Ethnography* 49 (3): 291–317.

Parsons, Elaine Frantz. 2005. "Midnight Rangers: Costume and Performance in the Reconstruction-Era Ku Klux Klan." *Journal of American History* 92 (3): 811–36.

Parsons, Elaine Frantz. 2015. *Ku-Klux: The Birth of the Klan during Reconstruction.* Chapel Hill: University of North Carolina Press.

Parsons, Talcott. (1951) 1991. *The Social System.* New York: Routledge.

Patton, Stacey. 2015. "Student Evaluations: Feared, Loathed, and Not Going Anywhere." *Chronicle of Higher Education,* May 19, 2015.

Peacey, Mike, and Michael Sanders. 2014. "Masked Heroes: Endogenous Anonymity in Charitable Giving." Centre for Market and Public Organization Working Paper Series, No. 14/329. http://www.bristol.ac.uk/media-library/sites/cmpo /migrated/documents/wp329.pdf.

Pearson, Jesse. 2009. "The Mystery of B. Traven." *Vice News,* December 1, 2009. https://www.vice.com/en_us/article/kw3m4y/the-myster-of-b-travern-270 -v16n12.

Peiser, Jaclyn. 2018. "How a Crowdsourced List Set Off Months of #MeToo Debate." *New York Times,* February 3, 2018. https://www.nytimes.com/2018/02/03 /business/media/media-men-list.html.

Perinbanayagam, R. S. 1991. *Discursive Acts.* New York: Aldine de Gruyter.

Peterson, Ashley Marie. 2012. "The Role of Surveyor-Perceived Anonymity within Social Network Sites." Master's thesis, Ohio State University. http://rave.ohio link.edu/etdc/view?acc_num=osu1343148703.

Peterson, David, and Daina Cheyenne Harvey. "Kafkaesque Bureaucracies as Natural Breaching Experiments: Interactional Failures and the Search for Institutional Agency." *Symbolic Interaction* 38 (2): 195–212.

Pitesa, Marko. 2013. "The Psychology of Unethical Behaviour in the Finance Industry." In *The Philosophy, Politics and Economics of Finance in the 21st Century: From Hubris to Disgrace,* edited by Patrick O'Sullivan, Nigel F. B. Allington, and Mark Esposito, 344–69. London: Routledge.

Plato. (~380 BCE) 1956. "The Republic." In *The Great Dialogues of Plato,* 118–422. Edited by Eric H. Warmington and Philip G. Rouse. Translated by W. H. D. Rouse. New York: New American Library.

Platt, Lisa F., and Sarah R. B. Milam. 2018. "Public Discomfort with Gender Appearance-Inconsistent Bathroom Use: The Oppressive Bind of Bathroom Laws for Transgender Individuals." *Gender Issues* 35 (3): 181–201.

Poe, Edgar Allan. 1842. "The Masque of the Red Death." https://www.gutenberg .org/files/1064/1064-h/1064-h.htm.

Poletti, Anna. 2011. "Intimate Economies: *PostSecret* and the Affect of Confession." *Biography* 34 (1): 25–36.

Polletta, Francesca. 2020. *Inventing the Ties That Bind: Imagined Relationships in Moral and Political Life.* Chicago: University of Chicago Press.

Pollner, Melvin, and Jill Stein. 1996. "Narrative Mapping of Social Worlds: The Voice of Experience in Alcoholics Anonymous." *Symbolic Interaction* 19 (3): 203–23.

Ponesse, Julie. 2013. "Navigating the Unknown: Towards a Positive Conception of Anonymity." *Southern Journal of Philosophy* 51 (3): 320–44.

Ponesse, Julie. 2014. "The Ties That Blind: Conceptualizing Anonymity." *Journal of Social Philosophy* 45 (3): 304–22.

Poster, Winifred R., Marion Crain, and Miriam A. Cherry. 2016. "Introduction:

Conceptualizing Invisible Labor." In *Invisible Labor: Hidden Work in the Contemporary World*, edited by Marion G. Crain, Winifred R. Poster, and Miriam A. Cherry, 3–27. Oakland: University of California Press.

Postmes, Tom, and Russell Spears. 1998. "Deindividuation and Antinormative Behavior: A Meta-Analysis." *Psychological Bulletin* 123 (3): 238–59.

Postmes, Tom, Russell Spears, and Martin Lea. 1999. "Social Identity, Normative Content and 'Deindividuation' in Computer-Mediated Groups." In *Social Identity*, edited by Naomi Ellemers, Russell Spears, and Bertjan Doosje, 164–83. Oxford: Blackwell.

Pozorski, Shelia, and Thomas Pozorski. 2015. "Graffiti as Resistance: Early Prehistoric Examples from the Casma Valley of Peru." In *Understanding Graffiti: Multidisciplinary Studies from Prehistory to Present*, edited by Troy Lovata and Elizabeth Olton, 143–57. Abington, UK: Routledge.

Preibusch, Sören. 2015. "Privacy Behaviors after Snowden." *Communications of the ACM* 58 (5): 48–55.

Price, Leah. 2003. "From Ghostwriter to Typewriter: Delegating Authority at Fin de Siècle." In *The Faces of Anonymity: Anonymous and Pseudonymous Publication from the Sixteenth to the Twentieth Century*, edited by Robert J. Griffin, 211–31. New York: Palgrave Macmillan.

Prus, Robert. 1987. "Generic Social Processes: Maximizing Conceptual Development in Ethnographic Research." *Journal of Contemporary Ethnography* 16 (3): 250–93.

Putman, Patrick. n.d. "What Is a Hacktivist?" *United States Cybersecurity Magazine*. https://www.uscybersecurity.net/hacktivist/.

Rappaport, Julian. 1993. "Narrative Studies, Personal Stories, and Identity Transformation in the Mutual Help Context." *Journal of Applied Behavioral Science* 29 (2): 239–56.

Reed, Isaac Ariail. 2017. "On the Very Idea of Cultural Sociology." In *Social Theory Now*, edited by Claudio E. Benzecry, Monika Krause, and Isaac Ariail Reed, 18–41. Chicago: University of Chicago Press.

Rehm, Rush. 1992. *Greek Tragic Theatre*. London: Routledge.

Reicher, S. D. 1984. "Social Influence in the Crowd: Attitudinal and Behavioural Effects of De-Individuation in Conditions of High and Low Group Salience." *British Journal of Social Psychology* 23 (4): 341–50.

Reicher, S. D., R. Spears, and T. Postmes. 1995. "A Social Identity Model of Deindividuation Phenomena." *European Review of Social Psychology* 6 (1): 161–98.

Reyes, Victoria. 2018. "Three Models of Transparency in Ethnographic Research: Naming Places, Naming People, and Sharing Data." *Ethnography* 19 (2): 204–26.

Ricoeur, Paul. 1991. "Narrative Identity." *Philosophy Today* 35 (1): 73–81.

Ridgeway, Cecilia. 2009. "Framed Before We Know It: How Gender Shapes Social Relations." *Gender and Society* 23 (2): 145–60.

Ridgeway, Cecilia L., and Shelley J. Correll. 2004. "Unpacking the Gender System: A Theoretical Perspective on Gender Beliefs and Social Relations." *Gender and Society* 18 (4): 510–31.

Ridout, Travis N., Michael M. Franz, and Erika Franklin Fowler. 2014. "Sponsorship, Disclosure, and Donors: Limiting the Impact of Outside Group Ads." *Political Research Quarterly* 68 (1): 154–66.

Riniolo, Todd C., Katherine C. Johnson, Tracey R. Sherman, and Julie A. Misso.

2006. "Hot or Not: Do Professors Perceived as Physically Attractive Receive Higher Student Evaluations?" *Journal of General Psychology* 133 (1): 19–35.

Robben, Antonius C. G. M. 2013. "The Hostile Gaze: Night Vision and the Immediation of Nocturnal Combat in Vietnam and Iraq." In *Virtual War and Magical Death: Technologies and Imaginaries for Terror and Killing,* edited by Neil L. Whitehead and Sverker Finnström, 132–51. Durham, NC: Duke University Press.

Rodriguez, Amardo. 2015. "On the Origins of Anonymous Texts That Appear on Walls." In *Understanding Graffiti: Multidisciplinary Studies from Prehistory to Present,* edited by Troy Lovata and Elizabeth Olton, 21–31. Abington, UK: Routledge.

Rogers, Alex. 2014. "What Anonymous Is Doing in Ferguson." *Time,* August 21, 2014. https://time.com/3148925/ferguson-michael-brown-anonymous/.

Rohter, Larry. 1990. "His Widow Reveals Much of Who B. Traven Really Was." *New York Times.* June 25, 1990. https://www.nytimes.com/1990/06/25/books/his-widow-reveals-much-of-who-b-traven-really-was.html?pagewanted=all&mcubz=0.

Roko, Ellyde. 2007. "Executioner Identities: Toward Recognizing a Right to Know Who Is Hiding Beneath the Hood." *Fordham Law Review* 75 (5): 2791–829.

Roose, Kevin. 2020. "What Is QAnon, the Viral Pro-Trump Conspiracy Theory?" *New York Times,* October 19, 2020. https://www.nytimes.com/article/what-is-qanon.html.

Rubenstein, Jeffrey L. 2003. *The Culture of the Babylonian Talmud.* Baltimore: Johns Hopkins University Press.

Rubenstein, Jeffrey L. (2005) 2019. "Introduction." In *Creation and Composition: The Contribution of the Bavli Redactors (Stammaim) to the Aggada,* edited by Jeffrey L. Rubenstein, 1–20. Tübingen: Mohr Siebeck.

Ruiz, Pollyanna, 2013. "Revealing Power: Masked Protest and the Blank Figure." *Cultural Politics* 9 (3): 263–79.

Ruiz-Junco, Natalia. 2017. "Advancing the Sociology of Empathy: A Proposal." *Symbolic Interaction* 40 (3): 414–35.

Ryder, Katie. 2016. "Walker Evans's Typology of the American Worker." *New Yorker,* April 25, 2016. https://www.newyorker.com/culture/photo-booth/walker-evanss-typology-of-the-american-worker.

Said, Edward W. 1978. *Orientalism.* New York: Vintage Books.

Saks, Michael J., and Thomas M. Ostrom. 1973. "Anonymity in Letters to the Editor." *Public Opinion Quarterly* 37 (3): 417–22.

Samarati, Pierangela, and Latanya Sweeney. 1998. "Protecting Privacy When Disclosing Information: *k*-Anonymity and Its Enforcement through Generalization and Suppression." *Proceedings of the IEEE Symposium on Research in Security and Privacy* (S&P). Oakland, CA, May 1998. https://dataprivacylab.org/dataprivacy/projects/kanonymity/index3.html.

Sanburn, Josh. 2014. "Creator of Lethal Injection Method: 'I Don't See Anything That Is More Humane.'" *Time,* May 15, 2014. https://time.com/101143/lethal-injection-creator-jay-chapman-botched-executions/.

Sanders, Teela. 2008. "Male Sexual Scripts: Intimacy, Sexuality and Pleasure in the Purchase of Commercial Sex." *Sociology* 42 (3): 400–417.

Sarat, Austin. 1999. "The Cultural Life of Capital Punishment: Responsibility and Representation in *Dead Man Walking* and *Last Dance*." *Yale Journal of Law and the Humanities* 11 (1): 153–90.

Saunders, Benjamin, Jenny Kitzinger, and Celia Kitzinger. 2015. "Participant Anonymity in the Internet Age: From Theory to Practice." *Qualitative Research in
Psychology* 12 (2): 125–37.

Savage, Neil. 2016. "Privacy: The Myth of Anonymity." *Nature* 537:70–72.

Scammell, Rosie. 2016. "Who Is Elena Ferrante? Novelist Issues Denial as Guessing Game Goes On." *The Guardian*, March 13, 2016. https://www.theguardian
.com/books/2016/mar/13/who-is-elena-ferrante-novelist-issues-denial-as
-guessing-game-goes-on.

Schafer, Tyler S., and David R. Dickens. 2016. "Social Marking in Memory Entrepre-
neurship: The Battle Over Zapata's Legacy." *Qualitative Sociology Review* 12 (2):
100–123.

Schappell, Elissa. 2015. "Elena Ferrante Explains Why, for the Last Time, You Don't
Need to Know Her Name." *Vanity Fair*, August 28, 2015. https://www.vanityfair
.com/culture/2015/08/elena-ferrante-interview-the-story-of-the-lost-child
-part-two.

Schechner, Richard. (1977) 2003. *Performance Theory*. London: Routledge.

Scheff, Thomas J. 1975. "The Labeling Theory of Mental Illness." In *Labeling Mad-
ness*, edited by Thomas J. Scheff, 21–34. Englewood Cliffs, NJ: Prentice-Hall.

Scheff, Thomas J. 1984. *Being Mentally Ill: A Sociological Theory*. 2nd ed. New York:
Aldine de Gruyter.

Scheper-Hughes, Nancy. 2000. "Ire in Ireland." *Ethnography* 1 (1): 117–40.

Schilt, Kristen. 2010. *Just One of the Guys? Transgender Men and the Persistence of
Gender Inequality*. Chicago: University of Chicago Press.

Schuppe, Jon. 2015. "Anonymous Hackers Threaten to Release Names of Ku
Klux Klan Members." *NBC News*. https://www.nbcnews.com/news/us
-news/anonymous-hackers-threaten-release-names-ku-klux-klan-members
-n453246.

Schutz, Alfred. (1932) 1967. *The Phenomenology of the Social World*. Evanston, IL:
Northwestern University Press.

Schutz, Alfred. 1962. *Collected Papers I. The Problem of Social Reality*. The Hague:
Martinus Nijhoff.

Schutz, Alfred. 1970. *On Phenomenology and Social Relations*. Chicago: University of
Chicago Press.

Schutz, Alfred, and Thomas Luckmann. 1973. *The Structures of the Lifeworld*. vol. 1.
Evanston, IL: Northwestern University Press.

Schwalbe, Michael. (2008) 2015. *Rigging the Game: How Inequality Is Reproduced in
Everyday Life*. New York: Oxford University Press.

Schwalbe, Michael L., and Kelsey Mischke. 2021. "Power and Interaction." In *The
Oxford Handbook of Symbolic Interactionism*, edited by Wayne H. Brekhus,
Thomas DeGloma, and William Ryan Force. New York: Oxford University Press.

Schwartz, Alexandra. 2016. "The 'Unmasking' of Elena Ferrante." *New Yorker*,
October 3, 2016. https://www.newyorker.com/culture/cultural-comment/the
-unmasking-of-elena-ferrante.

Schweingruber, David, and Ronald T. Wohlstein. 2005. "The Madding Crowd Goes
to School: Myths about Crowds in Introductory Sociology Textbooks." *Teaching
Sociology* 33 (2): 136–53.

Scott, David A. 2017. "Art Restoration and Its Contextualization." *Journal of Aesthetic Education* 51 (2): 82–104.

Scott, James C. 1990. *Domination and the Arts of Resistance: Hidden Transcripts.* New Haven, CT: Yale University Press.

Scott, Susan V., and Wanda J. Orlikowski. 2014. "Entanglements in Practice: Performing Anonymity through Social Media." *MIS Quarterly* 38 (3): 873–93.

Scott, Susie. 2011. *Total Institutions and Reinvented Identities: Identity Studies in the Social Science.* London: Palgrave Macmillan.

Scott, Susie. 2015. *Negotiating Identity: Symbolic Interactionist Approaches to Social Identity.* Cambridge: Polity Press.

Searle, John R. 1969. *Speech Acts: An Essay in the Philosophy of Language.* Cambridge: Cambridge University Press.

Sennett, Richard. 1974. *The Fall of Public Man.* New York: W. W. Norton.

Serracino-Inglott, Philip. 2013. "Is It OK to Be an Anonymous?" *Ethics & Global Politics* 6 (4): 217–44.

Shalev, Eran. 2003. "Ancient Masks, American Fathers: Classical Pseudonyms during the American Revolution and Early Republic." *Journal of the Early Republic* 23 (2): 151–72.

Shane, Scott. 2015. "Drone Strikes Reveal Uncomfortable Truth: U.S. Is Often Unsure about Who Will Die." *New York Times,* April 23, 2015. https://www.nytimes.com/2015/04/24/world/asia/drone-strikes-reveal-uncomfortable-truth-us-is-often-unsure-about-who-will-die.html.

Shang, Rong-An, Yu-Chen Chen, and Sheng-Chieh Huang. 2012. "A Private versus Public Space: Anonymity and Buying Decorative Symbolic Goods for Avatars in a Virtual World." *Computers in Human Behavior* 28 (6): 2227–35.

Sharpe, James. 2005. *Remember, Remember: A Cultural History of Guy Fawkes Day.* Cambridge, MA: Harvard University Press.

Silver, Andrew. 2000. "Making Minstrelsy of Murder: George Washington Harris, the Ku Klux Klan, and the Reconstruction Aesthetic of Black Fright." *Prospects* 25:339–62.

Simcovitch, Maxim. 1972. "The Impact of Griffith's *Birth of a Nation* on the Modern Ku Klux Klan." *Journal of Popular Film* 1 (1): 45–54.

Simko, Christina. 2015. *The Politics of Consolation: Memory and the Meaning of September 11.* New York: Oxford University Press.

Simmel, Georg. 1898. "The Persistence of Social Groups." *American Journal of Sociology* 3 (5): 662–98.

Simmel, Georg. (1903) 1950. "Metropolis." In *The Sociology of Georg Simmel,* edited by Kurt H. Wolff, 409–24. New York: Free Press.

Simmel, Georg. (1908) 1950. "The Stranger." In *The Sociology of Georg Simmel,* edited by Kurt H. Wolff, 402–8. New York: Free Press.

Simmel, Georg. 1950a. "The Field of Sociology." In *The Sociology of Georg Simmel,* edited by Kurt H. Wolff, 3–25. New York: Free Press.

Simmel, Georg. 1950b. "Quantitative Aspects of the Group." In *The Sociology of Georg Simmel,* edited by Kurt H. Wolff, 86–177. New York: Free Press.

Simmel, Georg. 1950c. "The Secret and the Secret Society." In *The Sociology of Georg Simmel,* edited by Kurt H. Wolff, 305–76. New York: Free Press.

Simmel, Georg. (1955) 1964. *Conflict and the Web of Groups Affiliations.* New York: Free Press.

Simmel, Georg. (1978) 2011. *The Philosophy of Money.* London: Routledge.

Simmonds, Gemma. 2000. "Spiritual Direction in Cyberspace." *The Way* 40 (3): 263–71.

Singh, Vikash. 2017. *Uprising of the Fools: Pilgrimage as Moral Protest in Contemporary India*. Stanford, CA: Stanford University Press.

Sluka, Jeffrey A. 2013. "Virtual War in the Tribal Zone: Air Strikes, Drones, Civilian Casualties, and Losing Hearts and Minds in Afghanistan and Pakistan." In *Virtual War and Magical Death: Technologies and Imaginaries for Terror and Killing*, edited by Neil L. Whitehead and Sverker Finnström, 171–93. Durham, NC: Duke University Press.

Smith, Adam. (1759) 2010. *The Theory of Moral Sentiments*. New York: Penguin Random House.

Smith, Adam. (1776) 2003. *The Wealth of Nations*. New York: Bantam.

Smith, Philip. 2003. "Narrating the Guillotine: Punishment Technology as Myth and Symbol." *Theory, Culture & Society* 20 (5): 27–51.

Smith, Philip. 2005. *Why War? The Cultural Logic of Iraq, the Gulf War, and Suez*. Chicago: University of Chicago Press.

Smith, Philip. 2008. *Punishment and Culture*. Chicago: University of Chicago Press.

Smithsonian Archives of American Art. 2007. "Oral History Interview with Guerrilla Girls Alice Neel and Gertrude Stein." Interview by Judith Olch Richards, December 1, 2007. https://www.aaa.si.edu/collections/interviews/oral-history -interview-guerrilla-girls-alice-neel-and-gertrude-stein-15841.

Smithsonian Archives of American Art. 2008a. "Oral History Interview with Guerrilla Girls Frida Kahlo and Kathe Kollwitz." Interview by Judith Olch Richards, January 19–March 9, 2008. https://www.aaa.si.edu/collections/interviews/oral -history-interview-guerrilla-girls-frida-kahlo-and-kathe-kollwitz-15837.

Smithsonian Archives of American Art. 2008b. "Oral History Interview with Guerrilla Girls Jane Bowles and Alma Thomas." Interview by Judith Olch Richards, May 8, 2008. https://www.aaa.si.edu/collections/interviews/oral-history -interview-guerrilla-girls-jane-bowles-and-alma-thomas-15838.

Snow, David A., and Leon Anderson. 1987. "Identity Work among the Homeless: The Verbal Construction and Avowal of Personal Identities." *American Journal of Sociology* 92 (6): 1336–71.

Snow, David A., Louis A. Zurcher, and Robert Peters. 1981. "Victory Celebrations as Theater: A Dramaturgical Approach to Crowd Behavior." *Symbolic Interaction* 4 (1): 21–42.

Sodaro, Amy. Forthcoming. "Contentious Pasts, Contentious Futures: Race, Memory and Politics in Montgomery's Legacy Museum." In *Interpreting Contentious Memory: Countermemories and Social Conflicts Over the Past*, edited by Thomas DeGloma and Janet Jacobs. Bristol, UK: Bristol University Press.

Somers, Margaret R. 1994. "The Narrative Constitution of Identity: A Relational and Network Approach." *Theory and Society* 23 (5): 605–49.

Spears, Russell, and Martin Lea. 1992. "Social Influence and the Influence of the 'Social' in Computer-Mediated Communication." In *Contexts of Computer-Mediated Communication*, edited by Martin Lea, 30–65. Hertfordshire, UK: Harvester Wheatsheaf.

Spears, Russell, and Martin Lea. 1994. "Panacea or Panopticon? The Hidden Power in Computer-Mediated Communication." *Communication Research* 21 (4): 427–59.

Spears, Russell, Martin Lea, Rolf Arne Corneliussen, Tom Postmes, and Wouter Ter Haar. 2002. "Computer-Mediated Communication as a Channel for Social Resistance: The Strategic Side of SIDE." *Small Group Research* 33 (5): 555–74.

Spears, Russell, Martin Lea, Tom Postmes, and Anke Wolbert. 2014. "A SIDE Look at Computer-Mediated Communication: Power and the Gender Divide." In *Strategic Uses of Social Technology: An Interactive Perspective of Social Psychology*, edited by Zachary Birchmeier, Beth Dietz-Uhler, and Garold Stasser, 16–39. Cambridge: Cambridge University Press.

Spears, Russell, and Tom Postmes. 2015. "Group Identity, Social Influence, and Collective Action Online: Extensions and Applications of the SIDE Model." In *The Handbook of the Psychology of Communication Technology*, edited by S. Shyam Sundar, 23–46. West Sussex, UK: Wiley Blackwell.

Speri, Alice. 2014. "KKK Missouri Chapter Threatens Ferguson Protesters with 'Lethal Force.'" *Vice News*, November 13, 2014. https://www.vice.com/en_us /article/59a83k/kkk-missouri-chapter-threatens-ferguson-protesters-with -lethal-force.

Spiegel, Jennifer B. 2015. "Masked Protest in the Age of Austerity: State Violence, Anonymous Bodies, and Resistance 'In the Red.'" *Critical Inquiry* 41 (4): 786–810.

Stark, Philip. 2013. "What Exactly Do Student Evaluations Measure?" *Berkeley Blog*, October 21, 2013. https://blogs.berkeley.edu/2013/10/21/what-exactly-do -student-evaluations-measure/.

Starr, Mark. 1990. "The Writing on the Wall." *Newsweek*, November 25, 1990. https://www.newsweek.com/writing-wall-205980.

Stein, Karen. 2019. *Getting Away from It All: Vacations and Identity*. Philadelphia: Temple University Press.

Steinbeck, John. 1939. *The Grapes of Wrath*. New York: Viking Press.

Strachan, Maxwell. 2018. "The National Enquirer's Plot to Assassinate Ted Cruz's Candidacy." *HuffPost*, October 31, 2018. https://www.huffingtonpost.com/entry /ted-cruz-ami-national-enquirer-donald-trump_us_5bd8a992e4b019a7ab57 d70e.

Strong, Tovah. 2021. "Mentally Ill and Sentenced to Death." *Texas Observer*, June 16, 2021. https://www.texasobserver.org/mentally-ill-and-sentenced-to-death/.

Sumerau, J. E., Ryan T. Cragun, and Lain A. B. Mathers. 2016. "Contemporary Religion and the Cisgendering of Reality." *Social Currents* 3 (3): 293–311.

Sweeney, Latanya. 2002. "k-Anonymity: A Model for Protecting Privacy." *International Journal on Uncertainty, Fuzziness and Knowledge-Based Systems* 10 (5): 557–70.

Tavory, Iddo. 2009. "Of Yarmulkes and Categories: Delegating Boundaries and the Phenomenology of Interactional Expectation." *Theory and Society* 39:49–68.

Taylor, Anne. 2022. "Audience Agency in Social Performance." *Cultural Sociology* 16 (1): 68–85.

Taylor, Verta. 1989. "Social Movement Continuity: The Women's Movement in Abeyance." *American Sociological Review* 54 (5): 761–75.

Tertullian. ~197–202. "De Spectaculis (The Shows)." Published on the Christian Classics Ethereal Library. https://www.ccel.org/ccel/schaff/anf03.iv.v.html.

Thompson, Dennis F. 1980. "Moral Responsibility of Public Officials: The Problem of Many Hands." *American Political Science Review* 74 (4): 905–16.

Thompson, E. P. 1974. "Patrician Society, Plebeian Culture." *Journal of Social History* 7 (4): 382–405.

Thompson, E. P. (1975) 2011. "The Crime of Anonymity." In *Albion's Fatal Tree: Crime and Society in Eighteenth Century England*, by Douglas Hay, Peter Linebaugh, John G. Rule, E. P. Thompson, and Cal Winslow, 255–308. London: Verso.

Thompson, Jerry L. 2016. "Walker Evans in 1946/Labor Anonymous." In *Walker Evans: Labor Anonymous*, edited by Thomas Zander, 7–32. New York: Distributed Art Publishers.

Time. 2009. "25 People to Blame for the Financial Crisis." http://content.time.com/time/specials/packages/article/0,28804,1877351_1877350_1877339,00.html.

Torpey, John, and Saskia Hooiveld. 2016. "Warfare without Warriors? Changes in Contemporary Warfare and the Demise of the Citizen-Soldier." In *Transformations of Warfare in the Contemporary World*, edited by John C. Torpey and David Jacobson, 134–52. Philadelphia: Temple University Press.

Tseëlon, Efrat. 2001a. "Masquerade Identities." In *Masquerade and Identities: Essays on Gender, Sexuality, and Marginality*, edited by Efrat Tseëlon, 1–17. London: Routledge.

Tseëlon, Efrat. 2001b. "Reflections on Mask and Carnival." In *Masquerade and Identities: Essays on Gender, Sexuality, and Marginality*, edited by Efrat Tseëlon, 18–37. London: Routledge.

Turner, Victor. 1967. *The Forest of Symbols: Aspects of Ndembu Ritual*. Ithaca, NY: Cornell University Press.

Turner, Victor. 1982. *From Ritual to Theatre: The Human Seriousness of Play*. New York: PAJ Publications.

Tverdek, Edward. 2008. "The Myth of Public Anonymity." *Public Affairs Quarterly* 22 (2): 197–211.

Tyler, Royall. 1987. "Buddhism in Noh." *Japanese Journal or Religious Studies* 14 (1): 19–52.

Ubelacker, Sheryl. 2018. "Anonymous Donor Give $100M to Canada's Largest Mental Health Hospital." *CTV News*, January 11, 2018. https://www.ctvnews.ca/health/anonymous-donor-gives-100m-to-canada-s-largest-mental-health-hospital-1.3755190.

Udaka, Michishige. 2010. *The Secrets of Noh Masks*. New York: Kodansha.

van den Berg, Zirk. 2011. "Is Emile Ajar the Greatest Writer Who Never Lived?" *Say Books*. https://www.saybooksonline.com/is-emile-ajar-the-greatest-writer-who-never-lived/.

Vasquez, Jose N. 2008. "Seeing Green: Visual Technology, Virtual Reality, and the Experience of War." *Social Analysis* 52 (2): 87–105.

Vaughan, Diane. 1992. "Theory Elaboration: The Heuristics of Case Analysis." In *What Is a Case? Exploring the Foundations of Social Inquiry*, edited by Charles C. Ragin and Howard S. Becker, 173–202. Cambridge: Cambridge University Press.

Veblen, Thorstein. (1899) 1918. *The Theory of the Leisure Class: An Economic Study of Institutions*. New York: B. W. Huebsch.

Vizel, F. 2012. "Breaking From Hasidism, Online." *Tablet*, July 10, 2012. https://www.tabletmag.com/sections/community/articles/escaping-from-hasidism-online.

Wagner-Pacifici, Robin, and Barry Schwartz. 1991. "The Vietnam Veterans Memorial: Commemorating a Difficult Past." *American Journal of Sociology* 97 (2): 376–420.

Waites, Rosie. 2011. "V for Vendetta Masks: Who's Behind Them?" *BBC News Magazine*, October 20, 2011. https://www.bbc.co.uk/news/magazine-15359735.

Walford, Geoffrey. 2018. "The Impossibility of Anonymity in Ethnographic Research." *Qualitative Research* 18 (5): 516–25.

Walker, Neil. 2017. "All or Nothing: The False Promise of Anonymity." *Data Science Journal* 16 (24): 1–7.

Wallace, Kathleen A. 1999. "Anonymity." *Ethics and Information Technology* 1 (1): 23–35.

Wallison, Peter. 2011. "Hey, Barney Frank: The Government Did Cause the Housing Crisis." *The Atlantic*, December 13, 2011. https://www.theatlantic.com/business/archive/2011/12/hey-barney-frank-the-government-did-cause-the-housing-crisis/249903/.

Walzer, Michael. 2016. "Just and Unjust Targeted Killing and Drone Warfare." *Dædalus* 145 (4): 12–24.

Wanshel, Elyse. 2016. "Someone Anonymously Slipped $8,000 into an Animal Shelter's Donation Box: There Are Good People in This World!" *HuffPost*, September 23, 2016. https://www.huffpost.com/entry/8000-thousands-anonymous-donation-box-animal-shelter-pasadena-humane-society-spca-mystery_n_57e55049e4b0e28b2b538a87.

Warman, Matt. 2013. "Online Anonymity: Impossible after Four Phone Calls." *Telegraph*, March 25, 2013. https://www.telegraph.co.uk/technology/news/9952841/Online-anonymity-impossible-after-four-phone-calls.html.

Warren, Frank. 2007. *The Secret Lives of Men and Women*. New York: HarperCollins.

Waskul, Dennis D. 2003. *Self-Games and Body-Play: Personhood in Online Chat and Cyberspace*. New York: Peter Lang.

Wasserman, Jason Adam, Jeffrey Michael Clair, and Chelsea Platt. 2012. "The 'Homeless Problem' and Double Consciousness." *Sociological Inquiry* 82 (3): 331–35.

Watson, Bruce. 2010. "Where Are They Now? Seven Villains of the Financial Crisis." *Aol*, September 15, 2010. https://www.aol.com/2010/09/15/villains-of-the-financial-crisis/.

Watson, Leon. 2012. "America's Deadly Double Tap Drone Attacks Are 'Killing 49 People for Every Known Terrorist in Pakistan.'" *Daily Mail*, September 25, 2012. https://www.dailymail.co.uk/news/article-2208307/Americas-deadly-double-tap-drone-attacks-killing-49-people-known-terrorist-Pakistan.html.

Weber, Max. (1903–17) 1949. *The Methodology of the Social Sciences*. New York: Free Press.

Weber, Max. (1915) 1946. "Religious Rejections of the World and Their Directions." In *From Max Weber: Essays in Sociology*, 323–59. Edited by H. H. Gerth and C. Wright Mills. New York: Oxford University Press.

Weber, Max. (1922) 1978. *Economy and Society: An Outline of Interpretive Sociology*. Berkeley: University of California Press.

Weber, Max. (1930) 1992. *The Protestant Ethic and the Spirit of Capitalism*. London: Routledge.

Weber, Max. 1948. "Politics as a Vocation." In *From Max Weber: Essays in Sociology*, 77–128. Edited by H. H. Gerth and C. Wight Mills. Abington, UK: Routledge.

Weingarten, Gene. 2007. "Pearls before Breakfast." *Washington Post*, April 8, 2007.

https://www.washingtonpost.com/lifestyle/magazine/pearls-before-breakfast
-can-one-of-the-nations-great-musicians-cut-through-the-fog-of-a-dc-rush
-hour-lets-find-out/2014/09/23/8a6d46da-4331-11e4-b47c-f5889e061e5f
_story.html.

West, Candace, and Sarah Fenstermaker. 1995. "Doing Difference." *Gender and Society* 9 (1): 8–37.

West, Candace, and Don H. Zimmerman. 1987. "Doing Gender." *Gender and Society* 1 (2): 125–51.

Westbrook, Laurel, and Kristen Schilt. 2013. "Doing Gender, Determining Gender: Transgender People, Gender Panics, and the Maintenance of the Sex/Gender/ Sexuality System." *Gender & Society* 28 (1): 32–57.

Whitehead, Neil L., and Sverker Finnström. 2013. "Virtual War and Magical Death." In *Virtual War and Magical Death: Technologies and Imaginaries for Terror and Killing,* edited by Neil L. Whitehead and Sverker Finnström, 1–25. Durham, NC: Duke University Press.

Whitlinger, Claire. 2020. *Between Remembrance and Repair: Commemorating Racial Violence in Philadelphia, Mississippi.* Chapel Hill: University of North Carolina Press.

Wiedeman, Reeves. 2018. "The Watcher." *The Cut.* https://www.thecut.com/2018 /11/the-haunting-of-657-boulevard-in-westfield-new-jersey.html.

Wiles, David. 2000. *Greek Theatre Performance: An Introduction.* Cambridge: Cambridge University Press.

Wiley, Norbert. 1994. *The Semiotic Self.* Chicago: University of Chicago Press.

Wirth, Louis. 1938. "Urbanism as a Way of Life." *American Journal of Sociology* 44 (1): 1–24.

Wolf, Talya. 2019. "Sober Together: Self- and Institutional-Reflexivity in Alcoholics Anonymous." Paper Presented at the Annual Meeting of the Eastern Sociological Society, Boston, MA.

Wolf, Z. Byron. 2017. "James Comey Confirms He's 'Reinhold Niebuhr' in the Strangest Possible Way." CNN. https://www.cnn.com/2017/10/23/politics /james-comey-twitter-account-reinhold-niebuhr/index.html.

Wong, Brittany. 2020. "Medical Workers Wear Pics of Themselves Smiling to Comfort COVID-19 Patients." *HuffPost,* April 10, 2020. https://www.huffpost .com/entry/medical-workers-pics-smiling-covid-19-patients_l_5e8f725bc5b 6b371812da523.

Wood, James. 2013. "Women on the Verge: The Fiction of Elena Ferrante." *New Yorker.* January 14, 2013. https://www.newyorker.com/magazine/2013/01/21 /women-on-the-verge.

Woolf, Nicky. 2015a. "Anonymous Plans to Reveal Names of about 1,000 Ku Klux Klan Members." *The Guardian,* October 29, 2015. https://www.theguardian.com /technology/2015/oct/29/anonymous-ku-klux-klan-members-reveal-names.

Woolf, Nicky. 2015b. "Anonymous Leaks Identities of 350 Alleged Ku Klux Klan Members." *The Guardian,* November 5, 2015. https://www.theguardian.com /technology/2015/nov/06/anonymous-ku-klux-klan-name-leak.

Woolf, Nicky. 2016. "Anti-Trump Campaign Sparks Civil War among Anonymous Hackers." *The Guardian,* March 24, 2016. https://www.theguardian.com /technology/2016/mar/24/anti-donald-trump-campaign-anonymous-hackers -debate-election-2016?CMP=twt_a-technology_b-gdntech.

Woolf, Virginia. ["Anon."] (1940) 1979. "'Anon' and 'The Reader': Virginia Woolf's Last Essays," edited by Brenda R. Silver. *Twentieth Century Literature* 25 (3/4): 356–441.

Wright, Joss, Susan Stepney, John A. Clark, and Jeremy Jacob. 2005. "Designing Anonymity: A Formal Basis for Identity Hiding." https://www.researchgate.net/publication/228735934_Designing_anonymity-a_formal_basis_for_identity_hiding.

Wrigley, Richard. 1983. "Censorship and Anonymity in Eighteenth-Century French Art Criticism." *Oxford Art Journal* 6 (2): 17–28.

Young, Tara M., Michael J. Marks, Yuliana Zaikman, and Jacqueline A. Zeiber. 2017. "Situational Influences on Condom Purchasing." *Sexuality and Culture* 21 (4): 925–41.

Zander, Thomas, ed. 2016. *Walker Evans: Labor Anonymous*. New York: Distributed Art Publishers.

Zerubavel, Eviatar. 1980. "If Simmel Were a Fieldworker: On Formal Sociological Theory and Analytic Field Research." *Symbolic Interaction* 3 (2): 25–34.

Zerubavel, Eviatar. 1982. "Personal Information and Social Life." *Symbolic Interaction* 5 (1): 97–109.

Zerubavel, Eviatar. 1991. *The Fine Line: Making Distinctions in Everyday Life*. Chicago: University of Chicago Press.

Zerubavel, Eviatar. 2003. *Time Maps: Collective Memory and the Social Shape of the Past*. Chicago: University of Chicago Press.

Zerubavel, Eviatar. 2006. *The Elephant in the Room: Silence and Denial in Everyday Life*. New York: Oxford University Press.

Zerubavel, Eviatar. 2007. "Generally Speaking: The Logic and Mechanics of Social Pattern Analysis." *Sociological Forum* 22 (2): 131–45.

Zerubavel, Eviatar. 2012. *Ancestors and Relatives: Genealogy, Identity, and Community*. New York: Oxford University Press.

Zerubavel, Eviatar. 2015. *Hidden in Plain Sight: The Social Structure of Irrelevance*. New York: Oxford University Press.

Zerubavel, Eviatar. 2016. "The Five Pillars of Essentialism: Reification and the Social Construction of an Objective Reality." *Cultural Sociology* 10 (1): 69–76.

Zerubavel, Eviatar. 2018. *Taken for Granted: The Remarkable Power of the Unremarkable*. Princeton, NJ: Princeton University Press.

Zerubavel, Eviatar. 2021. *Generally Speaking: An Invitation to Concept-Driven Sociology*. New York: Oxford University Press.

Zerubavel, Eviatar. Forthcoming. *Don't Take It Personally: Personalness and Impersonality in Everyday Life*. New York: Oxford University Press.

Zhong, Chen-Bo, Vanessa K. Bohns, and Francesca Gino. 2010. "Good Lamps Are the Best Police: Darkness Increases Dishonesty and Self-Interested Behavior." *Psychological Science* 21 (3): 311–14.

Zimbardo, Philip G. 1969. "The Human Choice: Individuation Reason and Order versus Deindividuation Impulse and Chaos." In *Nebraska Symposium on Motivation*, edited by W. J. Arnold and D. Devine, Vol. 17, 237–307. Lincoln: University of Nebraska Press.

Zimbardo, Philip G. 2021. "The Stanford Prison Experiment." https://www.prisonexp.org/the-story.

Zimbardo, Philip, Craig Haney, W. Curtis Banks, and David Jaffe. 1971. "The

Stanford Prison Experiment: A Simulation Study of the Psychology of Imprisonment." https://web.stanford.edu/dept/spec_coll/uarch/exhibits/spe/Narration.pdf.

Zuckerman, Mortimer B. 2010. "Who to Blame for the Financial Crisis." *U.S. News and World Report*, January 29, 2010. https://www.usnews.com/opinion/m zuckerman/articles/2010/01/29/mort-zuckerman-who-to-blame-for-the -financial-crisis-.

Zweig, David. 2014. *Invisibles: The Power of Anonymous Work in an Age of Relentless Self-Promotion*. New York: Portfolio.

# Index

Abu Ghraib prison, 144

A-culture, 59–60

Adams, John, 82

Adut, Ari, 186n85, 207n55

affirmative action, 146–47

African Americans. *See* Black Americans

agency, 10, 18–26, 108; of corporations, 111–12, 127–28; to impersonal systems, 109; to state system, 121

Ajar, Émile, 73. *See also* Gary, Romaine

Alabama, 121

Al-Anon, 56

Alcoholics Anonymous (AA), 34, 56–57, 189n8, 194n139, 194n151, 194n153; anonymity, as spiritual foundation of, 58; "Big Book" of, 194n154

Alexander, Jeffrey C., 26, 188n130, 188n132, 199nn78–79, 201nn118–19, 213n8

Al-Muslimi, Farea, 120

Al Qaeda, 118–19

al-Rashid, Harun, 187n111

altruism: as anonymous, 30, 44–46; ethic of selflessness, as core of, 44

American Civil Liberties Union (ACLU), 156

American Indian Movement (AIM), 100

American Medical Association (AMA), 125

American Psychiatric Association (APA), 1–2, 6; homosexuality as mental disorder, declassifying of, 3

American Revolutionary War, 120–21

Amy's soups, 129

Ancona, Frank, 177

Anderson, Elijah, 155

*Anonyma: Eine Frau in Berlin* (*A Woman in Berlin*) (film), 34, 188n4

anonymity, 4, 7, 65, 107, 109; in academic research, 52–55; and accountability, 14, 39, 64–65, 82, 101, 106, 110, 123, 133, 170; as achievable and precarious, 6; addiction and recovery programs, 30, 56; aggression, 69; alternative social norms, asserting of, 70; altruism, 30, 45; anyoneness of, 22, 178; anyones, 107; and Black bodies, 155; Catholic confession, 30, 47; celebrity, as antithetical to, 22; characteristics of, 3; charitable acts, goodness of, 44; as computer-mediated, 56, 58, 141, 183n24, 214n22; as contextually, situationally, relationally, and temporally bound, 6; as contingent and emergent, 5; correspondence, 21; cover representations, 12–13, 66; cultural codes, 26; democratizing of artistic identity, 76; disembodiment, 186n93; of economic exchange, 131; ethics of, 43, 170; of evaluations, 50–52, 54–55; everyoneness of, 23–24, 77, 178; of executions, 121, 123–25; false flag operations, 101; female music composers, 198n36; freedom of, 13–14, 185n56; high-status positions, 205n4; identity play, 49, 60; identity typification, as consequence of, 31–32, 135–40; as interpersonal, 13–14,

anonymity (*continued*)
26, 182n13; IP addresses, 16, 58, 62, 115, 186n80, 208n65; vs. invisibility, 5; of Ku Klux Klan, 85, 88–89, 97; lottery winners, 189n9; love letters, 13, 17; manipulation or deceit, potential for, 64; masquerade masks, 49; masquerade parties, 30, 49; as meaningful act, 170; meanings of, 5–6; misdirectional type of, 101; mystery, as core feature of, 19–20; namelessness, 9–10; naming, as antithesis of, 9; no oneness of, 25, 178; of online review platforms, 64; as performance, 5, 26–27, 178; performative accomplishment, 5; personal identifiability, in commerce, 61; personal identity, obscuring of, 4–6, 12; personalization, as antithesis of, 178; personal recognition, 133; philosophical pragmatism, 5; phone calls, 189n11; of political action committees (PACs), 114; political stability and social disruption, cultivation of, 19–20; power, dynamics of, 30, 83; power imbalance, 18, 32; and privacy, 16; protective, 30–31, 34–39, 44, 69, 170; pseudonymity, differences blurred, 12–13; publicity, as means to, 185–86n76; of racial characterization, 159–60; as racialized, 155; of racism, 155; of racist typification, 160; Reddit, 195n170; revolutionaries, 81–82; secrecy, differences between, 19; sincere representational form of, 100–101; as social, 61, 182n13; social characteristics of, 6–7; social and contingent character of, 6; social ethics of, 30, 43–44; on social media forums, 14, 55; social movement dramaturgy, 201n119; of social movements, 84, 90, 100–101; as social performance, 5–6, 170, 172, 182n13; of social systems, 106–9, 115–16, 125–27, 132–33, 171–72, 205n9; sociology of, 181–82n12; someoneness of, 21, 178; and speech, 38–39, 189n23; as subversive, 68–71, 171; subversive acts, 68–70, 76–78, 83–84; subversive dimensions of, 31,

66, 68, 71, 102–3; sunglasses, 214n46; support groups, 28–30, 56–58; surveillance, 62, 88–89, 98, 115–17, 169; surveilling others, 18; temporal dimension of, 10; tinted windows and visors, 18; and trust, 64; of typification, 135–40, 144, 146–50, 155, 157–60, 164, 166–68, 172, 176; unmasking of, 175; voyeuristic advantage of, 17–18
Anonymous (hacker network), 13, 24, 31, 77, 92–93, 95, 178, 187n110, 220n30; code of conduct, 203n162; cover representations, 98; Guy Fawkes mask, 90–91, 94, 99, 203n162; LULZ, 97–98; masking, 98; Operation KKK (Operation Hoods Off), 177; Project Chanology, 96; as social movement, 96; subversive activity, 96; subversive symbolism of, 98; uniform masks, use of, 96–97; vigilantism of, 98
anonymous, as word, 8
anonymous agency. *See* agency
anonymous altruism, 44–46
anonymous authorship, 12, 18, 21, 23, 34, 39–43, 71–73, 130–31, 190n53
anonymous communities and forums: A-culture, 59; computer-mediated, 58; crowdsourcing, 59; crude humor, 60; culture of reciprocal anonymity or pseudonymity, 55; dark web, 59; "don't ask, don't tell" practice, 57; hate speech, 60; identity play, 60; information-sharing sites, 59; liminoid zones of, 55; as protective space, 57–58; ritualized performances, engaging in, 58; shame and pride, 59; as therapeutic, 56; trolling, 60
anonymous consumption, 30–31, 60, 109–10; as depersonalizing, 61–62; third parties, 62–63
anonymous donors, 45–46, 176
anonymous evaluation, 50; double-blind peer-review system, 51; ethnographic ethics, 52–55; "extensive masking," 53; Institutional Review Boards (IRBs), 52–53; racist and sexist assessments, 51–52

anonymous executions, 121–25, 210n97, 211n110, 211n113

anonymous giving, "Secret Santa," 45–46

anonymous labor and production, 110, 127–32

*Anonymous Love Letters* (blog), 185n60

*Anonymous People, The* (documentary), 174

anonymous sex, 32, 150–52, 154; "girl-friend experience," 153. *See also* sex work

anonymous spectatorship, 56

anonymous speech, 38, 114, 171, 187n98, 189n23; bullying, 39; doxing, 39; flaming, 39; hate speech, 39, 60; libel, 39; public shaming, 39; trolling, 39

anonymous surveillance, 18, 88–89, 98, 114–17, 115–16, 169

Antifa, 77, 174, 203n160

any*body*, 186n93

anyone, 23, 47, 50, 54, 57, 76, 107, 119, 128; characteristics of, 22; generic social acts, anonymity of, 21–22; notion of, 18, 21–22, 26; random sampling, 22

anyoneness, 21, 34, 94, 108; of anonymity, 22, 178; as incognito, 22; social leveling, 22; of social movements, 83

Apple, 115

*Arabian Nights, or One Thousand and One Nights*, 187n111

Arab Spring, 90

Arbery, Ahmaud, 157–58

Arendt, Hannah, 44, 176

Arie, Sophie, 211n118

Arouet, François-Marie. *See* Voltaire

art restorers, 130

Asante, 216n110

Ashley Madison, 63

astroturfing, 64

Auerbach, David, 59–60

Augustine, 80

authorship. *See* anonymous authorship

autonomous movements, 203n160


Bacchus, 79, 80

Bachman, Richard. *See* King, Stephen

Baghdad, 120, 187n111

Bakhtin, Mikhail, 80–81, 98

Bakongo, 216n110

Bank of America, 112

Banksy, 12, 18, 76, 169, 178; as being distinctively unknown, 75; as being famous in his pseudonymity, contradictions of, 74–75; as "famous but unknown," 184n50; mysterious vandal, as international sensation, 75; personal fame, forgoing of, 75

*Barely Legal* (exhibition), 169

Batman, 35–36

*Battle of Algiers, The* (film), 94

Baudrillard, Jean, 73

Bauman, Zygmunt, 126–27

Bayer, Ronald, 181n5

Becton, Dajerria, 158

Bell, Acton. *See* Brontë, Anne

Bell, Currer. *See* Brontë, Charlotte

Bell, Ellis. *See* Brontë, Emily

Ben and Jerry's ice cream, 129

Benner, Joseph S., 187n119

Bentham, Jeremy: panopticon prison, 18

Berger, Peter L., 8–9, 136

Berkeley, CA, 84

Berlin, 33, 73

Bernstein, Elizabeth, 153

Biden, Hunter, 219n4

Biden, Joe, 219n4, 197n11, 197n14

big data, 115–17

big tech companies, 109, 114, 125

Bill W., 34, 194n151. *See also* Wilson, William

*Birth of a Nation, The* (film), 85, 91, 98; and Ku Klux Klan, 201n126

Bitcoin, 19, 62

blackface, 214n37

Black Hand (artist), 73

*BlacKkKlansman* (film), 214n24

blackness, 156, 166; as performative act, 159; as a type, 155

Blair, Eric Arthur, 40. *See also* Orwell, George

Bland, Sandra, 159–60

Blue Lives Matter, 67

Booz Allen Hamilton, 114

Borromeo, Archbishop Charles, 46

Bosk, Charles L., 53–54

Boston Tea Party, 82
Bourdieu, Pierre, 166
Bras, Juan Mari, 102
Brontë, Ann, 72
Brontë, Charlotte, 40–41, 72, 190n50
Brontë, Emily, 72
Brooklyn Museum, 74
Brooks, Ethel C., 132
Brown, Michael, 90, 177
Brown University, 73–74
BTK Strangler, 15
Burning Man festival, 200n100
Butler, Judith, 215n64
Byron, Lord, 40

Calame, Claude, 87, 199n78
Campbell's Soup, 128
capitalism, 25, 112, 127, 166, 202n149; cultural codes of, 111; globalized, 92, 94
carnival, 59, 71, 192n98, 201–2n133; actors and spectators, lack of distinction between, 81; in feudal era, 80; masking and costume, 78, 87, 173, 200n100, 201–2n133; subversive anonymity of, 80, 200n98; trickery and dark comedy, 97–98; Venetian, 16, 49
Casebolt, Eric, 158
categorical cover representation, 137
Catholic Church, 40, 81
Catholic confession, 30, 46–48, 191n80
Cato, 82
Central Park, 130
Central Intelligence Agency (CIA), 119
Centre for Addiction and Mental Health, 45
Chapman, Jay, 122
character: of anonymity, 6, 8, 16, 31, 34–35, 38, 52, 66, 69, 171; of anonymous acts, 6, 38; corporate, 74; of every-oneness, 83; as performative act, 45, 48; of pseudonymity, 11, 34
character, performance of, 5, 10–12, 15, 26, 39–40, 42, 45, 68, 73, 75, 78–79, 81, 83–84, 94, 98–99, 102, 124, 151, 172, 174, 199–200n85
character frame, 43
character-types, 140–46, 151, 153–55, 157–59, 162, 164, 167–68

charity, 30; as anonymous, 44–46
Chauvin, Derek, 149
Chavez, Matthew "Levee," 191–92n88
Chiapas, Mexico, 91–92
child sex trafficking, 68
Christianity, 18, 23, 44–45, 48, 68, 7–80, 85, 176, 201–2n33
Christopherson, Kimberly M., 214n22
Churchill, Ward, 102, 204–5n190
Church of Scientology, 90, 95–96
cisgender character-types, 162
cisgenderism, 160, 162–64, 166
Citizens United v. Federal Election Commission, 109, 113–14
Civil War, 89, 135
Clansman, The: A Historical Romance of the Ku Klux Klan (Dixon), 85, 91, 98
class, 45, 50, 52–53, 60, 72, 82–83, 138, 146–47, 150, 157, 164, 174, 192n95, 212n135; dominant, 77; of mainstream museums and galleries, 75; and occupation, 32, 149; power dynamics, 77; and typification, 148–49, 166–67
Clothesline Project, 191–92n88
Co-Dependents Anonymous, 56
COINTELPRO, 31, 99–102
COINTELPRO Papers, The (Churchill and Vander Wall), 204–5n190
Cold War, 33, 91–92
Coleman, Gabriella, 90, 204n179
Collins, Patricia Hill: matrix of domination, 138
Colombia, 189n13
colonialism, 143, 216n110
Columbia University, 73–74
Comey, James, 17
computer-generated avatars, 26, 120
computer-mediated anonymous forums, as alternative publics, 58–60
Common Sense (Paine), 81
community-supported agriculture (CSA) initiatives, 129
concealed voyeurism: segmented audiences, 18; to be seen without being seen or known, 16–18, 98
Confederacy, 99; Confederate soldiers, 87–89
confessions, 34, 58, 178, 191n80, 191n83;

confessional booth, 46–48; confessional screen, anonymity of, 47, 65; personal identity, 48; and sin, 48
conspicuous consumption, 60, 169
controlled exhibitionism: segmented audiences, 18; unwanted divulgence, risk of, 16
Cookenboo, John, 84
Cooley, Charles Horton, 13
copyright, 40–41
corporate organizations, as cover representations, 113, 175
corporate personhood, 31, 113
corporate surveillance, 116–17
corporations, 111, 113, 115; agency of, 112, 127–28
Coughlin, John J., 46
cover representations, 12, 14, 21, 23–24, 26, 28, 31–32, 36–37, 39, 41, 58, 66, 103, 131–33, 204n170; of Anonymous, 90–91, 94–96, 98; of corporate organizations, 113; of FBI, 101; as impersonal fronts, 10–11; of Ku Klux Klan, 85, 89, 98; as performative tool, 91; personal identity, 83; pseudonymous authors, 71; of retail companies, 131; social systems, 106, 109–10; symbolic uniformity, 83–84; typification, 137, 139–41, 146–47
COVID-19 pandemic, 57, 67, 69, 175
cryptocurrencies, 59; Bitcoin, 19, 62, 196n187
cryptomarkets, 59, 195n172
Cuba, 101–2
cultural sociology, strong program, 6
culture of reciprocal anonymity or pseudonymity, 55
Cuomo, Andrew, 217n133
Curb Your Enthusiasm (TV series), 176
Curlew, Abigail E., 14, 60, 182n13, 194n141
Cusk, Rachel, 12
customer service, outsourcing of, 131

Daredevil (character), 36
dark money, 114
dark web, 59, 174
Daughters of Bilitis, 1–2

David, Larry, 176
Davis, Kate, 159–60
death penalty, 210n97, 210n103; constitutionality of, 122; legal injection, 122–23
Debtors Anonymous, 56
Dede Bandaid (artist), 74
Deep State, 67–68
Deep Throat, 34, 189n8
dehumanization, 133, 209n91
deindividuation, 25, 70, 185n62, 214n26; antisocial behavior, 69
De Mendoza, Diego Hurtado, 190n36
Denzin, Norman K., 56–57
depersonalization, 50–51, 143
Detroit, 147
Deutsch, Stanley, 122
Día de los Muertos, 200n100
Diagnostic and Statistical Manual of Mental Disorders (DSM), 1
Diallo, Amadou, 157
Diaz, Jorge. See Mola, Carmen
digital media, disembodied character of, 21
digital technologies, 4, 11, 21, 59, 62, 98, 183n24
Dionysus, 78–80, 97
Discipline and Punish (Foucault), 208n59
disguise: false identity, 101; and masks, 101; and responsibility, 185n63
Dismaland (exhibition), 74
distance killing, 31, 109; as asymmetrical, 118, 120; civilian casualties, 119; "collateral murder," 120; depersonalized violence, 120–21; mass killing, 118; moral burden of, 208n75; M230 Chain Gun, 120; precision killing, 119; "respatialization dynamics," 118; targeted long-range, 118. See also drones
Dixon, Thomas, Jr., 85, 89, 91, 98
Doerhoff, Alan, 211n110
Don Juan (Byron), 40
Dostoyevsky, Fyodor, 185n59
"double wall" of avoidance, 57
Douglass, Frederick, 116
doxing, 39, 174, 177

Dr. Bob, 34. *See also* Smith, Robert
"Driving While Black" (ACLU report), 156
drones, 208n76, 209n88; as asymmetrical, 120; civilian casualties, downplaying of, 119–20; dehumanization, 209n91; operators, 118; operators, and post-traumatic stress disorder, 208n75; personal identities, of operators, 119; as personality strikes, 119; as signature strikes, 119. *See also* distance killing
Du Bois, W. E. B., 139–40, 155; double consciousness, 142; racism, lived experience of, 135; second sight, 135, 160; veil, metaphor of, 135, 142
Dupin, Amantine Lucile Aurore. *See* Sand, George
Durkheim, Émile, 25, 199n77

Easley, Alexis, 189n23
ego: aggrandizement, 76; deprecation of, 76, 83, 96
Eighth Amendment, 122
*Eine Frau in Berlin* (*A Woman in Berlin*), 33
Ejército Zapatista de Liberación Nacional (EZLN), 27, 77, 91–92, 98–99. *See also* Zapatista movement
Elijah the Prophet, 17
Eliot, George, 12, 40–41, 72
Ellison, Ralph, 155
Emerson, Ralph Waldo, 72
England, 20, 23, 73, 77, 91, 95
Enlightenment, 81–82, 218n143
Eren, Colleen, 206–7n37
essentialist logics, 137–38
ethic of charity, 45
ethic of institutional responsibility, 111
ethic of personal liability, 110
ethic of personal responsibility, 110
ethic of socialized liability, 111
ethnicity, 50, 52–53, 138, 146
Europe, 85, 121, 125–26, 143, 166, 201–2n133, 210n99, 216n110
Evans, Mary Ann. *See* Eliot, George
Evans, Walker, 147–48, 167, 215n66
Evers, Medgar, 204n174

everybody, 186n93
everyone: of anonymity, 23–24, 178; collective mass, evoking of, 23; as mass pseudonymous covers, 24; notion of, 18, 23–24, 26; universality, striving toward, 23
everyoneness, 23, 42, 76, 83, 94, 96
executions, 209n95, 210n99, 211n118; anonymity, 121, 123–25, 211n110, 211n113; as "concealed dramaturgics," 121; distance of executioner, 210n102; via drone, 118; executioners, public personality of, 122; firing squad, 122; hanging, 122; institution of modern medicine, sanctioned by, 124; lethal injections, 109, 122–23, 211nn110–11, 210n97; lynch mobs, 122; as performative accomplishment, 124–25; professionalization of, 121–22; as public spectacles, 121; state killing, ritual act of, 124–25
*Exit Through the Gift Shop* (film), 74
Eyerman, Ron, 203n159
*Eyes Wide Shut* (film), 197n30

face, concept of, 184n42
Facebook, 114–15
Fanon, Frantz, 154–55
Färberböck, Max, 34, 188n4
farmers' markets, 129
Fawkes, Guy: mask, significance of, 91, 94–96, 99; mask, subversive anonymity of, 91; reappropriation of, as meme, 94
Federación Universitaria Pro Independencia (FUPI), 101
Federal Bureau of Investigation (FBI), 19–20, 186n80, 187n103; back region, 102; COINTELPRO, 31, 99–102, 204n189, 204–5n190; deceptive misdirectional form, 101; divide-and-rule strategy, 101; subversive anonymity of, 100, 102
Federal Election Campaign Act, 114
*Federalist Papers* (Hamilton, Madison, and Jay), 81–82
Federal Reserve, 95
Feldman, Paula R., 190n38

Felt, Mark, 189n8

Ferguson, MO, 90, 177

Ferrante, Elena, 12, 39–40, 176, 178, 190n46; character frame, 43; cover representation of, 42–43; mystique of personal identity, as media-generated image, 42–43; as performative literary act, 43, 177; personal identity, obscuring of, 177; pseudonymity of, 41–43

Ferri, Sandra, 43, 190n46

Ferri, Sandro, 43, 190n46

financial crises, 110, 112–13

Fine, Gary Alan, 202n151; reputation work, 184n51

First Amendment, 38, 113

*First National Bank of Boston v. Bellotti*, 113

Floyd, George, 149

food cooperatives, 129

food movements, 129

food production, 128; branding of, 129; personalization of, 129–30

foreclosures, 110, 113; as performative, 111

Forrest, Nathan Bedford, 89

*Fortune* (magazine), 147–48

Foucault, Michel, 18; authorship, 40–41, 197–98n31; social systems of power, 25

4chan, 59, 67, 90, 94, 193n134, 194n138, 203n161, 204n180

Fourteenth Amendment, 113

Fourth Amendment, 217n121

France, 72, 82

Frank, Barney, 207n41

*Frantumaglia: A Writer's Journey* (Ferrante), 177

Fraser, Nancy: subaltern counterpublics, 195n163

French Enlightenment, 81

French Revolution, 82, 99, 122–23

Frois, Catarina, 53

Froomkin, A. Michael, 186n80

Fryer, John Ercel, 5, 181n5; as "Dr. H. Anonymous," 1–3, 6

Furber, Paul, 196n6

*Furman v. Georgia*, 210n103

Galbraith, Robert. *See* Rowling, J. K.

Gap, 131–32, 212–13n151

Garland, David, 124, 210n99, 211n112

Garner, Eric, 160

Gary, Romain, 72–73

Gatti, Claudio, 177

Gawande, Atul, 123

GayPA, 6

Geertz, Clifford, 219n165

gender, 50, 52–54, 75, 80, 138, 146, 148–49, 160, 198n36, 218n143, 218–19n155; gender identity, 1, 56, 72, 162–64, 218n151, 218n153

Georgia, 88–89

German Democratic Republic, Stasi agents, 19

Germany, 33

ghostwriters, 130

Gibbons, Dave, 24

Gittings, Barbara, 1–2

Gladwell, Malcolm, 157

Glaser, Barney G., 7

Global North, 92, 94

Global South, 92, 94

glory hole, 150–51

Goffman, Alice, 53

Goffman, Erving, 26, 181n10, 182n17, 187n110; face, 192n104; false front, 184–85n53; giving off an impression, 186n77; passing, 181n4; personal front, 184n41

Google, 114–15

Gordon, Lewis R., 154–55, 215n51

Gordon, Linda, 201nn121–22, 201n131

Gordon, Thomas, 82. *See also* Cato

graffiti art, 31; as aesthetically subversive, 73; alternative spaces, creating of, 74; as artistically subversive, 73; as "insurrection of signs," 73; as legally subversive, 73; as performative, 73; as politically subversive, 73–74

*Grapes of Wrath, The* (Steinbeck), 105

Greece, Greek theater, 79–80, 87

Greenspan, Alan, 207n41

*Gregg v. Georgia*, 210n103

Griffin, Robert J., 40, 184n45

Griffith, D. W., 85, 91, 98

Guantanamo Bay, 144

Guerrilla Girls, 75, 98–99; as anonymous movement, 76–77; as collective movement, 76–77

*Guerrilla Girls' Code of Ethics for Art Museums*, 75–76

guerrilla grafters, 74

Guillotin, Joseph-Ignace, 122–23

*Gulliver's Travels* (Swift), 18

Gunpowder Plot, 91

Guy Fawkes Day, 200n100

Guy Fawkes mask, 96, 203nn162–63; adopting of, by activists, 94; Anonymous, 91, 94–95; as anonymous political performance, 91; cover representation, as performative tool, 91; as "Epic Fail Guy" meme character, 203n161; in protest, 203n155; subversive actors, 94; V, character of, 91, 94

Habermas, Jürgen, 107

hackers, 16, 63, 90, 97, 174, 202n151, 208n65

hacktivists, as term, 202n151

Hamilton, Alexander, 81–82

Harcourt, Bernard E., 186n80, 208n63

Harvey, Daina Cheyenne, 105–6

Health Insurance Portability and Accountability Act (HIPAA), 61

*Hearts and Minds* (documentary), 215n54

Heffernan, Mary Beth, 175–76

Heilbroner, David, 159–60

Hellfire Missile, 119

hidden identity, 6, 26–27, 37–39, 43–44, 66, 69, 102–3, 169–70, 172, 178. *See also* identity; personal identity

Hillers, Marta, 33–34

Holocaust, 25

homelessness, 149–50; homeless people, visibility of, 216n78

Homer, 13

homogenizing portrayals, 137–38

homosexuality, 2–3; as mental disorder, 1

Hong Kong, 174

Hoover, J. Edgar, 99–100

House Subcommittee on Crime, Terrorism, Homeland Security, and Investigations, 174

housing crisis, 31, 110, 113; homeowners, 111–12

Iaccoca, Lee, 206–7n37

*I Am with You* (short film), 219n13

identity: 2–6, 8–10, 13–14, 19, 52–53, 57–58, 69, 146, 173, 175–76; affiliation of, 60; alternate, 76; ambiguity of, 48–49; artistic, 76; bogus, 73; character identity, 11–12, 15, 39, 42, 68, 73, 75, 78–79, 94, 98–99, 172; collective, 68, 76, 78, 81, 90, 118; concealed, 183n29; disguise of, 101; experimentation with, 34–35; false, 101; flexible, 79–80; gender, 1, 56, 72, 163, 218n151, 218n153; hiding of, 80, 82; hiding of, as uncivil, 82; identity cover, 38; "identity document," 181n8; identity insiders, 18; "identity knowledge," 181n8; identity play, 49, 60; narrative, 12; norms of, 49; personal reputation, 34; segmentation of, 152; sexual, 3; shielding of, 34, 95; social, 70; subversive, 203n160; subverting of, 68, 70; typification, 31, 137, 142. *See also* hidden identity; personal identity

impersonal agencies, 18–19, 25–26, 133

impersonal fronts, 10–11, 125

impersonality, 21–24, 31, 47, 50, 62, 83, 97, 108, 126, 139–40, 143, 150, 160–64, 170, 187nn106–7, 190n53, 196n186; impersonal brands, 128; impersonal labels, 137; impersonal medical authority, 124; impersonal social forces, 108–9, 120, 127; impersonal systems/institutions, 106–7, 109, 112–13, 115, 121, 125, 171–72

*Impersonal Life, The* (book), 23

incognito, 14, 148, 183n29, 187n111; as temporary anyoneness, 22

India, 214n24

Industrial Revolution, 118

information control, 6, 16, 18

information slippage, 186n77

Institutional Review Boards (IRBs), 52–53

*Invisible Man* (Ellison), 155

Iran, 73
Iraq, 144
Iroquois, 216n110
ISIS, 90
Islam, 44, 96

Jack the Ripper, 15
James I, 91
*Jane Eyre* (Brontë), 72
Japan: Noh and Kuogen theater, 199–200n85; Shinto rituals in, 78
Japenga, Ann, 209n95
Jay, John, 81–82
Jeems, Davie, 88–89
Jews, religious, 141–42
Johnson, James H., 173, 187n111
Judaism, 130–31

Kaczynski, Theodore "Ted": as Unabomber, 15, 20, 187n101
Kafka, Franz, 106
*Kagura* rituals, 78
Kameny, Franklin E., 1–2
Karp, David A., 182n13
Keller, Arthur I., 201n125
Kessler, Suzanne J., 162, 218–19n155
Kick-Ass (character), 36
King, Martin Luther, Jr., 19–20, 100, 187n103
King, Stephen, 17
Knight, Phil, 206–7n37
*Know My Name* (Miller), 175
Knuttila, Lee: culture of anonymity, 193n134
Kohler, Jeremy, 211n110
Kollwitz, Kathe, 76–77
Krampus, 81
Kubrick, Stanley, 24, 68, 197n30
Ku Klux Klan (KKK), 15–16, 31, 77, 90, 100, 177, 178, 202n143; anonymity of, 85, 88–89, 97; *Birth of a Nation*, 201n126; Boston Tea Party, as ancestor, 201n131; carnival, origins in, 87, 97; collective meaning system and social order of, 89; cover representations of, 85, 89, 98, 204n170; feudal-Christian influence, 201–2n133; fiery

cross, 85; as Invisible Empire, 89, 97, 99; Ku Klux Kreed, 201n123; masked rituals, 86–88; masking, 98; as performative, 85, 87–89; in public sphere, 85; revival of, 202n139; subversive activity, 96, 99; subversive symbolism of, 98; symbols of, 85; uniform masks, use of, 96–97; vigilantism of, 98; violence of, 85, 87–89, 97–98
Kwakiutl Indian communities, 199n76

labor: anonymization of, 127–32; as invisible, 127–28; online commerce, 132
*Labor Anonymous*, 147, 215n65
*La Casa de Papel (Money Heist)* (TV series), 23
LaFrance, Adrienne, 68
Larsson, Stieg, 202n151
*La vie devant soi* (Ajar), 73
Lehman Brothers, 110
*Leopard's Spots, The* (Dixon), 201n124
Lévi-Strauss, Claude, 199n76
LGBTQ community, 140
liminoid zones, 55
Lin, Maya, 50
Lloyd, David, 90–91, 94, 98, 203n155
Lofland, John, 121, 210n97
London, 74
Lone Ranger, 36
Los Angeles Police Department, 95
Luckmann, Thomas, 8–9, 136
LULZ, 97–98, 204n179
lynching, 85, 175, 210n99

Madison, James, 81–82
Madoff, Bernie, 206–7n37
Maimonides, 44
Manning, Chelsea, 120
Marcos, Subcomandante, 28, 92, 174, 188nn131–32
Mardi Gras, 200n100, 201–2n133
Markham, Sir Clements, 190n36
Marmo, Marcella, 176–77
Marmor, Judd, 2
Martin, James, 195n172
Martin, Trayvon, 157–58
Martínez, Augustín. *See* Mola, Carmen

Marx, Gary T., 181n8, 181n10, 181–82n12, 182n13, 184n45, 186n77, 189n13, 192n100, 193n135, 196n182, 213n8; masking moves, 184–85n53; surveillance, 207n55

Marx, Karl, 99, 128, 166, 200n101, 200n103; invisible and anonymous labor, 127

*Masked Singer, The* (TV show), 50

masks, 16, 35–36, 75, 77, 184n42, 186n85, 187n111, 199nn75–76, 199n84, 199–200n85, 200n100, 201nn112–13, 201–2n133; as anarchist groups, and black bloc tactics, 203n160; anonymous, 11; banning of, 82; carnival, 80–81, 200n100; as cover representation, 11, 23–24; deceit, coded with, 80; and disguise, 101; escaping surveillance, 98; Guy Fawkes mask, 90–91, 95–96; as iconic, 98; identity, flexible notion of, 79; identity, hiding of, 80, 101; masked performances, 78, 96–97, 99; Noh theater, 199–200n85; norms, suspending or subverting of, 78; as particular and pseudonymous, 11; personal identities, disappearing of, 79; personal identities, obscuring of, 81, 84, 97, 171; as political activism, 91–92; politically coded characters, 79; rituals, 86–88; social leveling, 22–23, 49; social movements, 24, 27–28, 83, 87, 203n158; social protest, 78, 81, 84; subversive activity, 96, 203n160; subversive anonymity, 80, 87; symbolism associated with, 27

"Masque of the Red Death, The" (Poe), 192n95

masquerade masks: anonymity, 48–49; carnival, roots in, 48; as subversive anonymity, 71

masquerade parties, 30; ethic of, 49

mass, accentuation of, 83–84

Massachusetts, 135

mass killings: memorials, personalizing of, 208n72; victims, as anonymous, 118

Matrix trilogy, 202n151

Mauss, Marcel, 181n7

McCorvey, Norma, 189n8

McDonald's, 128–29

*McIntyre v. Ohio Elections Commission,* 38–39

McKenna, Wendy, 162, 218–19n155

McKinney, TX, 158

McTeigue, James, 90–91, 94, 98

Mead, George Herbert, 13

Mercero, Antonio. *See* Mola, Carmen

Mesoamerican cultures, 78

Me Too movement, 73–74

Metropolitan Museum of Art, 74

Mexico, 24, 27, 91–92

Middle East, 18, 144–45

Milgram, Stanley, 125–26, 197n18

Mill, John Stuart, 82

Miller, Chanel, 175

Mills, C. Wright, 133

minstrelsy, 87

Missouri, 90, 121, 177, 211n110

mistypification, 146

modernity, 82, 196n186

Mola, Carmen, 141

Moore, Alan, 24, 90–91, 94, 98

Moore, Alfred, 23, 39, 181n10, 185–86n76; durability, 184n46; freedom online, 206n12; traceability, 186n80

Moore, Michael, 175

Movimiento Pro-Independencia de Puerto Rico (MPIPR), 101–2

*Mr. Robot* (TV series), 202n151

Mubarak, Hosni, 73

Mullan, John, 12, 173, 182n13, 184n45, 189n17, 204n179

mummers' plays, 87

Museum of Modern Art, 74–75

Museum of Natural History, 74

Nakamoto, Satoshi, 19

namelessness, 9–10

names, continuity of personal identity, 10

naming, 8; act of, 9; character, attribution of, 12; personal identity, 12; as same entity over time, 10

Napier, A. David, 80, 160, 199n76, 199n84

Narcotics Anonymous, 56

Natanson, Maurice, 154–55, 212n133; "anonymous transcendental ego," 21
*National Bird* (documentary), 208n78
National Memorial for Peace and Justice, 175
National Mobilization Committee to End the War in Vietnam (MOBE), 100–101
National Security Agency (NSA), 31, 109, 114–17
Native American ceremonies, 78
*Nature* (Emerson), 72
Nazis, 33–34, 125–26, 211n106
Neel, Alice, 76
Nelson, Kadir, 160
neoliberalism, 92, 94, 202n149
New Left, 100
Newman, Paul, 129
Newman's Own, 129
New Orleans, 200n100, 201–2n133
New York City, 74–75, 149, 160, 203n155, 208n72; "stop-and-frisk" policy, 156–57
Nielsen, Kirstjen, 186n97
Nixon, Richard M., 34
no*body*, 186n93
Noh theater, 199–200n85
no one, 18, 24–26; "Noman," 13, 24
no oneness, 108; of anonymity, 178; deindividuation, 25
North American Free Trade Agreement (NAFTA), 92
North Carolina Public Facilities Privacy and Securities Act (House Bill 2), 163

Obama, Barack, 105–6, 118–19
Occupy Wall Street movement, 90–91, 113, 203n155, 203n158
Oklahoma, 122
Olesen, Thomas, 92, 204n185
Olmsted, Frederick Law, 130
Open Research and Contributor ID (ORCID) system, 212n139
Operation Enduring Freedom, 144
Operation Onymous, 174
Oregon, 210n97
Ortiz, Ingrid, 112
Orwell, George, 40

other-typification, 139. *See also* typification
Ovimbundu, 216n110

Paine, Thomas, 81
Pakistan, 120
*paliacate*, 27–28
Paris, 74
Parsons, Elaine Frantz, 97, 202n147
Parsons, Talcott, 107
passing, 181n4
pedophilia, 68
peer-review system, double-blind, 51
Pennsylvania, 210n97
Pequot, 216n110
personal identity, 3, 9, 12, 15, 18–19, 22–23, 25–26, 37, 42–43, 46–47, 63, 65, 89–90, 108, 127, 135, 170, 175, 182n17, 186n93; anonymous communities and forums, 57; confession, 48; continuity of, 10; cover representation, 14, 83; evaluations, 50–51; of executioners, 122; exposing of, 40, 174; hiding of, as uncivil, 82; impersonal fronts, 10–11; incognito, 14; IP address, 186n80; mystery of, 173; obscuring of, 4–6, 31–32, 55, 66, 69–71, 74, 81, 84, 100–101, 107, 118–19, 121, 132–33, 154, 169, 171, 174, 177–78, 183n24, 197n18; performative dissociation from, 14; signifiers, blocking of, 6; social interaction, 13; as socially ignored and privately known, 48; subversion of, 68–69; subverting of, 31, 102; typification, 137; unmasking of, 173; in war, 117–19. *See also* hidden identity; identity
personality branding, 129–30
Peru, 189n13
Peterson, David, 105–6
Philadelphia Mummers Parade, 200n100
Plato, 5
Poe, Edgar Allan, 192n95
police brutality, 160
polytheism, 79–80
Ponesse, Julie, 4, 181–82n12, 182n13, 183n33, 185n62, 185–86n76
pornography, 60, 151

PostSecret project, 47–48, 191–92n88
Pride movements, 170–71
*Primary Colors* (Klein), 189n17
Prince, 45
PRISM program, 114
privacy, and anonymity, 16
profiling, 15, 62, 115, 138, 156
prostitution, 60, 151, 154
protective anonymity, 34, 40, 46, 60,
69; anonymous speech, 38–39; of
communities and forums, 58; of
confession, 47; cover representations,
65; deceitful actors, 63–64; of donors, 44–45; of evaluations, 50–52;
fictional superheroes, 35–36; fraudulent acts, 63–64; as liberating, 170;
marginalization, 170; multivocal, 38;
performing the need for protection,
37; performing while protected, 35;
personal shame, 171; safe spaces, 170;
selflessness, 44; snooping actors, 66;
of telephone hotlines, 65; as violable
and precarious, 63; whistleblowers,
35; witness protection programs, 35
pseudonymity, 4, 14–15, 21, 30, 65,
74–75, 164, 169, 173, 176, 178, 183n24;
anonymity, as blurred, 12–13; of
authors, 40; cover representations,
12–13, 66; cultural codes, 26; of evaluations, 50; freedom of, 13; graffiti
art, 73; IP addresses, 186n80; masks,
11; as meaningful act, 170; of online
review platforms, 64; as performance,
5; personal identity, obscuring of, 5;
personal identity, obscuring of with
specific name, 12; power, dynamics
of, 83; protective, 34–37, 39, 60; revolutionaries, 81–82; as social performance, 5–6, 170, 172; subversive acts,
68, 70; subversive character, 68, 102
pseudonymous actors, 12, 14–15, 26;
agency, 18; unmasking of, 173
pseudonymous acts, 170, 178
pseudonymous authorship, 42, 73; "By
a Lady" signature, 71–72, 140; as
categorical designation, 140; cover
representations, 71; gender identity,
72

pseudonymous characters, as famous
and unknown, 12
pseudonymous reputations, 12; social
control, 15
pseudonyms, 12, 184–85n53, 193n133; by
employers, 17; ethnographic research,
52–55; *nom de guerre* (name of war),
71; of popular authors, 17; of serial
killers, 15
psychoanalysis, 186n77
Publicola, Publius Valerius, 82
public sphere, 85, 171, 188n132, 195n164,
207n55
Publius, 81–82
Puerto Rico, independence movement,
73, 100–102
Puritans, 200n93

Q, 67, 174, 178, 196n6, 196n8; subversive
character, 68
QAnon, 31, 67, 174, 196n6, 197n11;
Christian apocalyptic theme, 68; US
Capitol, storming of, 197n14
Q clearance, 196n3
Q drops, 67
Quran, 44, 46

race, 50, 83, 85, 138–39, 146, 148, 154–55,
164; and policing, 156–57; suspicion,
156
racial characterization, anonymizing of,
154–55, 158–60
racial profiling, 156
racial typification: and criminality, 157,
159; darker skin color, as proxy of
criminality, 156–57; law enforcement,
155–59; vigilantes, 157–59
racism, 135, 215n51; as anonymizing
force, 155
Racists Anonymous, 56
Raja, Anita, 177
Ramos, Sheila, 113
Rate My Professor, 51, 192n104
Reconstruction, 87, 89, 99
Reddit, 59
restroom segregation, 163–64, 218n149
Reyes, Victoria, 193n133
Right to Know Act, 149

Rodriquez, Dirma, 112
*Roe v. Wade*, 34, 189n8
*Roger & Me* (documentary), 175
Roko, Ellyde, 209n95
*Romeo and Juliet* (Shakespeare), 49, 192n94
Rowling, J. K., 17
Rubenstein, Jeffrey L., 131

Said, Edward W.: Orient, idea of, 143
Sand, George, 72
Santagata, Marco, 176–77
Saudi Arabia, 37
*Say Her Name: The Life and Death of Sandra Bland* (documentary), 159–60, 217n132
"Say Her Name" campaign, 159–60, 175, 217n133
Scalia, Antonin, 39
Scarlet Pimpernel, 35–36
Schechner, Richard: performance theory of, 26
Scheper-Hughes, Nancy, 54
Schutz, Alfred, 135–36, 142, 148, 154–55, 165–66, 197–98n31, 213n6, 215n62
Schwartz, Alexandra, 42
Scotland, 85
Scott, James C., 77–78, 200n98
Scott, Susie, 58
Scott, Sir Walter, 42, 182n13
secrecy and anonymity, differences between, 19–20
"Secret Santa," 45–46
Seidenberg, Robert, 2
self-typification, 139. *See also* typification
semiotics of power, 139
Senate Subcommittee on the Constitution, Civil Rights and Human Rights, 120
Sendero Luminoso, 189n13
Sennett, Richard, 22–23
September 11, 2001, attacks, 144; 9/11 Memorial, 208n72
sexism, 75; and unmasking, 177
sex work, 151–54, 166, 216n86. *See also* anonymous sex
Sex Workers Anonymous, 56

shadow banking, 206n30
Shakespeare, William, 49
"Shitty Media Men," 37
Shtrimpkind, Shpitzle, 38, 189n21. *See also* Vizel, Frieda
Simmel, Georg, 101, 107, 136, 165, 185n56, 185n63, 187n107, 196n186; "The king never dies," 213n17; "noble individual," 44; secrecy, 186n94; stranger, notion of, 166
Simmons, William Joseph, 89, 99
Skype, 114
*Sleep No More* (theatrical experience), 186n85
Smith, Robert, 189n8, 194n151
Snowden, Edward, 114–17
social ethics of anonymity, 30
Social Identity model of Deindividuation Effects (SIDE), 70
Socialist Workers Party (SWP), 100
social leveling, 23, 38–39, 47, 49, 192n95; of anyoneness, 22
social logics, 124, 126, 162
social movements, 31, 79, 80–82, 96, 98–99; accentuation of the mass, 83; anonymity of, 84, 90; and deprecation of the ego, 83; and masked, 27, 77–78, 83–84, 100–101, 103; sincere representational form of anonymity, 100–101
social opacity, 108
social pattern analysis, 7
social sciences, 22, 52, 165
sociology, 25; comparative, 165
some*body*, 186n93
someone, 20, 22; anonymous agency, mystery of, 19, 21; notion of, 18–19, 21, 26
someoneness, of anonymity, 21, 75–76, 178
Son of Sam, 15
*Souls of Black Folk, The* (Du Bois), 135
South America, 19
Sowders, Edward R., 143
Spain, 40
Spanish Inquisition, 63–64
*Spartacus* (film), 24, 68
spectatorship, 186n85, 207n55

Spider-Man, 36
Spiegel, Jennifer B., 207–8n58
Stanford Prison experiment, 142–43
Steinbeck, John, 105–6, 112–13, 205–6n10
Steubenville (OH) High School, 90
Stevens, John Paul, 38
Stone, Grace, 217n129
Story of the Lost Child, The (Ferrante), 12, 43
Strauss, Anselm L., 7
street art, 73–74, 198n40
Student Nonviolent Coordinating Committee (SNCC), 100
subversive anonymity, 68–69, 78, 98, 100, 102, 171; accentuation of the mass, 83; carnival, key feature of, 80; deceptive misdirectional form of, 101; depreciation of the ego, 83; free speech and assembly, 171; graffiti art, 73; of Guy Fawkes mask, 91, 94; masked masquerades, 71; as performance, 71, 90, 94, 103; political dissidents, 71; social dynamics of, 71; symbolic uniformity, 83–84
subversive art, 73–77
Subway Therapy Project, 191–92n88
super PACs (political action committees), 114
surveillance, 3–4, 18, 88–89, 98, 114, 155–56, 169, 207n55, 208nn63–64; anonymity of, 115–16; asymmetry of, 207–8n58; by big tech, 125; corporate, 116–17; electronic, 31, 62
Swift, Jonathan, 18
symbolic interactionism, 5

Talley v. California, 38
Talmud, Stammaim, 130–31
Tattered Cover, Inc. v. City of Thornton, 63
Tavory, Iddo, 141–42
Taylor, Anne, 186n93
Taylor, Miles, 186n97
terrorism, 31, 118
Tertullian, 80
Texas, 121, 158, 160
third parties, 4, 11, 21, 45, 61–63, 184n45, 208n65

Third Reich, 33, 188n4
Thomas, Alma, 76
Thompson, Dennis F., 205–6n10
Thompson, E. P., 77, 199n71, 204n180
Tia Lupita's hot sauce, 129
Tor (web browser), 116–17, 186n80, 208n65
Toynbee tiles, 19
Traditionalist American Knights of the Ku Klux Klan (TAKKKK), 177
traffic stops, 156, 217n121
Traitor, The: A Story of the Fall of the Invisible Empire (Dixon), 89, 201n124
transcendentalism, 72
transgender, 163–64, 218n151, 218n153, 218–19n155
Traven, B., 19
Trenchard, John, 82
Trial, The (Kafka), 106
Trump, Donald, 19, 67–68, 96, 174, 186n97, 219n4
Tseëlon, Efrat, 80
Tupac Amaru, 189n13
Turner, Brock, 175
Turner, Victor, 26, 55, 182–83n21, 200n93
Tutelo, 216n110
Twelve Steps and Twelve Traditions (AA), 58
Twitter, 17, 37
typification, 178, 213n6; acts of self-typification vs. acts of other-typification, 139; of American labor, 147–48; analytic, 164–67; anonymity of, 135–40, 144, 146–50, 152, 155, 157–60, 164, 166–68, 172, 176; of anonymous sex, 150–54; of Arabs and Muslims, 144; of blackness, 159; categorical cover representation, 137, 139–41, 146–47; character-types, 140–41, 144–46, 153, 157–58, 167; cisgender, 160, 162–64; cisgender character-types, 162; of class, 148–49, 166–67; of cops, 149; eclipsing personal identities in meaningful ways, 137; essentialist logics, 137–38; of guards and prisoners, 142–43; heterogeneity, cloaking of, 137; of homeless, 149–50; homogeneity, accentuating of, 137–38,

146; human thought and knowledge, fundamental to, 138; and intimacy, 153; of Jews, 141–42; misrecognizing and mistypifying others, 146; nanny label, 146; of occupations, 148–49; people of color, mental conflation with criminality and guilt, 157; perception and knowledge, as function of, 167; as prepersonal, 162; public places, 149–50; public restrooms, 163–64; as racial, 154–60; racial signification, 154; within relations of power, 145; self-typification, acts of, 140–42; of skin color, 155; social semiotics of power, 139; of social types, 148; sociomental, 136, 158; sociomental distance, 136; strangers of a particular type, 136; as terrorists, 144–45; typification norms, reinforcing of, 138; typifier vs. typified, 139; of Vietnamese, 143–44; vocal, 214n24; of whiteness, 159; white people, mental conflation with lawful and innocence, 157; of working class, 147
typifier and typified, 139
Tyson (food company), 128
tzedakah, 44

Ukraine, 219n4
Undercover Boss (TV series), 17
United States, 19, 20, 67–68, 72, 85, 90, 99–100, 109, 110, 120, 124, 144, 154–55, 174, 204n189, 210n97, 210n99, 217n121; executions in, 121; lethal injection, 122; voting, 187n98
unmasking: act of, 173, 175–77; of anonymous actors, 173–74; during COVID-19 pandemic, 175; good deeds, 176; as performative, 176; politics of, 177–78; self-unmasking, 174–75; significance of, 32
Unmasking Antifa Act, 174

Vander Wall, Jim, 102, 204–5n190
Vaux, Calvert, 130
Veblen, Thorstein, 60
Venice, 187n111; Venetian carnival, 16, 49, 173

Verizon, 114
V for Vendetta (film), 24, 94–95, 98, 203n162, 204n174
V for Vendetta (Moore and Lloyd), 90–91, 94, 98, 203n155
vicarious ego aggrandizement, 76
Vietnam Veterans Memorial, 50, 208n72
Vietnam War, 100; "Charlie," as term, 215n52; "gook," as term, 215n53; VC, as acronym during, 143–44
vigilantes, 36, 98, 157–59, 163–64, 174, 210n99
Vizel, Frieda, 189n21. See also Shtrimpkind, Shpitzle
Voice, The (TV show), 50
Voltaire, 81
Voltaire, Jennifer Ryan, 113

Wachowskis (Lana and Lilly), 94
Wagner, Richard, 186n85
Walking Dead, The (TV series), 24
Wallace, Kathleen A., 4, 181–82n12, 189n13
Waller County, TX, 160
Walzer, Michael, 209n88
Warhol, Andy, 169
Warning, A (Anonymous), 19, 186n97
War on Terror, 144
Warren, Frank, 191–92n88
"Watcher, The," 17
Watchmen (TV series), 24
Watergate scandal, 34
Watkins, Ron, 196n6
Weber, Max, 107, 165, 187n107, 206n24, 213n17
Wells Fargo, 113
West Africa, Ebola in, 175–76
Westboro Baptist Church, 90
Westmoreland, William, 144
What's My Line? (TV show), 173
whistleblowers, 35, 115, 119, 120, 173–75
whiteness, 166; as performative act, 159
white supremacy, 85, 87, 89
Williams, Greg D., 174
Wilson, Darren, 177
Wilson, William, 189n8, 194n151
Wirth, Louis, 133
Wizard of Oz, The (film), 205n4

Wood, James, 41
Woods, Nathaniel, 121
Woolf, Virginia, 23, 190n53
working class, 108, 147, 166
World War II, 34

Yahoo, 114
Yik Yak, 59, 60
Yochelson, Vincent, 84
Yoruba, 216n110

Zapata, Emiliano, 98–99, 204n185
Zapata, Votán, 204n185
Zapatista movement, 77, 91, 174, 188n132;

anyoneness of, 94; balaclavas, 27–28,
188n131; cultural iconography of, 28;
everyoneness of, 24, 94; influence,
growth of, 94; masks of, 24, 27–28;
Occupy movement, 203n158; *paliacate*
(Mexican bandannas), 27–28, 92. *See
also* Ejército Zapatista de Liberación
Nacional (EZLN)
Zelenskyy, Volodymyr, 19, 174, 219n4
Zimbardo, Philip, 142, 197n18; de-
individuation, 25, 69–70, 214n26
Zodiac Killer, 15
Zorro, 36
Zuckerberg, Mark, 206–7n37